GREAT UNSOLVED
CRIMES

Dedicated to Jean Mote

GREAT UNSOLVED CRIMES

by
RODNEY CASTLEDEN

Futura

A *Futura* Book

First published by Futura in 2007

Copyright © Omnipress 2007

ISBN: 978-0-7088-0613-5

Produced by Omnipress, Eastbourne

Printed in India

Futura
An imprint of
Little, Brown Book Group
Brettenham House
Lancaster Place
London WC2E 7EN

Photo credits: Getty Images

CONTENTS

PART THREE: UNSOLVED CRIMES OF THE NINETEENTH CENTURY (1801–1900)

PART FOUR: UNSOLVED CRIMES OF THE EARLY TWENTIETH CENTURY (1901–1950)

PART FIVE: UNSOLVED CRIMES OF THE LATE TWENTIETH CENTURY (1951–2000)

PART SIX: RECENT UNSOLVED CRIMES
(2001–PRESENT)

INTRODUCTION

Of all crimes, the most worrying is the crime that is never solved. The perpetrator of the crime goes free, unpunished, often unidentified. Justice is not done. The friends and relatives of the victim – crimes always have victims – are left without closure. Often the parents, children and siblings of a murder victim live out the rest of their lives in a state of uncertainty, and sometimes fear or anger, because the crime went unpunished; their lives are often seriously damaged. Another unsatisfactory aspect of unsolved crimes is that whoever committed the crime is free to commit another. Police are very properly concerned about unsolved crimes for all of these reasons. Their concern has sometimes led to an excessive eagerness and haste in finding a suspect. The wrong person is suspected, and even convicted; so some crimes that at first appear to have been solved later turn out not to have been, and a double injustice has been done.

In past centuries, before forensic techniques and before the mass media, it was relatively easy for powerful people to commit large-scale crimes with impunity. In some societies, such as the absolute monarchies of the middle ages and the totalitarian regimes of the twentieth-century dictators, judicial murders were commonplace. But there were also crimes that were concealed, crimes that were presented as accidents; spin is not an invention of the Blair government.

With some crimes, the mystery is the age-old, central question: Whodunit? Many of the stories told in this book are whodunits. To find out who committed a crime, we need to examine the events that led up to the crime and investigate the lives, personalities, interests and motives of the various actors. Then, just as in an old-fashioned detective thriller, we need to assemble the suspects in the drawing room – and with a flourish expose the murderer. Each major unsolved crime story has the basic structure of a Poirot mystery, a Miss Marple or a Morse. Somewhere behind each crime lurks a criminal, a culprit waiting to be exposed. Where possible, I shall attempt to expose the villain and give my reasons for thinking that he (or she) is guilty. But there are many cases where, however hard we may try, the tidy ending of a well-tailored detective story, with its satisfying final scene, is not possible. Sometimes, no matter how many times the evidence is sifted through, it is impossible to establish who committed the crime.

The great unsolved crimes are of three major types. One is the crime that went unsolved at the time, and went unsolved for ever after – this is the ultimate crime mystery. The second type is the crime for which someone was blamed at the time, often punished, and the case was closed. Only later as new information became available did it emerge that the person blamed, convicted and sometimes executed was innocent of the crime, or alternatively had accomplices who were equally to blame or more to blame but went unpunished. The third type is an unexpected minority type – the crime that turns out not to have been a crime at all. Occasionally an incident is interpreted and presented as a crime when actually it is a legitimate act of war; occasionally a killing is not a murder but a legitimate act of self-defence; occasionally things simply happen by accident. And there are some unusual cases where it is assumed from circumstantial evidence that a crime has been committed when there has been no crime at all. Perhaps the most peculiar and spine-chilling case of this kind is the Chipping Campden mystery of 1660.

At the time when a particular crime is committed, forensic science is developed to a particular point where it may not allow the crime to be detected, or it may not allow the perpetrator of the crime to be identified. As time passes, forensic science moves on, new tests become available, and so-called 'cold cases' can be solved, sometimes years or even decades after the crimes were committed. Crimes that are initially unsolved, and may seem insoluble, can therefore be solved later. Equally, crimes that seemed once to have been solved conclusively, can turn out later not to have been solved at all, if it emerges that the convicted person could not have committed the crime after all. This is what has been emerging about the assassination of Robert F. Kennedy and Sirhan Sirhan, who was convicted of his murder.

The question 'Whodunit?' forms a major part of this book. But there are also crimes where there are other significant and highly charged questions. Often behind an assassination there is a conspiracy, and it is not always easy to find out who exactly was involved in that conspiracy. The classic political assassination has a mastermind, an originator who stands well back from the action and hopes to remain undetected, untraced; there is also a middle organization to act as a conduit (and a barrier) to information; then there is the assassin. The reasons for this structure are obvious. The assassin's presence at the scene of the crime makes it likely that he will be caught and identified, whereas the person who has ordered the assassination can, and nearly always wants to, remain unidentifiable. The only way of achieving this is to have an intermediary organization, which takes the contract from the originator and hires the killer. So, with many historic murders we know the names of the assassin, though we have to dig very deep indeed to discover who was behind them.

The failure to bring culprits to justice also generates many questions. Sometimes, when they fail to find or convict criminals, it can look as if the officers of the law or the judiciary are incompetent. Sometimes it can look as if they are conspiring to fail, as if there is some establishment conspiracy to obscure what has happened.

There are alarmingly large numbers of unsolved crimes, even today, when very sophisticated forensic procedures are available. There are still disturbingly large numbers of cases of disappearing boys and murdered girls that remain unsolved. There is often a suspicion, not only among the public but among the police officers concerned, that many may be linked, that they are the work of serial criminals. In Britain, now, there are teams of detectives working towards finding the links, identifying the serial crimes.

In the last few years we have entered a new phase of crime detection. The arrival of DNA testing has allowed some unsolved crimes, decades old, to be cleared up. Perhaps the most spectacular success resulting from the introduction of DNA profiling was the solving of the twenty-year-old Green River murders near Seattle, Washington. Many other cold cases, cases where the investigation has run out of steam or even been closed, can now be reopened and solved, thanks to DNA.

The DNA profile of convicted criminals is now routinely stored for future reference, in just the same way that fingerprints used to be taken. But in the UK there is some disquiet that the code of conduct relating to the keeping of DNA records is shifting towards the overriding power of the state and away from the rights of the individual. Until 2001, DNA profiles taken from people who were arrested but then not prosecuted, or prosecuted, tried and acquitted, had to be destroyed. Since 2001, any DNA profiles taken at the time of an arrest has been kept and permanently added to the National DNA Database (NDNAD). The result of this shift has been a huge expansion in the number of profiles acquired. The UK NDNAD is the biggest in the world, with more profiles in absolute numbers and more in proportion to the population than any other country. At the time of writing, the British government has 3.5 million DNA profiles on its database. This amounts to the DNA profiles of 5.2 per cent of the population, compared with 1.1 per cent for the European Union as a whole, and 0.5 per cent for the USA. This quantitatively defines the UK as a surveillance state.

Governments argue that the larger the database is, the better the chances of clearing up crimes, and the argument is hard to refute. The enthusiasm for resolving not only current cases but some long-closed cases by applying the new technique has raised some major ethical questions. How do we balance the need to conserve individual civil liberties with the desire to bring criminals to justice?

One cold case that might be solved in Britain is the 1963 murder of George Wilson in Nottingham. George Wilson was the landlord of the Fox & Grapes pub. He was unlocking the door to his pub when he was attacked and stabbed thirteen times. It was an apparently motiveless murder, and it prompted a large-scale investigation. Over 60,000 people were interviewed. Every dustbin in Nottingham was searched for the murder weapon. After nine days two boys playing in a ditch on the Nottingham to Radcliffe-on-Trent road found the knife in its sheath. At the time, forensic science was unable to extract from the knife the crucial information. Now, it may be possible. The knife is waiting to be examined using the latest DNA testing techniques.

In 1969, Annie Walker was battered to death in her home at Heather in Leicestershire. She had recently gone to her bank in Coalville and withdrawn £1,000. Probably she was followed from the bank to her home by her killer. The next day she was dead on the floor in her night clothes. The weapon she was struck with was never found, but police have now been able to extract DNA samples from the killer, left on items collected at the crime scene. All that is lacking is a match for the DNA profile.

In October 1970, a twenty-four-year-old teacher called Barbara Mayo hitch-hiked north from her home in London. Six days after she left, her body was discovered in a wood beside the northbound carriageway of the M1 motorway, within sight of Hardwick Hall. She had been raped and strangled. There were reports that a woman of Barbara's description had got into a Morris Traveller. No-one was ever caught for this crime. Then in 1990 detectives confirmed that Barbara was killed by the same man who raped and strangled eighteen-year-old Jackie Ansell-Lamb near the M6 in Cheshire in March 1970. So the DNA profiles from the two crime scenes confirmed that these were serial crimes. Detectives tried criminal record profiling to identify likely suspects. In 1997, they examined the DNA profiles of 250 'possibles' and were able to eliminate all of them. They are still waiting for the DNA profile that matches. Even after all this time, the killer of Barbara Jackie may be identified and brought to trial.

Clearly, the police have a marvellous tool for detection, and they would like to have a much bigger DNA database. As Prime Minister Tony Blair has indicated, if everyone in Britain was on the database, tens of thousands of cold case unsolved crimes could be solved.

But the successful solving of crimes is not just about the latest forensic techniques – it is about a lot of other things as well, such as comprehensive crime scene examination, and above all about objectivity and open-mindedness. In one case after another, the wrong suspect is pursued from the outset and, even if the right suspect becomes visible later on, the police are unable to backtrack and admit that they were wrong. Classic cases include the Rachel Nickell and JonBenet Ramsey murders. Not only did the murderers get away, but the wrongly accused prime suspects, Colin Stagg and the JonBenet's parents, had their lives ruined.

The determination of police officers to find a suspect, a single suspect, and ensure that all the evidence points unerringly towards that suspect's guilt, has caused unending misery and trauma to those wrongly accused. It has also led to the systematic wearing down of the suspect using refined interrogation techniques to force a confession. The worst (most meaningless) confessions are those extracted with some sort of promise of leniency in the courtroom – the practice known as plea bargaining. People are told they will get lighter sentences if they plead guilty, and many do. This is not the path to truth or justice. Although it may improve the clear-up rate as far as the police are concerned, it does not mean that the crimes are really solved. All too often the wrong people are sent to prison as a result. The most extreme example of the distorting effect of plea bargaining was the deal done between the Prosecuting Attorney of King County in Washington and Gary Ridgway. In exchange for confessing to more than forty murders in King County, he was offered his life. A statement of confession written under those conditions has no meaning, except to illuminate what Gary Ridgway understood the law officers wanted him to say.

PART ONE

MEDIEVAL
UNSOLVED CRIMES
(BEFORE 1500)

THE BURNING OF ROME: NERO OR THE CHRISTIANS?

The great fire that burned down most of the city of Rome broke out during the night of 18-19 July AD 64. It started in the commercial district, in the shops at the south-eastern end of the Circus Maximus. Town fires were not uncommon in cities, then or in later centuries. This one took its particular place in history because of its severity and because it was alleged, both then and subsequently, that the emperor himself had started it.

The flames were fanned by a strong summer breeze and spread quickly from district to district, burning down the wooden shops and tenements. The blaze raged for six days and nights before finally petering out. When it was over, ten out of Rome's fourteen districts were destroyed, seventy percent of the area of the city. Rome was a smouldering ruin.

Rumour spread, equally quickly, that the emperor Nero himself had ordered the city to be torched, and that he had stood watching the fire from the top of the Palatine Hill, playing his lyre as the city burned below and all around him. It was a powerful image, and one that has stuck to Nero's memory ever since.

The reality was that Nero was in his palace in Antium (Anzio) when the fire broke out. When he heard about the fire he rushed to Rome and ran about the city without his guards for the whole of that first night, personally directing the fire-fighting operation. But people preferred to believe that Nero had started the fire, and he looked for someone to blame. He used the Christians as scapegoats. The Christians were a small, fringe sect, and their obscurity laid them open to accusations of inexplicable antisocial behaviour. The perennial fear of the foreign meant that Nero's strategy worked. This led to a major persecution of the Christians. In spectacular 'games', Christians were fed to lions, crucified or burned as human torches to entertain the masses – and to remind them who started the fire. But suspicion that Nero had indeed been behind the fire grew when a lavish new building programme replaced the ruins with a city of marble, with wide streets, arcades for pedestrians and a newly designed water supply system. Debris from the ruins was cast into the surrounding malaria-ridden marshes. It began to look as if the clearing of a large area of the city for redevelopment had been carefully planned.

One of the main sources about the episode was the historian Tacitus. He was born in about AD 56 and was eight or nine years old at the time of the fire. He wrote his eye-witness account in *The Annals* in the year 116.

Now started the most terrible and destructive fire which

Rome had ever experienced. It began in the Circus, where it adjoins the Palatine and Caelian hills. Breaking out in shops selling flammable goods, and fanned by the wind, the conflagration instantly grew and swept the whole length of the Circus. There were no walled mansions or temples, or any other obstructions, which could arrest it. First, the fire swept violently over the level spaces. Then it climbed the hills, but returned to ravage the lower ground again. It outstripped every counter-measure. The ancient city's narrow winding streets and irregular blocks encouraged its progress.

Terrified, shrieking women, the helpless old and young, people intent on their own safety, people unselfishly supporting invalids or waiting for them, fugitives and lingerers alike - all heightened the confusion. When people looked back, menacing flames sprang up before them or outflanked them. When they escaped to a neighbouring quarter, the fire followed them - even districts believed to be remote were affected. Finally, with no idea where or what to flee, they crowded on to the country roads or lay in the fields. Some who had lost everything – even their food for the day – could have escaped, but preferred to die. So did others who had failed to rescue their loved ones. Nobody dared fight the flames. Attempts to do so were prevented by menacing gangs. Torches, too, were openly thrown in, by men crying that they acted under orders. Perhaps they had received orders. Or they may just have wanted to plunder unhampered.

Nero was at Antium. He returned to the city only when the fire was approaching the mansion he had built to link the

Gardens of Maecenas to the Palatine. The flames could not be prevented from overwhelming the whole of the Palatine, including his palace. Nevertheless, for the relief of the homeless, fugitive masses he threw open the Field of Mars, including Agrippa's public buildings, and even his own gardens. Nero also constructed emergency accommodation for the destitute multitude. Food was brought from Ostia and neighbouring towns, and the price of corn was reduced. Yet these measures, for all their popular character, earned no gratitude. For a rumour had spread that, while the city was burning, Nero had mounted his private stage and, comparing modern calamities with ancient, had sung of the destruction of Troy.

By the sixth day enormous demolitions had confronted the raging flames with bare ground and open sky, and the fire was finally stamped out at the foot of the Esquiline Hill. But before panic had subsided, or hope revived, flames broke out again in the more open regions of the city. Here there were fewer casualties; but the destruction of temples and pleasure arcades was even worse. This new conflagration caused additional ill-feeling because it started on Tigellinus' estate in the Aemilian district. People believed that Nero was ambitious to found a new city to be named after himself.

Tacitus may have witnessed the fire, but he was too young for his account to have much credibility. He must have relied on the accounts of others to assemble his own. Pliny was the only other Roman historian to live through that period to write about the fire, and he only mentions it in passing. There is a forged letter (forged by Christians) purporting to be from Seneca to St Paul, which includes the detail that '132 houses and four blocks' were destroyed in six days. If true, that implies that less than one-tenth of the city was really destroyed by the fire. But really nothing much can be learned from a forgery.

The historian Suetonius has Nero singing *The Sack of Ilium* dressed in stage costume as his city burned, but Suetonius was intent on portraying the Roman emperors as decadent and wicked. What he wrote about them cannot really be taken as historical fact. Cassio Dio tells a similar story, though it is interesting that Suetonius has Nero singing and playing as he watched from the Tower of Maecenas on the Esquiline Hill, while Cassius Dio places him on the Palatine Hill. Tacitus has him singing in private. There is enough variation among the accounts to justify discounting all of them.

The popular image of Nero fiddling while Rome burned clearly cannot be true, as the fiddle had not been invented. Nero could no more have played the fiddle than the electric guitar, a far more vivid image. He could, on the other hand, have sung and played the lyre, but he may have fallen back on this in despair on the second or third days, and only after he had realized that his efforts to quench the flames were futile. It is not at all unusual for people to seek refuge in music, poetry or prayer at times of personal crisis.

In the aftermath of the fire, Nero opened his palaces as shelters for the many people who had lost their homes in the blaze. He also organized emergency food supplies for the survivors. He did indeed redesign the areas of the city that had been devastated, but with a view to making them more fire-resistant. The wide roads were to act as fire-breaks. The new houses were built with gaps between them, again to stop fire jumping so easily from building to building. Where he made a major political error was in laying out a huge and expensive new palace complex for himself within the area cleared by the fire. This was obviously open to misinterpretation. The new palace was the Domus Aurea, a huge 300-acre development of villas and pavilions set in a landscaped park with an artificial lake. The complex also featured the Colossus Neronis outside its entrance, a bronze statue of Nero that soared over a hundred feet into the air. These extravagances inevitably made Romans wonder whether Nero had deliberately started the fire in order to create the new palace. If Nero had built a palace complex of this kind out in the countryside somewhere, it would probably have occasioned no adverse comment, but to build it in the city, where the land was clearly needed for commerce and housing, was an extraordinarily insensitive decision on Nero's part, and he would have known that under normal circumstances he would not have got the Senate's approval for it.

If Nero was to blame for the fire, he might have had more than one motive for starting it. One might have been to clear the site for the Domus Aurea and other redevelopment. Another might have been to destroy the houses of the senators who were troublesome to him. On the other hand, we know that Nero rushed back to Rome and spent all night trying to organize the fire-fighting. He also lost his own palace, the Domus Transitoria, which was a huge complex that stretched from the Palatine Hill to the Esquiline Hill. The Italian archaeologist Andrea Carandini has been excavating in Rome for twenty years and he has examined the layers of ash left after the fire of 64. His conclusion was that the destruction was very severe indeed. 'Everything was destroyed. Not a single house was left standing.'

Carandini also found that the area of the Forum where the senators lived and worked was destroyed. As a result the Roman aristocracy no longer had a place to live. The open avenue down the centre of the Forum survived, but that became a kind of shopping street, a commercial area built on the ruins of the Roman aristocracy. The way the fire struck had the effect of severely weakening the power of the senatorial class.

The ferocity of the fire has been corroborated by other evidence. Nails holding roof tiles down fell from roofs and melted. Large numbers of coins found in the Forum seem to have been the small change in the pockets of Roman citizens caught there in the firestorm.

We are left with four possibilities. The fire may have started deliberately on orders from the emperor Nero. It may have been started deliberately by the Christians. It may have been started deliberately by some unknown arsonist. It may have been an entirely accidental town fire. As many as a hundred small fires broke out every day in ancient Rome. Even major accidental fires were fairly common. The city was burned again in the time of the emperor Vitellius in 69 and in the reign of Titus in 80. The chances of the fire of 64 having broken out accidentally are quite high.

Tacitus argued that the fire could not have spread naturally because the wind was blowing in the wrong direction. In other words, the fire spread into the wind. In recent decades, our understanding of the physics of fire has improved to a point where this objection of Tacitus can be discounted. What happens in a big conflagration is that when the flames consume all the available oxygen in the area they will spread outwards into adjacent areas where oxygen is available – and that includes areas that are upwind. A large fire creates a strong updraft, and this in turn sucks air in from all around, creating a distinct microclimate that cuts across whatever the regional wind pattern might be.

Tacitus also argued that the fire spread through the stone and marble temples and the concrete dwellings of the rich just as easily as through the wooden tenements of the poor, and this pointed to deliberate arson. But even if buildings are made of non-flammable materials, wooden furniture, rugs, mats, wall hangings and curtains can still catch fire, especially if the windows are open. Roman buildings were particularly vulnerable in this respect, as the windows were usually left open and unshuttered, and they were designed for maximum ventilation. An archaeological experiment was carried out, in which a replica of an aristocrat's house was built inside a fire chamber. A small fire was set in one corner of the replica house. It soon spread to the furniture and consumed the whole house.

Suetonius and Cassius Dio both accused Nero of being the arsonist. Nero himself accused the Christians. It has for a long time been assumed that the Christians were innocent scapegoats, the victims of a cruel, sadistic and self-centred tyrant. But there is some evidence to suggest that Nero may have been right, that the Christians were the ones who started the fire.

Tacitus summarized the 'scapegoat theory' in the following way.

Consequently, to put an end to the report [that he himself had started the fire], Nero fastened the guilt and inflicted the most exquisite tortures on a class hated for their abominations, called Christians by the populace. Christus, from whom the name had its origin, suffered the extreme penalty during the reign of Tiberius at the hands of one of our procurators, Pontius Pilatus, and a most mischievous superstition, thus checked for the moment, again broke out not only in Judaea, the first source of the evil, but even in Rome, where all things hideous and shameful from every part of the world find their centre and become popular. Accordingly, an arrest was first made of all who pleaded guilty; then, upon their information, an immense multitude was convicted, not so much of the crime of firing the city, as of hatred against mankind. Mockery of every sort was added to their deaths. Covered with the skins of beasts, they were torn by dogs and perished, or were nailed to crosses, or were doomed to the flames and burnt, to serve as a nightly illumination, when daylight had expired.

Tacitus mentions that the Christians pleaded guilty, though as in many court cases of the modern day this may not be the same thing as an admission of guilt. It may be that that they pleaded guilty in the hope of more lenient treatment, a form of plea bargaining, or it may be that they were tortured into admission.

One reason for thinking that the Christians were to blame is that the fire started in an area where they were living. Another is that they believed that Rome would soon be destroyed by fire. Starting that fire would simply have been a way of making the prophecy come true. Professor Gerhard Baudy of the University of Konstanz has studied ancient apocalyptic prophecies, and discovered that Christians living in the poorer districts of Rome were circulating revenge-ridden texts that told of a raging inferno that would reduce the city of Rome to ashes. These were not submissive, meek and mild Christians, but Christians with a zeal for change. There is tendency to forget that early Christianity was quite unlike the religion that it became later. This was, after all, thirty years before the Book of Revelation was written, a book full of strange and frightening prophecies. And Revelation refers to the Whore of Babylon, an evil beast with seven heads. The text itself tells us that 'the seven heads are seven mountains' and Rome was famously the city of seven hills. Probably the writer of Revelation had the city of Rome in mind as the source of all evil. The constant mantra of the oracles of the Roman Christians was that Rome must burn. That was their objective.

With their interest in prophecies, those same Christians would very likely have heard of the Egyptian prophecy that the great city would fall on the day Sirius rose above the horizon. In AD 64, Sirius rose on 19 July. It was on that day that the great fire of Rome started. It could have been a coincidence, but in the context of the Roman Christians' own predictions of destruction by fire it does seem an extraordinary coincidence. Professor Baudy believes that the Christians were the deliberate instigators of the fire, and that Nero's accusation against them was right.

Even if Nero was innocent of starting the fire, he was unable to escape the political fall-out from the huge disaster. With both the senate and the army against him, within four years he was forced to flee from his rebuilt city and commit suicide.

WILLIAM RUFUS:
A HUNTING ACCIDENT?

On the face of it, the death of William Rufus, the second Norman king of England, looks an open and shut case of death by misadventure. The official account circulated at the time was that the king died as a result of 'friendly fire': an arrow fired by one of his hunting companions. Yet some people at the time had their suspicions that it was no accident, but murder.

The first Norman king of England, William the Conqueror, is one of those historical figures everyone has heard of; he invaded England, set up a new administration and a new aristocracy, replacing the Anglo-Saxon elite with Norman barons. By contrast his son and successor is a dim and shadowy figure, remembered mainly for his red hair and his mysterious death in the New Forest. That death, inadequately explained at the time as a hunting accident, has become an almost mythic event. We hold in our minds an iconic rustic image of deer running through an August forest, a medieval king on horseback, cantering in dappled sunlight beneath oak trees, felled without warning by a stray arrow during the chase. William Rufus has been turned into a figure from a pagan realm, where horned gods hold sway in the ancient forests and treacherous courtiers conspire against their kings.

But William Rufus was a genuine historical figure and historians have a great deal to tell us about him. Perhaps the key information about him is his deep unpopularity. He was enormously disliked as a man; he was even more disliked as a ruler. He shared many of his father's personality traits, and that may go some way towards explaining why William the Conqueror chose him among his sons as his successor; he was the favourite son. Rufus was also being rewarded for his unswerving loyalty to his father. During the Conqueror's lifetime, William Rufus was always at his side, supporting him during the rebellions stirred up by his elder brother Robert. But for those rebellions, Robert would have been the natural heir, and William I of England would have been succeeded by Robert I, not William II.

The date of William Rufus's birth is uncertain. He was probably born between 1056 and 1060, and he is known to have been a boy at the time of his father's momentous conquest of England. He was crowned king on 26 September 1087, following his father's accidental death. Outwardly, the Conqueror had left him a securely conquered kingdom, but he also left him with an insoluble problem with the power structure. The feudal lords in England also held lands across the Channel in Normandy, and leaving England to William and Normandy to Robert meant that these lords owed unswerving homage and loyalty to two masters instead of one. The problem was intensified because of the bitter rivalry between William and Robert; offering support, service and loyalty to one often meant antagonizing the other. It was not surprising that the barons became restless under the new regime, and not surprising that plots developed.

William Rufus was built like his father: short, muscular, stocky and rather fat. What made his appearance distinctive was his wild red hair and ruddy complexion. It was this that gave rise to his nickname, 'Rufus'. William had an unattractive personality. He disliked people, he was tyrannical, cruel, greedy, brash. Because he was the king, there were no constraints on his antisocial traits. He was given to violent fits of temper and vindictive paranoia, though as events turned out he may have been right to sense conspiracies gathering round him.

He caused offence to the Church with his blasphemies. He used his royal powers to exact heavy taxes from the Church. William was motivated by greed, not by any anticlerical mindset. He manipulated the feudal law in a similar way to benefit his treasury; shire courts were instructed to impose heavy fines, confiscation of property was used far more than before as a punishment, and very high inheritance taxes were introduced. In the same spirit, he treated the Church as the wealthy corporation it was, siphoning off its wealth for his own use. He also caused great offence to the Church by quarrelling with the Archbishop of Canterbury, Anselm, and driving him into exile.

Because of these transgressions, he was intensely disliked by churchmen. In the years after his death, William's reputation suffered greatly at the hands of chroniclers, most of whom were monks. In reading character sketches of the king, due allowance has to be made for the bias of the writers. William was also gay and sympathetic towards the Jews. A revisionist historian writing today might portray William in a sympathetic light, but these tendencies were disastrous for any public figure, especially a king, in an age that was strongly anti-semitic and strongly homophobic. They also made him even more of a hate figure as far as the Church was concerned.

One of the most critical of the monastic chroniclers was Peter of Blois, who blamed many of the problems on Ranulph, the Bishop of Durham, whose advice William acted upon. In Peter's eyes, it was Ranulph who was the cruel extortionist and the woeful oppressor of the kingdom, rather than William himself. William was criticized for holding 'in his own hands' the archbishopric of Canterbury, four bishoprics and eleven abbeys; he was 'keeping all these dignities for a long time for no good reason whatever', and of course taking all the income from the vast ecclesiastical estates. Peter of Blois painted a black picture of England under the rule of William and Ranulph. 'Chastity utterly sickened away, sin stalked in the streets with open and undaunted front and, facing the law with haughty eye, daily triumphed.' A godless kingdom was afflicted with alarming portents. 'There were thunders terrifying the earth, lightnings and thunderbolts most frequent, deluging showers without number, winds of the most astonishing violence, whirlwinds that shook the towers of churches . . . fountains flowing with blood, mighty earthquakes, while the sea, overflowing its shores, wrought infinite calamities to the coasts.' Today most people would attribute these phenomena to natural causes, but the monkish chroniclers saw them as expressions of God's displeasure; the disasters were the voice of God telling England that William was a bad ruler.

William Rufus's unpopularity carried with it profound political implications. The general dissatisfaction with William's regime made it much easier for his elder brother Robert to gain support. Robert Curthose had inherited the dukedom of Normandy from their father. Understandably, and almost inevitably, there was mounting rivalry between the two brothers over the throne of England, which must have appeared the greater prize. Many of the barons were ready to support Robert as a replacement for William as king. There was a rising of these barons in 1088, only a year after William came to the throne. It was organized by Bishop Odo of Bayeux, who wanted to replace William with his brother Robert. But William proved to be ruthless, strong and purposeful enough to crush this rebellion. There was another rebellion by the barons seven years later, in 1095.

Like his father, William Rufus had enormous military strength. He was able to fend off major open rebellions and maintain control over his kingdom. Given the extraordinary circumstances – an alien king, the younger son of a usurper, an unpopular ruler – it was remarkable that he hung onto power for a full thirteen years before meeting his death, whether it was accidental or not. He was even able to defeat the king of Scotland, Malcolm III, and replace him with a client-king, the Saxon prince Edgar Atheling. He also managed to gain control over his father's entire legacy when his brother Robert wanted to join the crusade. Robert mortgaged the duchy of Normandy to him, leaving him in charge there during his absence.

While Robert was out of the way on the First Crusade in 1095, William used the respite from sibling rivalry to secure his borders with Scotland and Wales. He ordered the building of Carlisle Castle and a chain of forts along the Welsh border to stem the raids on the marcher barons by Welsh brigands. William's barons continued to complain about his high level of taxation. In particular, they complained to William's younger brother, Henry, who had been waiting ever since their father's death to seize his brother's throne if ever an opportunity arose. William was under threat from not one but two brothers.

William never placed any trust in his barons, which may explain why he never won their loyalty, and he never trusted his brother Henry. Perhaps he had good reason. It was after all Henry who suggested the hunting trip in the New Forest. But the nagging question remains: why did William agree to ride off into the New Forest with a brother he profoundly distrusted and a band of noblemen whose loyalty he knew he could not depend upon? He must have known that any one of them could have killed him at any time. Or did William trust in the magic aura of kingship? Did he imagine the fact that he was the king was sufficient protection, that they would stop short of anything as terrible as regicide? That seems unlikely, as he had watched his own father invade England in 1066 and slaughter the incumbent Saxon king on a hill near Hastings.

The night before his death, William's sleep was disturbed by a nightmare. He dreamt that the men he was about to ride out with would kill him. At an unconscious level, then, William knew very well that he was taking a terrible risk. Yet still he went. The reasons why he acted as he did that day are still not known. The whole question of who shot the arrow that killed him – and why – form the core of the mystery. But whichever theory we support, the fundamental question remains that William took a huge and essentially avoidable risk in agreeing to go hunting with these men.

A contemporary account by Orderic Vitalis described the preparations for the hunt.

An armourer came in and presented him [the king] with six arrows. The king immediately took them with great satisfaction, praising the work and, unconscious of what was to happen, kept four of them himself and held out the other two to Walter Tirel, saying, 'It is only right that the sharpest be given to the man who knows how to shoot the deadliest shots.'

This may be accurate reporting, but the detail has too much dramatic irony about it to be credible, and perhaps a biblical reminiscence of Jesus's remarks to Judas, another friend and betrayer. Orderic was helping to assemble a mythic version of the murder.

During the fatal hunt, which took place on 2 August 1100, an arrow was shot that found its way to the king's chest. It is not known who shot the arrow, but it was said at the time that the culprit was a powerful Norman baron, Sir Walter Tirel, the Lord of Poix. We know from the account of Peter of Blois that Walter Tirel had recently arrived in England from Normandy and was welcomed to join the king's table. After the banquet was over, the king invited his new guest to join the hunt. The hunting party spread out through the woods near Brockenhurst as they chased some running deer. The king and Walter Tirel became separated from the others. That, according to Peter's account, was the last time the king was seen alive.

Walter fired a wild shot at a stag, a shot which missed its target and hit the king in the chest instead. It was not a fatal shot, but William fell from his horse onto the shaft, which drove deep inside him, piercing the lung. Walter tried to offer aid, but there was no help he could give the dying man. Walter feared he would be charged with murder, panicked, mounted his horse and fled.

It was said that the death of the king, William II, Rufus, was an accident, but there are several aspects of the story that arouse suspicion. One was the behaviour of the hunting party immediately afterwards. The entire body of men rode off to leave the king to die alone, quickly drowning in his own blood. Incredibly, the king of England's body was left unattended in the woods, abandoned at the spot marked today by the Rufus Stone.

Another reason for doubting that the shot that killed William was fired accidentally was Walter Tirel's reputation as a master bowman. Tirel was someone who was extremely unlikely to shoot wild, and some chroniclers said so at the time. He was unlikely to make the very basic mistake of shooting his (one) hunting companion. These two circumstances together make the incident look very much like murder and a conspiracy to murder at that.

The king's corpse was discovered by a local country-man, a charcoal-burner named Purkis, who took it to Winchester on his cart. The following day he was buried in a modest grave and with few signs of grief. These circumstances too point to an organized conspiracy. The contemporary chroniclers report that all his servants were busy attending to their own interests, as would be likely with a major change of regime, and that few if any of them cared about the funeral.

The king died unmarried and therefore without any legal offspring. His younger brother Henry succeeded to the English throne as he had been hoping and, we must suspect, planning. The speed with which Henry secured the treasury at Winchester and had himself crowned king, just three short days after his brother's death, suggests a fair amount of pre-planning. That in turn suggests that Henry knew in advance that William was going to die, and that means that the accident must have been arranged. Henry stood to gain most by William's death, so if there was a conspiracy to kill William, it is most likely that Henry engineered it. In the three-cornered struggle for the English throne, this interval when Robert was out of the way was the very best moment Henry could have chosen to have his brother assassinated. With William killed while Robert was away in Palestine, Henry was in the very strongest possible position to gain the English throne, and he made sure of it by having himself crowned immediately, before Robert could return. All of this points directly to a political coup engineered by Henry.

The Church chroniclers studiously avoided blaming Henry for the assassination. They were very pleased and relieved to have Henry on the throne, describing him as 'a young man of extreme beauty, much more astute than his two brothers and better fitted for reigning.' He was a safer king than William as far as the Church was concerned; he released the Church's estates, imprisoned Ranulph, the Bishop of Durham, and recalled Archbishop Anselm from exile. Possibly Henry did all these things precisely to buy the Church's approval, not out of piety. The Church could not condone a political assassination, so it turned a blind eye to it, preferring the more convenient interpretation of the events as an accident.

Shortly afterwards, Robert heard the news and came

racing back from the crusade. He mounted an invasion to try to unseat Henry and take the English crown for himself. Peter of Blois was keen to blame this too on Ranulph who, he said, escaped from prison, 'repaired to Normandy, and in every way encouraged the Duke thereof, Robert, the King's brother, to invade England.'

So, the dead king had two brothers, both of whom had excellent motives for killing him or having him killed, as both wanted to be king in his place. In theory Robert could have been involved in a joint conspiracy with his brother Henry. On the face of it, it would appear that only one of the brothers could have gained from William's death – only one could gain the throne of England. On the other hand, in 1096 Robert had pawned the duchy of Normandy to William for 10,000 marks in order to finance his participation in the First Crusade. It is not clear how Robert would have been able to buy back his duchy on his return. Certainly it was extremely convenient as far as Robert was concerned for William to die in 1100; on his brother's very timely death, Robert regained possession of his duchy without having to pay for it. So, while Henry gained the English crown, Robert regained his duchy at no cost. Both brothers after all had a great deal to gain from William's sudden death.

On the other hand, no definite evidence of Robert's implication in the conspiracy has emerged, and the fact that the murder happened while Robert was as far from England as it was possible to be, in the Holy Land, implies that the plot was instigated by Henry and his supporters. It is possible that there was some discussion between them before Robert left, and that Robert intimated that he would like to see William removed; Robert may have consented to a violent resolution to the problem and left Henry to organize it.

But was Walter Tirel really the hitman? The chroniclers were unequivocal about Walter Tirel. He was the man who officially shot the fatal arrow, but there is no record of any form of retribution against him. He was not tried; he was not executed; there was no retribution; there were no sanctions. These facts also point to a palace conspiracy. Indeed it is possible that all of those who went out hunting with the king that day wanted him dead, and Tirel was simply the one who drew the shortest straw.

More intriguing still is the possibility that Tirel did not kill William at all. One contemporary document has survived to indicate that he may not have been guilty. The document was written by one of the greatest men of the time, a man of impeccable honesty and with no political interest in vindicating or incriminating Walter Tirel. He was the great Norman Abbot Suger. Suger was a friend of Tirel's and he gave Tirel shelter during his self-imposed exile in France after William's death. The two men evidently liked and trusted one another. While he was Tirel's host, Abbot Suger had many opportunities to talk to Walter and they evidently had many conversations about the events of that fateful day. What Suger wrote down, summarizing these conversations, is very revealing.

It was laid to the charge of a certain noble, Walter Tirel, that he had shot the king with an arrow; but I have often heard him, when he had nothing to fear nor to hope, solemnly swear that on the day in question he was not in the part of the forest where the king was hunting, nor ever saw him in the forest at all.

This means that Walter was afterwards claiming that he was not alone with the king at all. He was apparently with the main party, elsewhere. If Walter was not alone with the king, there is the clear implication that someone else was, and that their identity had to be concealed. Given all the circumstances, the most likely suspect must be the king's brother, Henry. In the aftermath of the assassination, Walter may have been persuaded that someone had to take the blame for the shooting, and that Henry himself, now to be king, could not be tainted with the crime. For the good of the kingdom and the safety of his tenure of the English throne, Henry must seem to be blameless. The murder of William Rufus was a particularly shocking crime. It was a triple crime, not just murder but regicide and fratricide as well. The reign of the new king, Henry I, would have been blighted from the beginning if he had been suspected of his brother's murder. Usurpers often, though not always, went the way of their predecessors. Henry VII was a notable exception.

Walter Tirel was perhaps persuaded that, in the best

41

interests of the kingdom, he should accept the blame for the king's death. An official version of events reduced his culpability by making the shooting entirely unintentional, and this made it possible for him to retreat into self-imposed exile without punishment. Tirel was never given any advancement, but Henry was adamant that he should not be punished in any way for what had happened. That in itself implies that Henry knew that Tirel was innocent, and is consistent with Henry himself being the real assassin.

Henry and Walter Tirel are not the only suspects. There were many barons who had plotted against William during the previous decade and some were in the hunting party; one of them could have been the assassin. One family in particular was suspected at the time, and for that reason should be given serious consideration. The Conqueror put his trust in Richard de Clare, appointing him to his ruling council and giving him the title Chief Justiciar. In this exalted position, Richard acted as the king's regent while William was across the Channel in Normandy. Immediately after William the Conqueror's death, Richard de Clare took part in a barons' rebellion that was intended to oust William Rufus and put Robert on the English throne. The rebellion failed partly because Rufus was a powerful warrior, partly because a significant number of Norman barons in England still supported him at that time.

William Rufus attacked the rebels' strongholds at Rochester, Pevensey and Tonbridge. Tonbridge Castle was owned by Richard de Clare. After a two-day siege at Tonbridge, de Clare was obliged to surrender to the king and he was punished by having both his castle and the town of Tonbridge beside it burnt down. De Clare was in addition forced to retire to a monastery, where he died three years later. Richard de Clare's daughter Adelize, interestingly, was married to Walter Tirel.

Richard de Clare was succeeded by his son Gilbert, who was allowed to inherit the family estates, including the burnt-out town of Tonbridge and its wrecked castle. Gilbert was more circumspect than his father, though not necessarily out of any liking for the king. He fought beside the king in the campaign against the Scots and possibly against the Welsh, too. Gilbert de Clare and his younger brother Roger were both members of the fateful hunting party in the New Forest. Either one of them could have been persuaded to assassinate the king for Henry. Whether either of them fired the arrow, it is probable that they were privy to the conspiracy. There was a flurry of activity following William's death. Henry rushed to Winchester to gain control of the royal treasury; he had himself crowned king as quickly as possible. In this race to present both England and his elder brother with a *fait accompli*, Henry was given conspicuous support by the de Clare brothers. Access to the treasury was vital for a number of reasons, not least to enable Henry to buy off his thwarted brother with an annual pension of £2,000, the price of his compliance with the coup.

The de Clares were such conspicuous supporters of the new king, and their father Richard de Clare had been so flagrantly humiliated by William, that many people suspected at the time that the de Clares had plotted the murder with Henry. They were rewarded on a scale suggesting that this was the case.

It seems unlikely that the official Henrician version of what happened is true. If Tirel and the king were really the only two men in that part of the wood, who were the witnesses who supplied the colourful details about the king's death? Obviously the king himself did not live long enough to give any account of what happened, and we know from Abbot Suger's comments that Tirel himself repeatedly denied that he was anywhere near the scene, so he could not possibly have supplied the circumstantial detail either.

This is how William of Malmesbury described the event in the 1120s, just twenty years afterwards.

The sun was now declining, when the king, drawing his bow and letting fly an arrow, slightly wounded a stag which passed in front of him. The stag was still running. The king followed it for a long time with his eyes, holding up his hand to keep off the power of the sun's rays. At this instant Walter decided to kill another stag. Oh gracious God! The arrow pierced the king's breast. On receiving the wound the king uttered not a word, but breaking off the shaft of the arrow where it projected from his body. This speeded his death. Walter ran up, but as he found him senseless, he leapt upon his horse and escaped with the utmost speed. Indeed there were none to pursue him. Some helped his flight; others felt sorry for him.

Some details could have been reconstructed after the body was discovered, such as the breaking of the arrow shaft, but most of William of Malmesbury's account must have been fabricated – unless there were really several people present at the scene.

Even the location has been disputed. The three-sided Rufus Stone, actually a mid-nineteenth century replacement made of cast iron, is generally thought to be close to the spot in the forest where the king fell. It bears the following wordy inscription dating from 1865:

Here stood the oak tree on which an arrow shot by Sir Walter Tyrell at a stag glanced and struck King William the Second, surnamed Rufus, on the breast, of which he instantly died, on the second day of August, anno 1100. King William the Second, surnamed Rufus, being slain, as before related, was laid in a cart, belonging to one Purkis, and drawn from hence, to Winchester, and buried in the Cathedral Church of that city.'

But not everyone believes that the Rufus Stone was raised in the right place. Some believe the king met his end at the National Motor Museum at Beaulieu.

William Rufus was a horrible man, even by the standards of medieval rulers. He had two surviving brothers, one older and one younger than himself, who both wanted his throne. Both of them had the strongest of motives for wanting him dead. It is not at all surprising that there was a conspiracy to assassinate and replace him. The thing that is most surprising is that after ten years of staving off threats to his safety William went off willingly into the woods with his murderers.

A curious but significant fact that has been overlooked is that William's brother Richard died long before (in 1081) at the age of twenty-four – *in a hunting accident in the New Forest*. Perhaps Henry was remembering this portentous and life-changing event from their younger days when he set up the 'hunting accident' in the New Forest for his brother William.

EDWARD II

Like William II, Edward II was an English king who met his end under mysterious circumstances. While William's death was alfresco, out in the New Forest, Edward's was a claustrophobic death in a castle dungeon – or so it is thought. The appalling death of Edward II took place on 21 September 1327, in a chamber in Berkeley Castle. The deposed king was forty-three years old, constitutionally strong, and his murderers tried several different ways of killing him before he eventually died. The road to this terrible death was a long and complicated one, involving power struggles among nobles, personal rivalries, personality clashes, heterosexual and homosexual love affairs, and an adulterous queen who was ready to depose her own husband out of revenge.

Edward II was born in Wales. He was the baby born in Carnarvon Castle to Eleanor of Castile in 1284 and presented to the Welsh by Edward I as their Prince of Wales. He was seen as a weak king because he preferred quiet rustic pursuits to soldiery; indeed he would probably have been a happier man if he had been born a simple countryman. He enjoyed gardening, basket-making and ditch-digging, preferring them to the noble arts of government, warfare and jousting. His chosen hobbies were of the wrong class, and this made him an object of sheer contempt among his courtiers. When he chose a lover, it was not just the fact that it was a gay lover that drew contempt, but a *low-born* gay lover. In an age where birth and breeding meant everything, Piers Gaveston was just too low-born to be countenanced at the royal court. That Gaveston could beat any and all of them at jousting only served to make the situation worse. Gaveston was also arrogant and sarcastic.

In these ways, Edward II antagonized his barons very early in his reign. A group of barons, headed by Thomas, Earl of Lancaster, seized Gaveston and executed him in June 1312. Edward adopted two new favourites with the same name, Hugh Le Despenser, father and son. These were very different men from Gaveston. They were administrators, but Edward gave them far too much power, so that they too became objects of hatred among the barons. In 1322, Edward led an army against the rebellious Roger Mortimer, and succeeded in capturing him and imprisoning him in the Tower of London. Then Edward marched against Thomas of Lancaster, defeating, capturing and summarily beheading him.

The queen meanwhile began to cultivate a relationship with Roger Mortimer while he was imprisoned in the Tower. It was probably with Queen Isabella's help that Roger Mortimer escaped from the Tower; once free he was able to create new problems for the king.

In the end, Edward's most dangerous enemy turned out to be his queen, whom he had married when she was twelve. Even then, French observers at the wedding said that Edward loved Gaveston more than Isabella. Poor Isabella had to put up with Edward's very public slights and infidelities for many years. The last straw was when the Despensers tried to persuade Edward that Isabella was a bad influence. In 1325, she offered to undertake a diplomatic mission to her brother the king of France. This was really a ruse to escape from the English court.

Isabella arranged a treaty between the two kings, but indicated that Edward would have to travel to France to sign it. He was persuaded not to go by the Despensers, who were afraid that he might be turned against them if he spent a significant amount of time talking to other people; then they might lose their hold over him. They also feared what might happen to them, the Despensers, without the personal protection of the king. They had seen what happened to Gaveston. So, a compromise was to send the young Prince Edward, which was exactly what the conniving Isabella wanted. She then had her son safely with her and could mount a small invasion without fear of her son being taken as a hostage. In September 1326, with a company of only 700 men, Isabella landed at Harwich and succeeded in pulling off a *coup d'état*. Edward, her husband, fled to Wales rather than fight against her. The Despensers were hunted down and killed. Then the king himself was captured and imprisoned at Kenilworth Castle.

The usurpers, Queen Isabella and her lover Roger Mortimer, needed to get rid of Edward II so that her son Prince Edward could become king. Isabella approached Parliament with a request to depose her husband. They refused, but indicated that she might persuade him to abdicate in favour of her son. This she succeeded in doing. King Edward II abdicated five days later, on 25 January 1327. The ex-king was then taken to Berkeley Castle.

It is almost certain that Edward was murdered there. Two key questions remain to be answered: who carried out the murder and on whose orders?

In 1327, Lord Berkeley, the owner of Berkeley Castle, was commissioned jointly with Sir John Maltravers to guard the royal prisoner. Lord Berkeley was not residing at his castle at the time of the king's murder, but was ill elsewhere. Later he was to make much of this absence, when he found himself on trial, and it may well be that he deliberately distanced himself from his prisoner because he knew what was to follow and did not want to be blamed for it. If so, he must take his share of culpability for Edward's death. By providing his castle and washing his hands of the ex-king's fate, he was as guilty as the assassins.

It is not clear whether Queen Isabella or Mortimer – or the two of them together – had decided to have Edward killed from the start. Certainly at least one of them came to this decision after there was an attempt to rescue Edward. Obviously, all the while he lived he might be reinstated. In later years, this proved to be the problem with Henry VI, who was deposed, then reinstated, then deposed and murdered. It was foreseeable. It was too risky to let Edward live. The initial orders, which probably emanated directly from Mortimer or Isabella, were to keep Edward in such poor living conditions that he would just die of neglect. But this reckoned without Edward's strong constitution; he went on living, and so the living conditions were made even worse. Still he would not die. Finally, he was held down and a red-hot poker inserted into his bowels – a slow and agonizing death that would leave no outward mark on his body.

On the night of 21 September 1327, the inmates of Berkeley Castle were terrified by shrieks coming from the king's apartment. The next day the king was found dead. His body was put on display in Gloucester and people were encouraged to go and see the body. Roger Mortimer wanted everyone to believe that the deposed king really was dead and could never regain the throne. The citizens of Gloucester were rounded up to view this unceremonious lying-in-state, but they were kept a good distance back from the corpse. Was this because there were, after all, some tell-tale marks of violence on the body? Or was it because the body smelt so awful?

Given the peculiar circumstances of Edward's forced abdication, some people have inevitably proposed that the official version of his demise was fabricated. They suggest that Edward II was not killed at Berkeley Castle at all, but was instead rescued and lived out the rest of his life abroad. The body briefly displayed and then buried in a royal tomb at Gloucester might have been a substitute: a body, yes, but someone else's. That might be the reason why the crowd was kept at a distance. Mortimer's men did not want to risk someone spotting that it was not the body of Edward II. In the middle ages, ordinary people did not see their king very often, and there were no press photographs to make the king a familiar figure. Passing off a corpse of approximately the right build and hair colour would have been fairly easy.

There was a significant delay before Edward's funeral took place on 20 December 1327, but that can be explained by the military expedition in Scotland. One reason for believing that Edward lived on is that some of his contemporaries believed it. Edmund, Earl of Kent, said that Edward still lived and was imprisoned at Corfe Castle. There was even a plot to free him from Corfe, which led to arrests, treason trials and executions. The Earl of Kent himself was executed in 1330. Another piece of evidence that Edward survived is a letter dating from 1337, written by the papal notary Fieschi. Fieschi claimed in this letter that he actually met Edward II in Italy, describing his life on the run until he ended up at a monastery near Milan. The document could be a forgery, but there is no reason to think so; Fieschi may have been exaggerating when he said he met the ex-king, but the possibility remains that the story about Edward's macabre death at Berkeley

Castle was a sensational cover-up, designed by Roger Mortimer and Isabella to bring Edward's supporters to heel. If Edward was dead, he was literally a lost cause.

The case has to be left open, at least until such time as more solid evidence of Edward's escape and emigration to Italy emerges. For the moment it seems sensible to work on the hypothesis that he did indeed die at Berkeley Castle, not least because the story of the manner of his death was extremely destructive to the Mortimer cause. It inspired pity for the dead king and sympathy for his cause, anger and disgust at the queen and her paramour. If Mortimer and Isabella had wanted to invent a story, then a 'natural causes' death would have been far better. The story about the red-hot poker is too awful to have been made up. Thomas Deloney's *Strange Histories* (modernized spellings) give us the fully developed late medieval horror of Edward's protracted sufferings, beginning with the failed attempt to poison him, then going on to the foul-smelling pit before the final horror of the red-hot poker.

Loathing his life at last his keepers came,
Into his chamber in the dead of night:
And without noise they soon entered the same,
With weapons drawn and torches burning bright,
Where the poor prisoner fast asleep in bed
Lay on his belly, nothing under his head.

The which advantage when the murderers saw,
A heavy table on him did they throw:
Wherewith awaked, his breath could scarcely draw,
With weight thereof they kept him under so,
Then turning up his clothes above his hips,
To hold his legs, a couple quickly skips.

Then came the murderers, one a horn had got,
Which far into his fundament down he thrust.
Another with a spit all burning hot,
The same quite through the horn he strongly pushed,
Among his entrails in most cruel wise, forcing
    hereby most lamentable cries.

And while within his body they did keep
The burning spit still rolling up and down,
Most mournfully the murdered man did weep,
Whose wailing noise waked many in the town,
Who guessing by his cries his death grew near,
Took great compassion on that noble peer.

And at each bitter shriek which he did make,
They prayed to God for to receive his soul:
His ghastly groans enforced their hearts to ache,
Yet none durst go to cause the bell to toll:
Ah me, poor man, alack, he cried, and long it was
    before he died.

Strong was his heart and long it was God knows
Ere it would stop unto the stroke of death.
First was it wounded with a thousand woes,
Before he did resign his vital breath.

Once Edward's slow murder was completed, Lord Maltravers was the one who rode to court to bring the news that her husband was dead. He evidently expected to be welcomed and well rewarded, but Isabella wept and wrung her hands, calling him a traitor for killing her noble wedded lord. Maltravers was thoroughly shaken when he was turned away from court. He realized he had been tricked, and returned to tell Sir Thomas Gourney and the other murderers that the queen had outlawed them all. Suddenly their lives were in peril, and they had to leave England as soon as possible.

Then farewell England, where we were born,
Our friends and kindred which hold us in scorn.

At Lord Berkeley's trial, Sir Thomas Gourney and William Ogle were specifically named as the ex-king's murderers, but they had fled the country. There is no record of Ogle ever having been found. Perhaps he successfully changed his identity and vanished. Sir Thomas Gourney was detained in Spain and brought back to England, but there is no record of his having been punished. According to one version of the story, Gourney was taken ill after his arrest and died under guard, in France, while on his way back to England. According to another version, picked up by Thomas Deloney, he was returning to England voluntarily because he missed his wife and children, was recognized on the ship and beheaded before landing.

Commandment was sent by one called Lea,
He should be beheaded forthwith on the sea:
Alack and alack and alas did he cry,
That ever we forced King Edward to die.
Thus was Sir Thomas despatched of life,
In coming to visit his sorrowful wife.

Maltravers was accused of murdering Edward, acquitted, but later executed for committing a similar crime elsewhere. On balance it looks as if Berkeley knew beforehand what was going to happen in his castle, had qualms about regicide and made himself scarce so that later he could not be accused of murdering the king. All of those concerned in the plot except Gourney were eventually given formal pardons, which tells us nothing about their guilt. Gourney, Ogle and Maltravers were most likely the regicides, the men who actually carried out the murder that, if reported accurately, must rank among the cruellest in history.

These regicides could not conceivably have acted on their own initiative, though. They must have been acting on instructions. The order to do away with Edward can only have come from Roger Mortimer or Queen Isabella. Ultimately the responsibility for Edward's death must be theirs. What is still not known is the specific nature of the instructions. They could have been explicit, expressed in the form, 'The king must die.' Or they could have been expressed more ambiguously, leaving no doubt in Lord Berkeley's mind that he was expected to oversee the demise of the unwanted king, yet also enabling Mortimer and the queen the option of protesting later that that was not what they had wanted. Queen Isabella was certainly capable of that level of duplicity and cunning, as her histrionic and totally insincere reaction to Berkeley's news of her husband's death showed. It is very unlikely, given the exalted status of the ex-king, that Ogle, Gourney and Maltravers took it upon themselves to decide to kill him on their own initiative. Some order from above must have been given, whatever form of words was used. In assassination conspiracies of this kind, it is often possible to identify the assassins, but nearly always impossible to prove the identity of the instigators.

The highest level political assassination conspiracies of recent decades have been three-layered conspiracies. The three-layered conspiracy consists of a small team of assassins, an intermediary organization or middle man behind them and, carefully distancing itself from the operation, an originator. This was the structure used in the attempted assassination of Pope John Paul II in 1981, with

Mehmet Ali Agca and Oral Celik as the gunmen, a Bulgarian organization in the middle and the KGB as the originator of the plot. This structure means that even if the assassins are apprehended and identified the identity of the originator is protected. In the case of Edward II, we have probably identified the assassins correctly (Ogle, Gourney and Maltravers) and can be fairly sure that the plot originated with either Isabella or Mortimer (or both jointly). From his behaviour, Lord Berkeley may well have been the middle man.

THE PRINCES IN
THE TOWER

The uncrowned King Edward V and his brother Richard duke of York were the two young sons and heirs of Edward IV, the king of England from 1471 until April 1483. They are remembered as 'the Princes in the Tower' and are generally believed to have been murdered in the Tower of London in the summer of 1483. It is also generally assumed that they were murdered on the orders of their uncle, Richard, who then had himself crowned as Richard III.

When Edward IV died, suddenly and unexpectedly, he left his two sons as heirs at a vulnerable age. Prince Edward was twelve and his brother Richard was nine. Edward's conscientiously loyal younger brother Richard, Duke of Gloucester acted quickly to take the two boys into his protection, and that action has always been susceptible of two interpretations. He may have intended from the first to imprison and do away with them so that he could have the throne for himself. Or he may have taken them into his care for their own safety.

Whatever his motive, Richard arranged for the young king to be escorted to Stony Stratford, where he took personal charge of the two boys. The road from Northampton to Stony Stratford was lined with soldiers. From Stony Stratford he accompanied them to London and lodged them in the Tower. This is often seen as a sinister move, indicating Richard's malevolent intention, but the Tower was as much a royal residence as a prison, and it may have been chosen as the safest place to house the boys at a time of political uncertainty. At the same time, Richard took the precaution of arresting Richard Neville, Earl of Warwick, who was the young king's guardian, and imprisoning him at Pontefract Castle for plotting to kill the young king.

Richard declared himself Lord Protector and Chief Councillor. As the senior member of the Yorkist family it was natural that he should act as regent to the young king during his minority, so even that declaration need not be interpreted as sinister. Then Richard took an extraordinary step. At a meeting of the Royal Council in the Tower on 13 June 1483, Lord Hastings was arrested for treason. He was known anti-Ricardian. A few minutes later, he was executed by beheading outside. Three other alleged conspirators, Lord Rivers, Richard Grey and Sir Thomas Vaughan, where executed elsewhere.

After removing all possible opposition at court, Richard had a statement read out, declaring that he was the rightful king, that his brother the late King Edward IV had been illegitimate and that therefore the two princes must be excluded from the line of succession. The declaration was startling for many reasons; Richard was not just barring his nephew from the line of succession, but denouncing his elder brother as illegitimate as well – the brother he had served with unswerving loyalty.

A few days afterwards some evidence was produced, probably by Robert Stillington, the Bishop of Bath and Wells, to show that Edward IV's marriage to Elizabeth Woodville had been bigamous, and therefore all their children were bastards anyway. The bishop's information was a bombshell. It was all too believable that Edward IV was a bigamist. He was a great womanizer, like his father, and he later conducted a high-profile affair with Jane Shore. Stillington alleged that Edward had been secretly married to Lady Eleanor Talbot in 1461, and since Lady Eleanor was still alive when Edward married Elizabeth Woodville in 1464 that second marriage, to the mother of the two princes, was bigamous and invalid. Lady Eleanor withdrew to die in a convent in 1468.

Stillington's breathtaking allegation helped Richard III, but it was to get him into serious trouble two years later when Henry VII came to the throne. Henry needed to reverse the charge of bigamy because it made his own wife, Elizabeth of York, illegitimate and therefore weakened his own claim to the throne. Stillington found himself imprisoned for embarrassing the unexpected new Tudor king and queen in 1485. Not surprisingly, he espoused the cause of Lambert Simnel in 1487, but when that failed he found himself accused of high treason. Most surprisingly of all, Stillington died a natural death at Windsor in 1491.

If Edward's two sons were illegitimate, as Bishop Stillington's evidence showed, they could have no right to the throne. The children of George, Duke of Clarence, Richard's older brother, had lost their right to a place in the line of succession on account of their father's treason. That left Richard himself as the clear heir. He was crowned King Richard III at Westminster Abbey on 6 July 1483.

The two princes were seen a few more times in the Tower shortly after that, then never again. According to the Great Chronicle of London, the boys were seen several times in the summer of 1483, shooting and playing in the Tower garden. According to another account, by the French spy Dominic Mancini, they were seen less and less frequently that summer, at windows and behind bars, 'till at length they ceased to appear altogether.' The two accounts contradict one another and it is not possible to be sure what happened. It is usually assumed that the boys were murdered that autumn in the Tower, in secret, much as Shakespeare portrays it, but it is possible that something altogether different happened.

Certainly the boys were fully and completely in the power of their uncle Richard, the aspiring new king, and it is important to explore what sort of man he was. The main difficulty is that most of what we think about him comes to us by way of Shakespeare's play. Playwrights taking historical subjects often bend history to make a better play, and Shakespeare certainly 'improved' the case against Richard. The historical Richard, as opposed to the character in the play, was born on 2 October 1452 at Fotheringhay Castle near Peterborough. As far as the outside world was concerned, he was the fourth son of Richard, Duke of York, who himself had a strong claim to the throne of Henry VI, and his wife, Cecily Neville. Within the family it was an open but unspoken secret that his older brother Edward was illegitimate; his low-key christening ceremony was an admission that his birth was not altogether welcomed. Once that older brother became king, as Edward IV, it became a very dangerous secret.

During the turbulent period of the Wars of the Roses, the Yorkists were sometimes in great danger. In February 1461, their mother sent the nine year old Richard and his brother George overseas, to Utrecht, for safety. It was thought to be too dangerous for them to remain in England. The political situation was constantly changing; they were brought back a month later and at the coronation of Edward IV, Richard was created duke of Gloucester.

Richard's father was killed when Richard was still a boy, and after that he was taken into the care of Richard Neville, Earl of Warwick, 'Warwick the Kingmaker'. Warwick was strongly implicated in turning Henry VI off the throne and replacing him with Richard's oldest brother (or rather half-brother) Edward, as Edward IV, and therefore indirectly responsible for making Richard king, too.

Richard started to become a player of consequence in 1469, when at the age of seventeen he supported his brother Edward against Warwick, shared his exile and took part in his triumphant return. He fought loyally and effectively on his family's behalf, the Yorkist cause, in battle after battle in the Wars of the Roses.

During his brother's reign, Richard worked with steadfast loyalty, using his great skills as a military commander to support his half-brother the king, and was rewarded with huge estates in the north of England and the title Duke of Gloucester. He thus became the richest and most powerful nobleman in England. The other surviving brother, George, Duke of Clarence, was by contrast disloyal to Edward IV, who had him executed for treason. Shakespeare has Richard responsible for murdering Clarence, but the truth is that Edward had him executed in secret; the drowning in a butt of Malmsey was true, but it was Clarence's requested mode of despatch. Richard had nothing to do with it. It is possible that George tried to use his knowledge of Edward's illegitimacy as a justification for leading a full-scale revolt in an attempt to supplant him. Edward saw him as too dangerous and had him removed. Richard, meanwhile, showed patience. He played a more intelligent game, showing his older half-brother nothing but loyalty.

After the Battle of Tewkesbury, which the Yorkists won, Richard married Prince Edward's widow, Anne Neville. It was Richard and his brother George who in cold blood stabbed Prince Edward to death after the battle. Richard was also in the Tower of London shortly afterwards, on the night of 21 May 1471, when Henry VI was murdered, and may have been responsible for that assassination too. Oddly, Shakespeare does not use that fact, when making Richard a regicide would have made his anti-hero an even more spectacular villain.

With that CV, Richard III was certainly capable of killing to maintain his position, but his family loyalties were intense and strong, and from that point of view it seems unlikely that he would have murdered his nephews. There is also the hint that history was repeating itself. As a nine-year-old politically significant and vulnerable young aristocrat, he was 'disappeared', secretly spirited out of the country for his own safety by a close relative. Did he perhaps do the same for his nine- and twelve-year-old nephews? Did he perhaps not have them murdered at all, but arrange their disappearance overseas?

If they had disappeared but survived, it would not have been in the Tudors' interests for them to reappear. Richard III's reign was short – a mere two years – and he was replaced at the Battle of Bosworth by the usurper Henry VII. Henry had even less title to the throne of England than Richard, and therefore had an even more powerful motive for removing the two princes than Richard. Henry

VII's mother, Lady Margaret Beaufort, was a great schemer on her son's behalf. When she heard of the reported death of the two princes, she was delighted because she supposed 'that the deed would without doubt prove for the profit of the commonwealth.' If it was known that the princes were alive during the Plantagenet-Tudor regime change, they would have been a focus for rebellion. The Crowland Chronicle says that it suited the Tudors to spread the rumour 'that King Edward's sons, by some unknown manner of violent destruction, had met their fate.' In other words, it was actually said at the time that Henry Tudor and his supporters wanted the two princes to be dead, whether their fate was known or not. While the possibility that one or both of them were alive, Henry was not safe on his throne, simply because their right to it was stronger than his. For this reason, Henry Tudor (and his dynasty) promoted the idea that the two boys had died in the Tower – and at the hands of Henry's predecessor.

If the princes were murdered in the Tower, they could have been killed at the orders of Richard III or Henry VII. Confirmation of their murder seemed to emerge during building work in the seventeenth century. Two small skeletons were found under a stone staircase and it was assumed that these must be the remains of the murdered Edward V and his younger brother. The bones were found in a complex of buildings running along the southern side of the White Tower, and later demolished; the site has been cleared.

Sir Thomas More gives the most detailed account of the alleged murder, and he says that the bodies were removed from the place where they were initially buried 'at the stair foot' to a better (ie more dignified) site by a priest of Sir Robert Brackenbury, who then died taking the secret with him. But the position of the skeletons found in 1674 was 'at the stair foot', where they should no longer have been, which throws doubt on the rest of More's account, if indeed the remains belonged to the two princes in the first place.

When the bones were subjected to forensic examination in 1933, the results were inconclusive. The skeletons seemed to be closer together in age than the two princes were, and there was a strong chance that they belonged to two girls. In 1933, there was no chance of radiocarbon dating the bones – the technique had not been invented – and a firm date might have helped to resolve the issue.

The problem becomes even more complicated by the earlier discovery, in 1603, of another pair of skeletons, which were also at the time assumed to be the remains of Edward V and his brother. The 1603 bones were found in the substantial fore-building that then stood in front of the south-west corner of the White Tower, not far from the two skeletons that were to be found in 1674. Obviously all four skeletons could not be authentic, and maybe none of them were.

Given the absence of bodies and the absence of any credible evidence of murder, it remains a possibility that the two princes were not murdered on Richard III's orders. It is at least equally likely that Richard III did not kill his nephews but instead sent them abroad. He himself had needed to withdraw to Flanders as a boy, his flight arranged by his mother, and with that experience behind him he may well have sent the boys overseas to the care of his sister, the Dowager Duchess of Burgundy, who held her own independent court at Malines. It is likely that for a time the boys lived quietly with their mother at Gipping Hall near Stowmarket, which was also the home of the Tyrell family. Tyrell is named by Shakespeare as one of the princes' murderers, but he was in fact Richard's 'knight of the body', his secret agent.

Tyrell might well have been entrusted with looking after the princes for a time, while arrangements for shipping them across to the continent were made. That is the tradition in Sir James Tyrell's family. The princes lived at Gipping Hall 'by permission of their uncle', Richard III. There were, moreover, widespread rumours circulating in 1486, following Richard III's death at the Battle of Bosworth, that the princes had not been murdered, but were still alive. There are even documents dated 1484 among the Harleian Manuscripts which may tell us of the arrangements that were made for the secret transfer of the boys overseas. There is a tantalizing entry late in 1484 which refers to a journey made by Sir James Tyrell 'over the Sea into Flanders for divers matters greatly concerning our well-being.'

Although it is generally assumed that Perkin Warbeck (a pretender to the English throne) was an impostor, it is just possible that he really was, as he claimed, Richard, Duke of York. He may have been lodged with the Werbecque family of Tournai. What happened to the elder brother is less clear, and although chroniclers are able to say where Richard/Perkin went they seem to be unable to follow Edward. One chronicler actually says, 'I find no mention of the elder brother being in Flanders, but very frequent mention of his younger brother being there.'

There was a great deal of confusion over the identity of Lambert Simnel, the pretender who appeared in 1486. Four of the early chroniclers gave conflicting accounts of his claim. One said he was the genuine Earl of Warwick, son of George, Duke of Clarence; another said he claimed to be Edward V but was an impostor; another said he was an impostor claiming to be the Earl of Warwick; another said he first claimed to be the Duke of York and then changed his claim to Warwick. It has even been suggested that the original claimant (whoever he was and whatever he claimed to be) was killed in the Battle of Stoke in June 1487, when his army of supporters was annihilated, and that the Lambert Simnel who was afterwards treated as the claimant was a substitute. He must rank as one of the strangest figures in history: someone pretending to be another person who was pretending to be someone else.

The identity of Perkin Warbeck is a shade clearer though still uncertain. He looked strikingly similar to Edward IV, Edward V's father, spoke flawless English, carried himself in a princely manner. It was at the time, and still is, very hard to believe that he was the son of a Tournai boatman. After close questioning he was acknowledged by Margaret of Burgundy as her nephew and was acknowledged as the Duke of York by many other people too. It was only after he fell into the clutches of Henry VII that his fate was sealed. Henry VII eventually had him executed.

If the two pretenders were not Edward V and his brother Prince Richard, it is difficult to see what else might have happened to them other than an untimely death. If they were murdered, they might have been murdered at the orders of Richard III or Henry VII. When they were murdered, by whom and at whose orders is still entirely unknown, though it has usually been assumed that Richard III was responsible for ordering their murder. Richard was only in power for two years, and Henry VII, who would equally have wanted rival claimants out of the way, was around for much longer. Indeed Henry VII and Henry VIII systematically and ruthlessly weeded out aristocrats with any significant Plantagenet connections, simply to ensure the supremacy of their own dynasty. Within that culture, eliminating the sons of Edward IV would have been inevitable.

Shakespeare has conditioned us to believe that Richard III was evil, but he, Shakespeare, had little choice but to be a mouthpiece for Tudor propaganda. His play *Richard III* is in effect a justification for Henry VII's usurpation of the English throne; but Henry VII's claim to the throne, his pedigree, was not as strong as Richard's, as he himself must have known. Shakespeare blames Richard for the murder of his innocent brother, George, Duke of Clarence, but history records a very different story. Clarence did indeed plot against Edward IV and it was Edward himself who had him executed, and privately rather than secretly, in the Tower.

Some have excused the alleged murder of the two princes on the grounds that England needed to be governed by a man. There were, however, precedents for boy-kings – Richard II and Henry VI had been boy-kings – and they had regents or protectors to rule for them until they were old enough to rule for themselves. A well-established mechanism existed to get round the problem, as Richard III himself clearly understood. As for Bishop Stillington's accusation that Prince Edward, the boy-king, had no right to the throne: that turns out to have been doubly true. Edward IV was a bigamist, so his sons by his invalid second marriage to Elizabeth Woodville were both illegitimate. As illegitimate offspring they could not succeed to the throne.

Edward IV was himself illegitimate. His mother was Cecily, Duchess of York, but she conceived Edward on about 28 July 1441 while her husband the duke was away on campaign (14 July–21 August) and she was having an affair with an archer called Blaybourne. It was matter of general comment that Richard (Richard III) and George (Duke of Clarence) were men of slight build, like their natural father the duke of York, but Edward (Edward IV)

71

was huge. He was six foot four inches tall, the same build as his natural father, Blaybourne. It was an open secret. The French king Louis XI, laughed, 'He is not Edward IV! Everyone knows his name is Blaybourne!'

Richard III would certainly have known that his older 'brother' was an illegitimate half-brother, but kept quiet about it for safety's sake while his brother was alive. Once Edward IV was dead, it was a different matter. Then it was safe for him to expose the double illegitimacy of Edward's sons. Given his long and impeccable record of intense family loyalty down to that moment in 1483, Richard may even have seen it as his painful duty to bring out the skeletons in the family cupboard and try to purify the dynastic bloodline; he may have seen it as his patriotic duty to the integrity of the crown. What we see here is a very different Richard III from the crook-backed villain of Shakespeare's play, and someone really rather unlikely to have killed his nephews.

PART TWO

UNSOLVED CRIMES OF THE EARLY MODERN PERIOD
(1500–1800)

THE SUSPICIOUS DEATH OF AMY ROBSART

The scene of Amy Robsart's death was Cumnor Hall or Cumnor Place in Oxfordshire. In 1560 Cumnor Hall was a modest low-built house arranged round a quadrangle. It had been the sanatorium of the monks of Abingdon Abbey but after the suppression of the monasteries the property had been occupied by a royal physician called Dr Owen and then, from 1558, by Antony Forster, Treasurer of the Household of Robert Dudley, later to become Earl of Leicester.

On the evening of 8 September 1560, his wife, Amy Robsart, was found dead at the foot of a staircase at Cumnor Hall.

Her death was a great scandal. Not only was it a sudden and suspicious death that might well have been murder – Robert Dudley was the great favourite of the queen, Elizabeth I, and Dudley wanted to marry her instead. The death of Amy Robsart, or Amye Duddley as she signed herself in letters, was very timely as far as Dudley was concerned. The queen had her twenty-seventh birthday the day before Amy's death and she was clearly infatuated with Dudley. There had been speculation, not only in England but in courts all over Europe, that if Dudley should ever be widowed or divorced he would become Elizabeth's king-consort. It had been openly discussed and there was no surprise at all when Amy was found dead: only scepticism about the explanation that it had been an accidental fall.

A pamphlet of the time gave the common view of Robert Dudley. 'When he was in full hope to marry the queen, he did but send his wife aside to the house of his servant, Forster of Cumnor, where shortly after she had the chance to fall from a pair of stairs and break her neck, but yet without hurting of the hood that stood upon her head.' The 'pair of stairs' did not mean there were only two steps for her to fall down, which would have defied credibility completely, but a returning staircase with two flights and a landing halfway up. It was even so clearly a fall down a short flight of steps. In the circumstances, it was an accident that should have resulted in a few bruises at worst.

An inquest was held and its verdict was that Amy had died accidentally. Amy's body was buried immediately at Cumnor. Presumably her burial was recorded in the parish register, though this was subsequently destroyed. Later, Dudley arranged a full-scale funeral for his wife in Oxford, but the coffin buried afterwards in the Church of St Mary the Virgin in Oxford High Street was, when it was opened in the twentieth century, found to be empty.

What the queen made of Amy Robsart's death is not known for certain. She was fully aware of the political damage to herself of what appeared to have happened. She certainly did not want it to appear that she had connived with her favourite to marry him as soon as he had murdered his wife. She immediately acted against Dudley in Council, though the detail of this action are not known as the Council's minutes for that year have disappeared.

Many historians of the period are pro-Elizabeth to a point where they will not countenance the possibility that the queen knew what was in Dudley's mind, that she knew beforehand that he was going to arrange his wife's murder. One result of that has been a certain amount of bending of evidence, much of it involving adjusting dates. One Elizabethan scholar, for instance, described a conversation as taking place 'probably on 8 September' when it is known to have happened on 6 September, two days before Amy Robsart's death. This may sound like a minor detail of no importance, but there is a great deal of difference between discussing someone's sudden death on the Sunday, when they are known to be dead, and discussing it two days beforehand. Then it clearly shows foreknowledge. The fact is that Elizabeth was sufficiently infatuated with Robert Dudley to turn a blind eye to his plan to murder his wife.

Exactly how Amy Robsart was killed is not known. She may have died as a result of being strangled, smothered or having her neck broken. A fall down the stairs could not conceivably have been the cause, so we may suspect that an expert assassin was hired, though another suspect exists. On the day when Amy Robsart died it is known that there were two other people at Cumnor Hall with Amy: Mrs Odingsell and Mrs Owen.

Mrs Odingsell was described as 'the widow that liveth with Antony Forster'. She seems to have been Antony Forster's housekeeper. She was also the aunt of Richard Verney, who had been Dudley's page and was still devoted to serving Dudley's interests. It is probable that either Richard Verney or his hireling was the murderer. Verney had been summoned by Dudley in the previous April, when there were rumours that there was a plot to poison Amy. Verney had been for some reason unable to travel to see Dudley, and wrote him a letter of apology, adding that he would 'always be to my best power advanced in any your affair or commandment where opportunity offereth.' It may have been no more than elegant politeness, but he was saying that he would do anything to help Dudley.

A document of unknown provenance says: 'Sir Richard Verney who, by commandment, remained with her [Amy] that day alone, with one man only, and had sent away perforce all her servants from her, to a market two miles off, he, I say, with this man, can tell how she died.' The writer of the pamphlet said that the other man in question was killed in prison, where he was sent for some other crime, because he threatened to tell what happened. Verney himself did not live very long. He died in London after a period raving about devils. Verney's presence at Cumnor Hall would have aroused no suspicion. Accompanied by a friend, he was simply calling on his aunt at Cumnor Hall one Sunday. Mrs Odingsell wanted to stay in the house, even though there was a fair that day at Abingdon. It was Our Lady's Fair, and Amy made a point of sending all the servants to it.

One theory is that Amy used the fair as a pretext to get the house to herself, so that she could commit suicide by throwing herself down the stairs. But she did not in the end have the house entirely to herself. When Mrs Odingsell protested that she should not go to the fair but stay to be with her, Amy answered that 'Mrs Owen could bear her company at dinner.'

Mrs Owen was either the widow of Dr Owen the royal physician who had been the previous tenant, or his daughter-in-law. She was occupying some of the rooms at Cumnor Hall, which was still regarded as the family house in spite of its being let to the Forsters. Maybe Amy wanted the house emptied so that she could have a confidential conversation over supper with the one person she trusted, someone who was outside the circle of friends and retainers attached to or appointed by her untrustworthy husband. Mrs Odingsell herself may have been an accomplice to the murder. Her motive in wanting to remain in the house may have been to preoccupy Mrs Owen while her nephew and his friend killed Amy. Mrs Odingsell seems to have been successful in isolating Mrs Owen, because the body was not found until late evening when the servants returned from the fair. The murder probably happened much earlier in the day and the body was arranged in the position at the foot of the flight of stairs where the servants were to find it. Mrs Odingsell may only have needed to say to Mrs Owen that Amy had decided to go to the fair herself and that would been enough to confine Mrs Owen to her rooms.

The layout of Cumnor Hall was unusual. When it had become a private house earlier in the sixteenth century, several doors in the sanatorium had been sealed up. It was said that on some pretext Amy was persuaded to exchange her usual bedroom for one that had one of these blocked doorways at the head of the bed. It was easy to disguise or conceal doors at this time as it was common to cover walls with tapestries and other hangings. Amy was unaware that there was a secret door behind her bed. It was easy for her murderer to enter the room without her knowing, come up behind her and strangle or smother her before she knew what was happening. Significantly, in the aftermath of Amy's death, Dudley gave huge grants of land to Forster in as many as fifteen counties. With this wealth he was able to buy Cumnor Hall and almost completely rebuild it. This make-over ensured that all traces of the existence of secret doors were removed. Another precaution was the clause in Forster's will that enabled Dudley to buy Cumnor Hall from his heirs – and Dudley in due course bought it.

Amy had been twenty-seven when she died, the same

age as both Robert Dudley and Queen Elizabeth. Robert had known Amy since they were seventeen, but he had known Elizabeth since childhood. After the murder of Amy, Robert Dudley was lucky not to find himself in the Tower, even if only for appearance's sake. He had been in the Tower once before, at the time of the Lady Jane Grey crisis. Lady Jane Grey was the wife of Robert Dudley's elder brother, Lord Guildford Dudley. Robert Dudley had been deeply implicated in the thrust to put Jane on the throne; it was he who had proclaimed Jane queen at King's Lynn. When Mary Tudor prevailed, Jane, Robert's brother Guildford and Robert's father the Duke of Northumberland were all executed in the Tower. Robert himself was imprisoned, and very lucky to escape with his life.

While in the Tower, Amy administered the Dudley estates. She was allowed to visit him though it is not known how often she did so. While Robert Dudley was in the Tower, he met the princess Elizabeth, who was also a prisoner there, and it was then that they fell in love. On her accession to the English throne, Elizabeth made Robert Dudley her Master of Horse. This meant that he had to be in continual attendance on her at court, so it was a way of keeping him near her. The Spanish ambassador reported in the spring of 1559, 'Lord Robert has come so much into favour that he does whatever he likes with affairs, and it is said that Her Majesty visits him in his chamber night and day. People talk of this so freely that they go so far as to say that his wife has a malady in one of her breasts and the queen is only waiting for her to die to marry Lord Robert.' Because of the way the situation was developing, the Spanish sent a new ambassador to London that summer, Alvaro de Quadra, the Bishop of Aquila, with the special task of watching Dudley. He reported in the autumn, 'I have heard from a certain person who is accustomed to give veracious news that Lord Robert has sent to poison his wife. Certainly all the queen has done in the matter of her marriage is only keeping Lord Robert's enemies and the country engaged with words until this wicked deed is consummated.'

In January 1560, de Quadra reported that England was getting restive with the uncertainty over the queen's intentions and even more over Lord Robert Dudley's. It seems everyone was waiting for news of Amy's death. Dudley had tried to enlist the help of the Professor of Physics at Oxford, Dr Bayly, asking him to prescribe something for Amy, 'meaning also to have added somewhat of their own for her comfort.' Bayly, according to de Quadra, would have nothing to do with it, suspecting, probably correctly, that Dudley was planning to add something lethal to his medicine and that he, Bayly, would find himself taking the blame for Dudley's crime. When this version of events was published in a pamphlet, the cautious Bayly was still alive and he did not contradict it. De Quadra also reported that people in England in general were critical of Dudley's behaviour, because what he was planning to do would ruin the queen.

Dudley may have sensed that the queen was getting nervous about all the publicity and was on the brink of rejecting him to save her own position. That may have caused him to act when he did. There was also, just three weeks before the murder, the scandalous public accusation by Anne Dowe of Brentford that the queen had had a child by Dudley. There were widespread rumours that Dudley had slept with the queen. Dudley may have realized that he needed to be free of Amy so that he could marry Elizabeth without delay.

By the first week in September the quarrel between Dudley and William Cecil, the queen's secretary, had intensified. Cecil was so unnerved by what was happening that he spoke unguardedly to de Quadra.

I met the Secretary Cecil, whom I knew to be in disgrace. Lord Robert, I was aware, was endeavouring to deprive him of his place. He [Cecil] said the Queen was conducting herself in such a way that he thought of retiring. He said it was a bad sailor who did not enter a port if he saw a storm coming on, and he clearly foresaw the ruin of the realm through Robert's intimacy with the Queen, who surrendered all affairs to him and meant to marry him. He said he should ask leave to go home, though he thought they would cast him into the Tower first. He ended by begging me in God's name to point out to the Queen the effect of her misconduct and to persuade her not to abandon business entirely, but to look to her realm; and then he repeated to me twice over that Lord Robert would be better in Paradise than here. Last of all, he said they were thinking of destroying Lord Robert's wife. They had given out that she was ill; but she was not ill at all; she was very well and taking care not to be poisoned.

The next day, the Saturday, was the queen's birthday. The Spanish ambassador managed to have a conversation with her. He reported, 'The queen told me on her return from hunting that lord Robert's wife was dead, or nearly so, and begged me to say nothing about it.' If true, this was damningly revealing. The queen knew that Amy was 'nearly dead' on Saturday. Amy was found dead late on Sunday evening and official news of her death did not reach Windsor until Monday. By then, de Quadra had not sent his letter, and he was able to add a postscript as follows. 'Since this was written the queen has published the death of Lord Robert's wife and has said in Italian, Si ha rotto il collo. She must have fallen down stairs.' Why the queen should have made this comment in Italian is not known. It suggests to me that she was already trying to distance herself from what had been done. From de Quadra's comments, which there is no particular reason to distrust, it is clear that the queen knew what was going to happen and colluded with Dudley in his plan to murder his wife. Elizabeth, the queen, was an accessory to murder, an accessory before the fact. Once this is realized, the reason for Cecil's extreme anxiety about the queen's conduct becomes clear; he knew she was plotting with Dudley to destroy his wife.

There was widespread condemnation of Dudley and the queen. Nobody believed that Amy's death was accidental. A week afterwards, one of the great preachers of the time, Dr Leaver, wrote that 'the country was full of mutterings and dangerous suspicions, and there must be an earnest searching and trying of the truth.' When it emerged that Dudley fully intended to marry the queen as soon as possible, English ambassadors in France and Scotland frantically signalled that this must be prevented if the prestige of the English court was to be sustained abroad. The foreign courts were even more scandalized than the English. Throckmorton, the English ambassador in Paris, was so humiliated by what the French were saying about his queen and about England that he wanted to crawl away and die. He reported this back and was sternly rebuked from London, in a letter which he annotated before filing it, 'A warning not to be too busy about matters between the queen and Lord Robert.'

In January 1561, it looked as if the marriage would go ahead. Dudley's brother-in-law went to de Quadra with an outrageous proposal. In principle it was a plea for Spain to endorse and support Elizabeth's marriage to Lord Robert; in return, Elizabeth would return England to Catholicism. De Quadra was understandably astonished and bewildered by this, and had to refer back to Philip of Spain. The decision was made for a papal nuncio to come to England, meet the queen and hear from her direct what she had in mind. This was to take place in April 1561. Like a magician, Cecil cleverly produced a Catholic plot before that could take place. It was a very minor plot to re-establish Catholicism in England, but Cecil managed to make it sound sinister and threatening to Protestant lords. 'The way is full of crooks,' he wrote, and he knew because he was one of them. In Council, he managed to establish that anyone who met the nuncio when he arrived would be guilty of treason. The use of the word treason was enough to clinch the matter. The nuncio would not be met. The Queen would not offer to turn the country Catholic. The queen would not solicit the support of Spain, Dudley's single ally. The queen would not be able to marry Dudley after all.

In this cunning way, Cecil succeeded in blocking the marriage that the queen appeared to have risked so much to bring about. He took a remarkable risk. It has even been suggested by some historians that Cecil himself may have been responsible for organizing Amy Robsart's murder in order to precipitate the crisis. Cecil had gradually slid out of favour with the rise of Robert Dudley. Cecil knew that if Dudley were to become king-consort it was probable that all of his work would be undone. In fact relations between Cecil and Dudley had deteriorated to a point where it was unlikely that Cecil could survive if the marriage took place.

Cecil may have reasoned that he would save the queen from a politically disastrous marriage – and so save the kingdom – by sabotaging the courtship. That scotching the queen's marriage to Dudley would save his own position, and possibly save him from a miserable end in the Tower, was an added incentive. If he could make the malicious rumours that Dudley was plotting to do away with his wife come true, the queen would have to drop Dudley. In some ways, Amy Robsart's death was more to Cecil's advantage than to anyone else's. The scandal it was certain to cause would make it impossible for the queen to go ahead and marry Dudley. So perhaps it was Cecil who hired Verney or someone else to kill Amy. The snag with this theory is that there is absolutely no documentary evidence to support it.

Another theory that has been put forward is that Amy Robsart's death was linked with her medical condition. We are told that she suffered from some sort of chest ailment. This could have been breast cancer or perhaps an aortic aneurism. Breast cancer sometimes produces porous bones. If Amy's bones were unusually fragile, it would, after all, be possible for her to break her neck by falling a short distance down a low flight of stairs. The idea that Amy broke her own neck, committing suicide by throwing herself downstairs, is less plausible, as she could not have known about the porosity of her bones. She could therefore not have known that a fall down a short flight of stairs would be sufficient. It is a very unlikely mode of suicide.

The likeliest explanation for Amy Robsart's death remains deliberate murder at the orders of her husband, with the connivance of the queen. There was never any attempt by the queen to deny that Amy was murdered.

She always spoken of Amy's death in a heartless way. There can be little doubt that Elizabeth I knew that Amy was going to be murdered. She very likely encouraged Robert Dudley to hasten matters. Dudley very likely commissioned his ex-page Richard Verney to carry out the murder, and Verney in turn enlisted the help of another man (unnamed), who was later killed in prison after threatening to publish the truth of what had happened.

KIRK O' FIELD:
THE ASSASSINATION OF
LORD DARNLEY

When Mary became Queen of Scots, she was more than aware that she needed to marry and provide heirs to the Scottish throne. In July 1565, she made the fateful and as it turned out very destructive decision to marry her cousin, Henry Stewart, Lord Darnley, a weak and vain young man. Why Mary chose Darnley remains a mystery, as he was evidently too headstrong, volatile and unstable to occupy the extremely sensitive role of a prince consort, a king in name only. He was admittedly tall, superficially charming and fond of courtly amusements, but he never showed affection for her and from the beginning asked for more power than she was willing to allow him.

Less than a year after the wedding, Darnley became overwhelmed with jealousy because Mary was spending much of her time with a musician called David Rizzio. Rizzio had come to Scotland from Italy some years earlier on a diplomatic mission but remained at the Scottish court as a lute player and subsequently as Queen Mary's secretary. The more outraged Mary became over her husband's stupid, childish and licentious behaviour, the more she looked to Rizzio for consolation and support.

This was happening at a time when many Scottish Protestant lords were becoming restless under Mary's rule, and some of these noblemen claimed that Rizzio had usurped their proper places beside the queen – even that he was a secret agent of the Pope. They easily persuaded the gullible Darnley into believing that Mary and Rizzio were sexual partners, an accusation that seems to have no foundation in truth, not least because Mary was six months pregnant with Darnley's child. They nevertheless succeeded in inflaming Darnley's jealousy and persuaded him to take part in a plot to murder the Italian, and do it in front of the heavily pregnant queen. In fact, it may be that the conspirators intended to distress her so much by making her watch the brutal murder that she would miscarry. Given that this was the sixteenth century, a miscarriage would probably have resulted in her own death. Mary herself believed that Darnley was so angry because she had denied him the crown matrimonial that he wanted to kill her and the child. Making her witness a brutal murder would bring about her death and allow Darnley to succeed as King of Scots.

On the night of Saturday 9 March 1566, Lord Ruthven and a group of accomplices burst into Mary's chamber in Holyrood House. Rizzio was seated at her supper table and the assassins dragged him screaming from her side, stabbing him repeatedly, both in front of her and once they had succeeded in dragging him out onto the staircase. It is not clear whether Darnley himself inflicted any of the injuries, but he was certainly incriminatingly present in the chamber, as the queen's own vivid account of the murder makes very clear.

We were in our chamber at our supper. The King [Darnley] came into our chamber and stood beside us. Lord Ruthven, dressed in a warlike manner, forced his way into our chamber with his accomplices. We asked our husband if he knew anything of the enterprise. He denied it. Ruthven and his accomplices overturned our table, put violent hands on Rizzio and struck him over our shoulder with daggers. One of them even stood in front of our face with a loaded pistol. They most cruelly took him out of our chamber and gave him fifty-six blows with daggers and swords.

Following this outrageous crime, the nobles kept Mary prisoner at Holyrood Palace. She was desperate to escape. Somehow she won Darnley over and they escaped together. But Darnley's decision to help Mary to escape infuriated the nobles who had conspired to kill David Rizzio; now they wanted Darnley out of the way as well. Mary pretended to forgive Darnley and cleverly managed to separate him from the group of treacherous nobles who had organized the assassination of Rizzio, but she must have realized that she could no longer trust him. With Rizzio still fresh in the minds of the court, another threat to Darnley's fragile self-esteem soon took centre stage – another man.

James Hepburn, Earl of Bothwell, rushed to Mary's aid in putting down a rebellion of Protestant conspirators, even though he was a Protestant himself. Bothwell was Lord Admiral of Scotland. He had a reputation as a brave man of action, but he also had a reputation for lechery, brutality and lust for power. Tired of the vicious weakling at her side, Mary saw Bothwell, the strong new man, as her rescuer and he soon became her most trusted advisor. He gave her security. Under his protection, Mary was safely ensconced in Edinburgh Castle, where she had to face a strange rebellion from the Scottish lords. The lords who had been involved in the murder of Rizzio asked for her forgiveness. She gave it, not from her heart but from the sheer political need to maintain some measure of control over her kingdom. She never forgave Darnley himself, but for the moment she was prepared to put up with Darnley as a necessary evil. The forgiven lords were unhappy about Darnley because of his distinctly two-faced performance during the murder of Rizzio; he was supposed to be present at the murder to give Ruthven and the other assassins support, but when the moment came he did not give it wholeheartedly. The lords were therefore disenchanted with Darnley as well as Mary.

By the time Mary gave birth to James VI in June 1566, Darnley had slid back into his habitual life of debauchery, neglecting his royal duties and sullenly watching Mary's relationship with Bothwell develop. He disappeared from court for a time and this prompted talk of a possible annulment of the royal marriage. At Craigmillar Castle in December 1566, the Scottish lords openly proposed to Mary that she should get rid of Darnley; she should either divorce him or arrange his death. Her response, which could mean anything or everything, was that she was not prepared to consider either option.

When the queen learned that Darnley was seriously ill in Glasgow, she uncharacteristically showed great concern by travelling to his bedside and then arranging for a horse-litter to carry him back to Edinburgh to convalesce at Holyrood Palace. For some reason, perhaps fearing that he was being set up for assassination, Darnley decided not to move into Holyrood. Instead he quartered himself in a house at Kirk o' Fields in the Royal Mile, a few hundred yards from Mary's residence. For months Mary had spoken of her husband with nothing but contempt, and this apparently kindly gesture was out of character. It may be that she wanted her unreliable husband close at hand where she could see what he was doing. It may be that she was cold-bloodedly preparing his death.

A recent apologist for Mary has said that she would have to be a duplicitous character indeed to have constantly rejected all suggestions of assassination, and to have sent Darnley her own doctor if she had been secretly planning to have him murdered. But this level of cunning and duplicity is of course well within the possibilities of

Mary's complex personality, and indeed well within the norms of high-level power politics in the sixteenth century. Henry VII, Henry VIII and Elizabeth I were all capable of behaving with the same deadly duplicity when the occasion demanded. It must be regarded as highly significant that the letter Mary wrote to Archbishop Beaton, on the eve of her journey to fetch Darnley from Glasgow, showed absolutely no indication that she planned a reconciliation with her husband.

At two o'clock one February morning in 1576 there was an enormous explosion, and Kirk o' Fields was reduced to a heap of rubble. It looks as Darnley may have had some warning, as after the explosion his body was not found in the house but some distance away in the gardens. It was apparent from the lack of damage to the body that he had not been killed by the explosion, but had been murdered while trying to escape from it. Perhaps he heard suspicious sounds under his bedroom where large amounts of gunpowder had been secretly hidden, perhaps the sounds of unfamiliar activity on the floor below, the voices of strangers, or a tip-off from a servant.

A chair and a length of rope were found in the gardens; Darnley and his groom had used them to climb out of the first floor window and reach the ground. They both lay dead with just one dagger between them. A contemporary drawing vividly shows the bodies of Darnley and servant, just as they were found lying in the gardens. They were wearing nightgowns, but the garments were pulled up, exposing the naked lower halves of their bodies, as if the two men had struggled with their assailants on the ground as they were overpowered and throttled. On the right hand side of the drawing of the crime scene is a touching little invention, the infant James VI, Darnley's son, sitting up in his crib and praying, 'Judge and avenge my cause, O Lord.'

There is still, after centuries of discussion and re-examination of the evidence, no definite proof of who murdered Lord Darnley. At the time, most people assumed that Bothwell organized it; the only question was whether he did so with or without Mary's knowledge and complicity. Most modern historians take that same line too.

The incident scandalized Scotland, and there were calls for Bothwell to be brought to trial for the king's murder. The scandal spread across Europe. It was after all the most flagrant of assassinations. The exploding house covered the tracks of the assassins, making it impossible to prove anything. Indeed, when it came to court it was impossible to prove Bothwell's guilt, and he had to be acquitted. But most people knew that Bothwell was a ruthless opportunist, aiming at nothing less than the throne of Scotland; everyone knew that he was capable of murder.

But whether Mary herself was involved is less clear. In the wake of the murder she appeared apathetic, and this was taken at the time to indicate her guilt, though their were also reports that when she first heard of her husband's death she was grief-stricken. Even more incriminating were the famous 'Casket' letters, which were supposed to have been written by Mary to Bothwell in the three months leading up to Darnley's death. These were allegedly found under Bothwell's bed. There is contemporary evidence that at least two of them were forgeries commissioned by Protestant lords who were busily trying to entrap her; some of them may have been genuine, but they had their dates tampered with. Mary herself was never allowed to see them, which strongly suggests that they were not in her handwriting and she would have been able to disprove their authenticity. They disappeared altogether in 1584 and so never became available for scrutiny by historians. They cannot really be used as evidence against Mary.

But even if Mary had wanted her husband dead, that was no more than many of the rest of the Scottish nobility wanted, as they made clear to her at Craigmillar Castle, and therefore it still did not directly implicate her in his murder. She may have appeared apathetic because she was taken by surprise and shaken, and because she felt powerless to do anything about the situation developing round her.

The events following Darnley's murder were almost as spectacular and dramatic as the murder itself. In the immediate aftermath, Bothwell met Mary about six miles outside Edinburgh; whether by chance or by pre-arrangement is not known, but if the meeting was pre-arranged Mary must have known about Bothwell's intention to kill her husband. He had 600 men with him and he asked to escort Mary to his castle at Dunbar; he told her she was in danger if she went to Edinburgh. Unwilling to cause further bloodshed, and now terrified, Mary did as Bothwell asked.

According to Mary, Bothwell kidnapped and raped her before marrying her. Within days of her marriage, Mary was suicidal with despair at the abuse she had to endure from Bothwell. In the eyes of many people, in England as well as Scotland, her marriage to Bothwell made Mary guilty by association of the murder of Darnley. Marrying her murdered husband's murderer made her as good as (or as bad as) a murderess. Yet it is easy to see that her marriage to Bothwell was a practical necessity; ironically, behaving as if she was an accomplice before and after the fact by throwing in her lot with Bothwell was the only thing that she could do to ensure her safety.

Mary had enemies in the Scottish nobility and she needed a strong ally to protect her from them. Even with Bothwell's forceful help, it was less than a year before the Scottish lords forced Mary to abdicate and flee to England. For the next two decades she was held prisoner by Queen Elizabeth I and finally executed in England at Fotheringhay Castle in 1587, compromised and betrayed first by her enemies in Scotland, then by her enemies in England.

Three months later the baby who would become James VI of Scotland was born. Mary now had an heir, which strengthened her position somewhat. The unmarried and childless Elizabeth of England, ten years older than Mary, watched these events beadily from south of the border. She was intelligent enough to see that although Mary herself might be a doomed monarch, Mary's son would be not only her cousin Mary's heir but her heir as well.

Mary might have produced the next king of Scots, but the Scottish lords were still dissatisfied. They were angry that Bothwell would be all-powerful and decided to take up arms against him. Not long after the (possibly forced) marriage, the rebel nobles and their armies met Mary's troops at Carberry Hill, not far outside Edinburgh. The rebel nobles demanded that Mary must abandon Bothwell. She refused and reminded them of their own earlier advice, which had been to marry Bothwell. Seeing little alternative now, Mary turned herself over to the rebel nobles, who took her first to Edinburgh and then to Lochleven Castle, where she was held captive. With justification she feared for her life, and she was forced to abdicate in favour of her son.

Within weeks, the infant prince was crowned king and James Stewart, Earl of Moray, Mary's unscrupulous bastard half-brother, became regent. The appalling Moray seems to have been the architect of the plan to murder Rizzio. He also spread the unfounded and dangerous rumour that Rizzio and the king were plotting against him, in order to deflect suspicion. But the Earl of Moray got his just deserts when he himself was murdered just three years later. The next regents were also to meet sudden deaths; in fact, James himself as a teenager had one of his regents executed in 1580. The Scottish political landscape was a minefield – and not just for the Queen of Scots. Meanwhile, the Earl of Bothwell's extraordinary later life must have looked to many Protestant (and other) Scots like God's just reward for the murder of Darnley. He managed to escape from Scotland but ended his life in 1578, languishing in a Danish prison, virtually insane.

FIGHTING FOR THE SUCCESSION: THE GOWRIE CONSPIRACY

On the afternoon of 5 August 1600, two men were murdered, the Earl of Gowrie and his brother the Master of Ruthven. Exactly what happened may never be known, as much of the evidence was destroyed at the time. The one contemporary account that survives, written by King James VI of Scotland, is unlikely to be true, not least because King James went out of his way to suppress any alternative scenarios.

The Ruthvens had never been on friendly terms with the Stuarts. Patrick, Lord Ruthven, had been one of the ring-leaders in the murder of David Rizzio, and during that episode he had handled Mary Queen of Scots roughly. Patrick's son William was the Ruthven who had kidnapped James VI at the age of sixteen in the Ruthven Raid and kept him prisoner in Gowrie House until he agreed to sign a statement saying that he was there under his own free will. The young prince had managed to escape and turn the tables on William. He induced William to write a private confession on James's promise of a pardon. James then treacherously used the confession to have William executed.

The next generation of Ruthvens consisted of the twenty-two-year-old John, Earl of Gowrie, and the nineteen-year-old Alexander Master of Ruthven. These two young men naturally saw the thirty-four-year-old James VI as the murderer of their father. In mitigation, James had tried to explain that at the time he was not his own master, and he had restored the confiscated family estates to them. He wanted to show that he was a man of good faith. At the same time, James had good reason to fear and distrust the young Ruthvens. He owed them £80,000. The older brother had also formally opposed James's request for 100,000 crowns to pursue his negotiations for his succession to the English throne. Gowrie himself had a claim to the throne of England. Gowrie's direct descent from Henry VII through his mother made him the next in succession to the English throne after James and his heirs. It has emerged that Gowrie was in London in April 1600, and while he was there Elizabeth I granted him the guard and honours appropriate to a Prince of Wales, which suggests that she was nominating him as her heir. Or, as is more likely with the ageing Elizabeth, she was mischievously playing at naming her successor. On top of that, the Gowries were thought to be involved with witchcraft. James hated them – for all of these reasons.

In July 1600, James wrote secret letters to each of the

Ruthven brothers. The letters were destroyed, so it is not known what they contained. Possibly the Ruthvens' sudden return to Gowrie House in Perth from their castle in Atholl was in response to instructions in James's letters. Another unexplained journey was the Master of Ruthven's early morning ride from Perth to Falkland on 5 August. He rose at four that morning, rode to Falkland and had a secret conversation with the King at the stables, before the King started his day's hunting. James VI's version of this meeting was that the Master had come to inform him that he had imprisoned in a secret room at Gowrie House a stranger 'with a great wide pot full of coined gold in great pieces.' Ruthven had found this stranger wandering in the fields the previous evening.

Ruthven had ridden to tell James so that he should be the first to know about it. James said that the gold had not been found, so it was not treasure trove and the Crown had no right to it. Ruthven argued that if James would not take it, somebody else would. James said that as the coins were foreign they were probably brought in by Jesuits and the stranger was probably a priest in disguise. James said he would send a servant back with a warrant and that the magistrates could question the stranger about the treasure. The hunt went on until eleven, with Ruthven continually pestering James to ride to Perth with him.

When James recounted this bizarre novella to Lennox, Lennox said bluntly and with considerable courage, 'I like not that, sir, for it is not likely.' It was as polite a response as James deserved. The story was absurd from start to finish. Even if Ruthven had genuinely found the stranger and the gold as he said, why on earth would have he ridden at four in the morning to see the king, who was no friend, to tell him about it? If Ruthven had made it all up, James suggested, then he might be mad. Lennox rejected this interpretation. 'I know nothing of him but as an honest discreet gentleman.' Lennox must have suspected that it was James who had made the story up – the entire story. James's interpretation of it was that it suggested a 'treasonable device'. The implication (which James intended Lennox to draw) was that Ruthven had made efforts to draw James into some sort of trap or ambush.

James set off for Perth with twenty-five men including Lennox, Mar, Erskine and John Ramsay, his current favourite. When this party was within a mile of Gowrie House, the Master of Ruthven rode ahead to let his brother know they were approaching. The Earl of Gowrie, who was having dinner with three of his neighbours, was suspicious; he could think of nothing that would bring the king to Perth. Anyway, he rushed out to give the king a welcome, apologizing that there was not enough food in the house to supply dinner. James had to wait an hour while food was sent out for. During this hour, the king drank and chatted to the earl, who was uneasy.

The Gowrie steward asked the Master why the king had come. It was good question. The Master said, 'Robert Abercromby, that false knave, has brought the king here to cause His Majesty to take order for our debt.' James later suppressed this comment. Abercromby, the king's saddler, was not called in court to comment on the Master's remark, so it was probably true – at least to the extent that it was the reason given to the Master by the king. The stranger and the pot of gold were inventions of James.

After James had dined in the Great Hall, he went upstairs with the Master. The Master turned to the company and said, 'Gentlemen, stay, for so it is His Highness's will.' Lennox was suspicious, anxious and rose as if thinking of following the king. He was held back by the remark of Gowrie that the king had gone up 'on some quiet errand', discreetly implying that the king and the Master had gone upstairs for sex. The two went upstairs, along the Great Gallery, then through a heavy door which they locked behind them. They were in the gallery chamber with a turreted room leading out of it, and they stayed there for over two hours.

The rest of the company left the Great Hall and walked in the garden, talking and eating cherries. Then, some time after five o'clock in the evening, the earl's equerry announced that James was riding away from Perth. Gowrie sensed that something was wrong, shouted, 'Horse! Horse!' and went into the courtyard, where the porter assured him that the king had not left the house and he had the keys of all the gates. Gowrie went into the house to see whether James was there or not. Then he emerged to say that he thought the king really had gone.

The group was startled to hear the king's voice shouting, 'Help, my Lord Mar! Treason! I am betrayed! They are murdering me!' They looked up to the turret room window, where they saw the king, red-faced, with a hand clutching his mouth and cheek.

Lennox and Mar led the rest of the company up the stairs, only to find their way blocked by the locked heavy door. They worked at it for half an hour, but were unable to break it down.

Two people stayed apart from all of this, and their behaviour suggests that they were acting as part of some plan. One was the page, Ramsay, and the other was Erskine. If the unfolding plot was of James's making, only these two young men need have known about it. Ramsay was the one who gave out the false story about James having ridden away. Instead of following the rest of the company into the Great Hall, he had gone up a small spiral staircase called the Black Turnpike, and which led directly into the gallery chamber where the king and the Master were. Ramsay must have known about this route from the king, who knew the geography of the house well. Presumably the door at the top of the Black Turnpike had been unlocked by the king when he was left alone for a moment by the Master. The shouting from the window by the king was evidently for Ramsay's benefit, a signal to come up to the chamber via the Black Turnpike.

Erskine and his brother set upon Gowrie and tried to kill him. With help from his supporters, he managed to fight them off. Erskine ran back to the Black Turnpike and with three companions went up to join Ramsay. When Ramsay arrived in the turret room he saw James and the Master wrestling. The Master was almost on his knees, with his head under the king's arm, yet managing to hold his hand over the king's mouth to stop him shouting. When James saw Ramsay he called, 'Strike him low! Strike him low! He is wearing a secret mail doublet.' Ramsay instead slashed at the Master's neck and face. Then he and James pushed him down the little spiral staircase.

It is evident that if James had wanted to apprehend the Master he could easily have done so. Erskine found the badly wounded Master on the stairs, shouted, 'This is the traitor,' and killed him. Gowrie came running up behind. He stepped over his brother's body and entered the gallery chamber. There he met Ramsay and the three other men who had killed his brother. The king was hiding in the turret room. Gowrie looked about him and asked where the king was. Ramsay said he had been killed. At this stunning news – whether he thought it was good or bad scarcely matters – Gowrie lowered his guard and the assassins promptly killed him.

Within minutes everyone was in the gallery chamber. The king knelt by Gowrie's body and thanked God for his deliverance. Outside, the citizens of Perth were gathering, summoned by the tolling town bell. They were devoted admirers of Gowrie, and James and the other assassins could have been in serious difficulties if it had not been for the presence, by chance, in Perth of three hundred armed king's men. If they had not been there, James VI of Scotland might not have lived long enough to become James I of England. But James was remorseless. He sent after the Ruthvens' two young brothers, but their mother had the sense to take them quickly across the border. One died in exile. The other was arrested when James became king of England and imprisoned in the Tower, without trial, for twenty years.

The motive was fairly clear. By murdering the Ruthvens and virtually annihilating their family, James wiped out his debt to them. He was also able to confiscate their huge estates, so he turned a worrying and politically embarrassing debt into a large profit, some of which he used to advance his fellow assassins.

The uncertainties surrounding the incident were almost entirely of James's own making. The opening chapter about the stranger and the crock of gold was pure fabrication. James concocted a complete version of the murders, which was slanted so that he emerged as the victim, threatened and attacked by the maniacal Ruthven brothers who had devised a trap for him. His version was a lie, in that the trap was his own, and the Ruthven brothers were its victims. They were not the assassins; he was the assassin. Yet behind this simple true/false dichotomy lies something more complicated. The Ruthvens did pose a threat to James by holding his huge debt over him. They might have been safer if they had written off the debt; but that is said with the benefit of hindsight. Possibly the Ruthvens were plotting against James, and James anticipated their conspiracy.

William Cecil was involved in the discreet quest for a successor for Elizabeth I. In terms of bloodline and the pro-Catholic position that had been forced upon him, James was the obvious candidate. If Cecil had a freer hand and could follow his own preference for a Protestant candidate, Gowrie was his man. James was plotting with Essex; James's idea was to move his army to the English border just as Essex was attempting to gain control in London by insurrection, and demand an acknowledgement regarding the succession. James assumed London would accede to this demand, not wanting to fend off a Scottish invasion while dealing with the Essex rebellion. At that moment, Cecil would have like nothing better than to see James disappear.

Scottish kings were kidnapped all the time. Since Gowrie would be the alternative candidate for the English throne, with everything at stake, Cecil might entrust him with the task of kidnapping James VI. In support of this scenario, it is known that there was a large English ship lurking off the coast of Scotland at Dirleton near North Berwick. At Dirleton, Gowrie had a fully manned castle. The Governor of Berwick was in close contact with Cecil. All this points to a developing plot to kidnap James. It also shows that the Gowrie family was indeed a danger to James VI of Scotland; the Earl of Gowrie stood to succeed

to the English throne instead of James, and he was –
probably – being encouraged to abduct James.

Death of a Leveller: The Assassination of Colonel Rainsborough

In Doncaster at eight o'clock in the morning on Sunday 29 October 1648, Colonel Thomas Rainsborough was killed by a party of horsemen. That much is certain. Various versions of what happened exist, but they differ from each other in significant ways. The contemporary accounts that were printed at the time were produced by angry Parliamentarians, their view distorted by their anger, and none of them seems to have seen the assassination anyway. One version has the murderers entering Rainsborough's lodgings, where they stabbed him, dragged him to the door, cut his throat and pitched him down the stairs before leaving. Another version has Rainsborough quietly accompanying his murderers outside and the murder only taking place when Rainsborough started to resist abduction.

At the time, there were two leading figures on the Parliamentary side in the English Civil War. One was Oliver Cromwell, the other was Thomas Rainsborough.

In the previous autumn, Rainsborough shouted at Cromwell, 'One of us must not live,' and threatened Cromwell with impeachment for what was seen as his betrayal of the common cause. In Westminster, it was a matter of speculation whether Cromwell would survive. With hindsight, we see Cromwell as the man of destiny, the man of steel, but at the time it looked as Rainsborough was pre-eminent, and that Cromwell would fall.

The death of Rainsborough was one of those turning points in history that have been overlooked. If he had lived, he would probably have carried through Parliament the *Agreement of the People*. This was to the seventeenth century what the *Social Contract* was to the eighteenth century and the *Communist Manifesto* was to the twentieth. The *Agreement* would have created in one step the social levelling process that did not in fact begin to happen until 1884.

Rainsborough was also Cromwell's only rival, the political and military leader of the far Left of the revolutionaries. Fairfax represented the far Right, and Cromwell the Centre. The three of them acted out their separate roles, with, as late as the autumn of 1647, Cromwell working for the restoration of Charles I to the throne, though with himself wielding the unseen power. Rainsborough's position was more straightforwardly anti-monarchist. Once Rainsborough was dead, Cromwell was able to shift his own position smoothly to the left, towards the destruction of the monarchy and the total removal of Charles.

On that much evidence, Cromwell could well have been

the instigator of the assassination, but Rainsborough had many enemies. The royalists hated him for his ruthlessness at the siege of Colchester, where in defiance of all the rules of war he ordered the judicial murder of the leading defenders, Sir Charles Lucas and Sir George Lisle. At the end of the siege Rainsborough had Lucas and Lisle tried by court martial and sentenced to be shot. The two men died with great courage and inspired universal admiration; the incident generated boiling hatred for Rainsborough. So Royalists who wanted revenge for the Colchester atrocity, a murder for a double murder, might have been the assassins. In fact just a month after the execution of Lucas and Lisle an attempt was made to kill him on the road between St Albans and London; he was attacked by 'three men of the king's party'.

Rainsborough was equally hated by the Grandees, the right-wingers in the Parliament and the army, because of his extreme left-wing political stance. Once the Second Civil War was over, the bonding caused by the threat of a common enemy was loosened, and the differences within the Parliamentarian confederation became more overt and conspicuous.

In November 1647, Rainsborough took part in one of the great army debates in Putney Church, debates which became landmarks in English constitutional history. The key question was whether it was time to make a complete break with the past and set up a new form of government, a single chamber elected every two years and with universal male suffrage. The document in which this revolutionary principle was laid out was the *Agreement of the People*. Rainsborough defended his *Agreement* with enormous clarity and conviction.

The poorest He that is in England hath a life to live as the greatest He; and therefore truly, sir, I think it's clear that every man that is to live under a government ought first by his own consent to put himself under that government; and I do think that the poorest man in England is not at all bound in a strict sense to that government that he hath not had a voice to put himself under.

A speaker on Cromwell's (opposing) side suggested that Rainsborough's society might lead to the abolition of property. Because four-fifths of the people in England had no property, they would vote for the abolition of property. Rainsborough's counter-argument was that it was unethical for one-fifth of the nation to enslave the other four-fifths, but the threat to property ownership was still left hanging in the air, and Rainsborough was unable to get his Agreement carried at Putney. To avoid total defeat, Rainsborough proposed that the matter should be put to a gathering of the entire army.

Meanwhile, Rainsborough was engaged in a secret plot to kidnap the king from Hampton Court Palace, where Charles was living under Cromwell's protection. When Charles discovered that Rainsborough was after him, he panicked and fled to the Isle of Wight, an action which helped Charles towards the scaffold.

Rainsborough's great army rally was convened on 15 November 1647 at Ware, but Fairfax and Cromwell intimidated the troops into voting against the *Agreement*. Some regiments carried copies of the *Agreement* and stuck pieces of paper in their hats with the slogans 'England's Freedom! Soldiers' Rights!' written on them. Cromwell ordered them to remove the pieces of paper from their hats. When they refused, he charged them with a drawn sword, had the leaders arrested and tried. One was shot as an example. It was a far cry from a free vote. Rainsborough's *Agreement* stood little chance of succeeding under such coercive conditions.

Rainsborough tried even before the Ware fiasco to have Cromwell impeached for treason. After the failure at Ware, the tables were turned, and it was Cromwell who tried to silence Rainsborough. He allowed it to be known that he wanted Rainsborough out – 'from the House and the Army'. But just as it looked as if some concerted effort was going to be made to remove Rainsborough the Royalist menace was seen to be far more important. From January 1648 onwards, Rainsborough was busy, first as Vice-Admiral of the Fleet, then at the siege of Colchester. After Colchester, Rainsborough presented his *Agreement* in the House. It created a great storm and it almost looked as if there might be a renewed outbreak of the Civil War on the issue of the *Agreement*.

The assassination of Rainsborough could therefore have been a Royalist act of revenge for the judicial murder of

Lucas and Lisle, or an assassination by the Right wing of the Parliamentarians, or indeed an assassination by the Centre. Rainsborough was sent north to Pontefract, evidently for political reasons: anything, really, to get him away from London.

The commander in charge of the siege of Pontefract was Sir Henry Cholmley. He was a popular man, who did not take his duties very seriously. Fairfax sent Rainsborough in to replace Cholmley, and Rainsborough's approach was very different. Cholmley was not giving up his command without a fight, and the Northern Committee who sat at York and who had appointed Cholmley were not happy about the interference from London. Cholmley wrote to the Speaker of the House of Commons airing his grievance. Rainsborough at first behaved with unusual tact, proposing that he and Cholmley stayed in separate and equal commands until Parliament had decided what should happen. Unfortunately, on the second day he had second thoughts and told the Committee at York that he could not after all be less than commander-in-chief.

Sir Henry Cholmley at this point emerged as another enemy made by Rainsborough. Cholmley could have been an accomplice to the assassination. A newspaper report subscribed to the view that a band of Royalists escaped from Pontefract Castle and carried out the assassination; it clearly implicated Cholmley in the conspiracy.

At the return of the party to Pontefract [from Doncaster], there was a mighty shout in the castle and presently the governor sent a sealed letter (which is against the law of arms) to Sir Henry Cholmley saying that 'he had now decided the controversy about the command, for his men had left Rainsborough dead in Doncaster street'; at the reading of which the base, treacherous, perfidious Cholmley very much laughed and rejoiced for a long time together, so that it is more probable that Sir Henry was an absolute complotter in the murder from which, as they came back the same day about two o'clock in the afternoon, his guard of horse (consisting of between two and three hundred) let them quietly pass by in their sight, as their good friends, without discharging one pistol upon them.

An account of the assassination was published by someone very close to the conspiracy, a Royalist called Thomas Paulden, who decided to reveal what happened fifty-four years after the event, in 1702. Whether this makes the account more reliable is not certain, but at least the emotional charge of narratives written in 1648 is missing, as is the fear of reprisal. Thomas Paulden was the brother of William Paulden, who apparently organized the raid, although he may have acted on orders from someone of higher rank. Thomas Paulden was insistent that the Royalists who attacked Rainsborough were attempting to abduct him, not kill him. Their plan was to kidnap him in Doncaster, then hold him prisoner at Pontefract Castle as a hostage in exchange for Sir Marmaduke Langdale, who was being held captive in Nottingham Castle and who seemed likely to be executed in the style of Lucas and Lisle.

Paulden said that his brother William chose twenty-two men and, at midnight on Friday, 27 October 1648, they rode out of Pontefract Castle to Mexborough, about four miles from Doncaster. There they rested before crossing the river and sending a scout ahead to make sure that entering Doncaster was safe. The next morning they arrived in Doncaster at about seven and met a friend who was walking along the street with a bible in his hand, a pre-arranged all-clear signal. They passed the Parliamentarian guard, posing as members of Colonel White's regiment from Rotherham. They were allowed into Rainsborough's lodgings, where they told him he was their prisoner; they would not harm him if he was prepared to go quietly with them.

At first Rainsborough appeared ready to go along with the Royalists. They told him to mount and he started to do so. Then he spotted that there were only four Royalists close by and that two of his own men, still armed, were near enough to help him. He took a fatal chance, taking his foot out of the stirrup and shouting, 'Arms! Arms!' One of the Royalists, not wanting to kill him, dropped his pistol and sword and grappled with Rainsborough. While they were on the ground, Rainsborough's lieutenant ran the Royalist through with his sword. Another Royalist drew his sword and wounded Rainsborough in the neck.

Rainsborough grabbed the sword, got to his feet ready to fight, but was run through by Captain Paulden's lieutenant. Rainsborough fell down dead.

Thomas Paulden wrote a second account that was broadly similar but different in detail, so it is still very difficult to be sure what happened. The second account did not, for instance, mention the man with the bible. The accounts are believable because of some details that can be corroborated. They say that the Royalists got past the Parliamentarian guards by saying that they had a letter from Cromwell. We know from other sources that Rainsborough was in fact expecting a letter from Cromwell; he wanted the command of the siege of Pontefract sorted out in London, and expected to have instructions at any moment. Rainsborough was lodging at the main inn in Doncaster, on the north side of the market place.

It belonged to Mr Mawood, who had asked Rainsborough the previous evening whether he planned to dine there on the Sunday. The colonel had answered that he expected orders and was uncertain. What is interesting is that the assassins seem to know about this, and the informal nature of the siege at Pontefract was just one aspect of the very fluid nature of the relationship between Royalists and Parliamentarians in the area. It is also possible, of course, that Cholmley was involved in the conspiracy. It would have suited him very well for the Royalists to capture Rainsborough; it would leave him indisputably in command of the siege and disadvantage the intruder from

117

London in a very satisfying way indeed. The fact that the Royalist company was allowed such an easy escape from Pontefract Castle also suggests collusion by Cholmley. Cholmley himself may have supplied Paulden with the information that Rainsborough was expecting messengers from Cromwell at any moment. Without necessarily ordering or organizing the abduction of Rainsborough, Cholmley could relatively easily have made it happen in this way.

Collusion from the Parliamentarian side must be suspected because of the way the case was never followed up. When Pontefract eventually fell, no attempt was made to find or identify or punish the murderers. Rainsborough's family and other supporters were indignant that no efforts were made, complaining to Parliament that in fact they were being discouraged from searching for the prosecutors of 'so bloody and inhumane a butchery'. That suggests that the Parliamentarian authorities knew there was some Parliamentarian complicity, whether by Cholmley or someone higher up the chain of command. Simple revenge was out of the question.

Cromwell was himself personally involved in the closure of the episode. He arrived immediately after Rainsborough's murder to deal with the siege, which was odd, given that there were so many pressing matters to attend to in London; the execution of Charles I was being debated at Westminster and St Albans. Cromwell was there, at Pontefract, supervising the siege without bringing it to an end, for some time. His involvement there may have been in some way connected with the assassination, or indeed in covering it up. When Westminster heard of Rainsborough's death, Cromwell was instructed by Parliament to 'make a strict and exact scrutiny of the manner of the horrible murder'. Maybe that was why Cromwell arrived in person. Maybe he did find out who was to blame. But in the excitement of the impending execution of Charles I, any findings Cromwell may have reached about the Rainsborough murder were overlooked; it appears that Cromwell himself was uncharacteristically ready to overlook the matter.

When Lambert (Cromwell's successor at Pontefract) started negotiating the terms for Pontefract's surrender, he made it clear that there would be no pardons for Rainsborough's killers. Lambert was oddly apologetic about it. He said he knew they were gallant men and he wanted to save as many of them as he could, but he must have six of them surrendered to him and their lives were forfeit. They were Colonel Morris, Sir John Digby and four others. He regretted it. As far as he was concerned the raid in which Rainsborough died 'was an enterprise no brave enemy would have revenged in that manner'; Lambert did not want to do it, but Cromwell insisted on it. The garrison's response was to break out in two separate sallies, during which four of the wanted men escaped. The remaining two had themselves walled up in a chamber inside the castle, with enough food and water to last them a month. When the castle was surrendered, Lambert believed that all six had indeed escaped.

Interestingly, Cromwell was able to tell Lambert the names of the six men, which suggests that he had indeed made enquiries during his time at Pontefract. A manuscript compiled by the antiquarian Nathaniel Johnston, who got his information from the staff at Rainsborough's lodgings, named the six as Colonel Morris, 'Cornet' Blackburn, Marmaduke Greenfield, Alan Austwick, Sir Charles Dallison and Mr Saltonsal. Despite the fact that their names were known, and despite the high public profile of their victim, not one of the six men was ever tried or punished.

Rainsborough's body was taken to Wapping, his family home, and given a huge and spectacular funeral involving over fifty coaches and 1,500 cavalry. The preacher who gave his funeral oration said, 'I think he was one of whom this sinful nation was not worthy; he was one of whom this declining Parliament was not worthy.' He was a great national figure, yet the Parliamentarian establishment, now in full power with the King's death imminent, chose not to bring his killers to justice, deliberately left the case unsolved.

THE CHIPPING CAMPDEN MYSTERY: THE STRANGE DISAPPEARANCE OF WILLIAM HARRISON

The so-called Campden Wonder, as the poet John Masefield called it, is one of the strangest crime mysteries in English history. It sounds very small in scale – the disappearance in 1660 of an elderly steward in a Gloucestershire village – but the way the story unfolded implies that something complicated and peculiar might have taken place.

The steward was William Harrison and he was the servant of Sir Baptist Hicks, who had made his money as a mercer and moneylender. When James VI of Scotland arrived in London to mount the English throne as James I, Hicks took the opportunity to supply the new king with the best silks he could find and lend him £16,000. In return, James I gave him a knighthood. Hicks wormed his way through James's courtiers in the same way, supplying, lending and finding out a lot of secrets along the way. Hicks became very rich, rich enough to buy himself a peerage, after which he styled himself Viscount Campden.

At Chipping Campden he spent a huge sum building a three-storied mansion. It had a glass dome which was always lit up at night to help travellers who might be lost on the wolds. It also had two banqueting rooms linked by an underground passage under the Terrace Walk. He was keen on underground passages.

In 1645, sixteen years after Sir Baptist Hicks, 1st Viscount Campden, died, the great house was wantonly destroyed by Sir Henry Bard. Bard was, ironically, a friend of the Campden family, though it is hard to tell this from his actions. He held the house as a garrison for Charles I, and his soldiers were so rapacious that they completely impoverished the people of the surrounding area. As Charles marched to Evesham he ordered his garrison out of Campden House and, on leaving, Sir Henry Bard set fire to it, burning the whole building and turning it into a ruin.

Hicks's daughter Juliana had gone to live in Rutland with her son, the third Viscount Campden. In 1660, she was still there. Meanwhile, the old steward, William Harrison, stayed on among the ruins of Campden House with his family, living in the stable block, from which he administered the estate and forwarded the tenants' rents to Lady Juliana.

William Harrison did not get on with his wife. She was a supporter of Cromwell and was described as 'a snotty, covetous Presbyterian'. Harrison hid all his papers from her because he suspected her of being in touch with Parliamentarians. He also had difficulties with his son, a man of forty who wanted his job. It would appear that William Harrison did not lead a very happy home life, and he consequently leant heavily on the friendship of his devoted servant, John Perry. The Perry family lived in a cottage near the gates of Campden House. There were two brothers, twenty-four-year-old John and thirty-year-old Richard, their mother, who was thought to be a witch, and Richard's wife and two children. They were allowed to live there rent-free and their needs were supplied by the estate, through Harrison.

On 16 August 1660, just a few weeks after the Restoration of Charles II, William Harrison walked across the fields to Charingworth, three miles away to the east. He was collecting rents, while most of the villagers were in the fields harvesting. He did not return. As night fell, Mrs Harrison sent John Perry to meet him, but Perry did not come back that night either. At daybreak, Edward Harrison set off in the direction of Charingworth to look for his father and Perry. He met Perry coming back alone. Perry knew nothing about William Harrison's whereabouts and they walked together to Ebrington, a hamlet halfway between Campden and Charingworth.

Later in the morning a woman who was gleaning in the fields half a mile from Campden House found beside some gorse bushes some of William Harrison's belongings. She picked up a comb, a hat and a neckerchief. The hat and comb were cut and there was blood on the neckband. The villagers assumed that William Harrison had been murdered, stopped harvesting and started looking for William Harrison's corpse. They could not find it, but they were certain Harrison was dead. Increasingly they suspected John Perry of murdering him. The local magistrate, Sir Thomas Overbury, rode over from Bourton to question him; he was the nephew and heir of the far more famous Sir Thomas Overbury who was poisoned in the Tower of London.

Perry gave a detailed itinerary of his search, including the names of two countrymen he met on the way: Reed and Pearce. He had not liked wandering across the fields on his own at night, which was why he persuaded Reed and Pearce to join him. He had sheltered in a hen coop by a churchyard until midnight. Then the full moon appeared and it was light enough for him to see his way clearly. Then a mist rolled in and he could see nothing again, so he spent the rest of the night under a hedge. At dawn he set off again. He knocked on the door of a man called Plaisterer at Charingworth, and found that Harrison had collected £23 in rent there the previous afternoon. He called on another tenant, Curtis, and Harrison had called there too for rent, though Harrison had been less lucky as Mr Curtis had been out at the time and so he did not get his money. This being as much as he could do, Perry set off home, without William Harrison and without any idea where he might be.

John Perry's nocturnal journey sounded very odd, but Reed, Pearce, Plaisterer and Curtis confirmed that the bits of the story that related to them were perfectly true. On the other hand, there was no one to corroborate Perry's version of what he was doing (or not doing) between 9.30 at night and four in the morning. Overbury decided he had no choice but to detain Perry for a couple of days while he awaited more evidence. But there was no more evidence. Overbury questioned Perry again and Perry repeated the story. Then, very rashly, he changed his story. A travelling tinker had murdered Harrison, he said, then he thought up another scenario in which a gentleman's servant had robbed and murdered Harrison. The body was hidden in a bean-rick in Sheep Street, he said. The villagers searched the bean-ricks and found nothing.

On 24 August, Overbury questioned John Perry a third time. This time Perry said his mother and his brother Richard had killed Harrison when he returned from Charingworth. He said they had often asked him to tell them when Harrison was going to collect rents. He implied that usually he evaded the question, but this time he answered them. The result was that when William Harrison returned to Campden House after his rent-collecting, Richard Perry followed him. At first John Perry was not with them. When he joined them, he found Harrison on the ground and his brother Richard kneeling on him. Old Joan Perry was standing watching. Harrison had said, 'You rogues, are you going to kill me?' and pleaded with Richard not to kill him. Richard told him to hold his tongue, called him a fool and then strangled him.

Richard emptied the pockets, emptied the money into his mother's lap and then the two of them, Richard and the mother, dragged the body to the great sink beside Wallington's Mill.

John Perry insisted that he had nothing to do with the murder or the disposal of the body. All he did was to keep watch, and it was while he was doing this that he saw John Pearce.

The next day, Overbury interviewed Joan and Richard Perry. They denied John's allegations completely. The villagers searched the sink by Wallington's Mill, found nothing, searched the fish ponds and all the ruins of the house, and found nothing there either. There was no sign of William Harrison's body. In spite of this, Overbury decided that the Perrys must stand trial for murder. When the three were being taken to prison at Campden, Richard dropped a ball of string. The guard showed it to John, who immediately identified it as 'the string my brother strangled my master with.'

At the September Assizes at Gloucester, the case was brought before a judge, but the judge, Sir Christopher Turnor, threw it out on the grounds that there was no body and therefore no evidence that murder had been done. The Perrys were kept in prison, though, and at the next session, the spring Assizes, their case was heard. This time a different judge, Sir Robert Hyde, decided that the lack of a corpse was no hindrance.

Meanwhile, something else had happened. In the

February before William Harrison's disappearance there had been a robbery at Campden. On a particular market day when a famous preacher was visiting the town, and everyone in the area was either in church or at the market, there was a break-in at William Harrison's house. A ladder was placed against the wall to reach a second-storey window, an iron bar was ripped away with a ploughshare (which was flung down in the room) and the sum of £140 was stolen. The burglary was evidently carefully planned and carried out, and the culprits were never found, in spite of many inquiries.

There was a sequel to this crime three months later, on May Eve. Inmates of the almshouses and passers-by in Church Street could hear, from outside the high walls of Campden House, frantic screams for help from John Perry. Three men who happened to be passing in the street ran to the courtyard gate of the house, where they found Perry in a state of sheer terror. He had a pick in his hand and his coat pocket was slashed. He said he had been set upon by two men in white brandishing drawn swords, and that they would have killed him if had not defended himself with the pick. The pick bore recent cut marks to corroborate his story. A key in his pocket was similarly notched.

Perry's behaviour and the bizarre story he told made people think that in some way he and his family had been responsible for the earlier robbery of William Harrison. Perry was pretending to be a victim of criminals in order to divert suspicion. At the September Assizes, the Perrys had been more or less forced to plead guilty to the robbery because they would be pardoned immediately. Charles II had marked his Restoration in May by an Act of Pardon and Oblivion. They pleaded guilty and as expected, guaranteed by law, they were duly pardoned. But, as in many modern cases of plea bargaining, the result rebounded on them in that they now had a criminal record and were seen as a criminal family. If they were capable of robbery, then why not aggravated robbery with violence? Why not murder?

When it came to the spring Assizes of 1661, the Perry family took back their admission of guilt for the robbery. They had not been the robbers on that occasion. Nor were they guilty of murdering William Harrison. John Perry tried to retract all his stories, saying that he was mad and did not know what he was saying. The outcome was inevitable. There was still no body, no positive evidence of any kind that murder had taken place, the accused all pleaded not guilty; but they were found guilty and hanged.

The executions were carried out consecutively. Old Joan was hanged first. It was assumed she was a witch and had put a spell on her sons. Richard was hanged second, after appealing to John to clear their names. John did not do so, but he did say something significant before he too was hanged; 'I know nothing of my master's death, nor what has become of him; but you may hereafter possibly hear.'

And more than a year later, in August 1662, something utterly extraordinary happened. William Harrison appeared alive and well in Chipping Campden. Given what had happened during his absence – the trial, humiliation and execution of three innocent neighbours – Harrison was required to give an account of himself to Sir Thomas Overbury. This is what he said.

As I was coming home that Thursday evening, there met me a horseman and said, 'Art thou here?' and I, fearing he would have ridden over me, struck his horse over the nose, whereupon he struck at me with his sword several blows and ran it into my side while I, with my little cane, made what defence I could. At last another came behind me, ran me in the thigh, laid hold on the collar of my doublet and drew me into a hedge near the place. Then came another. They did not take my money, but mounted me behind one of them, drew my arms about his middle and fastened my wrists together with something that had a spring lock to it – as I conceived by hearing a snap as they put it on. Then they threw a great cloak over me and carried me away.

In the night they alighted at a hayrick, which stood near unto a stone-pit by a wall-side, where they took away my money. About two hours before day (as I heard one of them tell another he thought it then to be) they tumbled me into the stone-pit. They stayed (as I thought) about an hour at the hayrick, when they took horse again. One of them bade me come out of the pit. I answered that they had my money already and asked what they would do with me, whereupon he struck me again, drew me out and put a great quantity of money into my pockets and mounted me again in the same manner.

So far, it is clear just from the simple fact that Harrison was alive in 1662 that John Perry's story of his murder was totally untrue. Probably his account of his night wanderings was untrue as well. But the yarn Harrison was telling was obviously equally untrue. Why would armed men carry Harrison off in order to rob him of a few pounds of rent money? Why would they then stuff his pockets full of money? Presumably Harrison needed to disappear for some reason that he was not prepared to tell anyone, and for some very compelling reason too. The two men were both lying, and probably for the same reason; they simply could not say what was really happening.

Harrison's story continued:

On Friday about sun-setting, they brought me to a lone house on a heath where they took me down almost dead, being sorely bruised with the carriage of the money. When the woman of the house saw that I could neither stand nor speak, she asked whether or no they had brought a dead man. They answered, 'No, but a friend that was hurt and they were carrying him to a surgeon.' She answered that if they did not make haste their friend would be dead before they could bring him to one. They laid me on cushions and suffered none to come into the room but a little girl. There we stayed all night, they giving me some broth and strong waters.

In the morning very early they mounted me as before, and on Saturday night they brought me to a place where there were two or three houses, in one of which I lay all night on cushions by their bedside. On Sunday morning they carried me from thence and about three or four o'clock they brought me to a place by the seaside called Deal, where they laid me on the ground. And, one of them staying with me, the other two walked a little off to meet a man with whom they talked. In their discourse, I heard them mention seven pounds; after which they went away together and half an hour after returned.

The man (whose name, as I after heard, was Wrenshaw) said he feared I would die before he could get me on board; then immediately they put me into a boat and carried me to ship-board where my wounds were dressed. I remained in the ship (as near as I could reckon) about six weeks.

The fictitious six week voyage to 'Turkey' involved being chased by Turkish pirates, being captured and taken to Smyrna and sold in the slave market there. Harrison became the slave of an eighty year old Turkish doctor. He was given a little silver bowl to carry and was given the nickname 'Boll'. When the doctor died, Harrison sold the bowl and bought his passage home.

Most commentators on this remarkable episode have assumed that the seven pounds mentioned was the price Harrison fetched as a white slave. This is a preposterous idea. There were white slavers, but they were interested in kidnapping healthy young girls (and boys), certainly not old men of seventy-two in the wrecked state that Harrison seems to have been in by this stage, exhausted and covered in cuts and bruises. The whole kidnapping by white slavers yarn is an obvious cover story, the sort of borrowed melodrama that an uneducated person would come up with in the seventeenth century. What Harrison was trying to do was not only avoid telling the truth about his secret journey, but show that he was out of the country during the ordeal of the Perry family.

Harrison would certainly have heard about white slavers. The Mediterranean in particular was infested with pirates and in Turkey and North Africa there were thousands of white Christians from northern Europe who had been abducted. Only twenty-three years before the disappearance of William Harrison, Colonel Rainsborough's father, Captain William Rainsborough, was hailed as a hero for rescuing 339 men, women and children from one port. In the early seventeenth century, Barbary pirates regularly raided the coasts of Ireland, Wales and the English West Country, snatching scores of people who were then sold on as slaves. Although by the nineteenth century William Harrison's story looked utterly childish, the background his story was based upon was real enough. But Harrison was no spring chicken. He was far too old to be worth transporting anywhere for any kind of work. Nor was he in the right location. In the early seventeenth century, it was certainly risky to be living in an isolated village on the south coast of Ireland, where pirates could come ashore, take twenty people and be away again before the alarm was raised; such things happened. But Chipping Campden was a long way inland. Both age and geography are against William Harrison's story.

There is an understandable assumption that Perry and Harrison were both lying for the same reason, that Harrison had to disappear for a few months and a cover story had to be concocted, and that Perry would corroborate it.

When Harrison was presumed dead, his son lost no time in asking lady Juliana for his father's job. She agreed to this, and he was extremely unpopular. When Old Harrison reappeared, there was great relief because it meant that Edward Harrison would have to give way to his father. Edward was in the forefront of the witch-hunt against the Perrys. He may have been instrumental in having the Perrys brought to trial a fatal second time. He certainly arranged for John Perry's body to be hung in chains on Broadway Hill, 'where he might daily see him'. Mrs Harrison was not pleased to have her husband back. In fact, she committed suicide six months later.

For some reason which nobody in the family or the neighbourhood could know about, William Harrison needed to undertake a journey. He trusted John Perry absolutely, and Perry seems to have trusted him, too. Perry's trust in Harrison turned out to be misplaced, as Harrison did not return in time to save Perry's life. Harrison and Perry probably presumed that the lack of a body would mean that there could be no murder trial. The judge at the first Assize thought so, too. Unfortunately the judge at the second Assize did not. Maybe Harrison was away longer than intended because he really was abducted.

One writer who has studied the case has latched onto old Joan's reputation as a witch and the evident friction between William Harrison and his Presbyterian wife. It is just possible that William Harrison and the Perrys were members of a witch cult. It would certainly explain the extreme secrecy involved and the intense loyalty shown. But there may be a simpler solution.

Among the Campden family papers there is a letter from the third Viscount Campden to his mother, Lady Juliana. It was written from Algiers, which in itself carries reverberations of Harrison's description of a long voyage and being captured by Turkish pirates. Campden's letter at first appears mundane enough. It is a request for cash. Then there is a receipt for money received 'by hand of Harrison, oure good servant, who retourneth forthwithe, and as I will later.' Campden was a young Royalist and like many others of his kind he was living in safe exile abroad during the Commonwealth, and using the opportunity to take a Grand Tour. The letter is very close to proof that Harrison did indeed undertake a voyage to the Mediterranean, and it shows him characteristically pursuing his duties as Lady Juliana's steward. She trusted him to take her son the money that he needed.

The remaining problem is the secrecy and the deception. Why did Harrison need to conceal from his family and the neighbourhood this routine business trip? There was certainly no need for it in 1660. The Royalists were not being hunted any more; it was rather the reverse, with Parliamentarian regicides on trial for their lives. But between 1642 and 1660, journeys like Harrison's trip to Algiers would have been treated as treasonable. The eighteen years of doing family business in secret had become a habit. The voyage to Algiers had after all not needed to be secret, it was just that Harrison was an old man and he had got into the habit of extreme caution. On the other hand, Harrison had presumably not gone missing in this way before, or his family would not have reacted as they did. Presumably the Algiers trip was a one-off foreign trip, or Mrs Harrison would have known there was no need to worry. Or was Harrison in the habit of keeping everything from her, because of her Cromwellian sympathies and her general antipathy towards him?

Baptist Hicks had built caution and secrecy into the layout of his estate. He knew he had to protect his enormous wealth, especially in economically and politic-ally fast-changing times. There were underground passages leading to neighbouring houses, so that at times of crisis, such as impending raids, valuables could be taken out for safety. Occasionally the rumbling of barrows and handcarts in the tunnels could be heard. Before the commandeering and destruction of the house, William Harrison, helped by the Perrys, had successfully emptied it of most of the portable furnishings by way of these tunnels. Or it may be that many of the house's treasures were actually stored in the tunnels. If so they might have remained there after the house was burnt down. William Harrison's role as steward would then have extended beyond mere rent-collection; he was curating an unknown amount of treasure in the network of tunnels under and round the ruins. The swordsman's attack on John Perry and the break-in at William Harrison's house suggest that others had got to know that there were valuables to be had.

These are only suggestions about the nature of William Harrison's responsibilities. Lady Juliana had clearly entrusted him with some great task, which he partially delegated to John Perry. Harrison had to go away, to Algiers, to take money to Lord Campden, and for some reason – not enslavement - his return was delayed. It was the delay that proved fatal to the Perry family. But there are still many unsolved mysteries surrounding the case. What was John Perry really doing during his un-accountable nocturnal wanderings? Why was William Harrison's son so keen to see the Perrys suffer? Why did Mrs Harrison hang herself after William Harrison's return? Why did William Harrison take so long to return home?

THE MURDER OF SIR EDMUND BERRY GODFREY

The body of Sir Edmund Berry Godfrey was found in a ditch on Primrose Hill in London on Thursday 17 October 1678. Two men who had been drinking at the White House inn in the fields north of Marylebone that wet afternoon found the body towards 4 o'clock. It had a sword stuck through it, the neck was broken and there were massive bruises on the chest; he appeared to have been 'beaten with some obtuse weapon' or punched and kicked. A circular mark round his neck showed that he had been hanged or strangled. The surgeon who carried out the post mortem observed that the two sword wounds had been inflicted perhaps days after death, that 'there was more done to his neck than an ordinary suffocation', and that he had not eaten for two days before his death. He had wax stains on his clothes, which implied that he had been maltreated in the house of some well-to-do people: people who lit their house with candles. It did not look as if he had been murdered in the place where the body was found as there was no evidence of a struggle, though the ground had been trampled by a number of bystanders by the time the investigators arrived. Robbery was evidently not a motive as the body still carried money and rings.

The man who came to this strange, violent and apparently inexplicable end was a fifty-seven year old bachelor who had the reputation of being the best Justice of the Peace in England. He was magistrate for Westminster. He made his living as a coal merchant and lived in Hartshorn Lane near Charing Cross. He was a well-known figure in the neighbourhood, tall, thin, sad-looking, always dressed in black, but with a gold hatband and cane. Edmund Berry Godfrey had been knighted for his bravery in staying at his post regardless of the risk to himself during the Great Plague of 1665. In 1669 he had showed great courage once again in pursuit of his duty when he had the king's physician, Sir Alexander Fraizer, arrested for owing him money; Godfrey found himself briefly imprisoned for that solecism. He nevertheless was a very frightened man when he disappeared on 12 October 1678. He was missing for five days, with the whole of London out looking for him, before his body was found on Primrose Hill.

His murder was a complete mystery, and many different theories have been put forward. His injuries are inconsistent with suicide, unless of course he killed himself and then his brothers ran their swords through his body and beat him to make it look like murder; their motive could have been to avoid a suicide verdict at the inquest, in which case his estate would have passed to the Crown.

Three men were later hanged for his murder, though all

later commentators agree that they were not the murderers. On 21 December a Catholic silversmith called Miles Prance was arrested and taken to Newgate Prison. Prance's landlord John Wren said Prance had been out for four nights before Godfrey's body was found. At Newgate, Prance was tortured until in desperation he told his tormentors what they wanted to hear. On 24 December he admitted to taking part in the murder, but the main instigators had been Catholic priests, three of whom watched the murder in the courtyard of Somerset House. Under duress, Prance gave the names of three tradesmen, Robert Green, Henry Berry and Lawrence Hill. They all served at Somerset House, the Queen's residence, where the true perpetrators of the crime wanted to place the murder scene. In those days, Primrose Hill was known as Greenbury Hill, and it really cannot be a coincidence that the three names Prance supplied made up the name of the place where the victim's body was found. It seems to have been some kind of joke on Prance's part. It is utterly mystifying that the English justice system got as far as arresting three men called Green, Berry and Hill for killing a man whose body was found on Greenbury Hill, but it did, and went as far as finding them guilty and on 5 February 1679 and actually hanging them on Greenbury Hill.

Prance withdrew his confession and was thrown in prison. He naturally recanted his recantation, changed his mind twice more and ended up with his original story. It is an old story – a confession obtained under duress has no value whatever. Eventually Prance's story was discredited and he admitted perjury. The three men were hanged, but on false evidence, so the case is officially unsolved.

This was the time of the Titus Oates conspiracy. Oates claimed that he had discovered a Popish Plot. The Pope, Louis XIV, the Jesuit General and the Archbishop of Dublin were at the head of a plot to kill the Protestant king of England, Charles II, and set up his Catholic brother, the Duke of York, in his place. London would be set on fire and all the Protestants would be murdered in their beds. Charles II, to his credit, laughed in Oates's face when he first heard the story. It was totally incredible. Oates described the Commander-in-Chief of the Pope's army as tall and dark; Charles II knew the man in question, and knew him to be red-haired and short. Charles and his Secretary of State knew that Oates was a fraud, but were (rightly) concerned that he could do mischief.

In the country at large, Oates was widely believed. When Oates realized that he would get nowhere by trying to convince the establishment, he initiated proceedings in the ordinary courts. This was where Sir Edmund Berry Godfrey comes into the picture. On 6 September 1678, Oates went to Godfrey as a magistrate and swore the truth of a statement he had written outlining the Popish Plot. Godfrey conscientiously passed the information on to a friend, Edmund Coleman, secretary to the duchess of York, and Coleman was able to assure Oates that the king knew all about the accusations Oates had made and would take no action.

Oates refused to give up. Three weeks later, on 28 September, Oates went back to Godfrey with further information about the plot, swore to its truth under oath, and then took the additional information to Whitehall to give to the king, who saw that the story was now more than a lie: it was perjury.

Godfrey was now worried. He knew that Titus Oates was committing perjury and that Oates had no conscience about it. He also knew that there was no interest at all at court in pursuing the matter. But because Oates had approached him as a Justice of the Peace and made sworn statements he felt he had no choice but to proceed on Oates's behalf. He was duty-bound to act, even though he knew Oates was lying. Godfrey became even more worried when his friend Coleman was arrested. Godfrey said to other friends that he had taken the depositions from Oates very unwillingly and added, 'I think I shall have little thanks for my pains. Upon my conscience I think I shall be the first martyr.' He said he 'was master of a dangerous secret which would be fatal to him', though he did not say what the secret was. Subsequently it emerged that the secret, which he learned through Coleman, was that Shaftesbury and his Country party (the land-owning grandees who were anti-Catholic and anti-French and wanted to reduce royal power) were ironically in the pay of the French. As it happened both Louis XIV and the Country party wanted the same thing – major political disturbance in England. Receiving financial support from the French was nevertheless something Shaftesbury and his collaborators did not want to be known.

Godfrey now knew their dangerous secret, and he also knew, because his source, Coleman, had been arrested that they would know that he knew. He was in great personal danger. He told a trusted friend that he was not afraid of them if they 'came fairly' and that he would put up a fight for his life.

Evidently they did come for Sir Edmund, not fairly, and they maltreated him before killing him, but it is less evident who 'they' were. It is unlikely that Catholics were responsible. The mood of the moment in England was such that Catholics would be assumed to be responsible and the backlash would be extreme; English Catholics were painfully aware that for some time to come they were going to be the scapegoats for everything that went wrong. Godfrey was also signalling that he did not believe Titus Oates's allegations, and that was if anything a pro-Catholic gesture. He was indicating, like the king, that there was no conspiracy. Catholics were in the end hanged for his murder, and in the climate of the time that was probably inevitable, but the Catholics were the least likely people to have been his killers.

Both Titus Oates and the Earl of Shaftesbury had alibis. So they personally could not have been Godfrey's murderers.

On Friday 11 October, Godfrey had a letter that worried him intensely. It is not known who wrote the letter, but it was probably his murderer. He afterwards went out and turned down an invitation to dinner the next day, because he did not know he would be free. He then said, 'You ask for news? Why, I'll tell 'ee. In a short time you will hear of the death of someone.' When he returned home he spent the evening burning papers. The next day he got up rather early and dressed with unusual care. He first put on his best coat, then changed it for an older one. Some time after nine o'clock, Godfrey left his house. Shortly afterwards he was seen near St Giles-in-the-Fields, and heard asking to be directed to Primrose Hill. He was sighted near Paddington Woods.

He got home again from this country walk by midday and shortly after that one his fellow vestrymen met him in the Strand and asked him to dine with him. Godfrey was unable to accept as he was in a hurry. After two o'clock on the Saturday, he was never seen alive again; his body was found the following Thursday.

All London buzzed with speculation as to what had happened to Sir Edmund Godfrey. There were lots of wild stories, but what people kept returning to was the idea that he had taken the depositions about the Popish Plot; he was obviously the Popish Plot's first victim.

A pointer to the identity of the murderers was the remarks made by two bishops an hour or two before the discovery of the body. They said they had heard that Sir Edmund Berry Godfrey's body had been found, with a sword sticking through it, in Leicester Fields, in other words the open lands west of Leicester Square. The two bishops were strong supporters of the Country party, great friends of the Earl of Shaftesbury. This foreknowledge strongly suggests that Godfrey was murdered by members of the Country party.

One of the noble members of the Country party was the Earl of Pembroke. He was described as 'a madman when he was sober and a homicidal maniac when he was not.' The mad earl had drinking bouts that went on for days, and he died of drink at the age of thirty. At this time he was still in his mid-twenties. He was a very violent man, and he lived close to Leicester Fields. On 3 February 1678 he had killed one of his drinking companions by kicking him to death – in the chest. This was by no means his first murder. He had certainly murdered at least six people and perhaps as many as sixteen. Somehow, up to this point, he had evaded justice. Following the 3 February killing, the mad earl was indicted by a Middlesex jury. At the head of that jury, and therefore acting as prosecutor, was none other than Sir Edmund Berry Godfrey. Godfrey had shown exceptional bravery during the time of the plague. Leading the indictment against the murderously violent Earl of Pembroke was perhaps the bravest thing he did, and he may have lost his life because of it.

When the earl stood trial on 4 April in front of the House of Lords, he pleaded benefit of clergy. In Henry VII's time, a distinction was made between those in holy orders and those who, even though they were secular people, were 'clerks' to the extent that they could read.

Under Henry VII's odd ruling, these secular clerks were allowed to claim benefit of clergy only once. When they had claimed it, they were to be branded on the left thumb, so that the courts could see on future occasions that the benefit had been used up. Under Edward VI the branding was stopped and benefit of clergy was extended to all members of the House of Lords. Now any member of the Lords could escape punishment for any first offence except murder, even if he could not read – an early example of dumbing-down.

Pembroke was charged with manslaughter, not murder, so he was legally able to claim benefit of clergy. He was immediately freed, though the Lord Chief Justice warned him, 'Your Lordship must give me leave to tell you that no man can have the benefit of that statute but once; and I would have Your Lordship take notice of it as a caution to you for the future.' The Lords must have known Pembroke's record well, and the Lord Chief Justice was spelling out to him that he would not be able to commit any more serious crimes with impunity.

Godfrey knew that he was a marked man as far as the Earl of Pembroke was concerned. Pembroke was going to kill him. When Pembroke was released, Godfrey went abroad for the sake of his health. He had only just returned in September when Titus Oates came knocking at his door.

Some commentators on the episode have made the melancholy disposition of Godfrey their focus, with suicide as their solution to the mystery. But Godfrey had plenty to be melancholy about. He knew the earl of Pembroke's record and he knew that he must be the object of the earl's hatred. The Titus Oates depositions and his reticent handling of them made him an object of hatred by the Country party generally. And the earl of Pembroke was an enthusiastic member of the Country party. Pembroke now had two reasons for wanting to do him violence. Godfrey's behaviour immediately before his disappearance shows that he was expecting to die. His fellow-vestrymen would shortly hear of 'the death of someone'. He was not afraid if they 'came fairly' and he would put up a fight for his life. He spent an evening burning his papers.

The frightening letter that Godfrey received was probably an invitation that he was unable to decline. It has been suggested that it might have come from the desk of the Lord Chief Justice, saying that they needed to discuss the handling of the Titus Oates affair. The letter might have been from Pembroke, pretending to be the Lord Chief Justice, luring Godfrey into a fatal ambush.

It looks as if during the afternoon when he went missing Sir Edmund Berry Godfrey fell into the clutches of the earl of Pembroke, who held him prisoner. The strange pattern of injuries on Godfrey's body speak loudly of Pembroke. He had got his 3 February victim down onto the ground and kicked him to death in the chest. Godfrey too had massive bruising on his chest. Two years later, Pembroke murdered a man called Smeeth in exactly the same way. The method of killing had become so familiar to everyone that 'a Pembroke blow' was a stock phrase. There really seems little doubt that the bruises on Godfrey's chest were inflicted by a drunken earl. Pembroke got away with killing Godfrey. He got away with killing Smeeth too. There was a petition of mercy for him. The king took an unusual step in requiring the petitioners to sign, and lodging the signed petition in the patent roll; it is virtually a membership list for the Country party. The Country party evidently found Pembroke useful, in spite of his appalling behaviour, in spite of his terrifying record as a many times unconvicted murderer. And there was no doubt some satisfaction that Pembroke had murdered Sir Edmund Berry Godfrey, who had thrown cold water on the Popish Plot.

The Country party exploited Berry's murder (which they probably condoned, as Pembroke was not pursued) by giving him a lavish and highly politicized funeral. Godfrey's body was exposed to public view, to help inflame the public against his supposedly Catholic murderers. Seventy-two Protestant clergymen marched in front of the coffin in the funeral cortege and more than a thousand 'persons of distinction' walked behind it. In a particularly theatrical gesture, the preacher was flanked by two bodyguards in the pulpit, just in case the Papists should break in and try to carry out another murder.

The killing of Sir Edmund may therefore have been nothing directly to do with the Popish Plot, though the Country party used it to whip up anti-Catholic fear. Godfrey's death probably had much more to do with the earl of Pembroke's revenge. There can be little doubt that wherever Godfrey thought he was going that Saturday afternoon, he ended up a prisoner in Pembroke's house, where he was starved, abused and tortured for several days. At the end of his imprisonment, Godfrey was killed in Pembroke's accustomed manner – repeated kicks in the chest. The sword thrusts were added to distract attention from the chest injuries, which were now too well known as Pembroke's fingerprints. No doubt Pembroke's unquestioning servants were told to dump the body, as on many previous occasions, and they initially left it in Leicester Fields, where it was not unknown for the bodies of duellists and suicides to be found. Word passed round the Country party that that was what was happening. Then, perhaps sobering up early on Thursday afternoon, the seventh Earl of Pembroke realized that Godfrey's corpse had been left compromisingly close to his home, and ordered his servants to take it further away from his house and that was when it was moved to Greenbury Hill.

If this scenario is what really happened, several crimes were committed and several injustices were inflicted in relation to this case. Sir Edmund Berry Godfrey was cruelly and sadistically murdered. Three innocent men were wrongly convicted and hanged for his murder, apparently selected on the basis of their names recalling the name of the crime scene. The sadistic murderer, the seventh Earl of Pembroke, went entirely unpunished – not for the first and not for the last time.

THE MAN IN THE IRON MASK: CRIMINAL OR VICTIM?

In 1698, a mysterious prisoner was transferred to the Bastille, the notorious prison-fortress in Paris reserved for political prisoners, people who had fallen foul of France's autocratic ruler, Louis XIV. The transferred prisoner had already been in prison for at least eleven years. It was said that no one was allowed to know who he was and his face was hidden behind a mask. He lived on in his cell at the Bastille until his death in 1703, but rumours about his unexplained incarceration and his identity continued to develop during the next three centuries.

The masked prisoner was mentioned in a letter to an aunt from the Princess Palatine, the king's sister-in-law. She commented that the man was treated very well, but that two musketeers stood beside him at all times with orders to kill him at once if he took off the mask. He had to keep the mask on all the time, even when he was eating, even when he was asleep, even when he was dying. No one at court knew who he was.

The writer and philosopher Voltaire found himself a prisoner in the Bastille for several months in 1717, and this gave him an opportunity to speak to people who had served the Man in the Mask. Much later, in his 1751 book The Age of Louis XIV, Voltaire said the prisoner had been made to wear an iron mask as early as 1661, at which time he was held prisoner on the island of Sainte Marguerite. He was said to have been young, tall and handsome in 1661, though it is difficult to see how anyone could have known whether he was handsome or not if he was wearing a mask continuously. He wore lace and fine linen, played the guitar, and there was a clear implication that he was at least a gentleman, and probably an aristocrat.

In his later writings, Voltaire made tantalizing hints that the prisoner was Louis XIV's brother. The man was sixty years old when he died, Voltaire said, and he looked strikingly like 'someone very famous'. France's most famous face was that of Louis XIV, who was also in his sixties at the time in question. The same hints were being dropped by Joseph de Lagrange-Chancel, another writer, who resided at Versailles during the reign of Louis XIV and was imprisoned on Sainte Marguerite in the 1720s. According to him, Saint-Mars, the prison governor, was deferential towards the masked man and called him 'my prince'. Later in the century a descendant of Saint-Mars said that the masked man was called 'Tower' by the prison staff and that he did not have to wear the mask all the time, only when there were visitors or when he was being transferred. Prison officials removed their hats and remained standing in the prisoner's presence.

All of these details were intended to indicate that the prisoner was a very high-ranking nobleman indeed. The references to the mask vary. Some say it was made of iron. Etienne de Junca, deputy governor of the Bastille, said he never saw the prisoner without his black velvet mask. De Junca's journal notes that the masked man was buried under the name M. de Marchiel. Another writer discovered a death certificate, which gave the masked man's name as Marchioly and his age at death as 'about forty-five'.

Hints that he was Louis XIV kept resurfacing later in the eighteenth century. In 1789, a journalist called Frederic-Melchior Grimm claimed that he knew Louis XIV had an identical twin brother; his source was a royal valet. Louis XIII, the father of the twins, was afraid there would be a power struggle between the boys and decided to have the second of the two babies taken away to be reared in secret. The disinherited son was never told who he was, but when he was a young adult he saw a portrait of his royal brother and guessed. Once he knew the truth, he was confined and made to wear the mask, presumably because his exact likeness to the king would immediately give away who he was and so endanger Louis XIV's position. Many people believed the journalist's account, even though it was probably fictitious, and it was developed and embroidered with picturesque anecdotal detail by other writers as the years passed. It was said that when the Bastille was stormed by the people of Paris, the imprisoned prince's skeleton was discovered, still wearing its iron mask; there is no record that this actually happened.

It was a commonplace in France that Louis XIV might not have been the son of Louis XIII. Louis XIII and his wife Anne of Austria thoroughly disliked one another. Their marriage was certainly not consummated in the first four years, and there was a long wait of twenty-three years before their first child, Louis XIV, was born. It was seen as a miracle – or a trick. There were rumours that the child was really the son of the queen's lover, the Duc de Beaufort. He then became a candidate for the prisoner in the mask, imprisoned in case he should reveal the dangerous truth that the king was illegitimate, and not entitled to sit on the French throne. Others too had shared the queen's bed, the Duke of Buckingham among them. Perhaps the man in the mask was Buckingham's son. Another variation on this royal theme was that the man in the mask was really a woman, the daughter of Louis XIII and Anne of Austria. Louis XIII needed a son to inherit the throne, and swapped his unwanted daughter for somebody else's son. The daughter was then masked and confined.

The circulation of many of these stories was politically motivated. Louis XIV had many enemies and it suited them to cast doubt on his legitimacy. Just a year after giving birth to Louis XIV (if indeed she did give birth to Louis), Anne of Austria gave birth to his younger brother,

Philippe. Louis' enemies would have liked to see Louis toppled and replaced by his younger brother.

Louis XIV was invited to a house party at Vaux-le-Vicomte, the beautiful new chateau of his minister, Nicolas Fouquet. When he saw the palace he was deeply envious and resentful. Louis started work on his own big project after that – Versailles. Meanwhile, he had Fouquet arrested and imprisoned. Some believe that it was Fouquet who was required to put on the mask. Fouquet officially died in 1680; Louis, it was said, had promised to release him that year, but then changed his mind when he discovered that his mistress had also slept with Fouquet. In order to keep his vengeful change of mind secret, Louis had Fouquet's death staged and kept the poor man more severely confined by making him wear the mask.

In the nineteenth century, the Man in the Iron Mask became fiction, however much historical truth there may have been in the story at the start of the eighteenth century. Alexandre Dumas' novel and the various films based on it created the image most of us now have of the masked prisoner. Dumas was interested in many of the exotic by-ways of French history. This one may have been of special interest to him because his grandfather, the Marquis de la Pailleterie, grew up at the court of Versailles.

The identity of the man in the mask is still extremely elusive. The most popular theory, that he was the identical twin brother of Louis XIV, is in fact the least likely. The king wore platform shoes and high wigs and these created an illusion of height, but he was really quite a short man, rather like Lord Farquaad in the 2001 film Shrek. The man in the mask was described as tall. The death certificate for the man in the mask said he was about forty-five; the king was sixty-six. On this circumstantial evidence alone, the prisoner and the king could not possibly have been identical twins.

Most researchers believe the man in the mask must have been either a nobleman or the servant of a nobleman. One candidate falling into this last category was Eustache Danger, a valet arrested and imprisoned in 1669 for some unknown offence. It is just possible that the governor of the Bastille kept a prisoner selected at random in a mask just to impress others with the supposed importance of one of his prisoners, and therefore his own credit and status as governor.

Another candidate for the mask with a very similar name is Eustache Dauger de Cavoye. He was a French soldier, arrested in 1668 perhaps for taking part in satanic rituals and imprisoned indefinitely (again perhaps) because he knew that one of the king's mistresses was also a satanist. Alternatively, Dauger may have been confined because he was an illegitimate half brother of Louis XIV.

The Comte de Vermandois is another possibility. He was one of Louis XIV's illegitimate children, who is supposed to have died of smallpox in 1683, while on a military campaign. In the eighteenth century, some people believed the count did not die but was instead imprisoned for striking the king's legitimate son. This is very unlikely, as Louis made a point of treating his illegitimate offspring well.

The Duke of Monmouth is an English candidate for the celebrity prisoner. An illegitimate son of Charles II, Monmouth led a rebellion against James II, Charles's brother, and had to be sentenced to death for high treason. James, it was said, was unwilling to order the execution of his nephew, so in 1685 another convict was publicly executed in his place while Monmouth himself was spirited away to be secretly imprisoned in France.

There was a confusing welter of speculation about the identity of the prisoner in the eighteenth century. The most reliable information about him comes from the early correspondence between Saint-Mars, the prison governor, and his superiors. The earliest surviving records date from July 1669, when Louis XIV's minister the Marquis de Louvois, entrusted a masked prisoner to the care of Benigne D'Auvergne de Saint-Mars, governor of Pignerol prison. Louvois' letter gave the man's name as Eustache Dauger and the place of his arrest as Dunkirk. Louvois was concerned that no one should be able to hear what Dauger had to say and instructed Saint-Mars to prepare a cell with several doors to ensure that the cell was soundproof. Dauger was to be warned that he would be summarily executed if he talked about anything other than his immediate needs. Saint-Mars was to visit him once a day with food and drink, but the prisoner would not need much because he was 'only a valet'.

It was at that early stage that the first rumours started to circulate about the secret prisoner's identity. Some thought he was a high-ranking soldier, perhaps a marshal. Saint-Mars was holding other distinguished prisoners besides the mysterious 'Dauger'. He had Nicolas Fouquet in one cell and the Marquis de Lauzun in the cell below Fouquet's.

Isolating Dauger completely was impossible because of the social customs of the day. Wealthy and aristocratic prisoners usually had their manservants with them. Fouquet had one, a man called La Rivière. La Rivière was often ill, so Saint-Mars (after carefully applying to Louvois for permission in 1675) allowed Dauger to act as Fouquet's servant. Louvois agreed to this, but stipulated that Dauger could only attend Fouquet while Fouquet was alone; if the Marquis de Lauzun were present, Dauger must not be there. Lauzun was expecting to be released, and would therefore be able to tell the outside world about Dauger. Fouquet on the other hand was never going to be released, so it did not matter if he met Dauger.

The fact that Louvois, Saint-Mars, Fouquet and the prisoner were all prepared to go along with the idea of Dauger serving as a manservant is highly significant. It means that Dauger cannot have been a prince; he cannot have been the brother or half-brother of Louis XIV, still less the real Louis XIV.

When Fouquet died in 1680, Saint-Mars found a secret hole connecting Fouquet's cell with Lauzun's. This was clearly made so that they could communicate with each other, and that almost certainly meant that Lauzun knew about Dauger's existence and would have heard conversations between Fouquet and Dauger. Saint-Mars told Louvois what had happened, and Louvois gave instructions that Lauzun should be moved into Fouquet's cell and told that Dauger and La Rivière had been released. Instead Dauger and La Rivière were to be moved to cells on the opposite side of the prison. When Lauzun was released in 1681, Saint-Mars was transferred to another prison, the fortress of Exiles, and he took Dauger and La Rivière with him. In 1687, La Rivière died, still a prisoner, and in the May of that year Saint-Mars took Dauger with him to the island prison of Sainte Marguerite. It was during that journey that rumours about Dauger wearing an iron mask began. If Dauger's identity needed to be kept secret, then obliging him to wear some sort of mask while travelling might have seemed a good idea. In practice, it simply drew attention.

The final transfer came in September 1698, when Saint-Mars became governor of the Bastille in Paris, taking his celebrity prisoner with him. The man in the mask was installed in a furnished cell in the Bertaudière Tower. Many of the details about him from this phase came from one of the prison staff, Lieutenant du Junca. It was du Junca who reported that the prisoner was given preferential treatment, had to wear a mask at all times, and that the mask was made of black velvet.

Dauger, or whoever he was, died on 19 November 1703.

He was buried the next day under the name Marchioly. All his belongings were destroyed. The nature of Dauger's crime was still not revealed. It must be suspected, because of the kid-glove treatment he was given, that he was the victim of the crime of wrongful imprisonment. There were many such political prisoners. La Rivière shared Fouquet's fate – life imprisonment – just by being his manservant. The French state committed judicial crimes against such people.

There was a significant development in the 1890s. A French military historian, Louis Gendron, found coded letters and passed them to Etienne Bazeries, a military cryptographer. It took Bazeries three years to decipher some of the letters, which used Louis XIV's Great Cypher. One letter related to a prisoner identified as General Vivien de Bulonde. Another letter, from Louvois, revealed the nature of de Bulonde's crime. De Bulonde had been at the siege of Cuneo. Concerned about the impending arrival of enemy troops, de Bulonde had withdrawn in excessive haste, leaving behind munitions and his own wounded. Louis XIV was very angry and ordered his punishment; he was 'to be conducted to the fortress of Pignerole where he will be locked in a cell under guard at night, permitted to walk the battlements during the day with a mask.' The dates on the letters tally with the dates on the original records relating to the masked prisoner.

Some historians believe that this concludes the story. The identity of the man in the mask is revealed as General de Bulonde, and his crime was serious military impropriety, a kind of desertion, cowardice in the face of the enemy. There are nevertheless two snags with the de Bulonde scenario. One is that de Bulonde was not arrested in secret (it was in the press), and there was no reason for his detention or identity to be kept secret; that remains unexplained. There is also a discrepancy regarding the date of death. The man in the mask is recorded as dying in 1703, while de Bulonde died in 1709.

On balance, it is more likely that 'Dauger', the man in the mask, was General de Bulonde than any of the other candidates proposed, simply because there is more solid evidence. Many of the other stories, especially those implicating Louis XIV or those close to him, were politically motivated. Louis XIV was in such a powerful position as an absolute monarch that scandalous rumour-mongering that cast doubts on his legitimacy was the only way of weakening it. The only other realistic candidate is Count Matteoli, who was imprisoned for having sold to Spain the details of the negotiations between Louis XIV and Charles III of Mantua. The main reason for thinking Matteoli was the man in the mask is that the masked man who was buried in November 1703 was named in the burial record as 'Marchioly', which is phonetically very close indeed to the count's name.

THE APPIN MURDER: THE SHOOTING OF THE RED FOX

On 14 May 1752, Colin Campbell of Glenure was shot dead in a wood in Appin in the Scottish Highlands. The murder happened in the wake of the Jacobite Rebellion of 1745, the '45, in which Scotland was being held down by garrisons of English soldiers and the clans were suppressed. Lands of Highland chiefs loyal to the Jacobite cause were confiscated and handed over to Lowlanders loyal to the Hanoverian cause. The murder happened on the land of the Appin Stewarts, who had fought in the final battle of the rebellion, the Battle of Culloden, in the front line of the Jacobite army, alongside their neighbours, the Camerons, and against the Campbells, who had supported the Hanoverian cause. Culloden had been a virtual massacre of the Jacobites.

A Campbell mysteriously shot down in Appin Stewart country in the aftermath of Culloden and the retreat of Prince Charles Stuart looked suspiciously like a revenge assassination, and by whom else than one of the Appin Stewarts?

Charles Stewart of Ardsheal, who had led the Appin Stewarts at Culloden, escaped to France. Meanwhile his estate was confiscated. The Hanoverian government appointed the owner of the neighbouring estate, Colin Campbell of Glenure, to administer Stewart's estate and collect the rents. In a skilful and diplomatic manoeuvre, Colin Campbell appointed as his assistant James Stewart 'of the Glen', a farmer who was also half-brother of the exiled Charles Stewart. Having their rents collected by a Stewart might well be more palatable to the Stewarts than handing money over to a Campbell.

James Stewart was foster-father to one of his own younger relatives, Allan Breck Stewart, who had been assigned to James by the boy's dying father. In 1752, Allan Breck Stewart was about thirty years old and James was fifty; James would live to be no older. Allan Breck was a wild character. For excitement, he had joined the English army, then deserted in order to join the Jacobites. He fought alongside the rest of the Appin Stewarts at Culloden and after the battle, which was a virtual massacre, he had fled to France with Charles Stewart. Allan Breck Stewart came back to Scotland intermittently in order to recruit for the French army; he himself had joined a Scots regiment in the French army.

Allan Breck Stewart was in continuous danger when he was in Scotland. He was wanted by the English authorities for being a deserter, a Jacobite and a recruiter for King Louis; he could have been hanged for any of these offences. He was a tall, round-shouldered man with large dark eyes and a face pitted with smallpox – hence his nickname 'Breck', which means 'spotted'. In his French military uniform he was very conspicuous indeed. It consisted of a long blue coat lined with red and fastened with yellow buttons, a scarlet shirt, black breeches, tartan stockings and a feathered hat. He looked like a character out of a pantomime, and the outfit was far too conspicuous for him to wear it when in Scotland. He naturally swapped the uniform for some of his foster-father's clothes. Allan Breck Stewart was a man of unreliable character, a brigand. His own clan thought he was 'an idle, fair-spoken, clever rascal'.

When Allan returned to Scotland he was on the lookout for recruits, but he was also collecting money to support Charles Stewart in France. The tenants on the estate were loyal, and voluntarily paid their rent twice, once to Campbell of Glenure and once to Allan Breck for Charles Stewart.

Things were continuing uneasily but without aggression or violence until Colin Campbell, nicknamed the Red Fox, ordered the confiscation of James of the Glen's land in Glenduror in 1751. It was to be given to another Campbell. The government then went a step further, ordering that by 17 May 1752 all the Stewart tenants were to be evicted from their farms. Colin Campbell served notices to quit in April, giving the tenants until 15 May to get out. James of the Glen was incensed by this cavalier and inhuman treatment. He went to Edinburgh to put the case of the tenants to the barons of the Exchequer. Unfortunately the court was not in session. Instead he met one of the barons, Baron Kennedy, who expressed sympathy for the tenants' case and thought that they should be allowed to stay on their lands for the year while the matter was sorted out. But the fact remained that the barons would not be formally in session again until 3 June, by which time the evictions would already be over.

James managed to get a Bill of Suspension on 18 April, which would have delayed the eviction, but this was revoked by Lord Haining, a government supporter. James was still given to understand that there was a hope of saving the tenants' position if they were to make a formal protest in the presence of a lawyer and two witnesses. James was still trying to organize the presence of a lawyer when the whole process was interrupted by the murder of Campbell. It happened on 14 May, the day before the eviction, and James was in one of his potato fields, talking to a messenger he had sent to try to get hold of a lawyer. As they stood in the field talking, a rider came galloping up at high speed. As he passed, the rider shouted to them that Campbell of Glenure had just been shot dead in a wood four miles away.

James quietly commented, 'Well, whoever did the deed, I am the man they will hang for it.'

While James Stewart had been in Edinburgh trying to save the tenants from eviction, Colin Campbell had been there as well, working against him. Probably the intervention of Lord Haining, revoking the Bill of Suspension, was at Campbell's instigation. Once Campbell had his way over the evictions, he rode home, getting there on Saturday 9 May. On the Monday, two days later, he rode to Fort William, the nearest English garrison town in order to make arrangements for the forced evictions in Appin that were scheduled for Friday. He started back from Fort William on Thursday in the company of the sheriff-officer who was to supply the law-enforcement, his nephew Mungo Campbell who was an Edinburgh lawyer, and his servant Mackenzie.

The road they took was the long straight road south-west from Fort William, along the shore of Loch Linnhe. There was open water to their right, and the mountains of Cameron country to their left. The Camerons had fought on the same side as the Stewarts at Culloden. Like the Appin Stewarts, the Camerons had lost their estates to Colin Campbell of Glenure as their new administrator for the Crown. The Camerons had an additional grievance against Colin Campbell. He was, on his mother's side, himself a Cameron, so the Camerons saw Campbell as a traitor. As far as the Stewarts were concerned, Campbell was an enemy they might kill if they had an opportunity in an open fair fight. As far as the Camerons were concerned, he was someone who had put himself beyond any entitlement to fair play; they might kill him by stealth. They planned to do just that.

As Colin Campbell, the Red Fox, rode along the side of the loch, there were Camerons stationed all along the way, up on the hillsides, all armed, all looking for an opportunity to kill him. But Campbell had been tipped off that an ambush had been planned. There was no danger from the right, where there was a broad open expanse of water. But Campbell was vulnerable to his left. What he did was to make Mackenzie ride close beside him to the left; he was using him as a human shield, in the knowledge that the Camerons' code of honour would not allow them to risk shooting an innocent man. Campbell's party reached the Ballachulish ferry, where the road was broken across by the branch of the sea loch called Loch Leven. Beyond Loch Leven lay Appin Stewart country, and Campbell could feel safer there. Once he had made the short ferry crossing, Campbell said, 'I am safe now that I am out of my mother's country.'

They rode on and it was less than one mile into Stewart country when Campbell was shot. With his three companions he rode into the Wood of Lettermore, and it was there that he was ambushed, felled with a single shot by a sniper. Mungo Campbell described the incident a week afterwards.

Upon entering the middle of a thick wood, poor Glenure was shot, and had power to say no more than, 'Oh, I'm dead: Mungo, take care of yourself; the villain's going to shoot you.' On which I immediately dismounted and being a few paces before him I returned to where he was, and started up the brae where I imagined that the shot came from, and saw a villain with a firelock in his hand, who on seeing me, though unarmed, made off without firing. Glenure still kept his horse; and I removed him off, unable to utter a word, but opened his breast to show me the wound. We had two servants along with us but not a nail of arms among the whole. Immediately I despatched one of them to bring us some people. . . Judge then on my situation, in the middle of Appin, surrounded by my enemies, and the doleful spectacle of my uncle dead before us, expecting every moment to be attacked and entirely defenceless. In this situation, however, I continued about an hour and a half, when the Appin people flocked about me in shoals (none of whom but pleased at everything had I shared my uncle's fate). I got a boat and conveyed the corpse to a house in Appin Glenure.

Apart from Mungo Campbell, there was one other witness who saw the murderer. She was More MacIntyre. In her sworn statement she said, 'upon that foot road in the Wood I met a man running very hard, of whom I asked if he had seen Glenure. He told me he was a little before me on the road.' Mor MacIntyre was sure she had never seen the man before. Significantly, she was not called on to give her evidence at the trial. What she saw did not fit what would become the official version of events. The only evidence for identification that was admitted at the trial was Mungo Campbell's – and he diplomatically altered his description to fit what the authorities wanted.

The man the authorities wanted to incriminate was

Allan Breck Stewart. He would be their gunman, and he had James of the Glen as his accomplice. At the time of the trial, Allan was of course safely back in France, leaving James to hang alone. James knew, the moment he heard that Campbell had been shot, that he would be hanged for it. His speech at the trial, after sentence had been passed, was a model of dignity and restraint.

My Lords, I tamely submit to my hard sentence. I forgive the jury and the witnesses who have sworn several things falsely against me, and I declare, before the great God and this auditory, that I had no previous knowledge of the murder of Colin Campbell of Glenure and am innocent of it as a child unborn. I am not afraid to die, but what grieves me is my character, that after ages should think me capable of such a horrid and barbarous murder.

James of the Glen continued to maintain his innocence on the scaffold, and to make clear that none of the Appin Stewarts would have shot Campbell in an ambush.

To do my friends justice, as far as I know I do declare that none of my friends, to my knowledge, ever did plot or concert that murder; and I am persuaded they never employed any person to accomplish that cowardly action. . . there is none of my friends who might have a quarrel with that gentleman but had the honour and resolution to offer him a fairer chance for his life than to shoot him privately from a bush.

But could he really vouch for his wayward foster-son, Allan Breck? As it happens, Allan Breck's movements and clothing on that day are well known. The evening before the murder he spent at Ballachulish House, right beside the ferry and half a mile from the place where the murder took place. On the morning of the murder, he helped with farm work and then after a midday meal he decided to fish, took a fishing rod and went up to a stream on the hillside. He found a vantage point from which he could see all the surrounding country and also see the route Campbell would follow: the road coming round the hill to the north-west as he approached the ferry.

As if to remind everyone in the neighbourhood that he was there, Allan Breck came down the hillside in the afternoon, went to the ferry and asked the ferryman if the Red Fox and his party had crossed yet. He knew they had not, so he can only have had one motive in coming down – to show himself in front of witnesses. He went back up the hillside and disappeared into the trees, but without a gun.

Allan's motive in establishing so emphatically that he was there that afternoon is difficult to interpret. It is possible, indeed likely, that he knew just as Campbell knew that the Camerons were plotting to assassinate him somewhere along the Loch Linnhe lake shore. If he believed that Campbell was going to be murdered in Cameron country, and he also knew that he would be a prime suspect for the murder, he may have needed to establish his alibi. He made very sure that several people knew that he was on the south side of Loch Leven all morning and all afternoon, and therefore could not have assassinated Campbell somewhere to the north of the Ballachulish ferry.

Alternatively, he may have known, somehow, that the assassination would take place in the wood and was establishing a cover for someone else. If he was planning to leave for France immediately (as he evidently did), he may have agreed to take the blame for a murder someone else was about to commit. It made no difference to him now; he was already guilty of three capital offences. While his flaunted presence on the south side of Loch Leven would or should have ensured an acquittal on a charge of murder at some point north of the ferry, it would have damned him utterly if the murder took place to the south – which it did.

Could Allan Breck have been the murderer? He said repeatedly that he would welcome a chance of a fight with Campbell. He 'wanted nothing more than to meet him at a convenient place.' But, as his foster-father affirmed on the gallows, the Appin Stewart way was emphatically not to kill people in cold blood in an ambush. On the day of the murder, Allan Breck was wearing clothes borrowed from James, as he often did when on visits. He wore a short black coat with silver buttons and a scarlet lining. He also wore plaid trousers, in a striking blue and white striped pattern. This was not a stalking costume. This was not an outfit that any assassin would choose to wear when planning to lie hidden on a hillside. The boldness of the costume was designed, like his behaviour, to draw attention to him.

Does Allan Breck Stewart's borrowed clothing match Mungo Campbell's description of what the murderer was wearing? Mungo described him as 'a man with a gun in his hand, clothed in a short dun-coloured coat and breeches of the same.' He was evidently persuaded to change this for the trial, where the murderer became 'a man with a short dark-coloured coat.' This was clearly meant to tie in with what the law officers knew Allan Breck was wearing. But there is no possibility of mistaking blue and white striped trousers for dun-coloured breeches, so it is obvious that Allan Breck was not the murderer. That is reinforced by Mor MacIntyre's failure to recognize the man she saw on the road; she would have know Allan Breck well enough.

Some believe that Donald Stewart was the murderer. He was in the area at the time of the murder, lived in the district, knew Allan Breck and could therefore have been the man for whom Allan was covering. But there is no real case for believing that Donald was the killer. He was in an hysterical state as the day of James of the Glen's execution approached. He wanted to go to the gallows and give himself up to save James. His kinsmen tried to persuade him it would do no good, that it was too late and would only lead to a second hanging. In the end, they had to tie Donald up until after the execution was over. His behaviour is not evidence of guilt; only evidence of loyalty and love.

Donald's evidence at the trial nevertheless contains the clue we are looking for, the name of the assassin. Donald said he had gone to Allan immediately after the murder and accused him of being the murderer. Allan denied it, but said that he thought he would be accused of it. Because of that he would have to leave the country. Allan needed money, and asked Donald to get some from James for him. The next morning Donald went to James and in the course of the conversation he, Donald, had expressed regret that 'such an accident as Glenure's murder' should happen in their country. James replied that he had been told, presumably by Allan Breck, that 'one Sergeant Mor, alias John Cameron, had been threatening in France to harm Glenure.'

At the trial it was briefly mentioned that Sergeant Mor had not been seen in Scotland for ten years, but that does not allow for his returning in secret. Sergeant Mor was an even wilder character than Allan. After fighting on the Jacobite side in the '45, Mor organized a band of outlaws in the Western Highalnds. They robbed but never killed. Like Breck, Mor joined the French army. Like Breck, he hated Colin Campbell. The big difference, apart from the fact that Mor was even more of a brigand than Breck, was that Mor was a Cameron. As a Cameron, his attitude to the Red Fox was deadlier; he had no compunction about killing Campbell by stealth. Also, as a Cameron, he would not have seen that the murder of Campbell would have made things extremely difficult for the Stewarts, that it would jeopardize James of the Glen's careful negotiations, and probably not even cared much that James of the Glen would lose his life in his place. As a brigand, an outsider, Mor would be likely to overlook all that.

The only remaining problem is the location of the murder. Campbell breathed a sigh of relief when he crossed the Balluchulish ferry, knowing that he was now in Appin Stewart country. But the Cameron ambush was well planned. Armed Camerons were positioned at intervals all along the loch-side road from Fort William. Maybe they suspected that they needed a safety net, one more position just half a mile into Appin Stewart country. And what better place for an ambush than the Wood of Lettermore! Murdo Cameron, the man who organized the long ambush through Cameron country, had actually said that if the Red Fox escaped them there, he would not come alive through the Wood of Lettermore. This is as clear a statement as we are likely to find that there was one final sniper, a Cameron in the wood. That final, successful sniper must surely have been John Cameron, also known as Sergeant Mor.

PART THREE

UNSOLVED CRIMES OF THE NINETEENTH CENTURY

(1801–1900)

THE RATCLIFFE HIGHWAY MURDERS

Towards the end of the nineteenth century, in the 1880s, London was gripped by something like mass hysteria by the Whitechapel murders. The Jack the Ripper murders in a peculiar and distinctive way became part of the twentieth century equivalent of Penny Dreadful culture. What is now generally forgotten is that there was an even more intense wave of hysteria in London over another crop of murders, the Ratcliffe Highway murders. In Whitechapel in the 1880s there was a certain amount of fear in the air, but the risks were clearly contained as the murderer (and just one man, probably) was only interested in killing lone prostitutes who were out on the streets very late at night. If you were not a prostitute and stayed off the streets at night you were safe. The Ratcliffe Highway murders were altogether more terrifying, as people of both sexes and all ages were murdered in their own homes.

It was at midnight on Saturday, 7 December, in 1811 that London was shaken by the violent and inexplicable murder of an entire family. In spite of the lateness of the hour, the traders were only then shutting up shop for the night. Timothy Marr, who ran a draper's shop, was one of them. On the night in question, he was still behind the counter after a busy day, gathering up the lengths of cloth out on display in the shop and putting them away on the shelves, helped by his shop-boy, James Gowen. There were various types of cloth, rough worsted, dyed linen, canvas for seamen's trousers, serge for seamen's jackets and cheap printed cotton. Marr also kept stocks of silk and muslin for his better-off customers.

Timothy Marr sent his maidservant, Margaret Jewell, out to buy oysters for a late family supper, and she had left the shop door ajar because she expected to be back in a few minutes. It was midnight, but there were still shops open and it seemed safe to be walking the streets at that hour. Unfortunately, the shop where she was expecting to buy the oysters, Taylor's oyster shop, had shut for the night and she had to try elsewhere. This brought her back past Marr's shop, and as she walked past she looked in through the window and saw Mr Marr and the boy still at work. In the event she found no oyster shop open, though she was able to pay the baker's bill, which was another of Marr's errands.

A gang of criminals meanwhile walked into Timothy Marr's shop, pushed him to the floor and cut his throat. Then they grabbed hold of his shop-boy and murdered him too. Mrs Marr was in the kitchen, feeding her baby. She heard an extraordinary noise and scuffling upstairs, as she thought, so she laid the baby in its cradle and ran up to see what was happening. Then she was met by the men who had murdered her husband. She too was murdered – in the same way. The baby started crying in its cradle, and the intruders went in to silence it, fearing that the noise might attract the curiosity and concern of the neighbours; they cut the baby's throat as well.

Then the maidservant came back without the oysters. She found the shop door shut and locked, so she rang the bell. No one answered. But she did hear the soft tread of footsteps on the stairs, which she thought was her master coming downstairs to open the door for her. Then she heard the baby give a single low cry. Then nothing. No footsteps. Nothing. The watchman George Olney passed down the other side of the street, taking someone to the lock-up; he noticed Margaret standing at the door. She became angry that she had been locked out and frightened too. She could not understand why no one was answering the door. She started banging on the door and kicking it. Not knowing what to do, she just waited on the doorstep for half an hour, banging on the door from time to time.

In due course, George Olney, the watchman, came round again, calling the hour at one o'clock, and asked her what she was doing. She explained that she had been locked out and thought it very strange, and he agreed that the family must be in. He had seen Mr Marr putting the shutters up, but later had noticed that they were not fastened. Olney remembered calling out to Marr at the time and hearing an unfamiliar voice answering, 'We know of it'. Now he could see that the shutters were still unfastened. Olney knew there was something seriously wrong. He tugged vigorously on the bell and shouted through the keyhole, 'Mr Marr! Mr Marr!'. The intruders, who were still in the house at this time, realized that they needed to get away. They scrambled out of a window at the back of the house, across some mud and followed a route that showed an intimate knowledge of the area. It included passing through an empty house in Pennington Street. The man living in the house next to it heard a rumbling noise as 'about ten or twelve men' rushed through it from the back and out into Pennington Street.

The watchman wondered what to do. Mr Murray, a pawnbroker, lived next door. He was not a man to interfere in his neighbours' lives, but he and his wife were being kept awake by Margaret's banging on the door and wondered what was wrong, especially since there had been mysterious noises earlier on, including the cry of a boy or woman. Murray assumed that Marr was tired and irritated at the end of an exhausting day and was chastising the maid or the shop-boy.

Mr Murray went out to see what was going on and discussed the situation with Margaret and the watchman. Murray decided to climb over the fence separating Mr Marr's back yard from his own. This was quickly done and he got into the Marrs' house from the back. Inside it seemed very quiet and still. He saw a light from a candle burning on the first floor and went up. The door into the Marrs' bedroom was shut and he did not like to go in. He came back downstairs and found the first of the bodies. The fourteen-year-old shopboy James Gowen was lying near the door into the shop. The bones of his face had been shattered by blow after blow with a heavy object; his head had been beaten to a pulp. Blood and brains hung from the ceiling. This was the first of a series of the most appalling tableaux. He saw the body of Timothy Marr on the floor in the shop, and the body of his wife in the passage. The bodies were all still warm, still bleeding.

Murray was nauseated by what he saw. He managed to stumble to the front door and get it open. 'Murder! Murder! Come and see what murder is here!' In England in 1811, public hangings were regarded as major entertainments, and visiting crime scenes to view murder victims was quite normal behaviour. Someone asked him about the baby, which Murray had not seen. People crowded in from the street and saw the baby with its head almost completely severed.

The whole neighbourhood was soon in a state of alarm. The night watch mustered and a drum sounded the call to arms. By midnight a huge crowd had gathered in the street outside Marr's shop to hear what had happened.

One of the murder weapons was found in the Marrs' bedroom. The bed was undisturbed. Beside it stood a chair, and resting against it was a heavy iron mallet or maul, completely covered in blood and human tissue.

The bodies were laid out in the bedrooms and sightseers from all over the neighbourhood came to have a look.

Scores of people of every class tramped up and down the narrow staircase to see the bodies of the murder victims.

An inquest was opened on 10 December and a verdict of 'wilful murder by person or persons unknown' was brought in. The burial of the Marr family took place on 15 December 1811 at the Church of St George's in the East, attended by an enormous crowd, silent apart from groans of pity.

No one had any idea who could have done the murders, or why. Was it simple robbery? If so, why choose such a humble shop? Was it something to do with Timothy Marr's past, perhaps the settling of an old score? Marr was only twenty-four, but that was old enough for him to have had a past. He had been to sea with the East India Company, sailing his last voyage in the Dover Castle in 1808. He had not sailed before the mast but as the captain's personal servant. He was an agreeable young man, keen to please, but also ambitious. The captain, a man called Richardson, had promised to help him if he continued to serve him well. Timothy Marr wanted to leave the sea, marry the girl he was in love with, Celia, and set up a small shop. Ironically, he thought being a shop-keeper would be a safer life than his life at sea. When the Dover Castle docked at Wapping, Marr was signed off with a significant sum of money – enough to set him up in business. In April of 1811, Marr and his new wife found what they were looking for, cheap premises not far from the docks. Marr knew about the clothing needs of sailors, and there were huge numbers of sailors passing through the London Docks. Every year 13,000 ships passed through.

But the location Timothy Marr chose, close to the docks, was a dangerous one. The docks were a major focus for criminal activity. In 1800, it was estimated that around 10,000 thieves preyed on the ships that were docked on the open river. Things improved when the London Dock opened in 1805, but only a little. There were still huge numbers of criminals in the area. The warehouses that stored goods awaiting export and imported raw materials awaiting collection were a great magnet for criminals. Timothy Marr lived and worked within a stone's throw of all this crime. Very close to his shop was the twenty-foot high security wall of the London Dock.

The Marr murders were horrible enough, but they were soon to be followed by more. Everyone in the vicinity of the Marrs' shop felt vulnerable to attack by the merciless gang of murdering burglars, who were still at large, still unidentified; everyone was waiting for the same thing to happen again.

Just twelve days later, on 19 December, it did. At around eleven o'clock at night, Mr Williamson, the licencee of the King's Arms, No 81 New Gravel Lane, put up the shutters. He was fifty-six, a big, strong, burly man well able to deal with late drinkers or most kinds of troublemakers. It was a noisy, squalid area full of ship's chandlers, lodging houses, pawnbrokers and pubs packed out with sailors. It was said that every ninth building was a pub. New Gravel Lane was no stranger to disorder. The King's Arms had a tap-room and a private kitchen behind it on the ground floor, and a cellar with a flap-door opening on to the pavement for delivering barrels of beer. The Williamsons' bedroom and that of Kitty Stillwell, their fourteen-year-old granddaughter, were on the first floor. Above those bedrooms were a couple of attic bedrooms, one occupied by Bridget Harrington who worked behind the bar, and the other by a young lodger called John Taylor.

Williamson relaxed with a beer drawn by his wife and chatted with his neighbour, Mr Anderson, who was a constable. Williamson suddenly sat up, alert. There was something on his mind. 'You're an officer,' he said. 'There's been a fellow listening at my door, with a brown jacket on. If you see him, you should take him immediately into custody. Or tell me.'

Anderson said he certainly would, and for his own safety as well as Williamson's. He said goodnight to the Williamsons, then returned to his own house. The man Williamson described as listening at his door was at the inquest described by John Turner, who remembered Samuel Phillips calling in for a drink with Williamson at twenty to eleven. It was Phillips who told Williamson that 'there was a stout man with a very large coat on, peeping in at the glass door in the passage'. Williamson went off to challenge him, brandishing a candlestick, but came back having seen no one.

Twenty minutes after returning to his own house, Anderson was aware of a disturbance in the street. There were cries of 'Murder!' People started to gather in the street in front of the King's Arms pub. The shouts of

'Murder!' were coming from a near-naked man climbing down the outside of the house from an attic window on a rope of sheets, shouting and crying incoherently. The watchman stood below, holding his lantern and rattle. The half-naked man was John Turner. Anderson rushed back indoors to get his constable's sword and staff, and came out just in time to see John Turner come to the end of his rope. The last sheet ended eight feet short of the ground, and he fell this distance to be caught by the watchman, Shadrick Newhall. Then John Turner shouted, 'They are murdering the people in the house!'

Anderson quickly decided to force his way into the house through the cellar flap. This was done with the help of Mr Hawse, an axe-wielding butcher. Another man, Mr Fox, managed to get in through some wooden bars at the side of the house; for some reason he was carrying a cutlass. On looking round, the first thing they saw was the body of Mr Williamson, lying head downwards at the foot of the cellar steps, a terrible wound on his head, his right leg broken, his throat cut and a crowbar covered with blood by his side. They then went upstairs to the kitchen and found the body of Mrs Williamson, also with a head wound and a cut throat. Near her was the body of Bridget Harrington, her feet under the grate, with exactly the same injuries. Her throat had been cut right back to the neckbone. By some miracle, the granddaughter was still in her bed, unharmed, fast asleep. Someone carried her out into the street; she could not be left there.

Many enquiries, discussions and investigations followed, in the attempt to identify the criminals who carried out the two violent attacks. The Shadwell Police Office was very active in the investigation, as was Mr Graham of the Bow Street office.

This second set of murders seemed like a replay of the first set, but with one crucial difference. This time there was a witness – John Turner. Anderson reported that a tall man in a long Flushing coat had been seen loitering outside the King's Arms that evening. Turner saw a tall man dressed in just this way bending over Mrs Williamson's body. He had stayed in the doorway just long enough to take in what was happening, before tiptoeing back upstairs to make his rope of sheets. Initially, Turner had been taken into custody as a suspect, but it became clear that the murderer or murderers had got out of a window at the back of the house; there were bloodstains on the sill. Outside was a high clay bank with a footprint on it. The murderers, who would have clay on their clothes, must have got away over the waste land of the London Dock. Someone recalled that there were several points in common here with the Marr murders. The savage wounds inflicted, the timing, the escape route across back land, the lack of theft. Once again, money that could have been taken was left in the house.

Attempts were made to find links between the Williamsons and the Marrs, but there seemed to be none. Two men were spotted running away from the scene of the murder at the right time. One was tall. The other seemed slightly lame or exhausted by some exertion. The tall man had said something like, 'Come along Mahoney (or Hughie), come along'.

The law enforcers were under enormous pressure to find the perpetrators of these awful crimes. They needed to home in on a prime suspect. In situations like these, the wrong person has frequently been charged and condemned, and the unfortunate man the police settled on as the scapegoat for the Ratcliffe Highway murders was probably innocent. Of the many suspects interviewed, the one the authorities settled on was a man called John Williams. He was twenty-seven, five foot nine inches tall, slim, 'of an insinuating manner and pleasing countenance'. He had connections with both Marr and Williamson, which the authorities seized upon; he had sailed with Marr on the Dover Castle, and he had been seen drinking in Williamson's pub many times, including the fatal evening. They were slight enough connections, and they were not criminal connections either, but they seemed like a breakthrough. It was also to emerge later that Williams knew Jeremiah Fitzpatrick and Cornelius Hart, the carpenters at the Marrs' house. John Williams had returned from the sea in October 1811 and resumed his old lodgings at the Pear Tree pub, where he returned after all of his voyages. He treated Mr and Mrs Vermilloe as if they were his parents, with trust and respect. He handed over his earnings to Mr Vermilloe as his banker and was a tidy, clean and courteous lodger. He was a cut above normal seamen in his fastidious dress and education. He was occasionally mistaken for a gentleman.

But alongside these undoubted qualities, and in spite of his slightly weak and foppish appearance, Williams was extremely hot-tempered and easily got entangled in brawls. He was easily provoked and men found it entertaining to goad him. He not surprisingly had many female admirers, few male friends.

He was arrested as one of the gang of murderers, though it is very clear from the published evidence that there was no more evidence against him than there was against a hundred other men. The only reason for suspecting him was that he was acquainted with people who had connections with both of the households, which was very tenuous and not at all sinister. It was in the nature of the East End, then and later, and in the nature of seafaring that everybody knew everybody else. Certainly there was not enough to justify a guilty verdict or the sentence of death which is what, in effect, he got. There was a piece about him in The Times of 24 December 1811 that suggested there was no case against him at all. The piece sarcastically listed points against him including that he was short with a lame leg, that he asked a foreign sailor to put out his candle for him, that previous to the murders he had been short of money, that he was Irish. Unfortunately, the tone of the newspaper piece was a little too witty and sly to be effective, given the terrifying national demand for a scapegoat. And irony is a very risky device in the hands of any writer. The juggernaut of Justice was rolling towards Williams and nobody was trying to rescue him. The evidence was being allowed to pile up against him but without proper critical analysis. If, for example, John Williams was the shorter of the two men seen running away from the Williamsons' house, the lame man who had to be hurried up - why did the taller man call him Mahoney or Hughie? Neither of these names is anything like John or Williams.

Aaron Graham was meanwhile more interested in an Irishman called Maloney – much closer to the reported 'Mahoney' – after he had a letter from Captain Taylor of the frigate *Sparrow* at Deptford. Taylor reported that Maloney answered the description of one of the murderers. Graham sent for Maloney and was not satisfied with Maloney's account of himself. At Marlborough in Wiltshire the tall man was identified: he was a remarkably tall man with badly bloodstained clothing and it was alleged that there were letters connecting him with Maloney. He was named by the Home Secretary and the Prime Minister in Parliament as William Ablass, commonly known as Long Billy. He was a close friend of John Williams and had been to sea with him. The Times commented that Ablass looked remarkably like Williams, as if that were in itself a condemnation of the man. The torn and bloody shirt that had been noticed in Marlborough was explained by a pub brawl in Reading. Ablass in any case, for reasons not disclosed, had to be released.

The missing piece in the jigsaw as far as the authorities were concerned was a connection between the suspect, John Williams, and the murder weapon, the maul. Mr Vermilloe, the landlord of the Pear Tree, provided the connection. He had himself been in Newgate Prison for a debt of twenty pounds for seven weeks at the time, so the lure of a reward that would pay off the debt was probably a major factor in his evidence. What he said was that he could identify the maul, which was shown to him in Newgate, as having belonged to a German sailor who had lodged at the Pear Tree Inn. The sailor's name was John Peterson. Peterson had left his chest of tools with Vermilloe when he went to sea. Most of the tools were marked with Peterson's initials. Vermilloe would not perjure himself totally by saying that this maul was definitely one of Peterson's tools, but he had used one of the mauls for chopping wood and had himself broken the tip. The murder weapon had a broken tip. At a hearing in which the new 'evidence' about the maul was heard, John Williams tried to speak, but he was told by the magistrate to be silent. It is impossible to guess what he might have said; soon he would be silenced altogether.

The authorities hoped that by holding Williams long enough they could get him to tell them the names of his accomplices, so that they could round up the whole dangerous gang. Cornelius Hart was getting himself implicated. He looked like the gang member responsible for stealing the ripping chisel that was left in Marr's house, and he had secretly sent his wife to the Pear Tree to find out if Williams had been arrested, while denying that he was a friend of Williams.

But the holding plan went wrong. When the gaoler at Coldbath Fields Prison went to collect John Williams to answer questions before the Shadwell police magistrates, he found him dead in his cell, hanging from a beam. The investigation proceeded as if Williams had admitted his own guilt, though of course he may have committed suicide for some other reason, such as despair at being wrongly charged, or he may have been murdered. The Coroner, Mr Unwin, addressed the jury in terms that were strongly biased, unforgivably referring to John Williams as a 'miserable wretch' and accusing him of seeking to escape justice by recourse to self-destruction; by killing himself, Williams had proved himself a murderer, and so on. On the last day of the year 1811, Williams' body was moved, late at night, from the cell where he died to a watch-house near the London Docks, ready for burial.

The magistrate, Mr Capper, met the Home Secretary to discuss the possibility of departing from the usual custom of burying suicides at the nearest crossroads. They decided that something nastier and more barbaric was appropriate to satisfy public feeling – a public exhibition of the body through the neighbourhood where the crimes had been committed.

In line with this extraordinary decision, a procession led from the watch-house at half past ten in the morning, It consisted of several hundred constables carrying staves to clear the way, the newly formed patrol carrying drawn cutlasses, more constables, the parish officers of the three parishes concerned (St George's, St Paul's and Shadwell), peace officers on horseback, yet more constables, and then the High Constable of Middlesex on horseback.

Then, climatically, came the body of the 'miserable wretch', John Williams, stretched full length on a sloping board on the back of a cart, to give the best possible view of the murderer's body. Williams was dressed in blue trousers and a blue-and-white striped waistcoat, but no coat, just as he was found in his cell. On the left side of the murderer's head was displayed the maul, and on the right side the ripping chisel or crow bar; these were believed to be the murder weapons. The face of John Williams was awful to look at, and the condition of the corpse as a whole was too horrible for observers to describe in any further detail. Yet more constables brought up the rear.

This almost-medieval procession made its way slowly up Ratcliffe Highway, accompanied and followed by a huge crowd of people, all eager to get a good look at John Williams's body. When the cart reached Mr Marr's house, it was halted there for a quarter of an hour. Then the procession moved off towards Old Gravel Lane, Wapping, New Crane Lane and into New Gravel Lane. At Mr Williamson's house the procession again came to a halt for a while. Then it moved off into Ratcliffe Highway again, Cannon Street and St George's Turnpike, to the point where the road was intersected by Cannon Street. There, at the crossroads, a six-foot deep grave had been prepared. At about midday John Williams' body was untied from its platform and stuffed into the grave. A stake was driven through Williams' heart with the bloodstained maul, then the grave was filled and the paving stones replaced.

The authorities managed for a short time to sell the public the idea that John Williams was a lone killer, but it was obvious from many of the witness statements that at least two and possibly as many as twelve men were involved. Whether John Williams really was one of the murderers remains uncertain. And who were the others who were with him? There was a mystery surrounding the crowbar used as the second murder weapon. Mr Pugh was the clerk of works who had overseen the modernization of the shop for Marr. His carpenter had asked for a crowbar (or ripping chisel, as it was called) which Mr Pugh did not have, but borrowed one from a neighbour. When the carpentry job had been done the carpenter had been laid off, but he went without returning the chisel. Pugh asked the carpenter about it and the carpenter replied that he had left it in the shop, though Pugh could not find it. Some days later, Timothy Marr told Pugh that he had searched his house thoroughly and was sure the chisel wasn't there. On the day of Marr's murder the chisel was still missing from Marr's shop, only reappearing on the discovery of the bodies of Marr and Gowen, when it was seen lying on the counter. It is reasonable to suspect the carpenter of being one of the murderers. It was not immediately seen as a significant object because it was not covered in blood, but its return during the raid on the Marrs' house was a significant clue.

One peculiar aspect of the evidence is that The Times studiously avoided naming the carpenter. It would later emerge that there were three carpenters, Cornelius Hart and two joiners called Towler (or Trotter) and Jeremiah Fitzpatrick. Of the three, Cornelius Hart is the likeliest. Was he one of the murderers?

The motive seems not to have been simple robbery. There was cash to the value of £150 in the house, a considerable sum in those days, yet it was not taken. A score from Timothy Marr's seafaring days seems possible. It is also possible that there was some family rivalry. A man called Thomas Taylor said that he knew that Marr's brother had employed six or seven men to commit the murders. He also said he knew one of the men involved, who had been unable to cut the child's throat. Unfortunately, Taylor later said he had no memory of saying any of this and that he had been wounded in the head while serving in the forces; he admitted that he was sometimes so deranged, especially when drunk, that he did not know what he was saying. The magistrates agreed with him that he was insane and decided to let him go without taking any notice of his testimony. There were, even so, other witnesses who said Marr's brother hated him. There had been a lawsuit which Timothy Marr had won; the two men had not spoken to each other for years.

There were other leads, too. A week or two after the murders, when the bloodstained maul had been in the possession of John Harriott at the River Thames Police Office for some time, someone took a look at it with a magnifying glass. A detail had been overlooked. The caked blood and hair were carefully scraped back to reveal the initials I. P. punched in dots. Presumably these were the initials of the maul's owner. The description published at the time wrongly gave the initials as 'J. P.' and, thanks to that useful misprint, Mr Vermilloe's identification of the maul as belonging to John Peterson is seen to be a piece of pure perjury. (The Vermilloes got their £60 reward in due course.)

The other murder weapon, the knife or razor, was invisible through most of the enquiries. So also was the supposition that John Williams was the sort of man who cut people's throats. After his death, discreet investigations into his past revealed no violence with knives whatever. He may, through impulsiveness, have got involved in occasional fist-fights, but he was not a knife man.

The strange errand of Margaret Jewell may hold one of the keys to the mystery. She would certainly have been murdered if she had been in the house when the gang arrived; her life was saved by her fruitless search for oysters. But was she in fact sent out by Marr as she said? In one statement, she said it was Mrs Marr who had sent her out. The inconsistency suggests that perhaps neither of them sent her out, that it was her own idea to go out on a fruitless midnight shopping expedition. This may mean that she set it up, or had been bribed to go out, leaving the front door open. Her spectacular swoon at the inquest was seen at the time as quite consistent with guilt. She may have colluded with Marr's brother, assuming that some lesser crime was to be committed, maybe theft or some minor assault; finding out later that she had connived at the murder of the whole household might well have made her feel faint.

On the face of it, it looks like a remarkable coincidence that Margaret Jewell went out of the house for a short time, leaving the door unlocked, and in that short time the murderers entered, killed and left again. We shall come across exactly this kind of suspicious coincidental absence again, in the case of Billie-Jo Jenkins.

One of the investigators, Aaron Graham, followed the line of thought that Margaret Jewell was an accomplice, that she was somehow persuaded or bribed to go out and leave the door open, perhaps not realizing that mass murder was planned. Working on this hypothesis, Graham interrogated Marr's brother for two days. Marr had no interest in Margaret Jewell, had never even known her. Nor had there been a murderous family feud. Marr's brother also had an alibi. If he had planned the murder so meticulously, he would have an alibi; and there was nothing to stop him hiring others to do the job for him. But Aaron Graham's questioning was unable to get past Marr's alibi.

This whole line of enquiry began to disintegrate when the Williamson household was murdered. After John Williams's suicide, the investigators lost their way, having decided too soon that he was one of the murderers. What, in the end, did the most serious contemporary investigator make of it? In February 1812, Aaron Graham wrote his report. He concluded that two people had committed the Williamson murders, that Ablass was not one of them. He was sure that Cornelius Hart was involved in the Marr murders, but doubted if the case could ever be made to hold up in court; he had proved that Hart's statements contained lies. But it is a profoundly unsatisfactory report. He had to release his prime suspect, Ablass, yet he did not say why. He also missed the obvious point that John Turner, who saw the tall man, did not recognize him as Williams, whom he knew well and had seen earlier that evening. If the (relatively) tall man was not Ablass and, as Graham says, Williams's accomplice was shorter than Williams, then Williams must have been the 'tall' man seen at the King's Arms, and he does not really fit the description of the tall man either. The only conclusion can be that Williams was not there at all – indeed not involved in either of these horrible cases.

It is also possible that Williams himself was murdered. It would be obvious to the real murderers that if Williams came to trial and was acquitted, the man hunt would resume and they would still be in danger. If he appeared to commit suicide, his guilt would be taken for granted - as indeed it was. So it was simply a matter of bribing a turnkey in a prison with virtually no supervision to hang an already fettered prisoner. The state of Williams's body showed that he had 'struggled very hard' for life, yet when he was found his hands were free, his bed was close by and the iron beam was only five inches higher from the ground than he was; he could have reached up and held onto the beam while he found the bed with his feet. In view of the circumstances, it is very unlikely that he died voluntarily.

The two murders gripped the attention of the whole of England. The poet Robert Southey, avidly reading about them in the Lake District, declared that it was a rare case of 'a private event which rose to the dignity of a national event'. The Marrs were given a tall tombstone bearing a long inscription, relating how they were 'most inhumanely murdered in their dwelling house, No 28 Ratcliffe Highway, 8 December, 1811.

> *Stop, mortal, as you pass by,*
> *And view the grave wherein doth lie*
> *A Father, Mother and a Son,*
> *Whose earthly course was shortly run.*
> *For lo, all in one fatal hour,*
> *O'er came were they with ruthless power;*
> *And murdered in a cruel state -*
> *Yea, far too horrid to relate!*

NOT PROVEN: THE DEATH OF EMILE L'ANGELIER

Poison has always been the preferred weapon of the murderess; poison has been the death of choice. This may be because it does not require physical strength, but perhaps for a purely psychological reason, that it does not involve contact or physical confrontation. Poison is indirect. Poison was also a more intelligent way of killing people; in the days before forensic science, poison was often difficult to detect. Murder by poison was therefore also difficult to detect.

The two greatest Victorian poison cases are those of Madeleine Smith and Florence Maybrick. Both cases are complex, both, in spite of a hundred years of scrutiny, remain unsolved. What may look like a straightforward murder on closer inspection turns out to be an accident or a suicide. At the time of their trials, Madeleine Smith and Florence Maybrick were both branded murderesses, and they were both demonized, but did they commit murder?

Madeleine Smith was tried in Glasgow in July 1857. Her trial failed to establish whether she had committed murder or had been framed by her insane and suicidal lover. She was put on trial for the murder of her ex-lover Emile

L'Angelier, who died as a result of arsenic poisoning.

Madeleine was the elder daughter of one James Smith, a successful Glaswegian architect. He was able to afford to maintain a comfortable household with six servants, but like the head of many a Victorian paterfamilias he ruled it with a rod of iron. For much of the time there was nothing for Madeleine to do. Along with many other Victorian girls she was expected to occupy herself with lady-like pursuits such as painting and piano-playing.

Madeleine was bored stiff and ready for a romantic adventure. The adventure came in the unlikely shape of a packing clerk called Emile L'Angelier. She first saw Emile in the street, when their eyes met by chance. He later found an opportunity to send her a flowery message of love. She rather foolishly replied that she had worn it next to her heart. It would have been better if she hadn't.

A correspondence started that would prove very damaging to her at her trial. Conversations written down can be read out in court, as she was to discover to her great embarrassment. After the initial flush of novelty, she knew it was silly and she tried to break off the relationship, but Emile was by then obsessed. He wrote her a letter that appears to be reasoned and reasonable, but contained an alarming threat. Madeleine destroyed this and the other letters Emile wrote to her, and probably thought this meant there was no trail of incriminating evidence. In fact the obsessive Emile kept drafts of each letter, so we know exactly what he wrote to her.

Glasgow, 10 Bothwell Street. 18 July 1855

In the first place, I did not deserve to be treated as you have done. How you astonish me by writing such a note without condescending to explain the reasons why your father refuses his consent. He must have reasons, and I am not allowed to clear myself of accusations.

I should have written you before, but I preferred awaiting until I got over the surprise your last letter caused me, and also to be able to write you in a calm and a collected manner, free, from any animosity whatever.

Never, dear Madeleine, could I have believed you were capable of such conduct. I thought and believed you unfit for such a step. I believed you true to your word and to your honour. I will put questions to you which answer to yourself. What would you think if even one of your servants had played with anyone's affections as you have done, or what would you say to hear that any lady friends had done what you have – or what am I to (think) of you now? What is your opinion of your own self after those solemn vows you uttered and wrote to me. Show my letters to any one, Madeleine, I don't care who, and if any find that I mislead you I will free you from all blame. I warned you repeatedly not to be rash in your engagement and vows to me, but you persisted in that false and deceitful flirtation, playing with affections which you know to be pure and undivided, and knowing at the same time that at a word from your father you would break all your engagement.

You have deceived your father as you have deceived me.
You never told him how solemnly you bound yourself to me,
or if you had, for the honour of his daughter he could not
have asked to break of an engagement as ours. Madeleine,
you have truly acted wrong. May this be a lesson to you never
to trifle with any again. I wish you every happiness. I shall
be truly happy to hear that you are happy with another. You
desire and now you are at liberty to recognize me or cut me
just as you wish – but I give you my word of honour I shall
act always as a Gentleman, towards you. We may meet yet,
as my intentions of going to Lima are now at an end. I would
have gone for your sake. Yes, I would have sacrificed all to
have you with me, and to leave Glasgow and your friends
you detested so very much. Think what your father would
say if I sent him your letters for a perusal. Do you think he
could sanction your breaking your promises. No, Madeleine,
I leave your conscience to speak for itself. I flatter myself he can
only accuse me of a want of fortune. But he must remember
he too had to begin the world with dark clouds round him.

I cannot put it into my mind that yet you are at the bottom
of all this.

It is easy to imagine Madeleine's emotional response to
this, especially the thinly veiled threat near the end. 'Think
what your father would say if I sent him your letters for a
perusal.' Given the stern character of Mr Smith, this must
have frightened Madeleine. She was already virtually
imprisoned in the family home, and her father would

certainly be shocked if he was given her letters to read. They were full of barely suppressed sexuality, and this at a time when women in her class were supposed to put up with sex, not enjoy it. When L'Angelier lay dead and his lodgings were searched, more than five hundred steamy letters from Madeleine were found.

It was obvious from the letters that they had had sex. Emile explicitly addressed her as his wife. 'If we did wrong last night, it must have been in the excitement of our love. I suppose we should have waited until we were married.'

My dearest and beloved Wife Mimi,
Since I saw you I have been wretchedly sad. Would to God we had not met that night – I would have been happier. I am sad at what we did, I regret it very much. Why, Mimi, did you give way after your promises? My pet, it is a pity. Think of the consequences if I were never to marry you. What reproaches I should have, Mimi. I never shall be happy again. If ever I meet you again, love, it must be as at first. I will never again repeat what I did until we are regularly married. Try your friends once more – tell your determination – say nothing will change you, that you have thought seriously of it – and on that I shall firmly fix speaking to Huggins for Sepr. Unless you do something of that sort, Heaven only knows when I shall marry you. Unless you do, dearest, I shall have to leave the country; truly, dearest, I am in such a state of mind I do not care if I were dead. We did wrong. God forgive us for it. Mimi, we have loved blindly. It is your parents' fault

if shame is the result; they are to blame for it all.

I got home quite safe after leaving you, but I think it did my cold no good. I was fearfully excited the whole night. I was truly happy with you, my pet; too much so, for I am now too sad. I wish from the bottom of my heart we had never parted. Though we have sinned, ask earnestly God's forgiveness and blessings that all the obstacles in our way may be removed from us. I was disappointed, my love, at the little you had to say, but I can understand why. You are not stupid, Mimi, and if you disappoint me in information, and I have cause to reproach you of it, you will have no one to blame but yourself, as I have given you warning long enough to improve yourself. Sometimes I do think you take no notice of my wishes and my desires, but say yes for mere matter of form.

Mimi, unless Huggins helps me I cannot see how I shall be able to marry you for years. What misery to have such a future in one's mind. Do speak to your brother, open your heart to him, and try and win his friendship. Tell him if he loves you to take your part. And besides, my dear, if once you can trust, how pleasant it would be for you and me to meet. I could come over to Helensburgh when you would be riding or driving, or of a Sunday: I could join you in a walk of a Sunday afternoon. Mimi, dearest, you must take a bold step to be my wife. I entreat you, pet, by the love you have for me, Mimi, do speak to your mother – tell her it is the last time you ever shall speak of me to her. You are right, Mimi, you cannot be the wife of any one else than me. I shall ever blame myself for what has taken place. I never never can be happy until you are my own, my dear fond wife. Oh! Mimi, be bold for once, do not fear them – tell them you are my wife before God. Do not let them leave you without being married, for I cannot answer what would happen. My conscience reproaches me of a sin that marriage can only efface.

I can assure you it will be many days before I meet such nice people as the Seaverights, especially the daughter. I longed so much to have introduced you to her, to see the perfect Lady in her, and such an accomplished young person. My evenings, as you say, are very long and dreary. We must not be separated all next winter, for I know, Mimi, you will be as giddy as last. You will be going to public balls, and that I cannot endure. On my honour, dearest, sooner than see you or hear of you running about as you did last, I would leave Glasgow myself. Though I have truly forgiven you, I do not forget the misery I endured for your sake. You know yourself how ill it made me if not, Mary can tell you, my pet.

When they moved out to their country house at Row in the summer of 1856, Madeleine asked for a ground floor room. Then she could just step out of the window to meet Emile. They met again and again at night without Madeleine's parents knowing. But then a middle class suitor appeared on the scene, William Minnoch. He was a businessman in his thirties, and began 'calling on' Madeleine. She received these calls without finding Minnoch attractive, she told Emile. But Emile was not making things easy for Madeleine. They had sex repeatedly, which Emile wanted, but he also wanted her to feel guilty about it. He liked to chastise her afterwards, accuse her of being weak for giving in to him. It is not surprising that Madeleine tired of these games and decided to end them.

My dear wife, I could not take you to Lima. No European women could live there. Besides, I would live three or four thousand miles from it, far from any white people, and no Drs. if you were ill or getting a baby. No if we marry I must stay in Glasgow until I get enough to live elsewhere. Besides, it would cost £300 alone for our bare passage money.

I do not understand, my pet, your not bleeding, for every woman having her virginity must bleed. You must have done so some other time. Try to remember if you never hurt yourself in washing, &c. I am sorry you felt pain. I hope, pet, you are better. I trust, dearest, you will not be [pregnant?]. Be sure and tell me immediately you are ill next time, and if at your regular period. I was not angry at your allowing me, Mimi, but I am sad it happened. You had no resolution. We should indeed have waited till we were married, Mimi. It was very bad indeed. I shall look with regret on that night. No, nothing except our Marriage will efface it from my memory. Mimi, only fancy if it was known. My dear, my pet, you would be dishonoured, and that by me! Oh! why was I born, my pet? I dread lest some great obstacle prevents our marriage. If Mary did know it, what should you be in her eyes?

My Sisters' names are Anastasie and Elmire. I cannot help

doubting your word about flirting. You promised me the same thing before you left for Edin., and you did nothing else during your stay there. You cared more for your friends than for me. I do trust you will give me no cause to find fault again with you on that score, but I doubt very much the sincerity of your promise. Mimi, the least thing I hear of you doing, that day shall be the last of our tie, that I swear. You are my wife, and I have the right to expect from you the behaviour of a married woman or else you have no honour in you; and more, you have no right to go any where but where a women could go with her husband. Oh! Mimi, let your conduct make me happy. Remember when you are good how truly happy it makes Emile – but remember this, and if you love me you will do nothing wrong. Dearest, your letter to Mary was very pretty and good. I thought a great deal of it, and I like its seriousness. Fancy how happy I was when Mary told me the other day how Mimi was improving fast; she could tell it by her letters.

For Gods sake burn this, Mimi, for fear any thing happening to you, do dearest.

'I am sad it happened. You had no resolution.' Emile wanted to have sex with Madeleine but he also wanted her to be the model of Victorian purity. Madeleine must have sensed that there was no coherence, no future in her relationship with Emile. 'Only fancy if it was known.' There it was again: the veiled threat that Emile would tell people they had had sex.

At the end of that summer the Smiths returned to India Street in Glasgow. Secret meetings were more difficult there because Madeleine's bedroom was in the basement, with the window at pavement level covered by bars. There was no longer any possibility of slipping out to have sex with Emile. He came each night for a whispered conversation through the barred window, but it was scarcely enough. Emile went into a depression. Worse still, Madeleine's letters began to talk of their love as if it was over. She was seen in public with Minnoch and her letters to Emile were getting shorter. On 28 January she seems to have decided to marry Minnoch. This was a decisive moment. She had to end the affair with Emile. She wrote him a letter that was cold in tone. 'We had better for the future consider ourselves as strangers. I trust to your honour as a gentleman that you will not reveal anything that has passed between us.' And she asked him to return the deadly letters.

Emile became hysterical. He would not give her up. He would show her father the letters. If he couldn't have her, no other man would either.

My dear, sweet pet Mimi,
I feel indeed very vexed that the answer I recd. yesterday to mine of Tuesday to you should prevent me from sending you the kind letter I had ready for you. You must not blame me, dear, for this, but really your cold, indifferent, and reserved notes, so short, without a particle of love in them (especially

after pledging your word you were to write me kindly for those letters you asked me to destroy), and the manner you evaded answering the questions I put to you in my last, with the reports I hear, fully convince me, Mimi, that there is foundation in your marriage with another; besides, the way you put off our union till September without a just reason is very suspicious.

Madeleine in her turn became frantic when she realized that Emile was not going to return the letters. 'Hate me, despise me – but do not expose me.' In fact, Emile's hoard of letters is Madeleine's best defence. All the while Emile was alive, there was the hope that she would be able to get the letters back. Those who believe that Madeleine was innocent, and that Emile committed suicide, argue that she would have known that his death would result in police investigators finding the letters; her affair with Emile would be exposed. It is a strong argument, but by this stage, Madeleine was probably much more frightened by Emile's instability and his repeated threats to expose her – and saw his death as the best solution.

She agreed on 28 January to marry William Minnoch. She wrote to Emile, but he just returned her letter. This gave Madeleine the excuse she needed to end the affair. She wrote to Emile on 2 February, 'I felt truly astonished to have my last letter returned to me. But it will be the last you shall have the opportunity of returning. When you are not pleased with the letters I send you, then our correspondence shall be at an end, and, as there is a coolness on both sides, our engagement had better be broken . . . Bring my letters and likeness on Thursday eve., at seven.' The note shows a chillingly brutal side to Madeleine. Emile received Madeleine's letter on 3 February, but did not reply at once. Weeping, he told his friend Thomas Kennedy he would 'never allow her to marry another man as long as he lived.' Six more days passed, and Madeleine was getting irritated by Emile's failure to respond. She wrote a curt and sarcastic note on 9 February; 'I attribute it to your having a cold that I had no answer to my last note. On Thursday evening you were, I suppose afraid of the night air. I again appoint Thursday night first – same place – street gate, seven o'clock.' There was a crossing of notes. After she posted hers, a letter arrived from Emile threatening to show her letters to her father. She wrote again, this time pleading with him not to carry out his threat and telling him that if he did she would be disowned by her family.

Emile kept the appointment Madeleine had asked for, on 11 February 1857. Madeleine was playing a game with L'Angelier, playing for time, keeping his hopes alive so that he would not show her father the letters. She seems to have agreed to marry him in the autumn, which she cannot have intended to do.

A dangerous cat and mouse game was played out during the next month, leading up to Emile L'Angelier's death. But there is still uncertainty, a century and a half later, about who was the cat and who the mouse. Some commentators on the case believe that by this stage Emile had decided to commit suicide and use his suicide to frame Madeleine. There is a strong case for believing that Emile was fully aware of the symptoms of arsenic, knew he was being poisoned during those few weeks, and wanted to make sure that other people knew that he was being poisoned by Madeleine. He wanted to die, because he couldn't have Madeleine, and he didn't want William Minnoch to have her either. He would die of poison, and she would hang. In support of this scenario, there is Emile's diary. Just for these last few weeks, Emile kept a diary in which he recorded his mysterious illness.

Thursday 19 February: Saw Mimi a few moments was very ill during the night.
Friday 20 February: Passed two pleasant hours with M. in the Drawing Room.
Saturday 21 February: Don't feel well.
Sunday 22 February: Saw Mimi in Drawing Room – Promised me French Bible. Taken very ill.

The next day Emile told Kennedy he was very ill and visited a doctor. On 2 March, he told Mary Perry he had been very ill after his last visit to Madeleine, saying, 'Well, I never expected to see you again.' A week later, on 9 March, Emile took tea with Mary Perry and told her about a cup of chocolate that had made him very ill: 'I can't think why I was so unwell after getting that coffee and chocolate from her.' Mary Perry evidently did not pick up the hint, so he spelt it out for her. 'It is a perfect fascination I have for her – if she were to poison me I would forgive her.' He put on much the same performance when he visited Mr and Mrs Towers of Portobello on 16 March. He talked almost the whole time about his health, saying that he thought he might have been poisoned. One interpretation of this is that L'Angelier had decided to kill himself and he wanted Madeleine to be blamed for his death. He was framing her.

L'Angelier was certainly not lying about being ill. He was indeed being poisoned, but it is not clear whether by Madeleine or by himself. Mrs Jenkins, Emile's landlady, went to his room on 20 February to call him for breakfast and found that he was unwell. During the night he had been very sick after feeling violent stomach pains on the way home. Four days later Mrs Jenkins was awakened by Emile's groans. He had the same symptoms as before. The symptoms were those of arsenic poisoning. It emerged at her trial that Madeleine had been shopping for arsenic at exactly this time. The chemist gave it to her mixed with indigo according to the law as a way of making the normally white powder detectable if it contaminated food or drink. The chemist was surprised that Madeleine was concerned about the colour of it; why would it matter if she was giving it to rats, as she said? She clearly wanted the arsenic to be colourless and undetectable.

On 22 March, Emile arrived at his lodgings very late,

presumably after seeing Madeleine again. This time he was doubled up with pain. A doctor was fetched, but Emile died the next morning. Emile had enough arsenic in his stomach to kill forty men, and the presence of arsenic throughout his body showed that he had taken several doses.

At her trial, Madeleine pleaded not guilty and changed her explanation about the arsenic; she had bought it for cosmetic reasons. The prosecution explored the idea that she had used the dark-coloured arsenic to lace the coffee and chocolate and fed the drinks to Emile L'Angelier through the bars. She had got herself into such a difficult position that murder seemed the only way out. But the defending advocate argued that Emile was vain, unable to accept rejection. He had also boasted of being an arsenic eater. It is possible that in his depressed and desperate state Emile took the arsenic hoping to incriminate Madeleine. If he couldn't have Madeleine, no other man would have her either, as he had threatened. If he could commit suicide in a way that reflected badly on Madeleine, so much the better. If he could make it look as if she had murdered him, best of all.

There is also the possibility that Emile was not just an habitual arsenic eater, but that Madeleine knew he was and that had given her the idea of giving him additional doses, over and above his intended intake. It was the perfect way of getting rid of him. Perhaps they both killed Emile.

The coldness of Madeleine Smith at her trial was incriminating in itself. She showed no feeling when the sufferings of Emile L'Angelier were described. She showed the same indifference to William Minnoch's sufferings. The whole devastating affair had made Minnoch ill. Yet when asked about the welfare of the man she had recently said she would marry, she said, 'My friend I know nothing of. I hear he has been ill, which I don't much care.' The jury in Glasgow in 1857 could not decide – they gave a verdict of 'Not Proven' – and it is no easier for us to decide now. Could she possibly have committed that cold-blooded murder? If she did, she was indeed evil. It was noted at the trial that her defending advocate, normally a courteous man, pointedly left the courtroom after the verdict without so much as a glance at his client, implying that he thought her guilty.

Guilty or not, Madeleine Smith was a free woman. She moved to London, married an artist and led an interesting and fulfilled life. At the turn of the twentieth century she and her husband separated and the last years of her life are surrounded by mystery.

It is believed that she spent her later years in North America, where she survived under an assumed name and died, of natural causes, at the age of ninety-one. A problem with this theory is the discrepancy in the age of the old lady who died in North America and the age Madeleine would have been – a discrepancy of more than twenty years. On the other hand, Madeleine always looked much younger than her years, and she may well have lied about her age; she had already told a great many lies to save herself from the gallows. It is also possible that the '64' written on the death certificate was a result of a clerical error and that '84' was intended; '84' was a relatively small lie for a lady who was really ninety-one, and well within the bounds of social convention. It has been argued that that the fact that her death certificate gives her country of birth as England proves that she could not have been Madeleine, who was born in Scotland. This is a specious argument, because Americans often refer to Britain or the United Kingdom as 'England', as if Wales, Scotland and Northern Ireland were really counties within England. So an American document saying that Madeleine was 'born in England' does not preclude her having been born in Scotland.

Madeleine was posing as Lena Wardle Sheehy when her secret was discovered in New York in 1927. She was approached by a film company who wanted her to appear in a film about her life. Not surprisingly she refused. The slighted producer then revealed her secret to the press, and she was questioned by the US authorities, mainly because they were concerned about her ability to finance her declining years. Madeleine managed to convince them that she had enough money to support herself and it seems they left her alone.

Even in old age, Madeleine led a complicated life, full of mystery, misunderstandings, half-truths and deceptions.

There is a photograph of Madeleine Smith, taken when she was an old lady in North America. She is fastidiously and beautifully dressed, giving the camera a sunny, direct and guilelessly open smile. She looks happy, untroubled, innocent. But we are often deceived by appearances.

A FAMILY AFFAIR: THE KILLING OF SAVILLE KENT

Sixteen-year-old Constance Kent and her younger brother William were home from school for their summer holiday. It was June 1860. The Kents' home was Road Hill House in the village of Road (which these days is spelt Rode), on the Somerset-Wiltshire border about three miles north of the town of Frome.

Constance's father was Samuel Kent. He had several children and a new wife. He was socially ambitious and decided it would be advantageous to move close to Bath, which was still a fashionable city where his daughters might show themselves and pick up good husbands. Road Hill House, eight miles outside Bath, seemed ideally located for this purpose. It was a big house with stables, a fine garden, a shrubbery and pleasant views across fields and country lanes. It was a good place to bring up children.

Samuel Kent's household was affluent and respectable, but not happy. It was rigid and there was too little affection to share among the many children. Samuel Kent and his second wife had a new baby, Francis Saville Kent. They were besotted with him. Their affection for baby Saville seems to have completely displaced any affection they had

had for Constance, who was both aware of this and acutely jealous of Saville.

On 29 June 1860, Saville had been put to bed early. He slept soundly because he had been unable to sleep during the day; it was the day the chimneys had been swept.

The Kents kept two dogs. One was allowed to roam about inside the house. The other was kept chained up in the yard. Mr Kent went out into the yard at ten in the evening in his usual way to feed the dog. William and Constance went up to bed at the same time, as did their older sisters Mary Anne and Elizabeth. Mr and Mrs Kent stayed up talking for about another hour before they too went to bed. It was an evening like any other in the Kent house.

Mr and Mrs Kent slept through the night without being disturbed at all. Mrs Kent woke at dawn, when she thought she heard a sound like one of the drawing room windows being opened. During the night, a man out fishing in the River Frome heard a dog barking, apparently at the Kents' house. The village constable heard the dog barking, too. He also saw lights at the Kents' house, at the nursery window and in one of the downstairs windows.

The children's nurse, Elizabeth Gough, woke at five o'clock and saw that the four-year-old Saville was not in his bed. She saw that the sheets had been replaced neatly, and she assumed from this that Saville had been lifted from his bed by his mother, who was nursing him in her room. Thinking that nothing was wrong because Saville was safe with his mother, Elizabeth Gough went back to sleep.

Mrs Kent was pregnant, so when Elizabeth Gough got up at seven o'clock, went to Mrs Kent's room and got no answer to her gentle knock she returned unconcerned to her own room and read her Bible. An hour later the assistant nurse arrived, and Elizabeth Gough went back to Mrs Kent's room. To her consternation Saville was not there. Miss Gough explained what she thought had happened and Mrs Kent was angry with her for imagining that, in her condition, she would have gone wandering round the house at night looking for children.

Miss Gough was now seriously worried. She had no idea where the boy was and knew he must have been missing more than two hours. She went to the children and asked them if they knew what had happened to Saville. None of them knew anything. Miss Gough was getting frightened. She asked the parlour maid, Sarah Cox, if she had seen Saville. She had not, but she had found the drawing room window open.

At this point Elizabeth Gough raised the alarm. The boot boy was sent to the parish constable, then to the village constable, who always insisted that the parish constable should attend because the parish was mainly in Wiltshire while the village was in Somerset; there was a complicated division of responsibility. The two policemen duly arrived and came to the conclusion that the boy Saville Kent had been kidnapped. The policemen advised Mr Kent that the matter should be reported immediately to the Wiltshire police; Mr Kent rode off straight away to Southwick, just two and a half miles along the Trowbridge road (now the A361), to report the crime.

The villagers disliked the Kents and freely admitted it. Samuel Kent was a brusque incomer and had a high-handed attitude to the locals. He did not like the idea of his house being overlooked by the occupants of a row of cottages nearby, and he had had a high fence erected to block their view. He also insisted on having sole and exclusive fishing rights to a particularly rich stretch of the River Frome, which ran past the village to the west. The Kents' unpopularity was underlined by the behaviour of the village children, who were far from deferential; they jeered at the Kent children and openly taunted them.

In spite of this well-established and fully justified dislike of the Kent family, the villagers rallied to the family's support in its moment of crisis. The plight of a lost baby touched them and they set about trying to find it. Two of them, William Nutt and Thomas Benger, began searching the grounds of the Kents' house. Constance had once run away dressed as a boy, first cutting her hair and leaving her locks in an old privy in the shrubbery. Nutt and Benger went there and found an ominous pool of blood on the floor, but no splashes of blood on the privy seat. They peered down into the privy, but it was too dark to see down into the cess-pit, so Nutt went off to get a lamp. While he was gone, Benger's eyes gradually became accustomed to the dark and he saw something pale. He reached in and pulled it out. He found that it was a blanket, heavily bloodstained. The Nutt returned with a candle. With the help of its light they saw the boy. He was dead. His body was resting on a splashboard under the seat; the blanket had been covering the baby. The water was later drained from the cess-pit, revealing a bloodstained piece of flannel, a piece of women's clothing and a newspaper that had been used to wipe clean a knife.

There was no doubt now about what had happened to Saville Kent. He had been savagely murdered. Messengers were sent to fetch Mr Kent back from Southwick and the doctor, Mr Parson, from Beckington, another nearby village. By this time, Mr Kent had reached Southwick toll gate and was reporting that his child had been kidnapped in a blanket and asking that anyone seen with a child wrapped in a blanket was to be stopped. This was an odd detail to pass on; no one knew at that stage that a blanket was missing from the house, and the child had not been found together with the blanket in the privy until well after Kent had left for Southwick. How did Mr Kent know that his son had been carried to the privy in a blanket?

There was something else that was very peculiar about Mr Kent's ride to Southwick. The messenger who went after him to tell him the child had been found dead discovered that Mr Kent had only reached the toll gate. He had not reached Southwick, which itself was only two miles away, and yet he had been gone an hour and a half. Obviously people ride their horses at different speeds;

maybe Mr Kent stopped along the road to relieve himself. But even allowing for these variations more than an hour is left unaccounted for, and the lost hour was never explained. What exactly was Mr Kent doing during this crucial time, when he should have been riding as fast as possible to get help? Had he secretly returned to Road Hill House to destroy some incriminating evidence, or to confer with Constance? Or had he instead ridden to some other destination, to one of the other villages on some other errand, before he was ready to report the baby missing? These questions have never been answered.

Back at the house, the case had been taken over by Inspector Foley. Foley's police constable found a blood-stained shift, belonging to a woman, above the boiler in the kitchen, though for some reason this was left un-mentioned until three months later. All the night dresses in the house were inspected. Only one of them had blood on it and that, the doctor confirmed, was menstrual blood and therefore nothing to do with the murder. The investigators rapidly came to the conclusion that no outsider was involved. The murderer knew the layout of the interior of the house perfectly, knew that the drawing room window could only be opened in a certain way without creaking, knew about the old privy hidden in the shrubbery, and so on. It was what detectives in the twentieth century would call 'an inside job'.

The night dresses were inspected for blood because of the way the baby had been killed. The little boy had had his throat cut with a razor and died instantly. There was another injury too, one that was harder to explain. A weapon of some sort had penetrated the child's night gown and made a small wound in his chest. This had not bled. There were also two more tiny wounds in the boy's left hand; they too had not bled.

When the parlour maid collected the laundry, she took Constance's night dress along with the others. The girl followed her and asked if she would get her a glass of water. The maid later reflected that this was odd, as the girl had a jug of water in her room. When the maid returned she went on with her tasks, but the next day she discovered that Constance's night dress was missing. It was never found. The bloodstained shift in the kitchen was a different garment, and no one knows whose shift that was. This episode suggested that Constance deliberately diverted the parlour maid on the pretext of wanting a glass of water; what she really wanted was to get the parlour maid out of the way for a few minutes so that she could retrieve her night dress from the pile. The only conceivable reason for doing that was to prevent the parlour maid from examining her night dress; the maid would have seen bloodstains that seriously incriminated Constance. Presumably, once she had her bloodied night dress in her possession she secretly destroyed it. When asked why her night dress was not in the pile, Constance used the occasion to pour blame on the local village women who did the laundry for them; the Kents, she said, were always short of nightwear because the local laundresses were always losing their clothes. It was not surprising that the Kents were so hated by the locals.

The inquest on Saville Kent was opened in the Red Lion Inn. There was evidence that the amount of blood spilt in the privy was about a pint and a half, which was considered not enough given the nature of the wound. The jury wanted to question the children, who were clearly emerging as suspects, especially William and Constance, but among the crowd of spectators there was such a strong antipathy towards the children that the inquest had to be adjourned to the safety of the Kents' house. An element of unfairness had already crept into the proceedings. The children of Kent's first marriage were questioned, but Mr and Mrs Kent themselves were never questioned.

Constance said she knew nothing, had gone to bed at half past ten, had heard nothing unusual, knew of no resentment against the boy, and found the nurse always kind and attentive. William said much the same. The verdict was wilful murder – by person or persons unknown. That was a perfectly correct and legal outcome; even if the coroner and everyone else present had been convinced that they knew who the murderer was, that that person was present in the room, and that she was Constance Kent, the inquest verdict was still correct in stopping short of accusing her. Her guilt was for the courts to decide.

There was local outrage at the crime, and Scotland Yard was called in. Inspector Whicher from Scotland Yard quickly concluded that Constance had murdered her half-brother and charged her accordingly. She broke down in tears and pleaded her innocence. The nurse supported Constance. She had never known Constance behave other than well towards the child. She also made the point that the walls of Constance's room were so thin that she could not have gone out in the night without others hearing what she was doing. Constance mentioned giving the child a present and that they had played together.

At the committal hearing at Devizes in July 1860, two school friends of Constance gave a very different story. They said that Constance had told them how much she resented her stepmother's attitude, that her father and stepmother favoured the two youngest children and treated the children of the first Mrs Kent as servants. She said that William was made to use the back stairs like a servant, and was always compared unfavourably with the baby Saville. In adversity, Constance and William had always stuck together.

Overall, there was a powerful impression that Constance was guilty. There was insufficient evidence against her, especially since she had (apparently) succeeded in destroying the incriminating night dress, and the trial failed. The trial had been badly set up. The magistrate gave Whicher just seven days to prepare the case against Constance. Mr Kent hired a barrister to defend Constance, and the defence barrister dominated the proceedings. In spite of this unsatisfactory outcome, like many police officers in this situation over the decades, Inspector Whicher was sure she was guilty. Others were of the same mind. Constance was therefore not formally acquitted. Instead the trial was stopped, and she was released on bail, discharged into her father's care. There was clearly not enough solid evidence to continue with the trial, and it never reopened. Whicher was heavily criticized for incompetence. Later the local police had a go at bringing Elizabeth Gough to trial, but that too was a failure.

Constance's father, Samuel Saville Kent, had married Mary Anne Windus in 1830, when he was twenty-eight and she was twenty-one. They were both from middle class commercial families and to begin with they lived in London. Samuel Kent became ill and the doctor's advice was to move to the coast for better air, so they moved to Sidmouth, where Kent took a job as a factory inspector at £800 a year. A son, Edward, was born in 1835, but the four children born between 1837 and 1841 all died in infancy. The first Mrs Kent was herself not strong, and she had already shown symptoms of consumption when she was carrying Edward. She then started to show signs of mental instability. She took the children out and got lost. She also had a knife hidden under her bed.

The doctor advised Samuel Kent to hire a housekeeper, mainly to keep a close eye on his unstable wife. In 1844, Mrs Kent gave birth for the ninth time in fourteen years. This time it was Constance. Under the care of the new housekeeper, Miss Pratt, Mrs Kent gained strength and gave birth to William. By this time Mary Kent was completely insane. In characteristic Victorian style, Samuel Kent shut his wife away without any treatment and pretended that everything was normal. Then, in 1853, while Miss Pratt was away visiting relatives, Mary Kent developed a bowel problem and quickly died.

The children were used to Miss Pratt, who had been with the Kent family for a decade by this time, but they were nevertheless very shocked when their father announced that he and Miss Pratt were to be married. Edward was so disgusted by the idea that when he returned home from school he had a blazing row with his father about the marriage, left the house and went to sea.

It was then that Samuel Kent and his new wife moved to Somerset, but the problems simmered away. Constance was as angry and resentful of the marriage and its implications as Edward. She became hypersensitive to what were probably never intended to be slights. She became sullen, sulky and often rude. The jeering of the Road village children probably isolated her more, made matters worse, and she became paranoid.

The second Mrs Kent seems to have been a very patient woman, but she must have found Constance very hard to deal with. In the end, Constance just became a domestic nuisance and Mr and Mrs Kent decided she should go away to school in London, which she also deeply resented. When she returned from school on holiday, it was to find that her mother's successor had had another baby. This was the unfortunate Saville, and the Kents openly doted on him.

In 1854, the news came that Edward had been lost at sea, Mr Kent was distraught, Then, eventually, a letter came from Edward to say that other officers had died, but that he had survived. In 1858, he died of yellow fever. Only William was left, and like Constance he was sent away to school. The two surviving siblings were reunited in the holidays, and at the end of one of them they decided to run away rather than be separated again. Constance disguised herself as a boy and they walked to Bristol. They tried to book a room in a hotel but, not surprisingly, they were turned over to the police. Forced to explain herself to her father, Constance said she wanted to leave England and was not sorry.

Mr and Mrs Kent persevered. They found a school that was nearer to home, and her behaviour there was better, though she was still just as churlish and difficult when she was at home. After the murder of Saville, Samuel Kent sent his daughter to St Mary's Home for Female Penitents in Queen Square, Brighton. There, subjected to harsh discipline, she served as a probationer nurse. The Revd Arthur Wagner, who ran the home, initiated a series of interviews with Constance. He was determined to get to the bottom of the matter, and he had a strange hold over her. In the wake of her ordeal, Constance had developed religious leanings. She wanted to be confirmed, she wanted to take Holy Communion. The Revd Wagner refused to accept her as a confirmand 'because the stain of the suspicion of murder was still attached to her.' So she agreed to what Wagner required of her. In 1864, after a three-day interrogation by Wagner, Constance confessed to the murder of her half-brother Saville. The Revd Wagner wrote it all down and took the written statement to London to show it to the Home Secretary and insist that Constance be brought to trial (again). At Wagner's instigation, Constance made her confession to the murder public.

On Lady Day 1865, Constance appeared at Bow Street Magistrates Court dressed in black and made her public confession. Then she collapsed in tears. Her father, who evidently had not known that she was going to do this, read about the extraordinary confession, which was given a high profile in the English press, and decided to visit her. Following the Bow Street confession, she was sent to Salisbury to stand trial in 1865. Again she appeared in black, looking tall, grave and inappropriately noble. At her second trial for the same murder, Constance (in the written statement) added a few details to her confession.

She claimed she had taken a razor from her father's wardrobe a few days before the murder, though he had not noticed. She had placed candles in the privy, then went to bed, waited for everyone in the house to go to sleep. She went downstairs and opened the window shutters, Then she went to the nursery, picked Saville up from his bed, took out one of the blankets, replaced the other covers, then wrapped the boy in the blanket. She took the boy downstairs, put on galoshes, climbed out of the window, walked to the shrubbery and cut Saville's throat with the razor. She thought blood would gush out but it did not come. She thought this meant Saville was not dead, so she tried to stab him in the chest with the razor.

This was a peculiar claim because the post mortem showed that the chest wound could not have been caused by a razor. She put the body still wrapped in the blanket into the privy. This too was inconsistent with what the men had found; the blanket was definitely on, and not round, the body as they had pulled the blanket up first and only then seen the body.

Constance went on to explain in detail how she had only found two spots of blood on her night dress. This is almost incredible, given the act she claimed she had just committed. She washed the blood out herself and the next day her night dress was dry, which also seems unlikely.

The bloodstained shift in the kitchen was never explained, by Constance or anyone else. There are several disconcerting and unsettling things about Constance's confession, in addition to the details already mentioned. One is the fact that 'her' description of the murder – the murder that she committed – was recorded in the words of the Revd Wagner. The details she added were unconvincing attempts to explain things that no one else understood either. How could she have put on her galoshes and then climbed soundlessly out of a half-opened window while carrying a sleeping child wrapped in a blanket?

The trial was a very controversial one. Because Constance was the accused, she was, according to the law at that time, not allowed to speak. The only statement about what she had done was the 'written statement', which everyone knew was not in her own words but the Revd Wagner's. She was being condemned without an opportunity to say what happened in her own words. To make matters worse, Wagner absolutely refused to reveal in detail what Constance had said to him, claiming benefit of clergy. There were questions about this in Parliament and the Lord Chancellor made it clear that Wagner had no legal right whatever to conceal evidence, whether he was a priest or not. There was a general feeling that the trial was unfair. The outcome was in any case predetermined by Constance's public confession. She was found guilty, condemned to death.

There was a public outcry. There were wild allegations that Constance had only confessed in order to protect her father, who was the real villain; he not only killed the child but was having an affair with the nurse. The Home Secretary sensed that the conviction was unsafe because of the circumstances. Down in Brighton the Sisters of St Mary were abused in the streets by a mob and the Revd Wagner, who had goaded Constance into confessing and then shopped her to the Home Secretary, was set upon and badly injured. Public feeling ran so high that a reprieve was allowed. Constance was, after all, not to be hanged. Instead, she spent twenty years in prison at Portland and Millbank.

She was released in 1885 at the age of forty-one, into the custody of the Revd Wagner. After that, presumably with Wagner's help, she completely disappeared as far the English were concerned. One sensational theory is that she washed up in the East End of London three years later and, perhaps not using Papa's razor but someone else's, carried out the Whitechapel murders – not Jack but Jill the Ripper. The truth is more mundane, but in its way just as remarkable. Arthur Wagner seems to have helped her to emigrate to Australia, where she lived on under a new name.

Constance Kent may have murdered her half-brother, Saville Kent, out of hatred for her stepmother. Certainly she could have done the awful deed if she inherited her own mother's insanity and latent violence. She was profoundly unhappy with the ménage at Road Hill House, to the point where she had tried to run away with her brother. She had also used the privy in the shrubbery to conceal her misdeeds on that earlier occasion, and it looks as if she returned to this old haunt when she was looking for somewhere to kill Saville and dispose of his body. And she eventually confessed to the crime.

But, in spite of all of this, like several others who have looked at the details of her case, I am not completely convinced that in her confession Constance was telling the truth. Several points do not ring true:

1) When she cut Saville's throat he did not bleed. This is not consistent with the one and a half pints of blood found on the privy floor when Saville's body was discovered. Another puzzle is that one forensic test suggested that Saville died of suffocation and not by having his throat cut at all.

2) She stabbed Saville in the chest with the razor. The injury was not consistent with the use of a razor. Something else must have been used to make the small (and inexplicable) wounds in the chest and hands.

3) She climbed out of a half-open window wearing a night dress and galoshes without making any noise. If she attempted something like that without help she must have made a noise; perhaps someone else held the baby while she climbed out.

4) Her night dress had only two small spots of blood on it. Cutting the baby's throat produced a significant amount of blood, and she would have got more on her clothing.

5) She washed her bloodstained night dress after the murder and it was dry by the morning. Mrs Kent heard the drawing room window being opened at dawn, which must have been the time of the murder. The night dress must have been washed after that and could not have dried by the time it was seen only a few hours later.

6) She offered no explanation for the bloodstained shift left in the kitchen. No one has been able to come up with a plausible explanation for the shift.

Was Constance spinning this version of events in order to cover up for someone else? For her brother William, perhaps, or even her father? It is certainly not beyond the bounds of probability that she and William carried out the murder together.

But what lay behind Mr Kent's one hour delay in riding to the next village? Was it simply that he had ridden on through Southwick to Trowbridge, in order to inform Inspector Foley in person, and that the messenger encountering Kent back in Southwick did not realize that Kent had been on this extra journey? It is even so difficult to understand how Mr Kent knew so much about the circumstances of the disappearance. How did he know the baby would be found with a blanket? If Mr Kent was the murderer, what possible motive could he have had? If he committed the murder himself, it is hard to see why the churlish and discontented Constance would have confessed on his behalf – unless of course her inherited mental instability, the ordeal of being suspected of a crime and her time at St Mary's conspired to convince her that she had done something she had not. Perhaps she brainwashed herself into taking on the burden of the sins of the world, in imitation of Christ. Perhaps she was talked into it by the determined, high-minded and self-righteous Wagner. It is after all not all that uncommon for innocent suspects to sign confessions after they have been inter-rogated for a while by experienced police officers; priests and policemen are quite capable of persuading people that they are guilty when they are not.

Much speculation has surrounded Constance Kent's later life; she came out of prison when she was just over forty. Some painstaking recent research has revealed that in either late 1885 or 1886 she did indeed emigrate to Australia, where she joined her brother William, who had arrived there in 1884, and other family members; her half-brother Acland emigrated to Australia in 1885. Completely free at last, Constance launched on a long professional career in nursing. She went on working, amazingly, until her death at the age of 100 in 1945. Nobody in Australia knew about her extraordinary past, because there she was known as Ruth Emilie Kaye. She and her brother William were determined to leave their shared unhappy past (and possibly their shared crime) behind. William became an eminent naturalist and president of the Royal Society of Queensland. Constance trained as a nurse at the Royal Prince Alfred Hospital in Melbourne, then nursed at Prince Henry's Hospital in Sydney. For over a decade she was matron-superintendent of the Parramatta Industrial School for Girls. Her last venture was to manage a Nurses Home at Maitland. None of this makes up for murdering an innocent four-year-old boy, if that is what she did, but Constance herself may have seen her commitment to a selfless life of nursing as her only possible path to redemption.

THE TICHBORNE CLAIMANT

This story is not a story about murder, but about imposture. The crime was impersonating someone else for financial gain. The impostor was pretending to be Roger Tichborne, the elder of two surviving sons of Sir James and Lady Henrietta Tichborne. Roger Tichborne was born in Paris in 1829. Lady Henrietta, who was French, hated England and wanted to raise her son as a Frenchman. Roger therefore lived in France for his first fifteen years in Paris, while his father ran his estates in England. Roger naturally spoke French as his first language and English only with a French accent. This worried Sir James, as Roger was to inherit the estate and the English baronetcy. To make him more 'English' and fit into his eventual adult role, Sir James enrolled Roger at Stonyhurst, a Jesuit seminary in Lancashire. Because of the way he had been brought up by his mother, Roger had difficulties in making this switch into the English educational system.

Against his mother's wishes, Roger Tichborne went into the army in 1849, joining the 6th Dragoon Guards. He quickly discovered that he was not cut out to be an officer and the men understandably ridiculed his French accent. He resigned his commission and after that could not settle to anything. There was enough family money for him not to need to work, but he needed something to do. A second bad decision was to allow himself to fall in love with his first cousin, Catherine, a relationship that was doomed from the start.

At this point, Roger Tichborne decided to leave England and become an explorer in South America. His parents tried to talk him out of it, but he was insistent. One reason for leaving was the intolerable atmosphere in the family, with his mother and father always quarrelling. Roger once described his home life with them as hell on earth. He set off in 1854, fully aware of the hazards ahead, and making a will before he went.

Roger Tichborne had ample financial resources for his expedition. He had an allowance of £1,000 a year, a huge income in those days. He set off with the idea of spending eighteen months in South America, before going on to India. He was a great letter and journal writer and kept his mother continually informed of his travels. He also sent back a steady stream of animal skins, stuffed birds and other items back to Tichborne Hall to be added to the ancestral collection. His mother circulated his letters to the staff on the estate, who were fascinated by his travels.

Roger Tichborne's travels came to an abrupt end on 30 April 1855, on a voyage from Rio de Janeiro to New York aboard the British cargo schooner *Bella*. Four days into the voyage, the *Bella* foundered. The ship may have encountered bad weather or a badly stowed coffee cargo may have shifted in the hold, causing her to capsize. Whatever happened must have happened suddenly as no one survived. The only evidence of her existence and her end were an empty longboat and an area of flotsam. The *Bella*, her crew and her single distinguished passenger were declared lost at sea.

But Roger Tichborne's story was far from over. His mother characteristically refused to believe that he was dead. She had lost two children through miscarriages and could not bear the thought of losing another, especially when the remaining son, Alfred, was dismissed as a waster. Lady Tichborne took to leaving a lantern at the entrance to Tichborne Hall, so that when Roger returned he would be able to find his way to the door. Her husband Sir James died in 1862 and Alfred died in 1866.

She became more and more obsessed with finding Roger, hiring agents to comb docks and taverns for any information about him. Lady Tichborne's forlorn quest, worthy of Dickens, became well known among sailors. It was not unknown for sailors who were down on their luck to tell her stories of shipwreck survivors, raising her spirits and ensuring a sovereign for their trouble. Because she was willing to pay for information, it was not long before people started feeding her false reports that survivors from the *Bella* sinking had been picked up and taken to safety. One story had the ship itself surviving; she was hijacked by the crew, repainted, renamed and sold on in Australia.

Lady Tichborne knew then that her optimism had been right. She felt she was on the trail of her still-living son. She placed advertisements in newspapers offering a substantial reward for information about his whereabouts. These in turn led to newspaper articles about the case, emphasizing the illustriousness of the Tichborne family, owners of the ninth largest fortune in England.

The *Melbourne Argus* story was typical.

A handsome reward will be given to any person who can furnish such information as will discover the fate of Roger Charles Tichborne. He sailed from Rio de Janeiro on the 20th of April 1854 in the ship La Bella, *and has never been heard of since, but a report reached England to the effect that a portion of the crew and passengers of a vessel of that name was picked up by a vessel bound to Australia, Melbourne it is believed. It is not known whether the said Roger Charles Tichborne was among the drowned or saved. He would at the present time be about thirty-two years of age, is of a delicate constitution, rather tall, with very light brown hair, and blue eyes. Mr Tichborne is the son of Sir James Tichborne, now deceased, and is heir to all his estates.*

In 1865, Lady Tichborne wrote to a man in Sydney whose name she had spotted in connection with a 'missing friends' service. He was Mr Cubitt, and he posted advertisements in several Australian newspapers. In

October 1865, Cubitt had a response from an old acquaintance, a lawyer called Gibbes, who lived at Wagga Wagga. Gibbes wrote to say that he had 'spotted R. C. Tichborne' in Wagga Wagga. One of Gibbes's clients was a man going by the name of Thomas Castro and Gibbes reckoned that Castro was really Tichborne. This marked the start of one of the oddest legal tangles of the nineteenth century.

Wagga Wagga was a small town, where everyone knew everyone else. Gibbes in fact knew Thomas Castro very well. He was an old drinking companion. Castro was a butcher who had gone bankrupt and Gibbes was handling the bankruptcy arrangements. The idea that Castro the bankrupt butcher was the missing English aristocrat should have been rejected as absurd, but the outside world was surprisingly willing to believe it. Castro was affable and had told people that he came from a titled family and was living under an assumed name. Gibbes made the connection with the Tichborne case, and from a financial point of view it would have been opportune for Castro to be Tichborne in disguise; Castro owed a great deal of money to Gibbes, and if Castro inherited the Tichborne estate he would be able to pay his debt.

Castro was confronted with Gibbes's claim that he was Sir Roger Tichborne, and he laughed at the absurdity of the idea. But Gibbes would not give up the idea. He pressed Castro to write to the mother and make arrangements to return to England, just as if the pipe dream were true. Castro was in serious financial difficulty and decided to give it a try. He had a criminal background as a horse-thief and fence. He agreed to launch a correspondence with Lady Tichborne, at first via Gibbes. Roger was alive, bankrupt and needed funds in order to return home. When Castro started writing the letters himself, his poor education showed him up badly, but the fact that they arrived under the aegis of a solicitor somehow gave them a false credibility. And, of course, Lady Tichborne wanted to believe that her son was alive.

The Tichborne family generally became suspicious. Roger's reappearance in Wagga Wagga, the unlikeliest place in the circumstances, and after ten years, seemed improbable. They also knew that the sinking of the *Bella* was an established fact, and that there was no rational basis for Lady Tichborne's conviction that he was still alive. They quickly became convinced that the claimant was an impostor.

Thomas Castro was bare-faced in asking Lady Tichborne to send him cash, and she stopped short of doing that. Instead she wrote to Cubitt, 'You do not give any details whatever about the person you believe to be my son, you do not name even the town where he is, and you do not say anything about the way he was saved from the shipwreck.' No evidence, no money. She offered the man £200 if he could prove he was Roger. She sent Cubitt and Gibbes detailed biographical information about her son which they could use to question Castro. She assumed

Cubitt and Gibbes would act in good faith. But in practice Castro was given this information to help him flesh out his impersonation.

Castro discovered that the Tichbornes were Catholics, so his first act was to go to Goulburn to get himself remarried by a Catholic priest. He also studied Burke's Peerage to learn more about the family.

Castro wrote to Lady Tichborne to give an account of his rescue from the wreck of the *Bella*. She still was not completely convinced. She proposed to Cubitt that he should contact an African called Andrew Bogle; a rescued slave from Jamaica, who had known Sir Roger well, he was now living in Sydney. Another man living in Sydney who had known Sir Roger was Michael Guilfoyle, a one-time head gardener from Tichborne Park. Castro travelled to Sydney, where he was given red-carpet treatment. Suddenly he was a celebrity.

Bogle went to Castro's hotel and was startled to find the slim well-mannered young man turned into a rather rough fat middle-aged man. Yet it only took a few minutes for Bogle to change his mind. Guilfoyle was also easily persuaded that Castro was Roger Tichborne. Both Bogle and Guilfoyle were bowled over by Castro's comprehensive and detailed knowledge of the family and the estate. They duly wrote letters to Lady Tichborne to say that they had no doubt this was her son.

Castro was cunning. He did his preparation well, and he kept adding little bits of new information to flesh out his knowledge of the family he claimed to head. He was affable, and found it easy to get others talking. When he met members of the Tichborne family, he got them talking and collected their memories; he was good at utilizing odd crumbs of information to appear more knowledgeable than he really was.

Gibbes arrived in Sydney to find that Castro was a major focus of interest. Gibbes used his status as a lawyer to get Castro generous credit; between them they generated thousands of pounds in cash and goods. At last Gibbes was getting back the money Castro owed him. Castro meanwhile was wondering how much more money he could make out of this deception.

Andrew Bogle was apparently going along with Castro's deception for reasons of his own. After the death of his own master, Sir Edward Doughty, he was redundant. He had been given a good pension and Doughty had rescued him from slavery, but Bogle felt stranded in Australia, and cut off from the aristocratic lifestyle he had become accustomed to. He seems to have seen latching onto Castro-Tichborne as a way of getting to England and becoming ensconced at an English country house. He would certainly have known the difference between a butcher and a baronet, but it was in his interest to support Castro's claim. Bogle was able to offer Castro his services, and help him acquire the necessary social skills to enable him to act the part of a baronet. It is not known for certain, but there was probably a deal; probably Castro agreed to take Bogle with him to England and provide him with a position there, perhaps even agreeing to give him a percentage of the inheritance, in exchange for this crucial help. Interestingly, once Lady Doughty discovered how committed Bogle was to helping Castro, she stopped his annuity.

On 25 February 1866 Lady Tichborne accepted Castro as her son, though the rest of the family and her staff were unreservedly against her decision. The Tichborne party set sail, first-class, for England on 2 September, leaving £20,000 worth of debts in Roger Tichborne's name in Sydney. The voyage 'home' took four months and during that time Bogle worked hard to give Castro as full an education on the Tichborne's and English upper class behaviour as he could. It was turning Castro into a gentleman that was the hardest part. During the voyage, Castro had too much to drink, telling inappropriate stories and breaking wind at the dinner table. His behaviour was downright offensive to the other first-class passengers.

On arrival in England, Castro and his gang settled at Essex Lodge in Croydon. Now he faced his biggest challenge. In England, there were many people who had known Roger Tichborne, and all of them were sceptical about the claimant. His behaviour on landing itself aroused suspicion. He passed within a few hundred yards of the homes of relatives Roger had known and liked, yet he did not call on them. Instead Castro stopped in Wapping, where he tried to find out where his real family was.

Castro thought he was under surveillance, which is quite possible, so he took to wearing a heavy cloak and holding a handkerchief over his face. He contacted lawyers to search for the probate of Roger Tichborne's will, and got a copy made. He visited Lloyd's, to find out details of the *Bella* and the *Osprey*, the ship he claimed had rescued him. Suddenly Castro realized he needed much more knowledge to carry off the deception in London than in Sydney.

Castro, the now celebrated Claimant, next had to travel to France, which is where Lady Tichborne was. She had already put some distance between herself and the rest of the family, shunning them for their scepticism. She sacked her closest adviser, James Bowker, who had urged her from the start to be cautious. She had shown him the claimant's letters and he was forthright in pointing out the inconsistencies and improbabilities. Bowker was convinced from the start that it was a cycnical fraud, entirely motivated by money. She did not want to hear it.

After thirteen long years of waiting to be reunited with her son, Lady Tichbourne waited a little longer at the Place de la Madeleine. The Claimant lost his nerve, and lay on his bed saying that he was not well enough to see her. She abruptly entered the room, with its blinds half drawn. She leant over the butcher, kissed him and commented that his ears were like his uncle's. The Claimant was so worried about exposure that he lost the power of speech. Lady Tichborne sent for a doctor, whom she told that the man on the bed was her son.

Castro was stunned at how easy it had been. He relaxed. They became inseparable, eating, walking and chatting together. When she asked him questions he could not answer, he blamed memory loss on illness, alcoholism, head injury or the passage of time. But he could not remember any French, and that should have rung warning bells in the dowager's mind. But she wanted him to be her son, and she ignored the things that didn't quite fit. Her servants saw her smile and laugh for the first time in years.

The Claimant was less successful with the stream of visitors who had known Roger in his Parisian youth. Not one of them believed he was Roger. Roger's tutor and friend for many years, Monsieur Chatillon, was ready to be persuaded that he was about to meet Roger again. But he stopped dead as he was about to shake the Claimant's hand. 'No, my Lady, this is not your son!' She was not listening. 'You do not embrace Roger?' 'No, my Lady, it is not he.' Chatillon persevered with a long series of questions, through an interpreter, about their many shared experiences, such as holidays they had spent in Normandy and Brittany, but the Claimant could not remember anything at all. Chatillon was finally stopped by Lady Tichborne, and they agreed that they would continue another time, but the Claimant refused to meet Chatillon again. He was always unwell. Castro had prepared himself fairly well, but Bogle had no access to the first fifteen years of Roger's life, so Castro was totally exposed. Chatillon was a major problem.

Ignoring the clear evidence that a criminal deception was being practised, Lady Tichborne decided to return to England with the Claimant; she would set up home with her son in Croydon. She would also allocate him £1,000 a year in place of the control over the Tichborne estates. The Tichborne family in England were now very unimpressed. Their bankers in London had been contacted by creditors in Sydney about the huge debts the Claimant had run up. They naturally refused to pay the Claimant's debts. They also told Lady Tichborne they would not let the Tichborne Estate's trustees hand over authority to the Claimant before they were satisfied about his identity. This was the crux of the matter. The Claimant and his party knew now that they would have to go to court to win control of the Tichborne estate.

The Claimant was a very clever operator. He assembled an elaborate public relations machine and teams of agents to search out more information on the contacts of Roger Tichborne. He wanted to meet anyone who might be prepared to support him. His public relations machine was sophisticated in the extreme. It even put out disinformation. This claimed that the Claimant had rejected a secret offer from the Tichborne family that it would acknowledge him so long as the money was shared between him and the infant baronet (the true baronet). The family disputed this, of course, but the impression was cleverly created that the family had privately agreed that the Claimant was Roger, but wanted to do a deal on money. People in general were happy to believe that there was some sort of aristocratic conspiracy to defraud the Claimant.

While affidavits were collected from the many people who were prepared to support the Claimant, he carefully kept away from the family. His agents came back with more and more useful information. Now he was able to come out with the privileged knowledge that he (Roger) had gone off to South America in the wake of a failed romance with his cousin. Many of those who were ready to support him were people from the neighbourhood of Tichborne Park, who thought that there would be some benefit to them, socially or economically, when the Claimant was installed; it evidently did not occur to many of them that there would be a case against the Claimant. Some of the affidavits were evidently bought.

On 12 March 1868, Lady Tichborne died in London. The Claimant claimed she had been poisoned. He was thoroughly stranded now financially, as his £1,000 a year allowance came to a sudden end. The family saw this moment as their chance. They no longer had to respect the old lady's sentimental delusion, and the Claimant was more vulnerable now that he had no income. They opened a Chancery suit, Tichborne v. Castro to stop Castro seizing Lady Tichborne's property. They made it clear that he would have to go through the courts to win legal recognition as Roger Tichborne.

At the same time, the family wanted to avoid the cost of

using the courts to block the Claimant. They hoped to find an easier route by exposing him. They hired detectives in Australia and South America. In Wagga Wagga there were door-to-door calls. What they found was that Thomas Castro was indeed living in Wagga Wagga under an assumed name. They also found that his real name was not Roger Tichborne but Arthur Orton. They found that he had not come from Tichborne Park but from Wapping. He had lived as Arthur Orton in Tasmania as a Hobart butcher. The detectives found scores of people in Hobart who remembered him and recognized his photograph.

The Claimant had developed an incredibly elaborate knowledge of the real Roger Tichborne, but also became too used to improvising gap-filling. One really damaging story he told was that he (ie Roger Tichborne) had lived in Melipilla in Chile. Detectives hired in South America by the Tichborne family explored this story, travelling to the small town of Melipilla. They asked the locals if a young English aristocrat had been there. They replied that they had not seen any gringo there at all, and the only Englishman they could remember was a sailor who jumped ship in Valparaiso – and his name was Arthur Orton.

The coup de grâce was delivered by the Tichborne family when their agents found the Claimant's brother, Charles Orton. Charles Orton had been blackmailing Arthur for months after he realized Arthur had money to share round the family. Charles was getting money from Arthur, and gave up his job as a butcher on the strength of it.

Lawyers arranged a meeting of the two brothers, hoping that Charles would betray Arthur, but he refused to identify him. In return, the Claimant increased his allowance, on condition that he changed his address and his name. But Charles was greedy and impatient. He sold his brother out, giving the Tichborne family yet more information about Arthur Orton's past.

The Claimant's financial position was now very dangerous. He sold Tichborne Bonds, which were in effect shares in the Tichborne Estate. The Claimant addressed public rallies in music halls and London squares, urging the common people to help him overturn this upper class conspiracy – and gain a percentage of the estate. Really, the Claimant should have given up at this point, before going to court. The court case was long and complicated, and very expensive: it cost £200,000. Some of the greatest lawyers of the day were lined up on the opposing sides. The Tichborne family's legal team was led by the Solicitor-General, Sir John Coleridge. The Claimant was represented by Dr Edward Vaughan Kenealy. It became the longest running legal battle in British history, attracting attention from all round the world. Gilbert and Sullivan based their operetta Trial by Jury on the case.

The case against the Claimant was assembled out of all the blunders, large and small, he had made in reminiscing about the life of Roger Tichborne. Some points were very telling indeed. The Claimant had referred to Lady Tichborne, his supposed mother, in written statements as

Hannah Frances, when her real forenames were Henriette Felicité. However poor the Claimant's memory was, he could not have forgotten his mother's name. The Claimant's story about being rescued after the sinking of the Bella by the Osprey sounded all right, until, as the lawyers pointed out, it became clear that he was claiming that he had been taken to Australia after being rescued. Maritime law dictates that survivors picked up after shipwrecks must be taken to the nearest harbour, so it was utterly incredible that the Claimant was picked up in the middle of the Atlantic Ocean and then taken by the Osprey round the Cape of Good Hope and right across the Indian Ocean to be set ashore in Australia. Why not Cape Town?

In private, Kenealy advised the Claimant to give up the case and flee the country. But the Claimant would not listen. The jury had enough after 102 days in court. They intervened to say that there was no need for them to hear any further testimony from witnesses. They knew he was Arthur Orton and not Roger Tichborne.

The Claimant was then tried for perjury and found guilty after a trial lasting 188 days. He was found guilty and sentenced to seven years penal servitude for perjury and another seven for forging the Tichborne Bonds, the two terms to run consecutively. The Claimant later wrote that he felt the weight of the world lifted from him.

It was an extraordinary case that was somehow transformed from a despicable deception of a heartbroken old woman into a noble foray in the class war. It revealed many strange quirks of human nature. A glance told any unbiased observer that the Claimant was not Roger Tichborne – he looked nothing like him – yet there were scores of people, with many different motives, who were prepared to say that he was. Another curiosity of the case is that Arthur Orton had a very rare anatomical abnormality. His penis retracted right inside his body when not erect. It transpired, as the evidence was gathered, that he shared this abnormality with the real Roger Tichborne. The odds against that coincidence are enormous and it has made one or two historians wonder whether maybe the Claimant really was Roger Tichborne after all.

After his release from prison in 1884, Orton wrote a detailed confession, but changing his story only clouded the issue. When he died, in poverty, in April 1898, he was buried in a coffin bearing the name Sir Roger Charles Doughty Tichborne.

A BALHAM MYSTERY: THE POISONING OF CHARLES BRAVO

The poisoning of Charles Bravo was one of the great scandals of the nineteenth century. The world decided, perhaps rightly, perhaps wrongly, that he had been murdered by his wife. The world decided too quickly, though, without looking carefully at all the evidence that was staring it in the face.

Mrs Charles Bravo, born as Florence Campbell, was an unusually attractive young woman, small, pretty, with large widely set blue eyes and a mass of bright chestnut-coloured hair. She was brought up in a supportive and loving home. She had no difficulty in finding suitors, and at the age of nineteen in 1864 she married Captain Ricardo, a wealthy guards officer of twenty-three. But Ricardo's eligibility as a husband was superficial. He was unfaithful and a heavy drinker. Florence was at an early stage in their marriage subjected to stressful cycles of relapses, apologies, promises of amendment and brief reconciliations. It was completely unexpected and

Florence had not been in any way prepared for marriage to be like this. Neither was Florence the sort of young woman to accept it. She was spirited and pleasure-loving.

Florence Ricardo's way out was drink. Her mother tried to find some diversions for her and persuaded her to go to Malvern with her to try the water treatment. Captain Ricardo was to join them there. The water treatment was fashionable and well-established. It was run by Dr Wilson and Dr Gully. Gully's patients had included Alfred Tennyson and Thomas Carlyle. Florence had already met Gully and was fascinated by him; Gully in turn showed her profound sympathy and understanding, and was able to give her the support she needed. She fell in love with Dr James Manby Gully, even though he was old enough to be her father.

Ricardo's behaviour did not change, apart from the cycles of relapse and amendment, and Florence's parents pressed him to release Florence from what was clearly an unworkable marriage. In 1870, Ricardo agreed to a formal separation, giving her an allowance of £1,200 a year. Ricardo went to live in Cologne with a mistress, and died there suddenly and unexpectedly, without changing the will he had made on marrying Florence. This left her, at twenty-five, a rich widow with an income of £4,000 a year, and it also left her completely free of reliance on her parents. She was completely and exhilaratingly free. She was, curiously, also completely free of friends, which suggests a degree of self-centredness. She might have found friends a stabilizing and moderating influence.

She found herself in Malvern, with Dr Gully. Gully was a very busy man, close to the end of his professional life, with a wife and a son. On the other hand, his wife was in an asylum and he had been separated from her for thirty years – and the son was grown up. Florence was young, beautiful, unattached, determined. She laid siege to old Dr Gully, though in his sixties, and he gave in to her. They began an affair, of which her parents naturally strongly disapproved. Florence's mother refused to speak to her.

Florence and Gully enjoyed each other's company, but found that they were unable to enjoy that company in open society and increasingly found themselves isolated. Florence had no real friends anyway, so she employed a housekeeper-companion, Mrs Jane Cox, whom she treated as a friend and social equal. Janie Cox had three sons, and Florence paid her additional sums to maintain them, too.

After returning home from a holiday at the baths at Kissingen in 1872, Florence had a miscarriage. It was one of three miscarriages she was to have, and they may well have been caused by her heavy drinking. Gully attended her in his capacity as a doctor, and Mrs Cox did the nursing. Later, Gully would be suspected of carrying out an abortion. This traumatic experience brought Florence and Mrs Cox even closer together. In 1874, Florence decided to buy a house as a permanent residence. The house she chose was an early nineteenth century villa in Balham called The Priory. A few months later, Dr Gully discreetly bought himself Orwell Lodge, a house a few minutes away in Bedford Hill Road. He naturally had a key to The Priory and let himself in and out without troubling Florence's parlour-maid. Occasionally, when Mrs Cox was away, he stayed the night at The Priory. Florence was a similarly frequent visitor at Orwell Lodge. The butler there, Pritchard, saw that the two were still very attached to each other, but their existence was mundane and they had begun to quarrel routinely.

The Bravos, who had made friends with Mrs Cox, lived in Kensington. One day, Florence Ricardo dropped Mrs Cox at the Bravos and arranged to collect her later. On her return, she was invited inside to meet the Bravo family and that was her first meeting with the son of the house, Charles Bravo, a good-looking young barrister with an egotistical and aggressive air. They took little notice of one another at that first meeting.

In 1875, Dr Gully went abroad on a trip and Florence was bored. She decided on a trip of her own to Brighton with Mrs Cox. Quite by chance they met Charles Bravo there. On this occasion Florence fell for Charles's obvious charm. Florence was impulsive and strong-willed, and a romance quickly developed. In November, Charles Bravo proposed to Florence and she accepted. Dr Gully was initially angry. He had given up his practice to be at Florence's beck and call for five years, only to be cast off. But his anger was brief; he wrote Florence one angry letter, then settled for a quieter life without Florence. He was, after all, sixty-six. The hostility of Charles Bravo's parents to the match was not so fleeting; they saw Florence as flighty, wilful, worldly and sensual. Charles and Florence were frank with each other about their past lives. Florence told him about her affair with Gully, and Charles told her that he had had a mistress for four years.

The wedding was fixed for 7 December. Florence went into the marriage with her eyes wide open. There were at that time no Married Woman's Property Acts, so legally all of Florence's property would become her husband's. Florence was determined that this should not happen. She had after all been let down by one husband already. She had her solicitor arrange a prenuptial settlement to protect her property rights. Charles reacted very badly to this. Charles tried to compromise, by letting Florence include the income from her first husband in the settlement but excluding the house and furniture, which he would then later be able to claim as his. Florence resisted this. Charles said he would not sit on a chair that was not his own and threatened to break off the marriage.

Florence consulted Gully. He magnanimously agreed to give her advice, and his advice was that she should not jeopardize the marriage for such a matter; he advised her to give in to Bravo. He also returned his door key and told Pritchard that under no circumstances were Florence or Mrs Cox to be admitted to Orwell Lodge. As far as Gully was concerned the relationship with Florence Ricardo or Florence Bravo was at an end.

The wedding took place, though old Mrs Bravo could

not bring herself to attend. Not long afterwards, the seeds of trouble were sown. Florence did not mind spending money, and Charles was concerned that she was overspending. Did they really need to keep four horses, three gardeners, a butler, a footman, six women servants, a coachman and a groom? Then he questioned whether they really needed to employ Mrs Cox. He worked out that Mrs Cox was costing them £400 a year. Charles had no personal objection to Mrs Cox, in fact they were on very friendly terms, it was just that she was an expense that was hard to justify.

Even so, Florence and Charles were very happy together. The idea that his wife had been having sex with Dr Gully nevertheless increasingly irritated Bravo. Instead of leaving Florence's past behind, he allowed it to become part of the dynamic of their present love life. Bravo became jealous, cursing Gully as a wretch, and criticizing Florence for her affair with him. Gully meanwhile behaved with perfect propriety, kept well away from the Bravos, to the extent that Charles Bravo never once set eyes on him. Mrs Cox occasionally met him, though, and they exchanged news. Dr Gully mentioned that he knew of a cure for an ailment that was of interest to her, Jamaica fever, and would send a prescription for it to her if she liked. She agreed.

Unfortunately, Charles Bravo regarded opening the letters as one of the duties of the master of the house. When he picked up the mail, he met Mrs Cox and asked if he could open the letter addressed to her – as it was in

Dr Gully's handwriting. Mrs Cox said at the trial she was surprised that he recognized Gully's handwriting, and also surprised and affronted by his request. As a compromise, she opened the letter herself, in front of Bravo, to show him that it contained nothing more sinister than a prescription. Something lies beneath this odd incident that was not pursued at the trial, and that is the fact that Bravo did recognize Gully's handwriting. There is an implication that he had intercepted at least one earlier letter from Gully, presumably to his wife. Indeed, we might guess that that is why he had adopted the custom of opening all the mail himself. He wanted to be absolutely sure that his wife's affair with Dr Gully was over. Perhaps it was not.

Florence had another miscarriage shortly after this. Mrs Cox made it her business to keep Gully up to date with news of Florence when she met him. They had decided that Florence should take a house in Worthing to help Florence's convalescence. Mrs Cox went to Worthing to scout for one. Meanwhile, Florence went into town with her husband in their carriage. The carriage turned into Bedford Hill Road and when it passed Orwell Lodge Florence instinctively looked towards the house. It was a glance with no meaning, just a glance out of habit. Bravo noticed and asked her savagely, 'Did you see anybody?' She said not, and Bravo said something abusive about Gully. Florence told him it was unkind to bring up the past especially when he had promised he would not; he would not like it if she kept taunting him about his mistress. He softened, asked for a kiss, but she refused. Then he said something rather menacing. If she wouldn't kiss him, she would see what he would do when they got home. Then she did kiss him, but out of fear.

Florence went shopping, then returned to the Priory for lunch on her own, while Charles had lunch with a friend, returning to Balham in the afternoon. He was pleased when Florence gave him some tobacco she had bought for him that morning. He went for a ride and came back later badly shaken. The horse had bolted. Charles had dinner with Florence. It was the first dinner Florence had stayed up for since her miscarriage. Charles complained of stiffness and looked pale. Florence sent the butler upstairs to prepare a mustard bath for Charles.

Dinner was a little late because they had to wait for Mrs Cox. They had whiting, roast lamb and a dish of eggs and anchovies. Charles seemed out of sorts, unwell. Mrs Cox produced a photograph of the house she had chosen, but Charles brushed it aside. The butler noticed that Bravo was not himself, and put it down to the shock of the horse bolting. It is also possible that Bravo was suffering from toothache; he did not mention it that evening, but it was an ongoing problem. He drank three glasses of burgundy. The ladies drank almost two bottles of sherry between them.

At about half past eight, Bravo thought Florence had stayed up late enough. She agreed and went to bed, accompanied by Mrs Cox. Halfway up the stairs she asked Mrs Cox to bring her another glass of sherry. Mrs Cox went down to fetch it, then helped Florence undress because Mary the maid was having her supper.

At half past nine Charles Bravo went upstairs. Mary was on her way up to see Florence at the same moment, and noticed how distraught he looked. Normally Charles was good with the servants, and always had a friendly word for them. This evening he did not speak. He went into his bedroom and Mary went into Florence's. She was sent straight downstairs again to fetch yet another glass of sherry. She left Florence in bed and Mrs Cox sitting at her bedside, a common scene. Mary asked if anything was needed and Mrs Cox said no, just to take the dogs downstairs. It seemed like a fairly normal end of evening routine. Then, as Mary was taking the dogs along the landing, Bravo appeared in the doorway of his bedroom, obviously in a desperate state, shouting, 'Florence, Florence! Hot water!'

The maid scurried back to Florence's room, where Florence herself was in a stupor and Mrs Cox sat daydreaming, apparently not having heard Bravo's shout. But she too had consumed an entire bottle of Marsala and was probably quite drunk. The maid got Mrs Cox to rouse herself and they went to attend to Charles Bravo. By this time he was standing at the window, vomiting. Mrs Cox sent Mary down for some hot water. When the girl came back, she saw Bravo on the floor with Mrs Cox rubbing his chest. She told Mary to fetch mustard, as an emetic. As Mary ran off on this errand, she thought it was odd that Mrs Cox had not roused Florence, but Mrs Cox may have been considering the delicate state of Florence's health; as a convalescent there was not much she could have done to help. Mary nevertheless went in and roused her, managed to make her understand what was happening. Florence put on a dressing gown and rushed to see Charles. Her innocence was evident from her extreme anxiety. Mrs Cox had sent for Dr Harrison of Streatham, but Florence insisted on sending for Dr Moore because he lived much nearer.

When Dr Harrison arrived, Mrs Cox met him, saying that she thought Charles had taken chloroform. She said later that she had not mentioned this idea to Dr Moore because he was a local man and she did not want people in the neighbourhood to know that he might have done that. But neither Moore nor Harrison could detect any trace of chloroform on Bravo's breath. Following her miscarriage, Florence had been attended by Mr Royes Bell. Dr Harrison sent a note asking him to come and to bring someone else with him. The coachman set off and returned two hours later with Mr Royes Bell and Dr Johnson. Charles Bravo was now being attended by four doctors.

Florence was distraught, and had thrown herself down on the bed beside Charles, and fallen again into an alcoholic stupor; she had drunk something like a bottle and a half of sherry. Dr Harrison roused her and put her back in her own bed. After that Bravo came to and started vomiting again. 'I took some laudanum for toothache,' he said. Dr Johnson replied, 'Laudanum will not account for your symptoms.' Mrs Cox drew Mr Royes Bell to one side and told him that when she had first gone to Charles he had said, 'I have taken poison. Don't tell Florence.' Royes was astounded that she had kept this vital information back until now. 'It's no good sending for a doctor if you don't tell him what's the matter,' he said pithily, and hurried to tell his colleagues the crucial information. Dr Harrison was extremely irritated that Mrs Cox had not told him. Mrs Cox made the situation worse by saying that she had done so. 'I told you when you arrived,' she said. But Harrison was not having it. 'You did nothing of the sort,' he said angrily. 'You said he had taken chloroform.' He was unlikely to have misheard or misunderstood.

The condition of Charles Bravo did not improve during the night. At five o'clock in the morning, on 19 April, Harrison, Moore and Johnson went home, taking a vomit specimen for analysis. Royes Bell, who was agreed to be in charge of the case, stayed at the Bravos'. During the day, Charles had several bouts of intense pain followed by interludes of exhaustion. At noon, sensing that he was dying, he had a short will made, in which he left everything to Florence. At three o'clock the three doctors gathered again round his bed and pressed again to tell them what he had taken. They knew he must have taken poison. The butler overheard his master say weakly but irritably, 'Why the devil should I have sent for you if I knew what was the matter with me?'

Charles's parents arrived from St Leonards, bringing Mr

Bravo's brother-in-law, Dr Henry Smith, who was a surgeon, the surgeon's sister Miss Bell and their maid Amelia Bushell who had known Charles since childhood. Mrs Cox greeted them at the station with the news that Charles had poisoned himself. They didn't believe it for a moment. Mr Bravo said emphatically that such a thing was impossible. When they reached the sick room, Charles's mother asked Florence if she might take over, as she had always looked after Charles when he was ill in the past. Florence was so distracted that she agreed. She even gave up the double bedroom to Charles's parents and went upstairs to share Mrs Cox's room.

The next morning Charles Bravo was no better. In desperation, Florence sent Mrs Cox round to Orwell Lodge. She said afterwards that she had always though Dr Gully 'the cleverest doctor in the world.' She instinctively turned to him for help. When she arrived at Orwell Lodge, Pritchard understood the gravity of the situation, let her in and put her in the drawing room. When he told Gully that Mrs Cox was there, Gully said, 'You shouldn't have let her in,' but he went to see what the matter was. He suggested mustard plaster and small doses of arsenicum, and Mrs Cox quickly left.

Florence was by this stage distraught and making errors of judgement. She remembered that the eminent doctor Sir William Gull was a friend of her father's and summoned him, though without mentioning poison. It was a breach of etiquette to invite another doctor when she already had a doctor on the case, but Gull and Royes Bell agreed to overlook it. They drove out to Balham together, arriving at six o'clock in the evening. Sir William Gull ordered the sickroom emptied of everyone except the five doctors who were already assembled there. Gull examined Bravo and said, 'This is not a disease. You have been poisoned. Pray tell us how you came by it.' Bravo feebly insisted he had taken only laudanum for toothache. 'You have taken a great deal more than that,' Gull insisted.

Mrs Cox now made another of her surprising statements. She said to Sir William Gull that what Charles Bravo had really said to her was, 'I have taken poison for Gully. Don't tell Florence.' It is not known what Gull said to this, but presumably he did not know that Mrs Cox had already given two different versions of this conversation to others present in the room. They must have been very unnerved by this trickle of revelations. Sir William was, in the end, the only one of the medics who thought Charles Bravo had committed suicide.

Johnson's analysis of the vomit was useless. He only tested for arsenic, of which there was no trace, but there were other poisons for which he cold have tested. Gull looked out of the window where Bravo had vomited and saw traces on the leads below. He had some collected and took it away for analysis. Gull did not beat about the bush. Before he left with his sample, he told Charles Bravo that he was half dead already and the parents that he would not last through another night.

He was right. At four in the morning, on 21 April, Charles Bravo died. Mrs Cox was the only person in the household able to function among the grief and distress. She immediately got in touch with the East Surrey coroner, Mr Carter, knowing that there would have to be a post mortem and an inquest. She told him it was a suicide and that it was important to spare the family's feelings if possible. She went so far as proposing that the inquest could be held at The Priory and that refreshments would be provided for the jurors. Mr Carter fell in with Mrs Cox's arrangements. There was no notice sent to the press and there would be no reporters.

The inquest opened on 28 April, and it was evident that Mr Carter had taken for granted that it was a case of suicide. Then Sir William Gull's pathologist revealed that Charles Bravo had died from a large dose of antimony, taken in the form of tartar emetic. Dr Smith advised Charles Bravo's father to take the pathologist's report to Scotland Yard. It was important to trace any tartar emetic in the house. Scotland Yard sent an inspector, who completely failed to find any trace of the substance. Mrs Cox and Florence had stacks of patent medicines, but all harmless.

The evidence emerging at the inquest was not consistent with suicide, as witnesses testified to the affectionate relationship between Charles and Florence Bravo. Carter wanted to hurry his suicide verdict through, and refused to hear any testimony from Dr Moore and Dr Johnson, even though both of them wanted to speak. The jurors were by this stage thoroughly uneasy. They returned a verdict that Charles Bravo had died from a dose of tartar emetic but that there was no proof as to how he had taken it.

The following day, 29 April, the funeral took place at Norwood and the day after that Florence and Mrs Cox withdrew to Brighton, where Mrs Cox had found them an apartment at 38 Brunswick Terrace. Mr Bravo stayed on at The Priory, where he sealed up all his son's drawers, presumably pending the criminal investigation he anticipated. When Florence heard, she wrote to him at once reminding him that all Charles's belongings now belonged to her and that no one else had any right to touch anything. She tactlessly proposed that any money he had been in the habit of giving to his son should now be given to her; 'Poor Charlie told me that you promised to allow him £800 a year.' This was a very inappropriate thought to be passing through the mind of a grieving widow, and one who had plenty of money already. This kind of thing made her situation far worse. In fact when she next wrote to Joseph Bravo, she apologized for the disagreeable tone of her previous letter. Then she made it worse by adding that Royes Bell had persuaded her that poor Charlie had killed himself because his ex-mistress had been trying to get money out of him. This was very silly stuff, as there had been no trouble at all from that quarter, and Joseph Bravo must have known this.

The inquest had not gone well. Many people were now suspicious, as Florence knew from the flood of anonymous letters arriving at Brunswick Terrace. One of Charles Bravo's friends, present at the inquest, went to Scotland Yard to have the case investigated. Newspapers began to take up the story. Suspicion circled round Florence. New statements were taken from Florence and Mrs Cox, and as a result of Mrs Cox's statement in particular a new inquest was opened.

Before this could take place, Bravo's body had to be exhumed so that the jurors could view the body. Undertakers cut out a square of the coffin's lead casing so that the dead man's decomposed and black face was visible. The inquest on 11 July was packed with distinguished lawyers, yet rather an unruly occasion as the coroner was unable to control interjections from the public and the jury. Inevitably, Florence's affair with Dr Gully came out (thanks to Mrs Cox's statement) and much was made of it by lawyers who thought they could make it account for Bravo's committing suicide. Incredibly, Mrs Cox had not foreseen that the same evidence for the same relationship could be used equally to support a murder charge.

Florence Bravo made a spectacular impression when she appeared festooned in widow's weeds and appearing to be on the verge of breaking down. She was pressed hard to admit that she and Gully had been lovers while Gully was still in practice at Malvern. Dr Gully gave his evidence and it contained nothing that suggested he might be implicated in murder. The crowd at the inquest nevertheless treated him as if he was the murderer. At one point a lawyer tried to trap him into admitting that he had prescribed drugs to make Mrs Bravo miscarry, but Gully dismissed that; the prescribed drugs would not cause a miscarriage. So even the attempt to portray Gully as an abortionist, then a grave crime, failed.

The source of the tartar emetic was a puzzle. The police had found none at The Priory. Now it emerged that three months before Bravo's death there had indeed been tartar emetic at the property. The coachman, Griffiths, had bought some to treat Florence's horses. He had also used it at Dr Gully's stables at Malvern, though against Gully's wishes. In The Priory stables, Griffiths did what he liked, and bought a huge quantity of tartar emetic. Asked why he had bought enough for a hundred horses when Florence had only four, he said he liked to have things by him. Griffiths had been driving the carriage, with Florence and Mrs Cox on board, when it was involved in a serious collision. Possibly the accident was not Griffiths' fault, but Charles Bravo sacked him and Griffiths bore him a bitter grudge. But Griffiths insisted that he had poured down a drain all the tartar emetic in the stables before he left; it could not have been his tartar emetic that killed Charles Bravo.

Charles Bravo must have taken the poison, probably in a drink, some time after half past seven in the evening, and it must have been in either the burgundy he drank at dinner or the water bottle he kept on his bedroom washstand. He always drank a glass of water before going to bed. The medics thought it was more likely that the poison was in the water than the wine, because the wine was in the butler's sight from about seven o'clock when he had decanted it. But the water in his bedroom could have been poisoned at any time after Florence and Mrs Cox went upstairs and the appearance of Mary and Charles Bravo an hour later. The remains of neither the wine bottle nor the water bottle were available for analysis.

The upshot of the protracted inquest was that Charles Bravo had not died by misadventure, had not committed suicide, but had been poisoned; there was insufficient evidence to say who had poisoned him. The verdict was stunning. It meant that Mrs Cox's statement had not been believed, and if the jury had decided she was lying, that was as good as saying they thought she or Florence or possibly even Dr Gully had murdered Bravo. Remarkably, no one was ever charged.

Little is known of Florence's story afterwards, except that she died only a year after the second inquest. It has even been suggested that Florence herself may have been murdered. It is more likely that she knew why and how her husband had died, and the responsibility and the stress drove her to suicide; she died of excessive drinking. Mrs Cox somehow disappeared from view. Dr Gully, now exposed, in the eyes of Victorian society, as a thorough reprobate and rogue, lost his friends and his professional standing. His name was removed from the membership lists of all the societies to which he belonged. He lived on for another seven miserable years.

The shadow of suspicion remained over Florence Bravo and her friends. But who really was the murderer? After all this time, it is still uncertain. Given Dr Gully's extraordinary probity and sense of decency, he is really the unlikeliest suspect. He relinquished all hope of resuming his relationship with Florence the moment she decided to marry Bravo, and had indeed tried hard to keep both her and her companion out of his house.

It is possible that the death was misadventure, and that Charles Bravo could not tell the doctors what he had taken or how because it would incriminate him. He may have been trying to kill Florence. When he sacked the coachman, he was in a strong position to commandeer the stock of tartar emetic. He may then have fed the emetic to Florence in very small but regular doses in order to undermine her health. The classic way of poisoning people in the nineteenth century was to administer small doses over a long period to establish that the victim was sickly. When death eventually occurred, the doctor was likely to write it off as due to chronic illness such as consumption. Charles Bravo may therefore have had tartar emetic in his possession and secretly fed it to Florence; her health had been undermined ever since their marriage. Charles Bravo's motive would have been to make sure that he did, after all, own his wife's property, lock, stock and barrel. He was, as he said, taking laudanum for his toothache. He was probably suffering unusually badly from toothache on the evening when he took the poison, in fact so distracted by the pain that he drank from the wrong bottle.

The only problem with this is the failure of the police to find any trace of tartar emetic at The Priory. Someone must have helped him dispose of it during the three days he took to die. That person may have been his father, who was so keen after Charles's death to go through his belongings. Perhaps he was not trying to find evidence to incriminate Florence but attempting to remove any evidence that Charles had been trying to poison himself or Florence. It may even be that Charles's mother asked to be allowed to nurse her son in order to get Florence out of the way so that Joseph could search the bedroom thoroughly.

Another theory is that Florence poisoned him because he was working towards dismissing Mrs Cox to save money, and she wanted to keep Mrs Cox. Another is that it was Mrs Cox herself, who in a way stood to lose more than anyone if Charles Bravo remained alive. Jane Cox was an accomplished though not consistent liar and deceiver. She was also a very active organizer, someone who liked to control events, make things happen. She might well have seen herself having a very much happier life with her friend Florence if Charles Bravo was not around, and with Florence's income to support her, her sons' futures were assured too. The problem with identifying Mrs Cox as the murderer is that she and Florence were living hand in glove. If either one of them was guilty of planning the murder and carrying it out, the other is likely to have been complicit. On the other hand, if the behaviour of the two women in the hours and days after the poisoning are considered,

Florence Bravo's behaviour was that of a genuinely surprised and grief-stricken wife; Janie Cox's behaviour was controlled, controlling, manipulative, effective. Mrs Cox ran The Priory household from top to bottom.

Mrs Cox was not really seriously suspected at the time, though she must have aroused the suspicions of the clutch of doctors assembling round Charles Bravo's bedside. This needs to be explained. In the mid-nineteenth century, crimes like this one were seen as crimes of passion or marital crimes; husbands killed their wives, wives killed their husbands, husbands killed their wives' lovers. A purely economic motive, which is what we are visualizing for Mrs Cox, was not really allowed for. The likeliest suspect is Mrs Cox. Did she murder Charles Bravo – for social security?

THE PIMLICO MYSTERY: THE DEATH OF EDWIN BARTLETT

In 1886 Adelaide Bartlett found herself on trial at the Old Bailey for murdering her husband, Thomas Edwin Bartlett. Adelaide had mysterious origins. She was born in New Orleans in 1855, an illegitimate child who was probably the daughter of Adolphe Collot de la Tremouille, the Comte de Thouars d'Escury. Her mother is thought to have been an English girl called Clara Chamberlain. Adelaide spent her childhood in France and was then sent to England to live with a maternal aunt and uncle in Kingston on Thames.

It was at Kingston that she was introduced to Edwin Bartlett. He fell in love with her and decided to marry her. At thirty, he was eleven years older and he was moderately well off; he owned some grocery shops. Adelaide's parents in New Orleans approved of the marriage and her father provided a dowry.

As soon as they were married, Edwin took the odd step of sending his new wife off to boarding school to remedy the gaps in her education. She only saw her husband in the school holidays. Then Edwin sent her off to finishing school in Belgium. By 1878, he was satisfied that her education was complete and she was allowed to move in with him in an apartment over one of the grocery shops in Hern Hill.

Then a new problem developed. Edwin's father resented Adelaide's arrival, seeing her as coming between himself and his son. When Edwin's mother died, the father moved into Edwin and Adelaide's house. He promptly accused Adelaide of having an affair with his youngest son, Frederick. Edwin supported Adelaide and made his father formally retract his accusation in the presence of a solicitor.

The marriage had got off to a very poor start. Later, Adelaide alleged that she and her husband had only had sex once during their marriage. This was with the sole intention of making Adelaide pregnant – and it did. The midwife, Annie Walker, gave a different account of the marriage. She moved into the household a month before the baby was expected. She observed that the Bartletts always slept together and believed that the 'single act' Adelaide referred to was simply the one occasion when the Bartletts had unprotected sex.

Annie Walker saw that this would be a difficult delivery and that the baby's life was in danger. She recommended that a doctor should be summoned. Edwin objected that he did not want a man interfering with his wife, and only agreed to the doctor being present at the last minute. By then it was too late to save the baby, which was born dead. Adelaide decided then that she would not have any more children. Annie Walker remained on friendly terms with the Bartletts after the stillbirth. She testified at the trial that Adelaide complained that Edwin had written a will stipulating that she could not remarry.

In 1883, Edwin and Adelaide moved to East Dulwich, to live over another of Edwin Bartlett's shops. In 1885, they moved to Merton Abbey near Wimbledon. There they made friends with George Dyson, a Wesleyan minister. The three became great friends. Edwin encouraged displays of affection between Adelaide and George, to the extent of enjoying seeing them kiss in his presence. The relationship between Adelaide and George Dyson was probably platonic. Edwin made a new will, leaving everything he had to Adelaide, and this time not stipulating that she could not remarry; quite the contrary, he made it clear that if he died he expected Adelaide to marry Dyson.

In August 1885, Edwin and Adelaide Bartlett moved into two furnished rooms on the first floor of 85 Claverton Street, Pimlico. The house belonged to a registrar of births and deaths, Frederick Doggett. Edwin was still encouraging Dyson to visit Adelaide as much as possible, going so far as buying Dyson a season ticket from Putney to Waterloo to enable Dyson to visit frequently. Dyson was supposed to be teaching Adelaide Latin, maths, geography and history. The Doggett's maid on several occasion came upon Dyson and Adelaide in compromising positions; once she found them on the floor together.

By this stage, Adelaide was no longer sleeping with Edwin. They both slept in the drawing room. She slept on a couch, and he slept on a folding bed. One reason why Adelaide no longer wanted to sleep with her husband was his bad breath. Edwin suffered from tooth decay and an incompetent dentist had cut back the decaying teeth to the gums and fitted dentures over the stumps. In late 1885, Edwin was treated by a doctor for gastritis and diarrhoea. Another dentist removed the decaying teeth and stumps. This improved Edwin's health, but he was still depressed and hysterical.

Adelaide decided she needed to get a second opinion on Edwin's condition. She made the extraordinary statement, 'If Mr Bartlett does not soon get better his friends and relations will accuse me of poisoning him.' Dr Dudley looked at Edwin, said his gums were uninflamed, but declared his general health to be sound. Dudley recommended a daily walk. Now Edwin started to demand to have sex with Adelaide again. This was difficult for her, partly because Edwin had virtually forced her to get engaged to Dyson; his foul breath was also a great deterrent.

On 27 December 1885, Adelaide asked her friend George Dyson to buy some chloroform for her. In the hands of skilled medics, chloroform can be used as an anaesthetic, but a small dose can sometimes stop the heart and cause instant death. Dyson wanted to know why

Adelaide hadn't asked Edwin's doctor for the chloroform. She said Edwin had a complaint that caused paroxysms and that the doctor did not know about; she knew from past experience, she said, that chloroform would ease his pain. Dyson did as he was told, and bought two ounces from a chemist in Putney and another two ounces from another in Wimbledon. He combined his two purchases and gave Adelaide the four-ounce bottle. The chemists were told that the chloroform would be used to get rid of grease stains.

On 31 December 1885, Edwin had some dental treat-ment. When Adelaide returned home, she told Mrs Doggett she had regularly given Edwin chloroform to help him sleep. Early the next morning, Adelaide sent the maid out for Dr Leach. She then woke the Doggetts, telling Mr Doggett, 'Come down, come down. I think Mr Bartlett is dead.' She said she had tried to revive him by pouring brandy down his throat. Dogget went to the body, found it stone cold. Edwin had evidently been dead for several hours. A nearly full glass of wine stood on the mantelpiece close to Edwin's bed. Doggett thought it was brandy laced with ether. He also saw a glass half full of Condy's fluid was on a tray near the table. Condy's fluid was a disinfectant and deodorant. Doggett passed an unlabelled bottle on to the coroner's office. There was on the mantelpiece also a bottle of chlorodyne, which Adelaide said Edwin had used to rub on his inflamed gums.

Doggett refused to register the death until a post mortem

had been held. Dr Leach arranged for an autopsy, which Adelaide approved. It was carried out on 2 January at Charing Cross Hospital, but it failed to establish cause of death. Edwin's stomach contained liquid chloroform, as if drunk straight out of the bottle. Eventually it was decided that Edwin had died as a result of the intake of chloroform. Adelaide admitted to having chloroform. She objected to Edwin's attempts to have sex with her, and she had had to remind him of her pseudo-betrothal to George Dyson. Edwin had become insistent. She had got hold of the chloroform, intending to put drops on a handkerchief and hold it over his face. She had not actually used it at all, and had told Edwin what she had done on New Year's Eve. She showed him the bottle and he had put it on the mantelpiece. Adelaide fell asleep, and woke to find Edwin dead.

At the inquest, Dyson explained how the chloroform was bought, making it clear that Adelaide was the instigator, and the jury recommended that Adelaide should be arrested. The jury passed a verdict of willful murder against Adelaide. Dyson was arrested and charged with being an accessory before the fact.

The trial of the twenty-eight-year-old George Dyson and the thirty-year-old Adelaide Bartlett opened at the Old Bailey on 13 April. Adelaide's father instructed the prominent barrister Edward Clarke to defend her. The prosecution case was led by the Attorney General Sir Charles Russell. Once the charges were read, the prosecution withdrew its charges against George Dyson; the jury was asked to return a formal not guilty verdict on Dyson, and he was discharged.

Three possibilities were considered by the prosecution lawyers. Suicide was one, but that was considered unlikely. Misadventure was another, but that too was considered unlikely because the pain after swallowing the poison would have alerted the victim. The third, the only remaining, possibility, was that the poison was administered deliberately. The prosecution lawyers maintained that Adelaide had rendered her husband unconscious by putting drops of chloroform on a handkerchief, and then poured liquid chloroform down his throat.

When George Dyson gave evidence he said that Bartlett had some strange ideas, including the notion that he was terminally ill. If that was true, there was the possibility that Bartlett had committed suicide. Dyson also said that Adelaide had not asked him to conceal the fact that he had bought chloroform.

Dr Leach gave evidence that Adelaide had looked after her husband with great care and tenderness during his illness. He thought Edwin Bartlett was hysterical, unbalanced and this too supported the idea of his having committed suicide. Leach though Adelaide could not have poured the chloroform down Edwin's throat as this would have made him vomit; he had eaten a large meal shortly beforehand. In fact Edwin had not vomited.

Dr Thomas Stevenson, senior scientific analyst to the Home Office, said that he knew of no recorded case of murder by administering liquid chloroform. Pouring it down the victim's throat would have been very difficult, as it would very likely have gone down the windpipe. The autopsy showed that none had found its way into the windpipe. This tended to imply that Edwin Bartlett had taken the chloroform himself, while conscious.

For technical legal reasons, the defence was unable to call Adelaide to give evidence. Instead, her defence lawyer gave a closing speech lasting six hours. Edward Clarke pointed out the evidence that suggested suicide, and also the lack of motive for murder. When summing up, Mr Justice Wills mentioned that contraceptives had been found among Edwin's belongings, and drew the inference from these that Edwin and Adelaide had led an active sex life. That being so, Adelaide would not have needed to repel Edwin's sexual advances.

The jury was, even so, not persuaded. The jury had serious misgivings about Adelaide Bartlett. The foreman said, 'although we think grave suspicion is attached to the prisoner, we do not think there is sufficient evidence to show how or by whom the chloroform was administered.' The verdict was not guilty, and yet the jury evidently thought she might be guilty. There was applause in the court room. At the outset there had been strong public antipathy towards Adelaide, but by the time the verdict was reached, there was a general feeling that 'not guilty' was the right verdict.

What really happened to Edwin Bartlett is still not

known. Edward Clark thought Edwin had committed suicide, after hearing his dentist use the word 'necrosis', which he may have equate with gangrene. Edwin poured chloroform into the wine glass while Adelaide was out of the room and drank it. When Adelaide later returned to the bedside, she poured brandy into the same glass. But it is not clear why Edwin would have poured the chloroform into a glass – perhaps out of habit? Dr Leach later wrote that he too though Edwin had committed suicide, but inadvertently; he had taken a dose of chloroform to distress his wife, perhaps after she revealed her intention of dosing him with it.

The idea that Adelaide murdered Edwin is consistent with some of the known facts. She may by this stage have seen married life with Dyson as preferable to married life with Edwin. Her apparent tenderness and solicitude could have been an elaborate defensive act, an act carefully sustained in the knowledge that her behaviour would one day be scrutinized. She may have given her husband brandy first. The hot taste of the brandy would to a great extent immunize his mouth against the taste of the chloroform, which she offered him in the next glass. It is also likely that the diseased and inflamed state of his mouth rendered Edwin less sensitive to the taste of the chloroform.

It is also possible, given that there were several different medicines with reach, that Edwin simply took the chloroform by mistake. On balance, that does seem the likeliest explanation, but it is a close run thing. It is intriguing to note that once she was released from Edwin Bartlett Adelaide did not marry George Dyson. Instead she went back to New Orleans. Behind her she left one of the most puzzling unsolved poisoning cases of all time.

JACK THE RIPPER

The Whitechapel murders rank among the greatest and best known unsolved crimes of all time.

In the autumn of 1888, several prostitutes were brutally murdered, most of them in dark alleys, in the Whitechapel district of the East End of London. There was widespread panic and the police made a huge effort to catch the killer, but he was never found, never even identified. Even after scores of historians, journalists and police investigators have explored and re-explored the case, and more than a century has passed, we are still no nearer to knowing who the killer was.

The infamous Jack the Ripper murders were really just one manifestation of a low-life nineteenth century East End of London. The awful slum conditions bred disease, poverty and violence. There were huge numbers of prostitutes, there was high child mortality, high incidence of sexual abuse of every kind – and lots of murders. Prostitutes were particularly vulnerable, then as now, and prostitute murders were two a penny. Jack the Ripper was responsible for only five of these murders – a drop in the ocean – and his reign of terror in the East End was surprisingly brief, yet his name became notorious unlike any other murderer's before or since, a byword for gratuitous, sadistic violence. The Ripper murders made a huge impact on late Victorian England.

One minor mystery is exactly when the Ripper murders began. It is generally agreed that they happened within a fairly short time – but how short? Two early victims have been suggested: Emma Smith and Martha Turner. Emma Smith was described as 'a drunken Whitechapel prostitute' which might make her look like a classic Ripper victim, but there the similarities end. She was staggering home drunk to her lodgings in Spitalfields on 3 April 1888 when she was attacked. Before she died, twenty-four hours later, she was able to tell the police that she had been attacked by four men, the youngest about nineteen years old. She had been stabbed with something like a spike and robbed. It has never been suggested that any of the authentic Ripper murders was carried out by a gang.

The second possible early victim was Martha Turner, who was another prostitute. She was seen drinking with a soldier late one night before being murdered with thirty-nine stab wounds, nine in the throat, seventeen in the chest, thirteen in the stomach. It was a frenzied and vicious attack and looked as if it might have been done with two hands at once. Martha Turner was murdered on the night of 6-7 August 1888. Rather surprisingly, soldiers at the Tower of London had up until that time taken their bayonets with them when off duty. After the Turner murder that practice was stopped. All the soldiers at The Tower of London were lined up for an identity parade, but Martha Turner's friend, who had seen her with the soldier earlier in the evening of the murder, either could not or would not identify the murderer. Sir Melville Macnaghten, who was in charge of the CID after the last Ripper murder and had the job of wrapping the case up, discounted these two murders; he did not believe they were the work of the maniac who committed the Jack the Ripper murders.

The uncontested Ripper murders began on 31 August 1888. Mary Ann Nichols, a Whitechapel prostitute, was found murdered in an alley. The police thought from witness accounts that she had approached a tall stranger with the line, 'Want a good time, mister?' She took him into the dark alley for sex and had her throat savagely cut. The police surgeon who examined her body said, 'I have never seen so horrible a case. She was ripped about in a manner that only a person skilled in the use of a knife could have achieved.' This idea that skill had been used was to return again and again. When no definite suspect was found, people began to speculate that the killer might perhaps be a butcher or a surgeon: but that was grasping at straws.

It was a horrible murder, but 'one-off' prostitute murders were relatively common, and the police naturally assumed it was one of these. But a week later another prostitute, Annie Chapman, was found dead in Hanbury Street close to Spitalfields Market. She had not only had her throat cut, she had been disembowelled, and her possessions as well as her entrails laid out beside her body. The thorough dissection of Annie Chapman suggested that the murderer had an interest, however warped, in anatomy.

Then, on 25 September, came the first letter from the Whitechapel murderer. It was sent to a Fleet Street news agency.

Dear Boss,
I keep on hearing that the police have caught me. But they won't fix me yet . . . I am down on whores and I won't stop ripping them until I do get buckled. Grand job, that last job was, I gave the lady no time to squeal. How can they catch me now? I love my work and want to start again. You will soon hear from me with my funny little games. I saved some of the proper stuff in a little ginger beer bottle after my last job to write with, but it went thick like glue and I can't use it. Red ink is fit enough I hope. Ha! Ha! The next job I do I shall clip the ears off and send them to the police, just for the jolly. Keep this letter back till I do a bit more work, then give it out straight. My knife is nice and sharp I want to get to work right away if I get a chance. Good luck.

Yours truly, Jack the Ripper

Don't mind me giving the trade name, wasn't good enough to post this before I got all the red ink off my hands curse it. No luck yet they say I am a doctor now ha ha.'

Shortly afterwards, on 30 September, he murdered Liz Stride, another prostitute, in Berner's Street. Like the others, she had her throat cut, almost certainly from behind, but was not mutilated in any other way. The police, probably rightly, assumed that Jack had been disturbed during this murder and had run off before finishing the job. To compensate, he killed again a few streets away, in Mitre Square. This fourth victim was Catherine Eddowes. She was disembowelled.

Panic gripped Whitechapel. Women began to equip themselves with whistles to raise the alarm and knives to defend themselves.

The murder of Catherine Eddowes introduced a new dimension. Not only was it much bloodier than all the others – so far – but a trail of blood led to a wall in a tenement stairwell where a strange cryptic message was inscribed in chalk. It read, 'The Juwes are the men That Will not be Blamed for nothing'. Fearing reprisal attacks on Jewish men, the head of the Metropolitan Police Force, Sir Charles Warren, had the message scrubbed off. In doing so, he may have destroyed some vital evidence. It would be useful to know, for instance, whether the handwriting was the same as that in the 'Dear Boss' letter.

Warren's fears about reprisals were well-founded. All sorts of rumours were going round the East End about the identity of the murderer. One suspect was Michael Ostrog, a Russian-born doctor; it was rumoured he had been sent from Russia to incriminate expatriate Russian Jews.

Nevertheless, the spelling of 'Juwes' may suggest something else – the involvement of freemasonry. The disembowelling too may be connected with Freemasons' lore. The police were flooded with suspects nominated by the public, and the general atmosphere in the East End approached hysteria.

The Ripper's final victim was Mary Kelly, a twenty-five-year-old prostitute, who was murdered on 9 November in her rented room in Miller's Court. The following morning her landlord, Henry Bowers, called to collect her rent. He looked in through the window and saw the horrific sight of Mary's dismembered body lying on the bed. 'I shall be haunted by this for the rest of my life,' he told the police. The previous evening Mary had been desperately trying to earn her rent. She was seen approaching strangers for business. The last one she was seen approaching was tall, dark and wore a deerstalker hat.

There were no more Ripper murders after the death of Mary Kelly, and that is in itself one of the great unsolved mysteries about them. Compulsive psychopathic killers tend to go on killing until they are stopped, yet the police had not apprehended anyone. There was no arrest, yet there were no more killings. One possible explanation is that the Ripper was prevented from continuing by his own death, that he committed suicide. This has led to the identification of Montagu John Druitt as the Ripper. He was last seen alive on 3 December 1888, four weeks after the Kelly murder. His body was found floating in the

Thames a few days later. Druitt was a failed barrister who had fallen on such hard times that he had to resort to teaching to make a living. In favour of Montagu Druitt as the murderer are the history of mental illness within the family and Druitt's acquisition of basic medical skills as a young man.

Druitt was born on 15 August 1857 at Wimborne in Dorset. His father William was a distinguished surgeon, a Justice of the Peace, a pillar of the community. Montagu Druitt was sent to Winchester in 1870 at the age of twelve. At school he was successful, except as an actor. Even the school magazine slated his performance as Sir Toby Belch. His great passion was for cricket. He went on to New College Oxford to read Classics, graduating in 1880. His decision to become a barrister seems to have been the beginning of a decline. He fell back on teaching at a private 'cramming shop' in Blackheath. He went on playing cricket. Interestingly, he is known to have been playing in matches the day before or the day after several of the murders – whatever that proves.

In 1888, Montagu Druitt was going to pieces, and finally killed himself in December. It may be that he even gave the police his address too. On 29 September 1888, the Ripper wrote from Liverpool, 'Beware, I shall be at work on the 1st and 2nd inst., in Minories at twelve midnight, and I give the authorities a good chance, but there is never a policeman near when I am at work.' After the Catherine Eddowes killing he sent another letter from Liverpool:

ABOVE: *The Princes in the Tower, Edward V (1470–1483) and Richard, Duke of York (1473–1483), from an engraving by Stocks after a painting by Millais.*

ABOVE: *Mary Queen of Scots with her second husband and cousin Henry Stewart, Lord Darnley. The mystery surrounding the death of Darnley at Kirk o'Field is of such great magnitude that historians cannot even be certain how he died.*

ABOVE: *Doctor John Bodkin Adams. The terrible crimes he committed remain officially unsolved, simply because officially they were never committed in the first place.*

ABOVE: *Oscar Slater was accused of murdering eighty-two-year-old Marion Gilchrist in a brutal hammer attack in Glasgow in 1909. He was wrongfully convicted and served eighteen years in Peterhead Prison before being released, leaving yet another murder case unsolved.*

ABOVE: *Lord Lucan – by disappearing he created an almost unprecedented legal and ethical situation, where the verdict has to be suspended – apparently for ever.*

ABOVE: *The O. J. Simpson murder case is one of the most highly publicized crime cases of the last few decades. People were glued to the televison screen as the unique trial lasted for a period of 133 days.*

ABOVE: *Thirteen-year-old Billie-Jo Jenkins was brutally bludgeoned to death as she painted the French windows opening onto her own back garden in Lower Park Road, Hastings on 15 February 1977. The Sussex police have vowed never to close the Billie-Jo case.*

ABOVE: *A Jamaican newspaper headlining the murder of Pakistan national cricket coach, Bob Woolmer. He was found naked on the floor of his hotel bathroom, but it was not until four days later that the Jamaican police announced that Woolmer had not died of natural causes as first thought – he had been murdered.*

'What fools the police are. I even give them the name of the street where I am living.' Was Jack the Ripper really living in the Minories, a street near the Tower of London? Druitt had a relative called Lionel Druitt, who qualified as a doctor in Edinburgh in 1877, and he had lodgings near The Tower. It was at 140 Minories. Lionel seems to have moved in as a junior partner of Dr Gillard in Clapham Road in 1886, but it may be that the Minories rooms were passed on to his cousin Montagu, who was four years younger than him.

It was quite common for upper and middle class young men to go 'slumming' in the East End. Charles Dickens and Wilkie Collins had done it when looking for material for their fiction; others did it when looking for illicit sex. A room in a lodging house in the area would have been useful for the purpose. The connection between Montagu Druitt and the Minories is tenuous, but it is the one address he mentions in his letter.

It is also intriguing that Lionel Druitt left for New South Wales in Australia in 1886, yet he was able to produce, in 1890, a tantalizingly elusive document entitled *The East End Murderer – I knew him*. Since he was out of the country at the time of the murders, he can only have picked up the key information from other family members. Unfortunately, though the title and author of this document are known, no copy has so far been traced. In spite of having a promising career in both medicine and cricket in England, Montagu's brother Edward suddenly decided in

1889 to emigrate to Australia. Maybe, after his brother's murder spree and suicide, England was no longer so attractive. In 1889, he doubtless met Lionel and told hem everything, giving him the material for the 1890 monograph.

Dr Neill Cream is a known murderer who may have the Ripper murders added to his CV. Cream's career as an arsonist, abortionist and murderer was brought to an end in 1892, when he was convicted of the murders of four London prostitutes. He had picked them up in the boroughs of Walworth and Lambeth and poisoned them with strychnine. It is said that on the scaffold he exclaimed at the last moment, 'I am Jack the – ' just as he dropped. Unfortunately, as well as the hangman, who swore that this happened, there were others present, including Sir Henry Smith, who later boasted that nobody knew more about Jack the Ripper than he did, and he did not mention this key information. Actually, even if Cream had claimed at that crucial moment that he was the Ripper, it could have been a ruse to gain a stay of execution. If he had owned up to being Jack the Ripper, surely those with him on the scaffold would have wanted to hear more?

In fact, regardless of what Neill Cream shouted, or whether he shouted, Cream could not have committed the Ripper murders. From November 1881 until July 1891 he was serving a life sentence for murder in Illinois.

George Chapman is another convicted murderer often brought forward as a suspect for the Ripper murders. He was born in Poland in 1865 as Severin Klososwski. He was hanged in 1903 for the murder by arsenic poisoning of three women, Maud Marsh, Mary Spink and Bessie Taylor. He is linked to the Ripper cases by being, according to one source, in Whitechapel at the right time. He is said to have run a hairdresser's business at George Yard, which is where Martha Turner was murdered. Inspector Abberline, who led the Ripper enquiries, came to believe in his retirement that George Chapman was the Ripper. Abberline presumably suspected Chapman because he was living in the area (but a lot of other people were living in Whitechapel, which must have them suspects, too) and he fitted the description of the man seen with Mary Kelly on the night of her murder. But the nature of the Ripper killings is totally different from that of the Chapman killings. One murderer used a knife; the other used poison. They could not have been more different.

Some writers have proposed that the Duke of Clarence was the murderer, on the grounds that the Duke was mentally unstable and keen on London low-life, and was confined after the Ripper murders. The Duke's sexual proclivities seem to have lain elsewhere, though, and it is difficult to see how he could have been involved in slaying female prostitutes. Many other people have been named as Ripper suspects, including the painter Walter Sickert, though none carry real conviction. The Jack the Ripper murders seem destined to remain the great unsolved murder mystery of modern times.

A recent re-examination of the Whitechapel murders returns to the idea that we began with: that more than one murderer was at work. There were significant differences between the Emma Smith and Martha Turner murders and the series that came afterwards. In fact there were enough differences for us to be fairly sure that there was more than one prostitute-killer on the rampage. Before she died, Emma Smith was able to say that she had been attacked by four men, so we know from that one incident that there were at least four men who were killing prostitutes.

There were also variations between the later killings, again enough for it to be possible that more than one killer was involved. We have tended to treat the Mary Kelly murder as a grand climax to the earlier street killings, but the very fact that it happened indoors, in Mary Kelly's lodging, makes it a different crime from the others. It was also much more extreme. Mary Kelly was cut to pieces. This may point to the Mary Kelly murder as having been committed by a different killer. The case for there being several Rippers is convincing, especially since the copycat effect is well known in highly publicized and sensationalized crimes. It would also help to explain the widely differing descriptions of the killer that were given by witnesses.

On the other hand, the five classic Ripper murders happened within quite a short time span and there were many points in common. Until there is firm proof that more than one murderer carried out the killings, we should assume the simplest scenario – that just one maniac was responsible.

Who was he? At least we know what he looked like, because of one or two sightings of him immediately after the murders. The best description is the one given by a detective, Steve White, who saw a lone figure moving away from the scene of the murder of Catherine Eddowes in Mitre Square – a lone figure who was about to melt away into the night. This is his memorable, yet often overlooked, description of Jack the Ripper:

I saw a man coming out of the alley [where the body was found two minutes later]. He was walking quickly but noiselessly, apparently wearing rubber shoes, which were rather rare in those days.

He was about five feet ten inches in height, and was dressed rather shabbily, though it was obvious that the material of his clothes was good. Evidently a man who had seen better days, I thought. His face was long and thin, nostrils rather delicate and his hair was jet black. His complexion was inclined to be sallow and altogether the man was foreign in appearance. The most striking thing about him was the extraordinary brilliance of his eyes. The man was slightly bent at the shoulders, though he was obviously quite young – about thirty-three at the most – and gave one the idea of having been a student or professional man. His hands were snow white, and the fingers long and tapering. As the man passed me at the lamp, I had an uneasy feeling that there was something more than usually sinister about him, and I was strongly moved to find some pretext for detaining him; but it was not in keeping with British police methods that I should do so . . . I had a sort of intuition that the man was not quite right. The man stumbled a few feet away from me, and I made that an excuse for engaging him in conversation. He turned sharply at the sound of my voice, and scowled at me in surly fashion, but he said 'Good-night' and agreed with me that it was cold.

His voice was a surprise to me. It was soft and musical, with a touch of melancholy in it, and it was the voice of a man of culture – a voice altogether out of keeping with the squalid surroundings of the East End.

When Steve White's vivid description is compared with Montagu Druitt's photograph, there is not much doubt that the two are strikingly similar. White got Druitt's socio-economic class right. He even got Druitt's age right. The rubber-soled plimsolls were consistent with Druitt's sporting activity. Immediately after the detective's encounter with Jack the Ripper, he was called urgently by one of the other officers to 'come along' and look at the body of a woman he had just found in the alley. Steve White went and looked, remembered the man he had just seen and ran back after him as fast as he could.

But of course he didn't catch him. Nobody ever did catch Jack the Ripper.

GAVE HER MOTHER
FORTY WHACKS?
THE LIZZIE BORDEN CASE

Lizzie Borden was born on 19 July 1860 in Fall River, Massachusetts, into a seriously dysfunctional family. When Lizzie was only two, her mother Sarah died, leaving her father Andrew to care for Lizzie and her elder sister Emma. The big trouble started when Lizzie was five years old – and Andrew Borden remarried.

The new wife, Abby Durfee, was a short, heavy and rather withdrawn and reclusive woman. Local rumour had it that this was a marriage of convenience, and that all Andrew wanted from Abby was the services of a maid and childminder. Nevertheless, the rumour may have been wrong and Andrew Borden seems to have cared for his new wife, who was one of life's non-starters. It is also possible that Andrew Borden may not have had many alternatives to choose from; he was not a likable character.

The problems arose from the poor relationship that developed between the two girls and their new stepmother. Emma hated Abby, and she was justified in fearing that Abby would rob her of her inheritance. As the two girls grew older, things got steadily worse and they refused to eat meals with Abby, pointedly calling her 'Mrs Borden'. In a particularly nasty and revealing incident, Lizzie decapitated Abby's cat after it annoyed her.

Andrew Borden, who was now seventy, had become wealthy as a result of his investments but, in spite of being one of the richest men in town, he and his family lived frugally in a small house in an unfashionable district of Fall River. In fact, the unnecessary frugality may have been one of the sources of Lizzie's simmering anger.

Another problem was the narrow focus of Lizzie's life. At the age of thirty-two, she still had no job, no husband, no love life, nothing to distract her from the long-simmering grievance against her father and his second wife. She did some voluntary work and taught Sunday school, but these were not enough to distract her from the frustrations that were intensifying in her mind.

In 1892, her feud with her parents erupted into physical action. On one occasion when Andrew returned from an outing, Lizzie reported that Abby's bedroom had been broken into and ransacked by a thief who had stolen a watch and jewellery. Mr Borden called the police, then dismissed them halfway through their investigation once he realized that Lizzie herself was the culprit. After that he kept his and Abby's bedroom door locked. In the same year, the Borden's barn was broken into – twice. Andrew Borden again assumed that Lizzie was behind the petty crime. He retaliated by cutting the heads off Lizzie's pigeons, probably as a reminder of what Lizzie had done to Abby's cat. It is not known how Lizzie reacted to this vicious and spiteful punishment, but the Bordens tended to sit around fuming in silent malevolence for days after domestic incidents like these. Probably Andrew Borden's fate was already sealed, but the double murder of Lizzie's parents did not come until the following summer.

Lizzie Borden was known to have 'funny spells'. There were days when she behaved totally unpredictably, and those days became more frequent during the unusually hot year of 1892, when all New England steamed and suffocated. The local drugstore noticed that Lizzie was regularly buying small doses of prussic acid, which was well known as a lethal poison. By the end of July, the entire Borden household was afflicted with stomach upsets. These were probably nothing to with prussic acid, but more likely to do with the fact that fresh food was going off faster than normal in the high temperatures.

Abby Borden was still convinced that she had been poisoned after she suffered a long bout of vomiting. She made one of her rare trips out, to see the doctor who lived over the road. When she came back she was told off by her husband for her nonsensical behaviour. The doctor pointed out that the whole family was retching, including the maid. Lizzie's hatred grew; so did Abby's apprehension; so did Andrew's irritation. In the afternoon of 3 August, Uncle John Morse arrived without any luggage.

He was ostensibly there just to borrow a bed for the night so that he could visit friends across town the next morning; at least that was the reason he gave for being there. In the evening of 3 August, the evening before the death of her parents, Lizzie Borden visited her friend Alice Russell. Alice described Lizzie as agitated. She was worried about some threat to her father, concerned that something was about to happen. When Lizzie returned home at about nine o'clock, she could hear Uncle John and her parents talking loudly (by implication arguing) in the sitting room. Because the front stairs ran straight up from the hallway inside the front door, Lizzie was able to go upstairs to her room without speaking to any of them.

The hot summer's day of 4 August 1892 began like any other, only hotter. It was the hottest day of that whole summer. By mid-morning Andrew and Abby Borden would be dead. Exactly what happened in between is still not known. It is uncertain whether Lizzie committed the murders – and some investigators have suggested other culprits, such as a discontented employee, or the maid Bridget – but such evidence as there is points directly to Lizzie.

Luckily for her, Lizzie's sister Emma was out of town, or she too might have died. In the wake of a blazing row with their father over his gifting of the family property, both Emma and Lizzie had gone away on extended holidays to cool off; Lizzie had returned first. Uncle John was up first that fateful morning, at about six o'clock. The maid, Bridget Sullivan, followed him down to start her chores, but she had to stop to be sick: the effects of the food poisoning. By half past seven, Abby and Andrew were dressed and sitting at breakfast with Uncle John. Just over an hour later, Uncle John went into town to see his friends. Lizzie came down for a light breakfast, Bridget went outside to clean the windows and Abby got on with some dusting.

One peculiarity of the day was the heavy involvement of Dr Seabury Bowen. He was naturally called when Andrew Borden's body was discovered, and after that he prescribed a tranquillizer for Lizzie and assisted in the autopsies. But he had already visited the Borden household earlier in the morning, to treat everyone for food poisoning. Abby Borden had been in a distressed and fearful state when she had been to see him the previous day, 3 August, claiming that she and Andrew were being poisoned. Bowen put her symptoms down to food poisoning. Given what happened twenty-four hours later, her fears were well-founded; somebody did have it in mind to kill her. The high profile of Dr Bowen on the day of the murders has led some investigators to see him as in some way complicit in the murders, but there is really no reason to see his behaviour as suspicious; he was simply a conscientious GP.

At about nine o'clock in the morning, a youth called with a note and Andrew Borden went into town. He visited the bank, where he was a stockholder, and then visited a shop that he owned. He was having it remodelled and he wanted to check on the progress the carpenters were making. He left there at twenty to eleven and arrived home perhaps five minutes after that. While Andrew Borden was out, a second young man arrived and hung about outside the Borden house. He seemed agitated, then he disappeared. He was never identified. It is possible that was a sighting of the murderer and that when he disappeared he disappeared into the Borden house with the intention of killing Andrew Borden.

Inside Number 92 Second Street nasty things had already begun to happen. At half past nine someone had crept up behind Abby Borden while she was dusting the guest room and brought a hatchet crashing down on her head. She was killed instantly, but the attacker, whoever he or she was, carried on raining blows on her. There was no noise, at least not enough sound to alert anyone else in the house that anything untoward was happening. It was well after that, at about a quarter to eleven, that Andrew Borden arrived at the front door, hot and tired after his walk back from town. The door was locked from the inside, with three locks, and Bridget had to let Mr Borden in. As she was fumbling with the locks, she heard Lizzie laughing from the upstairs landing. Laughing? At a maid having difficulty unlocking a door? At a father who had become fanatical about security after the two mock-burglaries she had staged? Or laughing with elation because the much hated Abby was lying dead on the bedroom floor a few feet behind her? Lizzie characteristically told the police a completely contradictory story – that she had been in the kitchen when her father came home.

Andrew Borden went into the sitting room and took the key to his bedroom off the mantelpiece and went up the back stairs to his room. Since the burglary a year earlier, Andrew Borden had systematically kept the door to his (and Abby's) bedroom locked. Lizzie set up the ironing board and started ironing. Bridget went back to washing windows, but stopped at five minutes to eleven to go upstairs to lie down. At that time Andrew came down to the sitting room and settled himself for a rest on the sofa. Lizzie was self-incriminatingly vague about what she was doing and where during these moments leading to her father's death. She was in the yard, or the barn or the barn loft – and she was there, according to her own testimony, for twenty minutes or so before returning.

The temperature had soared to 86°F (30°C), though it was not yet midday. Andrew Borden was too exhausted by the heat to take off his heavy morning coat. He slumped back diagonally on the mohair-covered sofa, carefully keeping his boots on the floor so that the upholstery would not be spoilt. His head was very close to the door into an adjacent room. He dozed in the heat, unaware that his wife lay on the floor upstairs, and had already been dead for an hour and a half. As he dozed, he too was brutally hit over the head by an unseen hand, from behind, from through the doorway.

At ten past eleven Lizzie 'found' the body of her father sprawled on the sofa in the sitting room. Half of his head was shorn away by blows from an axe, and blood was still trickling down from his wounds. From the back door, Lizzie called Bridget down the back stairs and sent her to get the doctor. One of the neighbours, Mrs Adelaide Churchill, could see from the disturbance that something distressing was happening and called across to Lizzie to ask if anything was wrong. Lizzie called back, 'Oh, Mrs Churchill, please come over! Someone has killed Father!' Mrs Churchill asked where her mother was and Lizzie replied that she did not know; she said her mother had had a note asking her to go and visit a sick person, so she did not know where Mrs Borden was. That was odd, because Abby very seldom went out – and where was the note? Later, when questioned, she said she might have inadvertently burnt it. She told Mrs Churchill that Bridget could not find Dr Bowen, so Mrs Churchill offered to send her handyman to find a doctor; the handyman would also telephone the police. The police got his call for help at a quarter past eleven. So Lizzie had not delayed; she had taken every appropriate action from the moment she found her father's body.

Even when the police and the doctor arrived, the body of Abby Borden remained undetected upstairs. Then Lizzie 'remembered that she thought she had heard Abby coming back from town' and a curious neighbour went upstairs to look. It was only then that the body of Abby Borden was found on the floor beside the bed in the guest room. Dr Bowen found that Andrew Borden had been killed probably with a hatchet, where he lay on the sofa.

He had suffered eleven axe blows to the head, delivered from above and behind. Abby had similarly been attacked from behind as she cleaned the bedroom. The much-hated Abby received eighteen blows to the head. She had probably died at about half past nine, Andrew at eleven.

In spite of the heat, a crowd was gathering in the street outside the Borden house. Then a man came strolling up the street. It was Uncle John. It was his behaviour that now seemed remarkable. Instead of seeing the crowd and hurrying to see what had gone wrong at the Borden house, which would have been most people's response, he slowed right down. When he at last reached the house, instead of going in, he went round to the back garden, picked some fruit from a tree and ate it. Even with the evidence of some domestic disaster unfolding round him, Uncle John was in no hurry to find out what it was. Did he perhaps already know?

Once he was inside the house, Uncle John was a changed man. His story of the morning's events cascaded out of him. His alibi was so watertight – too good to be true – that he immediately became the principal suspect. When he emerged from the house, the crowd had already decided it was him, and they chased him back inside. When the police had finished with the Borden household for the day, they left a cordon round the house to keep away the crowd of curious onlookers which had gathered at the front of the house.

Emma was out of town, visiting friends, and Lizzie and Bridget were the only people left alive in the house.

Bridget told the police she had been washing windows most of the morning, and then gone up to her room to lie down. She was still lying there when Lizzie had called her down. Bridget hurried downstairs to find Lizzie at the back door. Lizzie stopped her from going into the sitting room; 'Don't go in there. Go and get the doctor. Run.' Bridget ran across the street to fetch their doctor and neighbour, Dr Bowen. He was out, so Bridget told Mrs Bowen that Mr Borden had been killed before running back to the house. Then Lizzie sent her to fetch her friend Alice Russell, who lived a few streets away.

Bridget was a straightforward young Irish woman of twenty-six. She had emigrated from Ireland in 1886 and found herself in a disadvantaged and discriminated class – the Irish immigrant community of Massachusetts. Her testimony, which was eventually published in full, comes across as honest, truthful, consistent. Interestingly, it neither incriminates nor vindicates Lizzie.

Bridget did not spend the night following the murders at the Borden house, but at a neighbour's. She spent the following night (Friday) in her second-floor room there, but left on the Saturday, never to return. It is not known what the circumstances of her departure were. One theory is that she was paid off by Lizzie, that Lizzie gave her enough money to go back to Ireland. That is possible, but Bridget returned to North America a few years later, marrying and moving to Montana, where she died in 1948.

Bridget's story never changed, but Lizzie kept on

contradicting herself and giving versions of events that could not have been true. She said she was in the barn loft for twenty minutes before discovering her father's body, but when the investigators went up to the loft they saw that the floor was covered with an undisturbed layer of dust: nobody had been up there for a long time. She had lied. In the cellar they found four hatchets. One of them had no handle and was covered in ash; this would be presented as the murder weapon at Lizzie's trial. The murder investigation, including the gathering of evidence, was an unusually incompetent affair; it was largely thanks to this that Lizzie was acquitted. When Lizzie came to trial the case against her was circumstantial. Even the identification of the murder weapon was entirely arbitrary; there was no good forensic reason why the investigators should have thought one hatchet was used for the murders rather than another. No bloodstained clothing was found or presented.

The next day, the day following the double murder, Emma hired a lawyer. The District Attorney Hosea Knowlton, resisted the pleas from the police to arrest Lizzie; as he said, 'You don't have any evidence against her.' Five days later, after an inquest had been held, Lizzie Borden was arrested, charged and taken to Taunton Jail. If it had been someone outside the family circle, an intruder, that intruder would have been incredibly lucky to hit a moment when Bridget was outside cleaning windows and Uncle John happened to be out. This was the same reasoning used by the British police when they charged

Sion Jenkins with murdering Billie-Jo. Of course, the 'too-great-a-coincidence' argument can be turned round if the hypothetical intruder was watching the house, simply waiting until the coast is clear before going in and committing the crime.

A preliminary hearing opened on 7 November. One of the Bordens' friends, Alice Russell, gave evidence; she had seen Lizzie burning a dress after the murders. On 2 December, Lizzie was formally charged on three counts of murder, one for the murder of Andrew, one for the murder of Abby, one (curiously) for the murder of them both.

The main trial opened on 5 June 1893 and lasted fourteen days. Witnesses for the prosecution testified that Andrew Borden was drawing up a new will. He intended to leave half his estate to Abby, the rest to be divided between his daughters. Another witness testified that Lizzie had tried to buy ten cents' worth of prussic acid from Eli Bence at a drug store which she could have intended to use, or actually used, to poison her parents. It certainly tied in with Abby's remark to Dr Bowen. The defence took only two days to present its case, calling witnesses who said that they had seen a mysterious man loitering near the Borden house. Emma Borden – who was not the most impartial of witnesses, since she hated Abby as much as Lizzie did and for the same reasons – confirmed that Lizzie had no motive for killing their parents. Was Emma protecting not only Lizzie but herself? Did she perhaps know that Lizzie was planning the murders? Did they perhaps collude? They both stood to gain equally from the deaths of Abby and their father.

A leading question related to Lizzie's visit to the outbuilding during the twenty minutes when her father was being murdered. What was she doing in the outhouse? 'To look for a piece of metal with which to mend a window screen, also to get some lead suitable for fishing weights.' Detectives searching the house found no broken screens and no lead that could be used for fishing weights. She also claimed that she had eaten three pears while she was in the outbuilding, even though it had been stifling and she had a queasy stomach. None of this sounded true.

In her favour was the lack of bloodstained clothing. If she had committed the two murders, she would have been soaked in blood, twice in the space of ninety minutes, yet when the house was searched all of Lizzie's clothes were found to be spotless. Alice Russell told a slightly different story. Before the second police search was carried out, Lizzie tore up an old dress and burnt it in the kitchen stove. That was on 7 August. She asked Lizzie why she was doing it. Lizzie said, 'Because it was all faded and paint-stained.' Alice said, 'I wouldn't let anybody see me do that, Lizzie, if I were you.' Alice could not see any paint on the dress and obviously suspected that the dress was stained in some more sinister way. It may have been a Freudian slip that made Lizzie mention stains. On the other hand, if Lizzie was destroying incriminating evidence, why on earth did she do it in front of a witness?

Why did she mention stains, when she could have said the garment was old, worn out or badly torn? And why did she wait until three days after the murders to dispose of it?

The court gave two rulings on points of order, and these proved to be decisive as far as the jury was concerned. This is unusual, in that the points of order were technical rather than substantive.

Lizzie's inquest testimony was disallowed as trial evidence on the grounds that when she made the statement she had not been formally charged. The evidence of the drug store assistant was also disallowed because the matter of the poison was irrelevant to the case. No poison had had been involved in the murders. These rulings evidently impressed the jury, who were left feeling that the case for the prosecution had been heavy-handed, illegal, unfair, oppressive. It took only half an hour for the jury's sense of fair play to prevail. They found Lizzie Borden not guilty on all three counts of murder. The court room reverberated with applause. That night she was guest of honour at a celebration party. She laughed over the scrapbook of newspaper cuttings of the trial that her supporters had compiled for her.

If Lizzie was innocent, then who had committed the murders? Was it the agitated young man seen by the neighbour outside the Borden house? And who was he? If it was him, how did he get through the locked front door?

Lizzie Borden was found not guilty, but that does not necessarily mean that the jury believed she was innocent.

Not guilty does not mean the same thing as innocent. In fact it has been suggested that, given the mores of the time, the jury did not like to think of a woman murdering her parents and in such a bloodthirsty way; that they found her not guilty because they wanted her not to be guilty. The closing speech of her defence lawyer, George D. Robinson, played up the idea that the murder was grotesque and diabolical, evidently relying on Lizzie's very ordinariness to point up the fact that she could not have done it. She did not look like the sort of person who would commit 'one of the most dastardly and diabolical crimes that was ever committed in Massachusetts. Who could have done such an act? In the quiet of the home, in the broad daylight of an August day, on the street of a popular city, with houses within a stone's throw, nay, almost touching, who could have done it?' Obviously somebody did, but the jurors did not want that person to be Lizzie.

Lizzie Borden was acquitted and released, but in spite of that acquittal the suspicion that she had killed her parents hung in the air at Fall River. Lizzie and Emma had to leave the neighbourhood, though surprisingly they stayed in Fall River. Five weeks after the trial, the sisters moved to a house in a more fashionable neighbourhood, and called the house Maplecroft. Lizzie took to calling herself Lizbeth which, in a similar way, was a sort of break with the past but not really enough to make any difference.

Lizzie's underlying deceitfulness and criminality, which seem to have been there all along, emerged in a small way again in 1897, when she was accused of shoplifting two paintings. The matter of $100 was settled out of court. Or, if we do not want to call it criminality, perhaps, as one writer has proposed, Lizzie suffered from temporal epilepsy, which would account for what the family called her 'peculiar turns'.

Lizzie Borden's lifestyle underwent a transformation when she met a young actress called Nance O'Neill. Nance moved into Maplecroft and Lizzie started throwing parties for Nance and her new-found theatrical friends, who were no doubt fascinated to meet the notorious Lizzie Borden. Emma did not like any of these new developments and moved out. She may have felt that Lizzie was tempting fate by inviting attention on this scale. She never spoke to her sister again. Lizzie Borden died at the age of sixty-six on 1 June 1927, following gall bladder surgery. A week later, her sister Emma died falling down stairs. Lizzie left her money to animal welfare organizations.

The Borden double murder remains unsolved. The maid, the doctor, an illegitimate brother demanding money, a mad stranger, Uncle John – all have been blamed by various authors, but Lizzie herself still looks like the obvious culprit. The Borden family was a profoundly dysfunctional family, and it is clear that both the daughters had a strong financial motive for resenting Abby's intrusion and their father's declared intention to draw up a new will in her favour. Abby could have been killed out of hatred; Andrew because he would have avenged Abby's murder; Andrew had to die before he could draft and sign the new will. There was no need to look outside the immediate family for suspects or motives. We also know enough about Lizzie's criminal tendencies (the faked burglaries, the shoplifting) and her violence (the beheading of Abby's cat) to sense that she was capable of both murder and criminal deception.

It is possible that someone else, a nameless stranger, or a disaffected neighbour, was guilty of the break-ins, and that Lizzie was incensed that her father should blame her for them. Anger at her father's unjust accusations could easily have fuelled her frenzied attack on him.

But there something else that happened that morning. The often forgotten figure of Uncle John was there for a particular purpose. Andrew Borden had already transferred a piece of property to Abby's name and it had led to a massive row, with Lizzie protesting that she was being disinherited. Uncle John was there to assist in the transfer of a second property, out of Lizzie's and Emma's reach: a farm that the two young women had come to think of as their summer home. No wonder they were angry.

A young man called at about nine o'clock in the morning with a note. He may have left the note just before or just after Andrew Borden left for the bank. Neither Andrew nor Uncle John would have wanted to upset the property arrangements by telling Lizzie, but it may be that the note was for Andrew, concerned the contentious property transfer and arrived just after Andrew left. Lizzie might well have read it and realized its significance; she was going to lose her holiday home and have her share of her father's wealth reduced even further. She could easily have flown into a towering rage and gone straight upstairs and killed Abby there and then. That makes more sense than temporal epilepsy. If it had been temporal epilepsy, Lizzie would have been quite certain she hadn't committed the murders and would probably have gone on living in Second Street.

Not only has Lizzie Borden become part of the fabric of American folk history, the house on Second Street has become a kind of heritage site. Restored to its 1892 condition, it is currently open for bed and breakfast. An earlier restoration of the house turned up – a hatchet.

Lizzie Borden was guilty, beyond all reasonable doubt. That was the general perception in the United States at the time, and the country delivered its own sentence on Lizzie Borden by turning her into folklore. She became, like the Big Bad Wolf, a nursery rhyme hate figure:

Lizzie Borden took an axe
And gave her mother forty whacks.
And when she saw what she had done,
She gave her father forty-one.

She became a jolly cautionary tale, a skipping rhyme. Lizzie Borden quickly turned into a kind of joke-evil which still persists and is in a strange way far worse than the guilty verdict which comes from a court of law – and which, of course, she should have had. Those who think she could not have done it should remember what she did to Abby's cat. A woman who is capable of beheading a cat is certainly capable of killing her father.

PART FOUR

UNSOLVED CRIMES OF THE EARLY TWENTIETH CENTURY

(1901–1950)

THE MURDER OF MARION GILCHRIST: SHERLOCK HOLMES TO THE RESCUE

Miss Marion Gilchrist was battered to death in her apartment in Glasgow on 21 December 1908. Miss Gilchrist was eighty-two and what used to be called 'a maiden lady'. She was looked after by a servant called Helen Lambie and the violent murder happened during the very short time when Helen was out buying a newspaper. Helen was out for as little as ten minutes, yet in that time an assailant managed to get into Miss Gilchrist's apartment, beat her to death and make off with a small diamond brooch. One peculiarity of this case is that the police discovered that only the one small diamond brooch was stolen, when Marion Gilchrist had a large collection of jewellery.

The family in the apartment underneath Miss Gilchrist's, the Adams family, heard noises, unusual noises, and Arthur Adams went upstairs to investigate. It had sounded like three knocks on the ceiling. Miss Gilchrist was an old lady and was perhaps in difficulties of some kind, possibly having a stroke or a heart attack or possibly she had fallen over and broken her leg; maybe she was signalling for help. When Mr Adams reached Miss Gilchrist's door he rang the bell. There was no answer, though he could hear noises inside the apartment. He went downstairs again, but was urged by his sisters to check that Miss Gilchrist really was all right. He went back upstairs and was standing in front of the door when Miss Lambie arrived back from her errand. It was at this moment that they both saw a man down in the hallway of the building. This was a semi-public area, so it did not strike either of them as unusual: perhaps another tenant or a visitor. There was no reason to connect this person with Miss Gilchrist.

Mr Adams told Miss Lambie what he had heard and the two of them went into the apartment. Together they found Miss Gilchrist; she was lying near the fireplace with her head brutally smashed in.

Oscar Slater, the man who emerged as the chief police suspect, had been living in Glasgow for about six weeks with his French girlfriend. He claimed to be a diamond cutter. Whether he was or not, the police – and others – thought he was a 'bad lot'. This assessment of Slater was based mainly on the lowest of prejudices; Oscar Slater was German, he was Jewish and he had a French mistress – a triple condemnation. But it must be admitted that he was also running an illegal gambling operation.

The day after the murder, Mary Barrowman, a girl of fourteen, told the police that at about the time when the murder had been committed she had bumped into a man hurrying out of the Gilchrist address. Mary described this man as tall, young and wearing a fawn cloak and a round hat. This description was evidently of a different man from the one Mr Adams and Miss Lambie saw. They described their man as 'about five feet six inches, wearing a light grey overcoat and a black cap'.

The police found out that Oscar Slater tried to sell a pawn-ticket for a diamond brooch just four days after the murder, and assumed that this brooch must be Miss Gilchrist's brooch. Even more suspicious was the fact that Slater and his girlfriend had then sailed for the United States on board the Lusitania, and Slater had used an assumed name for the passenger list. The police had been under a great deal of public pressure to find the villain who had committed this murder. Within five days they had their man, or at least a man. They cabled the police in the United States to take Slater into custody and then showed a picture of Slater to the three witnesses. The two girls, Helen Lambie and Mary Barrowman, obligingly identified Slater as the man they saw immediately after the murder; Mr Adams did not. It was the two girls who were sent off to the United States, on a free return trip, for the extradition proceedings. The expenses-paid trip to the United States for the girls looks suspiciously like a bribe.

Slater turned out to be very accommodating. He was willing to return to Scotland to answer the accusation. He knew he was innocent, could prove it and was positive that this 'misunderstanding' could be cleared up relatively easily. He could not know that the authorities were already determined to pin the murder on him and would stoop to any depth to secure his conviction. He could not know how close he would come to being hanged.

The initial British court hearing was in the Edinburgh High Court on 3 May 1909, over four months after the murder. The police had by this time decided not only that Slater had committed the murder, but that he had committed it with a small hammer that he owned. They had also mustered a dozen witnesses who claimed to have seen Slater near Miss Gilchrist's apartment on the day of the murder. This was hardly significant as Oscar Slater and Marion Gilchrist lived only four blocks apart.

This evaporation of the evidence against Oscar Slater is another of the hallmarks of his case, especially in view of the apparent determination of the authorities to get a conviction. That Slater should have been seen a number of times on the streets of Glasgow two hundred yards from his own home could hardly be presented as significant evidence tying him to the murder, at least not in any trial that was fair. The pawn ticket turned out to be even weaker evidence against him. The defence lawyer was able to show that the pawn ticket belonged to a brooch pawned several weeks before the murder, so it could not possibly have been the one stolen from Marion Gilchrist. Similarly, the voyage to North America had been booked six weeks before the murder; it was very far from being a moonlight flit.

Slater said in court that he had been at home with his girlfriend and her servant at the time when the murder was committed. This alibi was simply swept aside. The Lord Advocate, Alexander Ure, decided that Slater must be hanged. The jury was not so sure. It was not a unanimous verdict, but a majority found him guilty. Oscar Slater was sentenced to be hanged on 27 May 1909.

There was widespread public disquiet about the verdict, and about the evident determination of the authorities to pin the murder on Slater. A petition for clemency was launched immediately, raising 20,000 signatures. Two days before the execution was due to take place, the sentence was commuted to life imprisonment, with hard labour. Slater escaped the gallows. He had his life, but he still had to endure a cruel and unjust sentence. Naturally he wanted to prove his innocence and get out of prison. Sir Arthur Conan Doyle had read about the Oscar Slater case some years later in the book Notable Scottish Trials and had been struck then by the fact that Slater had been convicted on suspicion based on no more than prejudice; it had been based on no solid evidence whatever. Doyle did not approve of Slater as a person. He thought him a reprobate, but he was sure he had not committed the murder for which he was convicted.

It proved a long, slow process and many people felt that even if he had not committed the murder he probably had something to do with it. He was an unpleasant person and he was generally regarded as immoral. Doyle took his time. He spent three years thoroughly researching the case and in 1912 produced a book called The Case of Oscar Slater. It went through all the evidence raised against Slater at his trial and showed, detail by detail, how it simply could not be made to prove Oscar Slater's guilt.

The matter of the assumed name, for instance, was less suspicious than it was made to appear in court for the simple reason that Slater was travelling with his mistress. Slater was trying to avoid being detected by his wife, not evading the police. Slater had indeed possessed a small hammer as mentioned in the trial, but it was far too small to have inflicted the wounds on Miss Gilchrist's head. Doyle said that a forensic investigator at the crime scene had declared that a large chair, which was found dripping with blood after the crime, seemed by far the likeliest murder weapon. The matter of Miss Gilchrist opening the door and letting someone she knew into her apartment strongly suggested that the murderer was well known to her in some capacity or other. Oscar Slater and Marion Gilchrist did not know one another at all. Everything pointed away from Oscar Slater as the murderer.

Sir Arthur Conan Doyle's book raised a storm of indignation against the injustice that had been done against Slater. Now many people were ready to demand either a pardon or a retrial. But the authorities were adamant that nothing was going to be changed. Even Doyle's book made no difference as far as they were concerned. Then, much later, in 1925, William Gordon was released from Peterhead Prison; unknown to the authorities, Gordon was carrying a desperate message written on greaseproof paper, hidden under his tongue. The desperate message was Oscar Slater's cry for help to Sir Arthur Conan Doyle. Slater hoped to reactivate his old ally and enlist his help in getting justice for him.

Doyle was moved by this desperate plea and tried once again to help Slater. He fired off a fusillade of letters. But there was no new evidence that Doyle or Slater knew of. They were no further forward.

But even after this long period, it was possible for new information to emerge. In 1927 a new book about the case came out, The Truth About Oscar Slater, written by William Park, a Glasgow journalist. Park decided, just as Doyle had done, that Miss Gilchrist had known her murderer and went on to speculate that Miss Gilchrist had had a disagreement with the man about a document that she possessed. Park inferred this from the fact that Miss Gilchrist's documents had been disturbed and rummaged through, presumably by the murderer. During the argument she was pushed and hit her head. Her attacker then had to decide. He could leave Marion Gilchrist to recover and then probably have him charged with assault – or he could make sure she did not recover, in other words kill her. He decided to kill. The laws of libel made William Park hesitate and stop short of naming the killer, but he clearly believed that this was a family squabble, and that it was Miss Gilchrist's nephew who had murdered her.

The book was a sensation. The newspapers were full of the story and it was then that significant new information – or information long withheld – started to come out. A grocer called MacBrayne confirmed Slater's alibi; he had actually seen Slater on his own doorstep at the time of the murder, when he had said he was at home. Mary Barrowman and Helen Lambie were traced. Now they were ready to admit that they had been bribed and coached by the police to make a false identification. One cannot help wondering how many innocent people, over the centuries, have been sent to their deaths or to long prison sentences by bribed perjurers like these two women.

The official records show that several police officers perjured themselves, deliberately lying in order to make the case against Slater stick. One police officer stood out as a man of integrity throughout, and that was Detective Lieutenant John Trench. He said he didn't believe Helen Lambie's identification. Trench's persistence led to a closed (ie secret) enquiry into the police conduct of the case in 1914. The enquiry merely protected the existing state of affairs by announcing that there were 'no grounds for recommending that the conviction be overturned.'

Trench had been concerned about the Slater case for several years. Dismissed by the Chief Constable and hung out to dry by the Secretary of State, he could see no way forward – other than to go public. He consulted a lawyer, David Cook, and a journalist, William Park. Before he went further, Trench wanted to protect himself against further reprisals and approached Dr Devon, who was one of the Prison Commissioners. Devon was impressed by the evidence and wrote to McKinnon Wood on Trench's behalf. Wood replied on 13 February that he would give Trench's written statement his 'best consideration' – weasel words that meant nothing.

For stepping out of line, he was victimized by fellow officers and suspended from the force on 14 July 1914. The specific reason given for his suspension was that he had, without the express permission of his Chief Constable, communicated with persons outside the police force information he had acquired in the course of his duty. On 14 September, Glasgow magistrates found Trench guilty as charged and he was dismissed from the police force. Trench thought he had acted properly in passing information to the Secretary of State for Scotland, McKinnon Wood, and accordingly wrote to him to say that he saw 'your invitation to send the information and your acceptance thereof as ample protection against any breach of discipline.' McKinnon did not reply.

War broke out and (the now elderly) Trench joined up as a drill instructor. He was preparing to leave with his regiment for the Dardanelles when he was arrested on a charge of handling stolen property. The lawyer David Cook was arrested simultaneously on the same charge. Clearly the vendetta and the corruption were continuing. Trench and Cook were acquitted in August. The judge directed the jury, 'There is no justification at all which

324

would enable you to return a verdict of guilty.' The episode nevertheless did frighten Trench and Cook into making no further comment about the Oscar Slater case. Trench died at the age of fifty in 1919 and Cook died two years afterwards. Neither of them really recovered psychologically from their betrayal by the police force.

But as the trickle of new information, especially about the Barrowman and Lambie evidence, was published in the newspapers it became impossible for the authorities to keep Slater in prison any longer. On 8 November 1927, the Secretary of State for Scotland issued a statement: 'Oscar Slater has now completed more than eighteen and a half years of his life sentence, and I have felt justified in deciding to authorize his release on licence as soon as suitable arrangements can be made.' A few days later, Oscar Slater was released, though not pardoned.

Sir Arthur Conan Doyle despaired at the sheer wickedness of the Scottish authorities who refused to admit that they had been wrong. But he also despaired of Slater. It says much about Conan Doyle's probity that he was prepared to put himself to considerable trouble and expense to help a man he really disliked intensely. Because Slater was released but not pardoned, his case had to be reopened and re-tried if he was to be exonerated. It would be only then that Slater could apply for compensation for the eighteen years of wrongful imprisonment.

Conan Doyle and others gave money so that Slater could pay the legal fees. In the end, Slater was cleared of all the charges brought against him and awarded £6,000 in compensation. Conan Doyle naturally assumed Slater would pay back his supporters for the legal fees they had given him, which is what the honourable Sir Arthur would have done in the same circumstances. But Slater was embittered by his time in prison, and resented the fact that he had been put in a position where he had been forced to buy a re-trial; he should not have been asked to pay anything. He regarded the £6,000 as his. Conan Doyle was a wealthy man and did not really need to have back the £1,000 he had put into Slater's fund, but he was shocked that Slater was not prepared to pay him back. Slater was not an honourable man. Conan Doyle wrote to Slater, 'You seem to have taken leave of your senses. If you are indeed responsible for your actions, then you are the most ungrateful as well as the most foolish person whom I have ever known.'

When Oscar Slater died in 1949, the newspaper notice read, 'Oscar Slater Dead at 78, Reprieved Murderer, Friend of A. Conan Doyle'. Conan Doyle and many other people had gone to a lot of trouble to prove that Slater was not a reprieved murderer. They had gone to a lot of trouble to prove that he was not a murderer at all. It is doubtful whether Conan Doyle ever thought of Slater as a friend, either. But then, not everything we read in the newspapers is true.

Oscar Slater certainly did not kill Marion Gilchrist, but somebody did. Who was the real murderer? Nobody knows who killed Miss Gilchrist. It remains a great unsolved crime, though several theories have been floated. There are some significant pieces of evidence that point to the possible motive and the curious 'coincidence' of Helen Lambie's popping out to buy a newspaper just when the murderer was about to call.

Marion Gilchrist was well off. She had collected jewellery for years. By the time she was murdered she had a collection worth £3,000 then, and probably worth £60,000 in today's money. To build this collection, she often bought from shady backstreet dealers. It may possibly have been one of these who attacked her. Helen Lambie also revealed that she was expected to make herself scarce whenever one of these less than legitimate dealers was due to call. Was there rather more than coincidence to Helen Lambie's absence from the building at the time of the murder? Had she been asked to make herself scarce by Miss Gilchrist so that she could have a confidential conversation with a caller she was expecting? Or was she asked to make herself scarce for the murderer himself? Either way, it seems likely that Helen Lambie knew more about the situation than she ever revealed.

The murderer was also able to let himself in with his own door key, or was let in by Miss Gilchrist; either way, he must have been well known to the old lady, probably a regular dealer, a friend, or a relative who hoped to inherit. Maybe the theft of the brooch was meant to put the police off the scent and make them think the motive was robbery, when the real motive was something else, such as inheritance. And that brings us back to William Park's intriguing theory about the unnamed nephew.

SINKING OF THE *LUSITANIA*

On 7 May 1915, at a time when Britain and Germany were at war, the passenger liner RMS *Lusitania* was torpedoed off the Irish coast. Over a thousand lives were lost and there was consternation in the United States at what appeared to be an unprovoked attack on American civilians sailing on an unarmed passenger ship. It was an undeclared act of war. It was an atrocity, or at least so it was described at the time. The question in many of the cases discussed in this book is who committed the crime. In this case it much more a question of the nature of the crime and whether a crime was committed at all.

The ship was a huge luxury liner, built by John Brown on Clydeside and launched in 1906. With her identical twin sister ship the *Mauretania*, she was the flagship of the Cunard fleet, sailing on her maiden voyage across the Atlantic in 1907. The two ships were built specifically to compete with the big German liners of the time. Just as the British and German militaries competed with each other in an arms race, the big commercial companies were locked in economic war. There was in effect, before the First World War broke out, already a commercial war going on in the North Atlantic.

The *Lusitania* and *Mauretania* were built to be big, beautiful and fast. They were to be a little smaller than the White Star's Olympic class ships, the sister ships *Olympic, Titanic* and *Britannic*, but faster. The speed of the transatlantic crossing was vital to commercial success. The current fastest liner was said to hold the Blue Riband; the *Lusitania* won the Blue Riband in 1907. Once the White Star Line, Cunard's main British competitor, announced their Olympic class trio, Cunard decided to add a third ship. She was to be the *Aquitania*. She would be slower but bigger and more luxurious, and therefore bear comparison with the *Titanic*.

There was yet another war going on, too. American businessmen were keen to buy into this prestigious transatlantic race, and were not prepared to let the German liners go on winning. The American financier J. P. Morgan planned to buy up all the North Atlantic shipping lines he could, including the British White Star Line. In 1903, the chairman of the Cunard Line, Lord Inverclyde, used these threats, which were in effect threats to Britain's political as well as commercial prestige, to Cunard's advantage. Inverclyde lobbied the Balfour government for a huge loan to enable him to build two fast ships. The government agreed, but with the conditions that Cunard remained exclusively British and the two ships met Admiralty specifications. The British government also agreed to pay Cunard an annual subsidy of £150,000 to maintain the *Lusitania* and *Mauretania* in a state of readiness for war. This was a very significant step, given the events of 1915, when the official British and American position would be that the *Lusitania* was not a warship but an innocent merchant vessel. The fact was that the British government intended from the time when the *Lusitania's* keel was laid in 1904, ten years before the outbreak of war, to use her for war work. The huge annual payments for her upkeep proved that. The British government agreed to pay an extra £68,000 a year to have the two ships carry Royal Mail.

The ship was launched in 1906, which marked the completion of her hull, and in July 1907 she underwent her sea trials. It was found that when she steamed at full speed violent vibrations were set up in her stern and she was taken back to the yard to have stronger braces fitted in the stern. In August she was delivered to Cunard for service. The White Star's Olympic class ships were planned but not yet built, so at the time she went on her maiden voyage the *Lusitania* had the distinction of being the largest ship afloat.

In October 1907, the *Lusitania* took the Blue Riband from North German Lloyd's *Kaiser Wilhelm II*. This brought to an end the German domination of the North Atlantic. Was there now, perhaps, a score to settle in the minds of some German mariners? In 1909 the *Lusitania* handed the Blue Riband to her sister ship, the *Mauretania*, but the loss of the Blue Riband from a German flagship to the British *Lusitania* may still have remained a source of grievance. The Blue Riband would not return to Germany, ironically, until some time after her humiliating defeat in the First World War.

The *Lusitania* made an average speed of 24 knots on the westbound crossing, or 44.4 km per hour. It was partly confidence in this speed that led to a serious risk being taken in 1915. It was thought she could outrun any U-boat, and steam out of danger. She could comfortably steam 10 knots faster than a submarine, even with one of her boilers shut down. This complacency was misplaced, as it completely overlooked the possibility of an ambush, which is what happened, whether by design or by chance.

The *Lusitania* was sunk by a German U-boat, the U-20. For such a big ship, it sank surprisingly quickly, going down in only eighteen minutes. The huge loss of life was due in part to this rapidity: 1,198 of the 1,962 people on board were drowned.

The rapidity of the sinking is hard to understand. The *Titanic* was very badly damaged over a large area of her starboard side below the water line and probably her bottom too, but managed to remain afloat, thanks to her watertight bulkheads, for two and a half hours before sinking. Why did the *Lusitania* sink so quickly? The *Titanic* and her sister ships had transverse bulkheads, running across the ship. The *Lusitania* had transverse bulkheads, but she had longitudinal bulkheads too, running along each side, separating the boiler and engine rooms from the coal bunkers that ran along the sides.

When the British commission investigated the *Titanic* disaster in 1912, they heard evidence that the flooding of bunkers on the outside of longitudinal bulkheads along a significant proportion of the ship's length could exaggerate listing when they became flooded. This conclusion was reached after the *Lusitania* was built, after the *Titanic* had sunk, but three years before the *Lusitania* was sunk. What was predicted about the effect of longitudinal bulkheads in 1912 is exactly what happened in 1915, and with the predicted disastrous effect: the *Lusitania* developed an exaggerated list which made it almost impossible to lower the lifeboats on the upturned side because the hull was in the way.

The sinking of the ship turned many Americans from being confirmed neutrals keen to stay out of the European war to being strongly anti-German. It marked a significant step towards bringing the United States into the First World War two years later, which in itself was a major step towards the Allied victory.

The Germans regarded the *Lusitania* as a legitimate target when they torpedoed it. The British and Americans presented the vessel as a harmless merchant vessel but to an extent the Germans were right. The *Lusitania* had been built to Admiralty specifications, so that her decks were structurally strong enough to support deck guns if required. The *Lusitania* may not have been a warship at the time when she sank but her design meant that she could be requisitioned and quickly converted into an

Armed Merchant Cruiser. On the other hand, the *Lusitania* had not been so requisitioned, for economic and practical reasons. She was a big ship, used far too much coal compared with a custom-built cruiser and would have put too many crewmen at risk. As a result the British government were more interested in converting small liners into AMCs. The large ships were either left unrequisitioned or used for troop transport or used as hospital ships. The *Mauretania* became a troop transport. The *Britannic* became a hospital ship. The *Lusitania* conspicuously remained a transatlantic passenger liner.

On 4 February 1915, Germany declared that the seas surrounding the British Isles (ie Britain and Ireland) a war zone. From 18 February onwards any Allied ships would be sunk without warning. This meant that British ships might be sunk, though not American, because the Americans were still neutral. The British Admiralty issued the captain of the *Lusitania* with instructions on how to avoid submarines when the ship arrived in Liverpool on 6 March. The seriousness of the danger to the *Lusitania* was fully understood at the Admiralty, and two destroyers were sent to escort her, HMS *Louis* and HMS *Laverlock*; the Q ship HMS *Lyons* patrolled Liverpool Bay. Unfortunately Captain Dow did not know he was getting a naval escort, thought the destroyers might be German vessels and took evading action. He nevertheless arrived safely in Liverpool.

The *Lusitania* left Liverpool on 17 April and arrived in

New York on 24 April. Some German-Americans planning to return to the United States were unsure about travelling on the *Lusitania* because of the possibility of U-boat attack and consulted the German embassy. The advice from the German embassy was not to travel on the *Lusitania*. The German authorities were once again clearly signalling that they saw the ship as a military target, well before her final sailing. That final departure, from Pier 54 in New York, came on 1 May 1915. Before she sailed, a newspaper warning was published next to the advertisement for the ship's never-to-be return voyage, advising people not to travel because of the danger of U-boat attack. This was a reminder of the warning issued by the German Embassy in Washington on 22 April.

NOTICE!

TRAVELLERS intending to embark on the Atlantic voyage are reminded that a state of war exists between Germany and her allies and Great Britain and her allies; that the zone of war includes the waters adjacent to the British Isles; that, in accordance with formal notice given by the Imperial German Government, vessels flying the flag of Great Britain, or any of her allies, are liable to destruction in those waters and that travelers sailing in the war zone on the ships of Great Britain or her allies do so at their own risk.

IMPERIAL GERMAN EMBASSY, Washington DC April 22, 1915.

The *Lusitania's* fifty-eight year old captain, Bill Turner, made light of the danger. He told one passenger the *Lusitania* was 'safer than the trolley cars in New York City'. Shortly after embarkation, three German spies were discovered on board. They were arrested and detained.

As the *Lusitania* approached British waters, the British Admiralty tracked the movements of the German U-boat U-20 by picking up its wireless signals. The U-20, captained by Walther Schwieger, was off the west coast of Ireland and moving south, as if to intercept the *Lusitania*. On 5 and 6 May the U-20 sank three ships near the Fastnet Rock. The Royal Navy sent a warning to all British ships, 'Submarines active off the south coast of Ireland.' Captain Turner was given this message twice on the evening of 6 May. Turner responded by closing the watertight doors in the bulkheads, doubled the lookouts, ordered a blackout at night and had the lifeboats swung out on their davits so that if they were torpedoed the boats could be lowered at speed.

At eleven o'clock in the morning on 7 May Turner responded to another radio warning by altering course to the north-east. He assumed U-boats would be more likely to patrol the open seas, less likely to come close inshore. The *Lusitania*, he thought, would be safer steaming close to the Irish coast. Captain Schwieger was about to take the U-20 off duty. The submarine was low on fuel and he needed to take her home. He was taking the U-20 at top speed on the surface when, at one o'clock, he saw a ship on the horizon. This is his diary entry;

Ahead and to starboard four funnels and two masts of a steamer with course perpendicular to us come into sight (coming from SSW it steered towards Galley Head). Ship is made out to be large passenger steamer.

It was too good an opportunity for a conscientious U-boat captain to miss. He ordered his crew to take up battle stations and took the submarine down to thirty-six feet.

The *Lusitania* was heading for the port of Queenstown when she crossed right in front of the U-boat at ten past two. It was an ambush by chance. When his U-boat was just 700 yards away from the *Lusitania*, Schwieger gave the order to fire one torpedo, which hit the *Lusitania* right under the bridge and blew a hole in the side of the ship. Then there was a much bigger second explosion, which blew out the starboard bow. The two explosions have puzzled historians for a long time. There were definitely two explosions, but Schwieger's log shows that he only fired one torpedo. Some have argued that, in the wake of the international condemnation that followed the sinking, the German government doctored Schwieger's log to make it look as if he only fired once. Firing twice might have made it look like a massacre, especially since the ship sank so fast. On the other hand, the accounts of U-20 crew members agree with Schwieger's log entry: only one torpedo was fired. In fact it now looks as if the torpedo explosion on its own would have sunk the ship; the off-centre large-scale flooding would have caused the ship to capsize. All the ships' portholes were open, for ventilation, and that too would have speeded the sinking as the ship heeled over.

The wireless operator sent out an SOS straight away. Captain Turner gave the order to abandon ship, though this was difficult. The torpedo damage had made the ship list sharply and the damage caused by the second explosion made the bow sink under the water; at the same time, the ship was still moving forward at some speed. Launching the lifeboats under these conditions was difficult and dangerous. The lifeboats on the starboard side were swinging well away from the ship, making it difficult for passengers to step onto them. On the other side of the ship it was possible to get into the lifeboats quite easily, but hard to lower them. The hull plates were fastened together with big rivets and as the port side lifeboats were lowered they caught on the knobbly rivets and were in danger of being broken apart by them.

Some of the lifeboats overturned before they reached the water, spilling passengers into the sea. Some reached the water and were then overturned by the convulsing motion of the ship. Some, as a result of the incompetence of the crew, crashed onto the deck and killed passengers. Following the *Titanic* disaster, there were more than enough lifeboats for the number of people on the ship, but of the forty-eight lifeboats on the *Lusitania* only six reached the water and stayed afloat.

Captain Turner saw that land was in sight – in fact a six-year-old boy watched the entire tragedy unfold from the Old Head of Kinsale, eight miles away – and tried to take the ship towards the coast to beach her. All around him there was panic and chaos. Captain Schwieger watched this through his periscope. It seems not to have occurred to him to go to the aid of the passengers and crew of the *Lusitania*. Perhaps he regarded them as fools for sailing in the first place, in the face of all the warnings from Germany. At twenty-five minutes past two, he decided he had watched enough of the sinking of the *Lusitania*, dropped his periscope and headed for the open sea. In his war diary he implies only that he regretted being unable to fire a second torpedo.

Since it seemed as if the steamer would keep above water only a short time, we dived to a depth of twenty-four metres and ran out to sea. It would have been impossible for me, anyway, to fire a second torpedo into this crowd of people struggling to save their lives.

Captain Turner stayed on the bridge until it dipped under the water. He saved himself by grabbing a floating chair. The ship was sinking bow-first in shallow water. Her bow hit the seabed and she turned right over onto her side before sinking. The boilers blew up, one of the explosions causing the third funnel to collapse; the other three funnels snapped off one by one. The liner sank at twenty-eight minutes past two, sucking people, debris and water down with her. She hit the bottom and two minutes later there was a great up-welling of water, debris and people. In the event, 1,198 people died, including nearly a hundred children.

The second explosion was responsible for the ship sinking so fast, and therefore raising the death toll. One theory is that the *Lusitania* was carrying arms, which not only caused the second explosion but justified the German view that the ship was participating in the war effort. On the other hand there is only evidence from the wreck site of small arms ammunition (15,000 bullets), which could not have caused the explosion. Schwieger himself noted a possible cause in his war diary.

Torpedo hits starboard side right behind the bridge. An unusually heavy explosion takes place with a very strong explosion cloud (cloud reaches far beyond front funnel). The explosion of the torpedo must have been followed by a second one (boiler or coal or powder?).

The huge force of the first explosion may have stirred up a lot of coal dust in what must have been largely empty coal bunkers along the outside of the longitudinal bulkhead. It is well known that a mixture of coal dust and air makes a highly explosive gas. This, exploding on the outside of the longitudinal bulkhead could have blown a big hole in the ship's starboard bow.

Others believe this was almost impossible because the initial torpedo explosion would have sent huge quantities of seawater sideways into the coal bunkers. The coal dust would have been instantly saturated. A likelier alternative is an explosion in the steam-generating plant, as immediately after the second explosion the forward boiler room filled with steam and the steam pressure dropped dramatically.

There was outrage in Britain and the United States. The US government was indignant because 128 Americans had been killed by an act of hostility at a time when their country was neutral. In Britain, there was a hope that the United States would abandon neutrality and declare war on Germany. Some conspiracy theorists have even proposed that the First Lord of the Admiralty, Winston Churchill, set it all up. He arranged to sabotage the *Lusitania* specifically in order to force the Americans into the war. But there is no evidence whatever to support this.

President Woodrow Wilson still did not want to take that step, not least because many Americans were of German origin. Instead he sent a formal verbal protest, for which he was branded a coward in Britain. In fact Wilson's restraint was remarkable in view of the wave of anti-German anger in America. The American reaction was so strong that the German government decided to impose a ban on U-boat attacks against large passenger vessels; the Germans did not want to goad the Americans into becoming a British military ally.

In Munich, in August 1915, the metalworker Karl Goetz struck a commemorative medal to satirize Cunard's greed.

The German view of the *Lusitania* was that she was smuggling contraband under the cover of American neutrality. The medal carries the critically incorrect date of 5 May. British intelligence got hold of a copy and saw a way of turning its propaganda value upside down. The wrong date, possibly just a mistake, was made to imply that the sinking of the *Lusitania* was a premeditated crime, a crime in cold blood. Selfridge's were commissioned to make a quarter of a million exact copies of the medal, but with English lettering. They were sold in aid of the British Red Cross. Goetz realized too late that he had made a terrible mistake and issued a corrected medal bearing the date 7 May. After the war he admitted to having made the worst propaganda blunder of all time.

It is impossible now to find out what Schwieger thought he was doing – possibly, like so many other officers in wartime, just carrying out orders – as he died not long after the sinking. He was killed two years later when his submarine, the U-88, struck a mine. In the wake of the sinking of the *Lusitania*, he was branded a war criminal in Britain and the United States. But did he really commit a crime? While it might be argued that the attack on Pearl Harbor by the Japanese was unprovoked, an act of undeclared war, the same could not be said of the attack on the *Lusitania*. The *Lusitania* was a British ship; most of the personnel on board were British; Germany and Britain were formally at war; Germany had declared the waters round Britain to be a war zone; Germany had given several very explicit warnings that U-boats would attack British shipping, including a specific warning to those thinking of sailing on the *Lusitania* on its last voyage.

In the end, the British authorities believed they could get away with sending the *Lusitania* through seas patrolled by U-boats because she was so much faster than they were. She could outrun them. Why the Admiralty did not pause to consider the possibility that a U-boat might simply lie in wait off the Old Head of Kinsale, perhaps even stationary, and fire a torpedo into the side of the *Lusitania* as she passed, is beyond comprehension. There is the question of escorting vessels. The Admiralty for some reason took the precaution of sending a naval escort to accompany the *Lusitania* from the Irish Sea into Liverpool on an earlier voyage, but not to help her through the far more dangerous waters off the southern coast of Ireland. It could be argued that the Admiralty showed criminal negligence in failing to provide a very obvious target for German submarines with an escort.

But, even if the firing of the torpedo was not a crime, and even if the sinking of the *Lusitania* was not a crime, Captain Schwieger remains open to criticism. As he lowered his periscope, having seen enough, he knew that a thousand people were struggling for their lives in the water. He made no attempt to help them. It is also questionable whether he just happened to be in the right place at the right time by chance. Given that the sailing time of the *Lusitania* was public knowledge in New York, that her route was publicized, and that there were both a German embassy and German spies in New York, the German naval command would have known almost to the minute when to expect the *Lusitania*'s arrival in Queenstown. I firmly believe the U-20 was directed there, to wait for the *Lusitania*. In the wake of the tremendous wave of angry condemnation, this cold, calculated and premeditated ambush had to be presented as a U-boat captain's lucky break.

THE MAN FROM THE PRU: THE MURDER OF JULIA WALLACE

At some time between half past six and a quarter to nine in the evening on 20 January 1931, Julia Wallace was bludgeoned to death in her own home in Liverpool. It became known as the perfect murder. James Agate thought so; the crime writer Raymond Chandler thought so, too. The chief suspect was her husband. If he killed Julia, then the fact that he was released on appeal means that he succeeded in evading the death penalty and escaped justice. If someone else killed her, they were even more successful in that they succeeded in evading suspicion. One peculiarity of the case is that there was no conceivable motive. If, as most people believed at the time, Julia's husband William Wallace did it, what possible reason could he have had? The couple had lived together in what seemed to be perfect married harmony, if rather muted and in a minor key, for seventeen years.

William and Julia Wallace were an ordinary, lower middle-class couple living in a small drab house in the

Anfield district of Liverpool. They were a quiet, childless and rather sad pair. He was a cold, dull man with a mournful drooping moustache. He had been making a living for sixteen years as a life insurance agent for the Prudential; she was quite cultured, fastidious and rather more aspiring, hoping for something more from life. They lived in a small Victorian terraced house, No 29 Wolverton Street, which Julia had worked hard to make a genteel, middle-class home.

On the night before Julia Wallace died, her husband received a telephone message at the City Cafe in North John Street, the cafe he regularly visited because it was the venue of his Chess Club. The mysterious caller who was to change the lives of both of the Wallaces so melo-dramatically spoke to the club's captain, Samuel Beattie. He identified himself as Mr R. M. Qualtrough. He left a message asking Wallace to call and see him, apparently about an insurance policy, at 25 Menlove Gardens East at half past seven the next evening, 20 January 1931.

The next evening, Wallace accordingly set off to meet the mysterious Mr Qualtrough, who has never to this day been identified, leaving his house in Wolverton Street, as he later told the police, at a quarter to seven. It is known from an independent witness that William Wallace boarded a tram about three miles away in Lodge Lane at ten past seven, so the time that Wallace gave in his police statement is probably correct. Rather oddly, on the tram, Wallace kept reminding the conductor of his destination.

This was later to be interpreted by the police as an effort on Wallace's part to collect witnesses for his journey; he was setting up his alibi. But it may be that Wallace was merely over-anxious about keeping the appointment. After getting off the tram at Menlove Gardens West, he went on a futile search for Qualtrough's house; it turned out in the end that the address Qualtrough had given him was false; it just did not exist. During the search for 25 Menlove Gardens East he called at a newsagent, 25 Menlove Gardens West, and asked a policeman as well, making a point of asking people the time.

Satisfied that 25 Menlove Gardens East did not exist, Wallace gave up the search and made his way home. He arrived back home at quarter to nine to find the house in darkness. Feeling his way into the parlour, the front room, Wallace found the battered body of his wife lying face down on the floor on top of his mackintosh. She was lying rather too neatly to have fallen like that; it looked as if someone had straightened the body up and laid it on the raincoat. There was also some money missing.

The police photographs of the crime scene have survived. They show the pathetically genteel home that Julia had created, with its traditional set-piece fireplace and a large mirror above. Framed family photographs line the mantelpiece and four large pictures fill the wall on each side. It is a shock to see Julia's body lying so tidily on the carpet, her feet near the fireplace and head towards the door. This position suggested that she was not afraid of whoever killed her; the murderer must have been well into the room, struck her from behind so that she fell towards the door – unless of course the body was moved from a very different position, which is possible.

The police arrived, found no sign of a forced entry, and found Mr Wallace in a remarkably detached and composed state. He said something about a poker being missing from the fireside set. They suspected at once that he had done it. There was something odd about his account of entering the parlour at quarter to nine, in near total darkness, apart from the glow from the fire, and going to the gaslights on each side of the fireplace to light them; only then, he claimed, or so the prosecution said, did he see Julia's body. That is peculiar, because Julia's body, as the crime scene photographs show very clearly, filled the space between the doorway and the fireplace. It would scarcely be possible to enter the room and reach the gaslights without tripping over the body. On the other hand, Wallace would not have incriminated himself particularly if he had said that he saw on entering the room that there was someone lying on the floor and that he stepped over them to put the lights on. His account was nevertheless peculiar and two weeks later, when Wallace was staying with his sister in Aigburth, the police arrested him and charged him with Julia's murder.

The case for the prosecution hinged on the police view of Wallace as a cold, calculating, scheming man. It was easy to portray him in this way. He had discovered his wife's body at a quarter to nine. Only fifteen minutes later he was able to speak to PC Williams about this moment of discovery in unusually matter-of-fact terms.

At 6.45 p.m. I left the house in order to go to Menlove Gardens, and my wife accompanied me to the backyard door. She walked a little way down the alley with me, then she returned and bolted the backyard door. She would then be alone in the house. I went to Menlove Gardens to find the address which had been given me was wrong. Becoming suspicious I returned home and went to the front door. I inserted my key to find I could not open it. I went round to the backyard door: it was closed but not bolted. I went up the backyard and tried the back door, but it would not open. I again went to the front door and this time found the door to be bolted. I hurried round to the back and up the backyard, and tried the back door, and this time found it would open. I entered the house and this is what I found.

He sounded like an entomologist showing a colleague a specimen. What he was actually indicating to the policeman was the appalling aftermath of his wife's murder, her battered head lying in a pool of her blood. He was just too cool and calm to be true.

The prosecution maintained that there was no such person as Qualtrough. The 'Chess Club Murderer' had set up the Qualtrough alibi himself from start to finish. It was Wallace himself, the prosecution alleged, who had phoned the City Cafe and left the message. The lengthy journey and the nonexistence of the address given would explain why he was out of the house for such a long time, round about the time the murder was committed. But the prosecution argued that Wallace could have committed the murder at the beginning of the evening, before setting off to catch the tram. They also alleged that Wallace's persistent reminders about the stop at Menlove Gardens where he wanted to alight were simply a device to make the tram conductor remember him. In a similar way, asking for confirmation of the time in the newsagent's and asking a policeman to direct him to the address he was looking for were ways of ensuring that there were witnesses for his alibi.

The prosecution had more trouble explaining the lack of blood on Wallace's clothing. The scenario the counsel for the prosecution presented in court was as follows. Julia Wallace was in the parlour. Her husband, perhaps upstairs, took all of his clothes off and then came into the parlour wearing only his mackintosh. He then bludgeoned his wife to death, sending spatters of blood in all directions. He spread the mackintosh on the floor, put his wife's body on top to 'explain' the spots and splashes of blood on it, then went upstairs naked to wash the blood off. Then he put his clothes back on and went off for the meeting with Qualtrough.

There were in fact many difficulties with this scenario. One of them was that Wallace was known to have boarded the tram at ten past seven, and at a point three miles from the house. It would have taken Wallace a full twenty-five minutes to cover the three miles, making it likely that he was telling the truth about leaving the house at a quarter to seven. Could he have bludgeoned Julia to death, washed and dressed and been out on the streets by a quarter to seven? The 'forensic' report gave the estimated time of death as earlier than six o'clock, but it seems likely that the police indicated to the pathologist their preference for a time of death that would fit the scenario they were assembling. A major problem with having Julia dying at six o'clock or earlier is that she was seen, alive, by a delivery boy at half past six. That means that there was only a window of fifteen minutes – at the very most – in which Wallace could have committed the murder and done all the cleaning up. It was simply not long enough.

There were other problems with the prosecution's hypothesis. The bath was completely dry. There was no sign that anyone had taken a bath in the recent past. If Wallace had indeed committed the murder naked, then climbing into the bath would have been the obvious and only way of making absolutely sure every spot of blood was removed. It is inconceivable that Wallace would have risked missing blood splashes by having a mere washdown. None of the towels were damp either, so no-one had had a bath or a washdown in the previous few hours.

The area round the body in the parlour was found to have been sprayed with Julia Wallace's blood. The murderer must have been covered in it. Yet there were no drops of blood outside the parlour. If Wallace had hurried, naked and blood-spattered, out of the parlour to go and wash upstairs, there would be some spots of blood elsewhere. The forensic investigators were delighted when they found one drop of coagulated blood on the rim of the lavatory bowl. This was taken by the prosecution to prove that Wallace had indeed gone to the bathroom to wash. But the single drop of blood could easily have been picked up by one of the police officers on his coat hem, and accidentally transferred from the parlour to the bathroom as he made a tour of the house. The fact that it was a coagulated blob of blood suggests that it was moved a couple of hours after the murder rather than immediately after, and probably transferred on the hem of a detective's raincoat as the house was investigated – an unintentional plant. All in all, the prosecution case was unconvincing. Yet, in spite of the evidence, after only one hour's deliberation, the jury found Wallace guilty. He was sentenced to death.

Legal history was made when William Wallace appealed. His case was heard on 18 May by the Lord Chief Justice, Lord Hewart, who ruled that the verdict must be overturned on the grounds that it had been made against the weight of the evidence. Lord Hewart commented, 'We are not concerned here with suspicion, however grave, or with theories, however ingenious. Section 4 of the Court of Criminal Appeal Act of 1907 provides that the Court of Criminal Appeal shall allow the appeal if they think the verdict of the jury should be set aside on the ground that it cannot be supported by the evidence. The decision is that the case against the appellant was not proved with that certainty which is necessary in order to justify a verdict of Guilty.' Wallace's conviction was quashed. But the wording chosen by Lord Hewart makes it very clear that he was far from exonerated, that 'grave suspicion' still hung over him.

On the evidence as presented at the trial, Wallace should have been acquitted. Wallace came within a hair's breadth of the gallows, and was then freed. He tried to go on living at 29 Wolverton Street, and tried to go on doing his life insurance job, too, but the whispering and the gossip just would not stop. People would cruelly call, 'Julia! Julia!' in ghostly voices through his letterbox, just as he had himself that night late in January. He realized that he could not go on living in Anfield. He had to move away. He went to live in Cheshire, where he died only two years later of renal cancer.

The murderer of Julia Wallace was never caught, and never even identified. The police only considered one suspect, her husband, and there was insufficient evidence against him. But over the years since 1931 a prime suspect has emerged. His name is Gordon Parry. He had worked with Wallace in the insurance business and was a frequent visitor to the Wallace house. At the time of the original murder investigation, Gordon Parry was one of the names given to the police as someone Julia Wallace would have felt safe inviting into her house. She would have opened the door to Parry. The police even got as far as asking Parry where he was on the evening in question, but they were satisfied with his answer.

Gordon Parry was tracked down in the 1960s by two crime writers, Richard Whittington-Egan and Jonathan Goodman, when Parry was living in London. Parry would not let the two writers into his home – but then again why should he have trusted two strangers? How many of us would allow into our homes two men who want to accuse us of murder? The two investigators were surprised how much Parry knew. He seemed to know everything about everyone involved in the murder investigation. That in itself does not strike me as odd. The Wallace murder case was a sensational news story of its time. As a work associate of Wallace and a 'friend' of sorts to both Wallace and his wife, he would naturally have taken a great deal of interest in the case and its media coverage, even if he himself was entirely blameless.

Gordon Parry did however give the investigators one snippet of information that was suggestive. He told them that Wallace was 'sexually odd'. What that meant is very hard to tell, but on the whole people in 1931 did not normally discuss their sex lives; it was not the 1960s. The Wallaces seem very unlikely people to have shared this sort of information about themselves in the course of a social conversation, even with someone they regarded as a friend. So, if it was true that William Wallace had unusual sexual tastes, how did Gordon Parry know about them? One possibility is that Parry's relationship with Julia was more than just a friendship. If they were flirting, possibly even more, maybe Julia revealed one of her reasons for being dissatisfied with her husband. It was found that Julia was not wearing normal ladies' underwear when she was killed, but a nappy, and perhaps that was part of the 'oddity' that Parry was referring to.

In 1980, a radio presenter called Roger Wilkes researched the Wallace case. Startlingly, after almost fifty years some new evidence had come to light. A new witness came forward, a car mechanic called John Parkes. He had been given a car to clean by Gordon Parry on the night of the murder. While he was cleaning the interior, he found a bloodstained glove, which Parry snatched away from him, muttering, 'That could hang me'. Parkes did not say anything to the police at the time because he was afraid of Parry, who had a violent streak and a nasty temper. Parry was a dangerous man to cross. Unfortunately, Wilkes made this breakthrough just too late to confront Gordon Parry with it. Parry had died in North Wales a few weeks earlier.

Parry fits the profile of Julia's killer well. He had worked with Wallace and evidently harboured some sort of resentment against him. He had been in the same insurance business and knew about the pattern of collection. The Prudential worked on a weekly cycle that ran from Wednesday to Wednesday. It was not unusual to be storing a significant sum of money in the cash box on a Tuesday night, representing the week's takings, as Wednesday was account day, when the money was banked. If anyone who understood the insurance system was going to rob someone like Wallace, Tuesday night was the night to do it. Julia was murdered on a Tuesday evening. Parry, as a former work associate of Wallace, would have known all about the pattern of takings. As it happened, Parry or whoever else it was, only got away with £4 from Wallace's cash box, but the attack on a Tuesday does not look random. We also know that Parry was a dangerous thug with a criminal record, easily capable of beating someone to death with a poker.

Although it has been alleged that there is something suspicious about Wallace's account of his discovery of Julia's body, there is not. He did not, as the prosecution alleged that Wallace claimed, cross the darkened room, crossing the area where Julia was lying, to turn on the gas lights before he saw the body. In his police statement, Wallace said, 'I then came down and looked into the front room and struck a match and saw my wife lying on the floor.' So there was nothing suspicious about his account.

The wild goose chase looking for Qualtrough's nonexistent house could as easily have been set up by Gordon Parry, to lure Wallace away from his home for a good hour or two, giving Parry time to go in, kill Julia, take whatever money was there and, in effect, frame Wallace for murdering his wife. A marvellous revenge.

Why did Wallace remind the conductor that he wanted to get off at Menlove Gardens? The explanation may be very simple and ordinary. It may be that Wallace had had the bad experience of being whisked past the stop where he wanted to get off, and having to waste time and shoe leather walking back. He was keen not to be late for the appointment. That in turn explains why he kept asking people to verify the time for him: he had an appointment to keep. There is no more to it than that.

But there was a side to Wallace that does generate suspicion. After he was released, but only then, people in Liverpool began to turn against Wallace. It was mainly because of an autobiographical sketch, his *Life Story*, which he had published in the local press. Its style was a distinct contrast to the cool statements he made to the police and at his trial; it was emotional, mawkish and sentimental. The wheedling tone seemed designed to elicit sympathy. He did not get it. A more significant problem was that Wallace's *Life Story* contained details that were untrue or at best extremely misleading, even on matters that were unimportant. A typical detail is the claim that he was brought up in the Lake District. A childhood in Millom on the Duddon estuary hardly qualifies for the Wordsworthian upbringing in the 'glorious country of mountain, lake and fell' which he claimed. It was not a lie, but many reading Wallace's self-account were uneasy at the evident concealments and duplicities. He came across as evasive and devious, someone who had evaded justice.

In *Life Story*, Wallace described the happiest years of his life as beginning in 1911 in Harrogate, where he met his future wife. Wallace was a minor political activist for the Liberal Party, and enjoyed addressing meetings, though he was conscious of his lack of polish, poise and education. At Harrogate, Wallace consciously insinuated himself into literary and artistic circles as part of his programme of self-improvement.

Julia Wallace remains a shadowy figure, and the little that is known about her derives from Wallace's *Life Story* which, in the circumstances, cannot be quoted uncorroborated. He described her as 'a lady of good birth and social position. She was an excellent pianist, no mean artist in watercolour, a fluent French scholar, and of a cultured literary taste.' The reality was that Julia was an unexceptional lower middle class woman of perhaps slightly higher social class than Wallace. As usual, Wallace gilded the lily.

In *Life Story*, Wallace says that he lost his job as Liberal Party agent because of the outbreak of war, but as he was immediately replaced by Mr A. Cotterill, he must have lost his job for some other reason. It may have been that Wallace had fallen into debt, but the crucial fact is that whatever the reason was for losing his job Wallace concealed it. Overall, William Herbert Wallace comes across as a vaguely dislikeable man, a cold, metallic and unsympathetic man.

I do not like thee, Dr Fell;
The reason why I cannot tell:
But this I know, and know full well:
I do not like thee, Dr Fell.

But whatever reservations we may nurse about Wallace as a person, his release on appeal was perfectly proper. The fact that neither the police nor the lawyers could come up with any other suspect at the time does not mean that (by elimination) Wallace must have been the murderer. Now that another suspect has emerged, in the shape of Gordon Parry, Wallace recedes significantly.

The murder of Julia Wallace, with its mysterious, nebulous, unidentifiable Qualtrough lurking in the background, gripped the newspaper readers of the day and has gone on exercising the imaginations of crime writers ever since. It was made into a film in the 1990s, *The Man from the Pru*, starring Jonathan Pryce and Anna Massey. Was Gordon Parry the evil genius behind it all, the envious murderer who killed Julia, who widowed and robbed Wallace and then framed him? Or was Wallace, the cold and cunning Chess Club murderer, the real culprit all along, just as the police believed at the time? Raymond Chandler described the Julia Wallace case as 'unbeatable'. For him it was the perfect murder. No one was ever convicted for it, and still, even after seventy years, it is no nearer being solved.

THE BRIGHTON TRUNK MURDER: ANOTHER PERFECT MURDER?

To murder someone and conceal their body in a trunk is an extraordinary thing to do, simply because detection is certain. Sometimes the identity of the victim is obvious, and sometimes it has to be deduced as a result of forensic investigation. Usually there are enough clues on or in the body to point to a killer. The trunk itself may furnish clues to the killer's identity. A trunk murder is therefore one of the oddest crimes, almost a self-advertizing crime, an exhibitionist crime.

The senior police officer in Brighton was optimistic of success when on 17 June 1934 he went to the left-luggage office at Brighton station to look at the naked torso of a woman. The remains had just been discovered in a plywood trunk. The clerks could remember nothing about the man who had left the trunk there on Derby Day, which was ten days earlier, on 6 June. It had been the busiest day of the year.

Even so there seemed to be lots of clues. The renowned pathologist and forensic expert Sir Bernard Spilsbury

360

looked at the human remains, which were incomplete. She had been a young woman, probably in her early twenties. Her general physical condition suggested that she belonged to the middle or upper classes; she was well nourished, with a good figure, no slack flesh, and well-toned muscles that implied plenty of exercise. The golden brown of the skin also suggested that she could afford to spend a good deal of time in lower latitudes; that suggested wealth. At the time of her death she had been pregnant.

The Brighton police sent out an alert to all other left-luggage offices in England to search for mysterious abandoned packages. At King's Cross station in London, the young woman's legs were found in a suitcase. Each leg had been severed at the thigh and the knee, and they were the legs of a well-proportioned and athletic young woman. Some clues were emerging as significant. The body had been wrapped in brown paper and on one sheet was the suffix '-ford'. It looked as if it was the second half of a place-name, perhaps Guildford. In the trunk, there were two newspapers, copies of the *Daily Mail* for 31 May and 2 June. They were of an edition only circulated within fifty miles of London.

Then a porter remembered helping a man to carry the trunk on Derby Day. The man had travelled from Dartford to Brighton. Dartford was a place name ending in 'ford' and it was a place where the London edition of the *Daily Mail* might be bought. It began to look as though the murderer was a Dartford man. It also began to look as though the case was about to be solved. A girl who had sat in the same train compartment as the man from Dartford was able to give a general description of him. Five cheap day returns had been bought that day, and the ones that could be traced were eliminated by the police. The makers of the trunk and the suitcase were traced, but they were unable to connect the items with particular purchasers. Suddenly the trail had gone stone cold. There were no more leads.

The pathologist said the young woman had died on about 30 May, a week before the trunk was left at Brighton station. The man who killed her must have had plenty of spare time, and presumably a home where he could safely conceal a body for a whole week without detection; this would have to be a man with a large property or a single man who had (and expected) no visitors. The fact that a whole week went by before the body was dumped suggested that the murder was not premeditated; the disposal of the body had not been planned, and it had taken several days for the murderer to work out how to do it. A certain amount of reconstruction was possible.

A fairly well-off, strong and athletic man had a secret love affair with a rather similar girl – also well-off, strong and athletic. He lived in Dartford, in the stockbroker belt. The girl became pregnant. On 30 May she called on him to ask him what to do about it. His reactions perhaps revealed that he had no serious intention of marrying her. There was a quarrel, perhaps developing into a fight, and he hit her over the head with something heavy that happened to be to hand. The young woman's head was never found, but there were no injuries to the rest of the body, so it can be assumed that she died of some head injury.

The man was severely shaken by the girl's death, which he never intended or wished – he probably loved her and was very distressed at what had happened, but could not face the exposure of the affair or the accusation that he had murdered the girl. He needed time to decide how to dispose of the body. He decided to dismember it. He deposited the trunk in Brighton, travelling on a third-class ticket so as to lose himself in the crowd and not be remembered by witnesses. He deposited the suitcase containing the girls' legs at King's Cross. Probably after that, he left the country, knowing that it was only a matter of days before the body parts would be discovered.

In theory, the crime should have been solved by finding out which Dartford resident emigrated immediately after Derby Day. The sports clubs and riding stables of the Dartford area would almost certainly reveal both the missing man and the missing woman. In reality, the police investigation revealed nothing whatever that led to the Brighton trunk murderer. None of the obvious leads led anywhere at all. Careful searching of left-luggage offices did not reveal the whereabouts of the young woman's head, which was never found – though they did uncover the bodies of three children, opening up other murder enquiries. From that day to this, the Brighton trunk murder has never been solved. There is not even so much as the name of a suspect or the name of the victim.

THE SINISTER GP: DR JOHN BODKIN ADAMS

In July 1983, an elderly retired doctor died in Hove. A lot of retired people, especially from a genteel profession like his, end up in Hove. But this was no ordinary doctor. This eighty-four-year-old general practitioner was firmly believed by the police to be nothing less than a serial killer, and not only that but a serial killer who had successfully eluded the law for decades.

Because the law of libel is framed as it is, it was only after the old man had died that the newspapers were able to open their dossiers about Dr John Bodkin Adams and level the accusations anew. It was rather like the flood of revelations about Robert Maxwell that followed his death; while he lived, few journalists were prepared to risk litigation to tell what they knew. In a smaller and less sensational way, biographers had to wait until Sir Laurens van der Post was dead before the shadier side of his past, which had long been known about, could safely be revealed.

Dr Adams had been tried at the Old Bailey for the murder of one of his patients, a seventy-two-year-old widow called Edith Morrell. If he had been convicted on that charge, he would certainly have been charged with further murders. Two more charges had been confidently prepared and the Crown Prosecution Service believed they had enough evidence to bring successful prosecutions in another three cases. The police, in other words, were sure that Adams had murdered at least six of his patients. Some officers believed the figure was nine or maybe even as high as twenty-five. Detective Superintendent Charles Hewitt of Scotland Yard believed quite early on in the investigation that the death toll had been that high.

But at the Old Bailey, only the one case was ever discussed or fought over. Dr Adams was acquitted after a classic legal duel between two barristers, Sir Reginald Manningham-Buller, the Attorney General, and Adams's defence lawyer, Geoffrey Lawrence.

Geoffrey Lawrence was a thorough-going professional. He disliked his client, thoroughly disliked him in fact, but took his side ferociously and uncompromisingly in the courtroom. His adversary, Sir Reginald Manningham-Buller, was sure he could destroy Adams once he had him in the witness box. Lawrence's advice to Adams was to remain silent and avoid cross-examination. The counsel for the prosecution and the police believed that that was what saved Adams from the death sentence. Manningham-Buller had staked everything on cross-questioning Adams, and when the opportunity was not given to him the basis for the prosecution case collapsed. The jury therefore more or less had to acquit. After a forty-five minute deliberation, that was their verdict – and Adams walked free.

The Adams trial was such a disaster that the Director of Public Prosecutions had no confidence that any of the other similar charges could be made to stick either, so he announced that there would be no further action. It was, in the view of the police who had collected the evidence, a disaster for British justice. A dangerous multiple murderer had gone unpunished: worse still, he had been released.

As was customary in all cases in the English courts, the jury had no knowledge about the many parallel cases that were very similar to Edith Morell's, and also ended with the victim's death. If they had known that the police had investigated as many as 400 possibly suspicious deaths with which Adams had been associated, they would almost certainly have been less willing to give him the benefit of the doubt. A recent case that has some similarities is that of Dr Harold Shipman, another patient-slaying doctor. But Adams was a different sort of killer from Shipman; Adams killed purely and simply for financial gain. He got the old ladies to change their wills in his favour, and then he killed them.

Over a period of thirty-five years in general practice in Eastbourne, Dr Adams had been named as a beneficiary in the wills of as many as 132 of his patients. Most of the bequests were modest, but in all he had amassed £45,000 in cash, which would be worth perhaps ten times as much today, something approaching £500,000. He had also been left jewellery, silver, furniture and cars, including two Rolls Royces.

It could be argued that a sympathetic doctor with a good bedside manner and a genuine concern for his elderly patients might well be acknowledged in the wills of old ladies, especially old ladies with no-one else to leave their money to. There need not be anything sinister about the matter. There need not be anything exactly sinister about it even if Adams himself had dropped heavy hints about wills or openly asked the old ladies to change their wills in his favour. The key question is – did he kill them?

He was certainly a very popular doctor in Eastbourne, and had made the care of the elderly his speciality ever since he was a young doctor. He arrived in Eastbourne almost straight from medical school in Northern Ireland. He was an unprepossessing little man, only five foot five inches tall, but weighing eighteen stone. His face was pink and fleshy, with small eyes and thin lips. His flabby chin spilled out over the celluloid collars he liked to wear. He looked like Mr Toad. There was no doubt about it – John Bodkin Adams was ugly. Yet he managed to charm all his old ladies. He stroked their hands and even combed their hair for them.

The year-long investigation by Sergeant Hewitt and his superior officer, Detective Chief Superintendent Bert Hannam of the Murder Squad, was to show that there was a much darker side to Adams than the tender loving care that he liked everyone to see. He prescribed addictive drugs for his elderly patients and made them dependent on the drugs. He in effect turned his genteel old ladies into morphine and heroin addicts. Because he was the supplier, their dependency on the drugs could very easily be turned into dependency upon him. He was then able to alter their wills in his favour. Once that was done, he was able to ease them gently on their way out of this world by administering an overdose of the drugs they craved.

The Murder Squad's investigation showed that for all the patients for whom Adams signed death certificates sixty-eight per cent were alleged (according to what he wrote on the certificates) to have died of cerebral haemorrhage or cerebral thrombosis. This was a very high percentage – incredibly high.

Well before the outbreak of the Second World War there was gossip going round Eastbourne that Adams did his rounds with a bottle of morphia in one pocket and a blank will form in the other. In 1936, Dr Adams had a windfall from the will of Mrs Alice Whitton, who left him £3,000, a large sum then. Mrs Whitton's niece contested the will, but the court decided in Adams's favour and he kept the money. The gossip in Eastbourne continued through the 1940s and into the 1950s. Dr Adams's racket was an open secret. But it was not until 1956 that the police decided to investigate and then the circumstantial evidence started to build up. The problem was that most of the evidence was circumstantial.

There was the case of William Mawhood, where Adams made a bad miscalculation. He reckoned without Mrs Mawhood. William Mawhood was a wealthy steel merchant and also a long-standing friend of Adams. He had lent Adams £3,000 to buy his first house. When Mr Mawhood was dying, Adams visited him and asked his wife Edith to leave them alone for a moment. She was suspicious and listened outside the door to what was being said. It was just as well she did. She heard Adams telling her husband to leave his estate to him, Adams, and he would look after her.

Edith Mawhood was incensed. She burst back into the room, grabbed her walking stick and struck out at the wicked doctor, chasing him round the bed. He scuttled out of the room and down the stairs. Mrs Mawhood threw her stick down the stairs after him. She missed her target and broke a flower vase instead. She shouted after him to get out of the house. She never wanted to see him there again.

It was scandalous behaviour on Dr Adams's part, and he might perhaps have been charged with unprofessional conduct and maybe even struck off for it. But it was a far cry from that level of misbehaviour to proving that Dr Adams would have hastened the death of his other patients. Dr Adams was obviously a very nasty character, but was he a murderer?

The case of Emily Mortimer was similar to the Mawhood case. In the Mortimer family there was a strict tradition by which the family members intended to keep the family fortune intact. Whenever a Mortimer died, the bulk of the estate was divided among the surviving members of the family. In that way, each time there was a death, the money was recycled within the family. Adams persuaded Emily Mortimer to make a break with tradition. The year she died, she changed her will, transferring £3,000 worth of shares from the family (who would have been expecting that sum) to the doctor. Shortly before she died, she changed her will again so that Adams received £5,000 and the Mortimer family was cut out of the will altogether. Emily Mortimer's death certificate gave as the cause of death 'cerebral thrombosis'.

There was a rather different case of two old ladies who owned the house that they lived in. Adams persuaded them to sell their house and move into a flat – for the good of their health, he argued. He refused to hand over the money he made from the house sale until two years later, and then only when forced to do so by a writ.

The police investigation was very thorough. The Murder Squad had obtained statements from local solicitors and bank managers, which showed Dr Adams's intense concern with the wills of his patients. There were many irregularities. Adams was making visits to banks with his patients to oversee the changes he wanted them to make to their wills. He was making phone calls to solicitors demanding that they come out immediately to change a will or draw up a new one. There was even one patient who was so near to unconsciousness that he could only sign his changed will with a cross. There were also several changes of wills to stipulate cremation instead of burial, which could only have been made so that there could be no exhumation later on to test for levels of morphine or other drugs in the body.

One of the most damning findings of all was the sequence of thirty-two cheques payable to Dr Adams, totalling £18,000, and all drawn out of one old lady's account during the last few days of her life. The signatures also looked as if they had been forged, presumably by Dr Adams.

But all of this was circumstantial evidence, evidence of Adams's way of thinking, evidence of his determination to get his hands on his patients' money. What evidence did the police manage to find of murder?

They did manage to find evidence that some of the death certificates contained information that Dr Adams must have known was untrue. Clara McNeill-Miller was an elderly single lady who had lived with her sister Hilda for thirteen years. When Hilda died, she left everything to Clara. About a year afterwards, Clara too died, leaving nearly everything to Adams. The sum amounted to £5,000. Three years later the bodies were exhumed and post mortems were carried out. Clara had not died of coronary thrombosis as Adams had written on the death certificate, but of pneumonia. This was odd in itself, but then the police were able to interview one of the other guests in the rest home. This is what she told the police:

Dr Adams was called to Miss Clara the night before she died. She was suffering from influenza. He remained in her bedroom for nearly forty-five minutes before leaving. I later became worried as I heard nothing from the room. I opened the door and was horrified by what I saw.

This was a cold winter's night. The bedclothes on her bed had been pulled back and thrown over the bedrail at the base. Her nightdress had been folded back across her body to her neck. All the bedroom windows had been flung open. A cold gush of wind was sweeping through the room. That is how the doctor left her.

It was now very clear to the police from this vital witness evidence that Adams had tried to accelerate the death of Clara Neil-Miller – and probably succeeded. She died the day after this ordeal. The police also found that in the weeks running up to her death Clara had made out large cheques to Adams; these could not have been for medical treatment or medicines.

Adams also had a financial interest in the residential home where Clara died. He sent many of his patients there. Mrs Sharp, the woman who ran it, was likely to be able to advance the police enquiry significantly. Hewitt remembered her later. 'Mrs Sharp was on the point of talking when we left Eastbourne for a week's conferences with the Attorney General in London. She was the witness we needed. She knew much of what went on between Adams and his patients. She knew where the bodies were buried and she was scared. When we left, she was about to crack.'

Hewitt was sure that with just one more interview, Mrs Sharp would reveal a lot more. He was devastated to find that she had died while he was away in London, and drew the obvious conclusion: that Adams had got to her, killed her, silenced her. Experienced as he was, Hewitt was unable to pin any of this on Adams. By the time Hewitt got back to Eastbourne, only a week after leaving, Elizabeth Sharp was dead and cremated – on Dr John Bodkin Adams's orders. Hewitt sensed that Adams had played a key role in Elizabeth Sharp's death but was unable to prove a thing.

Julia Bradnum was another of Adams's patients. She was a strong and healthy eighty-two-year-old, but woke up one morning with a pain in her stomach. Dr Adams was called and stayed in the room with her for five minutes, presumably administering drugs. Ten minutes later she was dead, presumably of a drugs overdose. Julia Bradnum's body was later exhumed, but it was by then too badly decomposed to show anything other than that she did not die of cerebral haemorrhage, which is what Dr Adams had written on his certificate. Julia Bradnum was, of course, leaving money in her will to Dr Adams, He had been there only a few weeks earlier with a new will for her to sign.

Harriet Maud Hughes was another of Dr Adams's patients. She was a mere sixty-six when she died. Adams had only begun to treat her three months before she died. Once again, he declared on the death certificate that death was due to 'cerebral thrombosis'. She spoke of changing her will in his favour. She became seriously ill a few weeks before she died, then recovered just enough to make a trip to the bank with her doctor, who asked the bank manager to make him the executor of her will. Afterwards, she said to her domestic, 'You should have seen the bank manager's face. He was most surprised at my choice of executor.' She made two codicils to her will. One was the instruction that she should be cremated. The other was a bequest of £2,000 to Mr and Mrs Thurston, two friends of Adams, but police later discovered that Adams actually took 90 per cent of this sum, giving the Thurstons a 10 per cent 'commission' for the use of their name.

Another Adams case (unusually a male patient) was a well-heeled retired bank manager, James Downs, who nine times during the last few days of his life tried to put his signature to a will. On the tenth occasion, Mr Downs succeeded in writing a cross, but only with Dr Adams guiding his hand across the paper. It almost goes without saying that the will in question left Dr Adams £1,000 richer. Mr Downs was being treated for a broken ankle, but under Dr Adams's care he quickly went into a coma and within a month he was dead.

Another case was a widow called Annabelle Kilgour. She had been ill for several weeks, during which time she was being looked after by a State Registered Nurse, Miss Osgood. Adams arrived one night and announced to the nurse that he would give Mrs Kilgour an injection to help her get a good night's rest. Miss Osgood watched helplessly as Adams gave Mrs Kilgour what she could see was an excessively large dose. Adams said, 'That will keep her quiet.' Then he left. Mrs Kilgour fell immediately into a coma and died the following morning. He had certainly kept her quiet.

Adams returned to the scene and the nurse told him bluntly that he had been responsible for killing Mrs Kilgour. She later told the police, 'I have never seen a man look so frightened in all my life.' Adams signed the death certificate in his usual way: the death, he wrote, was caused by cerebral haemorrhage. It would have been more accurate to write, 'death was caused by me.' Adams's behaviour was flagrant. He was quite openly killing his patients, one after another, sometimes even in front of witnesses.

Another case was Margaret Pilling, who was suffering from nothing worse than flu when Dr Adams was called out, but within a fortnight she had fallen into a coma. Her family insisted she should stay with them. Her daughter, Irene Richardson, afterwards said that they imagined their mother was dying of cancer and that the doctor was being kind by not telling them the diagnosis. But they quickly realized that things were not as they should be, and called a family conference. The decided that the treatment was unsatisfactory. In particular they were unhappy that their mother was so heavily drugged and that her condition was worsening fast. Irene Richardson and her family decided to take Mrs Pilling away to a house at Ascot, and she began to improve. Irene Richardson later said, 'Had I not taken her away, I am sure she would have died.'

In this instance, one of Dr Adams's patients survived, but only because she was taken out of his clutches before he could kill her. Case after case pointed to Dr John Bodkin Adams as a murderer. The police and the Director of Public Prosecution's office were spoilt for choice. For the police, the clinching case was that of Bobbie Hullett, Bobbie was a lively forty-nine year old widow. It seems likely that Adams first killed her husband, Jack, in 1955. Jack Hullett was a retired Lloyds underwriter who had developed a heart condition. Adams gave him a dose of morphia and Jack Hullett died seven hours later, leaving £700 to Adams and the rest to Bobbie. Bobbie was grief-stricken and the friendly doctor was on hand to give her sympathy and drugs to help her sleep. The doses Adams prescribed were excessive and it was noticeable that Bobbie was staggering under the effects of the drug when she got up in the morning.

The comedian Leslie Henson was a close friend of Bobbie Hullett's and he was distressed to see her disintegrating under the effect of the addictive drugs. Henson and his wife invited her to their house, to try to get her away from the source of the problem, but she had to go back – for more drugs. Another of her friends was the Chief Constable, Mr Walker. When Bobbie died, both he and Leslie Henson were very upset, and Walker was in a strong position to make discreet enquiries. Walker found that a few days before Bobbie Hullett fell into a coma she had given Adams a cheque for £1,000, and that Adams had fed this into his bank account within hours. By this stage Adams had accumulated £35,000 in his bank accounts and a further £125,000 in investments.

The coroner's inquest on Bobbie Hullett did not go well for Dr Adams. The coroner asked him why he had not told his medical practice partner about the patient's history of depression. Why had he not put his patient into a nursing home? Why had he not called in a psychiatrist? Why had he stuck to his diagnosis of cerebral haemorrhage after a pathologist had suggested poisoning might be involved? The coroner was unimpressed by Adams's answers, commenting on 'an extraordinary degree of carelessness'. The reality was much worse than carelessness, and the inquest did not take that critical next step, which was to accuse Adams of killing Bobbie Hullett.

As events turned out, when the case against Adams was assembled, the prosecution decided to focus not on the death of Bobbie Hullett but on the death of Edith Morrell, the seventy-two-year-old widow of a Liverpool shipping merchant, instead. The prosecution lawyers chose this case because they thought it was a very clear-cut and obvious case of murder, though the police investigators – Sergeant Hewitt especially – were alarmed by the choice as they thought other cases were stronger, especially those where there were bodies to supply forensic evidence. Mrs Morrell's body had been destroyed; it had been cremated. This meant that there was no possibility of bringing in Francis Camps, the foremost forensic scientist of his time.

It was Manningham-Buller's decision, and he made it against the advice of his junior counsel, Melford Stevenson, and against the advice of Mr Leck at the Director of Public Prosecutions' office. Manningham-Buller knew John Bodkin Adams was a very frightened man and could easily be worn down in the witness stand. In the event, Adams did not take the stand and therefore escaped being reduced by Manningham-Buller. Manningham-Buller completely miscalculated the situation, bungled the prosecution of one of the worst and most flagrant serial killers of the twentieth century, and must be held responsible for letting him get off scot-free.

The trial of Dr John Bodkin Adams opened on 25 April 1957. This was six years after the death of Mrs Morrell, which in itself took the edge off the evidence. The prosecution brought witnesses who gave evidence that over a period of six weeks Adams had prescribed a huge quantity of drugs: more than 4,000 grains of barbiturate and heroin. The standard recommended maximum daily dosage of morphia was a quarter grain, yet in the final day of Mrs Morrell's life Adams injected eighteen grains. The witnesses were giving strong evidence that Adams had administered a huge drug overdose – one that he must have known would be fatal.

This damning evidence was nevertheless overturned by Adams's defence counsel, Geoffrey Lawrence. He had managed to find the nurses' daily record books. These seemed to show that the nurses' memories were at fault; in the six years that had passed they had exaggerated the doses of drugs Dr Adams had administered. They may have thought they were improving the case against Adams, but they were in effect ensuring his release. Geoffrey Lawrence then played his trump card, which was not to put Adams in the dock. He made it appear that there was no case for him to answer, and denied Manningham-Buller the chance to break Adams down by aggressive cross-questioning. The case against Adams – at least as far as the death of Mrs Morrell was concerned – just fell apart.

To the huge disappointment of the police investigators, who knew that Adams had killed dozens of elderly people, Adams was acquitted. But irregularities had been uncovered about Adams's professional life that could still be pursued. Three months after he was acquitted, Adams was in the dock at Lewes Assizes on fourteen minor charges over matters such as forging National Health Service prescriptions and bad record keeping in relation to dangerous drugs. The police were determined, at the very least, to remove Dr Adams from general practice. He pleaded guilty to these charges, perhaps hoping that the investigation would stop there, and he was right.

Adams was fined £2,400. Later in the year he was struck off by the General Medical Council. This meant that he was no longer able to practise. Remarkably and inexplicably, on 22 November 1961, Adams was allowed back onto the medical register. The police had not forgotten that he was an unconvicted serial killer, and the Home Office had not forgotten either; the Home Office refused to give him a licence to dispense drugs.

People in general, though, seemed to have short memories. Dr John Bodkin Adams, who should by this stage have been hanged as a murderer and buried in an unmarked grave, was back in business and his practice in Eastbourne gradually picked up. Almost astonishingly, in 1965 a grateful patient left him £2,000 in her will. Now Adams really was back in business. Somehow, and perhaps uniquely in legal history, Adams completely escaped retribution. He retired to Hove and eventually died there, a constant living reminder to a frustrated police force and legal profession that he had got the better of them. He even had a brass plate placed outside his front door flaunting his continuing presence: 'John Bodkin Adams, MD. At home 5 p.m. to 7 p.m.'

Judge Melford Stevenson reminisced about the case in his later years to his friend the novelist Kingsley Amis. 'How many did he do?' Amis asked. 'The police knew he'd done thirty-two,' Melford Stevenson said emphatically. 'There was some doubt about number thirty-three, his mother.'

Dr John Bodkin Adams was that very rare being, the serial killer who got away with murder, and in spite of being identified by the authorities got away with it over and over again. The terrible crimes he committed remain officially unsolved, simply because officially they were never committed in the first place. There were no crimes. Officially, all of Adams's victims died as he stated on their death certificates. Their relatives were often uneasy, and in many cases they were certain murder had been done. The police were certain murder was being done. Looking back on that time from a vantage point fifty years on, we can be certain that murder in cold blood was committed over and over again. Yet, officially, because of loopholes in the law, those deaths remain unsolved crimes.

THE GOLD-DIGGER, THE DUKE AND THE PLAYBOY: SIR HARRY OAKES

On the night of 7–8 July 1943 on Nassau in the Bahamas, Sir Harry Oakes was brutally murdered in his bed. A storm raged that night, and heavy rain coming in through the open bedroom window doused the flames that engulfed his body. At seven o'clock in the morning, Harold Christie, one of his friends, discovered Sir Harry's badly burnt remains. He had been murdered and his body soaked in petrol before being set on fire. There was a lacquered Chinese screen close to the bed; it was partly burnt and also covered in bloody handprints. Although some of the body was charred, the head was not, and it was clear from the blood and injuries there that Sir Harry had been bludgeoned to death before being set on fire.

Christie was both shocked and puzzled. The self-made millionaire Harry Oakes was generous and well liked. Who would have wanted to do this to him? Harry Oakes was a member of the social elite on Nassau, which included the Duke of Windsor, then Governor of the Bahamas. There was a great deal of speculation about the identity of the murderer. Suspicions surrounded a range of people, from a notorious Mafia boss to a flamboyant French playboy. Really it is only possible to understand what happened, or may have happened, by examining Sir Harry Oakes's colourful life.

Harry Oakes was born in 1874, the third of the five children of Edith and William Pitt Oakes of Sangerville, Maine. As a boy, Harry daydreamed about striking it rich one day. He went to Syracuse Medical School, but he was still gripped by the idea of acquiring wealth. He became obsessed with news of a Klondike gold rush, and in 1896 abandoned his medical studies to go off and look for gold. When he reached the Klondike, the gold rush was petering out, and he fell back on work as a medical assistant. He was shipwrecked off the Alaskan coast and for a time imprisoned by the Russians. After these adventures, Oakes went to Australia, working his passage as a deck-hand. Then he went to New Zealand and California, each time failing to find gold. He encountered many hard and unscrupulous men, which made him more self-reliant and tough but also increasingly bitter.

In 1911, Oakes went to Swastika in Ontario, Canada, following a rumour of gold. He lodged with Roza Brown, a strikingly ugly, smelly and foul woman who held prospectors in contempt but for some reason took a liking to Harry Oakes. She knew a little about the geography and geology of the area and gave him some tips. In 1912, in collaboration with the four Tough brothers and acting on

Roza's advice, Oakes began digging at Kirkland Lake. This time he struck gold. Inevitably a quarrel broke out about the distribution of shares in the gold, and eventually Oakes sold his shares. Oakes decided to mine underneath the lake itself. He was funded by his mother and he again struck gold. Suddenly he was rich. His Lake Shore Mines became one of the biggest producers of gold in the Western Hemisphere, and Oakes was earning $60,000 a day, quickly becoming the richest man in Canada. He gave generous shares in his mining company to family members and friends, and they became rich, too.

In 1919, Harry Oakes built himself a chateau over-looking his mines, quickly adjusting to the lifestyle of the very wealthy. But he was also restless. In 1923, he set off round the world. During the cruise he met a young Australian woman called Eunice MacIntyre. She was tall, elegant, sensitive, attractive, twenty-four. He was forty-eight and in many ways her antithesis; nevertheless they fell in love. When they reached Sydney they married. Over the following years they had five children and they acquired Canadian citizenship. In the late 1930s, Oakes changed citizenship again, becoming a Bahamian when he moved to Nassau to avoid taxation.

Harry Oakes's arrival on Nassau transformed the island's economy. He bought up half the property on the island and started developing it, building mansions, an airport, a country club and a golf course. Oakes often came across as a difficult and truculent man, but he was at the same time very generous, giving large sums to help the island economy, easing unemployment and building a new wing on the hospital. He also funded training schemes for the islanders, to help them get work. This display of civic responsibility led to Oakes's knighthood in 1939.

But there were other rich and successful islanders on Nassau, and maybe we should look to them as potential suspects for his murder. One of Oakes's social circle was the Governor of the Bahamas, the Duke of Windsor, the ex-King Edward VIII of England. With him was his new Duchess, the profoundly dissatisfied and bitter Wallis Simpson, who looked on her stay in the Bahamas as a kind of exile; she found life there very dull and hated the heat. Another irritation was the small allowance offered by the British government to refurbish the government house they were to live in. The Windsors nevertheless threw lavish parties which ran up enormous bills. There was a presumption that the Duke was getting money from other sources. One source says that he received more than two million dollars from Axel Wenner-Gren.

Wenner-Gren was another wealthy Bahamian with a shadowy past. He made friends with the Windsors, but this relationship was to cause them problems because he had links with the Nazis. He was a Berlin-educated Swede who had worked for a light-bulb company in New York. He had converted his sales commissions into shares, which then sharply increased in value. He eventually gained control, buying out the company. He set up other companies in Germany and by 1939 he was worth an estimated $100 million. He was able to buy himself an enormous yacht in which he set sail for the Bahamas at the outbreak of the Second World War. With his American wife and children, he set up home on Nassau, living in a mansion called Shangri-La.

While on Nassau, Wenner-Gren made friends with the Duke and Duchess and Sir Harry Oakes. He was also a close friend of Hermann Goering, and it is possible that this relationship made it possible for Sweden to remain on good terms with Germany and retain its neutrality. Wenner-Gren boasted that he was a friend of Mussolini too. Wenner-Gren was on lists of suspect people in both Washington and London; both the Americans and the British believed him to be a spy. They also believed Wenner–Gren was working his way towards controlling the economy of Mexico. As a result, agents of Britain and the United States froze his bank accounts while his activities were investigated. Wenner-Gren was obliged to stay in Mexico, as it was no longer safe for him to return to the Bahamas. During the investigation, it was found that he had financial dealings with Sir Harry Oakes, Harold Christie and the Duke of Windsor.

Harold Christie was born and brought up on Nassau, and started out poor. He acted as a selling agent for property on the island, persuading his employers to give him commission in land rather than money. In time, the value of the land increased and Christie was able to use the profits to buy larger plots. Christie rapidly became very wealthy. It was Christie who sold Harry Oakes more than half the property on Nassau, which gave him an enormous profit. Christie enjoyed his personal wealth, but he also had a vision for the development of Nassau, hoping to increase the tourist trade. He particularly wanted to open up the air service from Miami to Nassau and build more hotels. Christie and Oakes were really very similar in their ambitions and methods, and they quickly became friends.

There were other businessmen, mainly American, who were interested in developing Nassau, but with less altruistic motives. One of them was Frank Marshall, whom Christie met in the early 1940s. He represented a group of American businessmen who wanted to open gambling casinos on Nassau. Marshall knew that the law prohibited casinos, but also knew that Oakes and the Duke of Windsor could have the law changed; Marshall thought Christie would act as a go-between, to facilitate the legalization of gambling. Christie thought the casinos would be profitable, but that it was unlikely the law would change. Christie gradually discovered that the American investors represented by Marshall were connected with Lucky Luciano, the Mafia boss. This worried Christie enormously. In spite of this anxiety, Marshall talked Christie into agreeing to discuss the casino proposal with Oakes and the Duke. Marshall realized that Christie was not interested enough to argue his case convincingly, so he arranged to meet Oakes and the Duke in person shortly afterwards. Marshall was disappointed to find that Christie had indeed spoken to them, but had persuaded them not to support the idea. In fact Oakes and the Duke were opposed to the idea anyway. Marshall became irritated, tried to persuade the three men that there was a lot of money to be made, and was put under increasing pressure from his American associates to bring off the deal. It may be the mounting pressure over the casino deal that led directly to Oakes's murder.

Another member of Sir Harry Oakes's social circle was Count Marie Alfred Fouquereaux de Marigny. He came from Mauritius to Nassau shortly before the Second World War. He liked to dissociate himself from his aristocratic pedigree. He liked to be called Freddie de Marigny. He shared Oakes's love of adventure. Freddie ran a profitable chicken farm on the island, and also owned several apartment blocks. He enjoyed yacht racing, and won almost every race he entered at the Nassau Yacht Club.

Freddie was divorced from his first wife, separated from his second, and regarded as an eligible playboy. He had a lively social life and was seen with a different woman on his arm every time he went out partying. He was good-looking, six foot five, charming. He stood out from the other Nassau residents and was both liked and disliked for this reason. At a ball, Freddie met Nancy, the red-haired seventeen-year-old eldest daughter of Sir Harry Oakes. Freddie knew Sir Harry and Lady Oakes would not approve, and the relationship developed in secret. When

Nancy was eighteen, they flew to New York for a secret wedding. Nancy de Marigny phoned her parents to tell them. They were shocked and angry, upset that they had been completely excluded. The Oakeses had little choice other than to accept the situation, and accept Freddie into their family.

This was very difficult, as Sir Harry knew that Freddie had already had two wives, divorced both of them, and was a terrible womanizer. Sir Harry did not keep these feeling to himself, either. On several occasions, Freddie de Marigny and Harry Oakes were seen quarrelling in public. The whole of Nassau knew that Oakes and de Marigny were at loggerheads. The rift between the two men could have led to Sir Harry's murder.

When Harold Christie found the body he made several phone calls for help. He tried a neighbour, who did not answer, and then his brother Frank. Christie asked Frank to call a doctor out immediately. When he hung up, there was an incoming call from a reporter called Etienne Dupuch, who had an appointment for an interview later that day. Christie was still in a state of shock and shrieked at the reporter, 'He's dead! He's been shot!' The reporter naturally made the most of his story and the headline swiftly went via the news agency round the world. The Duke of Windsor hoped to confine news of the murder to the island, but thanks to Christie was unsuccessful, but he immediately blocked any further news about the case for the next two days.

Perhaps the Duke of Windsor was conscious that this was potentially a scandal that could ensnare him. A thorough police investigation might reveal his own as well as Sir Harry's financial wheeling and dealing. For whatever reason, the Duke took complete control of the investigation. His first initiative was to sidestep the Bahamas Criminal Investigation Department and the Nassau Police Department. He instead·brought in two detectives from Miami to lead the investigation. Naturally, once the news leaked out that the Duke had tried to stifle news of the investigation and also had overridden his own police departments, there was widespread suspicion about his motives.

The Miami detectives, James Barker and Edward Melchen, were chosen by the Duke because they were regarded as two of the best fingerprint experts in the United States. Melchen had also served as the Duke's personal bodyguard and the Duke had been impressed by his resourcefulness and loyalty. It was said that the Duke's brief to the two men was that they should confirm that the death was a suicide. If that is so, it is peculiar because he was well aware that Oakes had been murdered. It was an inauspicious beginning to what was one of the worst murder investigations of modern times.

Barker and Melchen arrived at the Oakeses' house a few hours after the murder. They found a bizarre scene: Sir Harry Oakes lying on the bed on his back, half burnt and covered in feathers from his pillow. The left side of his head was covered in blood, which ran from four dents in his scalp down towards his nose. The direction of blood flow showed that when the blows were delivered Sir Harry was lying face down, or indeed sitting with his head leaning forwards, perhaps while reading a book. The Chinese screen stood by the bed, covered in blood and fingerprints. The wall beside the bed carried a single bloody handprint. There were muddy footprints on the stairs up to the bedroom. Not only was it very obviously a murder, not a suicide, but there looked to be more than adequate forensic material to identify the murderer.

Unfortunately, the two detectives had left behind in Miami their camera for taking photographs of latent fingerprints, which straight away reduced the amount of information they were able to collect from the crime scene. Another error of judgement was to allow into the house several of Nassau's social elite to see the room where the body was found, once it had been removed. No trouble was taken to stop these sightseers from handling objects at the crime scene.

Sir Harry was murdered while his family was away on holiday. His wife was waiting for him to arrive at another property they owned in Maine, where he was expected to arrive the day after the discovery of the body. The children were travelling round North America. Only one member of the family could possibly have been a murder suspect.

The detectives interviewed Harold Christie, who had slept in the next bedroom on the night of the murder. He claimed he had not heard any unusual or suspicious sounds on the night of the murder. This seems extraordinary. There had clearly been a struggle between Oakes and his killer, he had been hit over the head four times, petrol had been splashed about, and a small fire started. It is hard to believe Harold Christie heard nothing at all.

The detectives also interviewed Freddie de Marigny. After that, they resumed their search for fingerprints and found their best piece of evidence, a fingerprint on the screen, which Barker claimed belonged to the murderer. It belonged to Freddie, who was charged with murdering his father-in-law and taken to Nassau jail. There was a surge of anger and hatred on the island directed at Freddie de Marigny. The Duke ordered the fire brigade to stand by the jailhouse to protect him if necessary.

Freddie's wife Nancy, the daughter of Sir Harry, thought the idea that Freddie would or could kill her father was ridiculous. She knew him very well, and considered him incapable of committing a crime like that. Nancy recruited her own detective, Raymond Schindler, to prove that Freddie was innocent. The detective agreed on condition that Freddie agreed to submit to a lie detector test. Freddie agreed; Schindler found a fingerprint and lie detector expert, Professor Keeler, and flew with him to Nassau.

When Schindler and Keeler arrived at the crime scene, they were staggered to fine police officers there scrubbing the bedroom walls – they had removed the bloody handprint by the bed. They had no idea whose handprint it was. Schindler asked why they were destroying fingerprint evidence, and the policemen answered that they were not Freddie de Marigny's and therefore were of no interest. Either the Nassau police were unbelievably incompetent or someone had specifically given the order to destroy evidence that pointed to the true murderer. Someone in authority was protecting the murderer and concealing his identity.

Barker had taken photographs of the walls in the bedroom, including the single bloody handprint. He flew back to Miami with the plates to have them developed. Those plates were destroyed by accidental exposure to light, so the identity of the owner of the hand that left the bloody handprint could now never be established.

Meanwhile, the body of Sir Harry Oakes was shipped aboard a plane to Bar Harbour for burial, but the plane had to return to Nassau so that Barker could take new photographs of Sir Harry's fingerprints. These fingerprints were essential so that any prints at the crime scene that were Sir Harry's could be eliminated. But at the same time, the crime scene was being cleansed of fingerprints, so collecting Sir Harry's prints was pointless. It is not known who gave the order for the removal of the fingerprints. Schindler suspected that someone powerful was manipulating the situation. He suspected that his phone was being tapped. To test this out, Schindler dialled an unknown number and said he would meet the person at a particular location. He thought whoever was tapping his phone would show up at the named location. He went to the location, watched from a vantage point, and two police cars appeared. This confirmed that someone powerful was not only following the investigation, but trying to ensure that it failed to reach the truth.

The trial of Freddie de Marigny started on 18 October 1943 at the Bahamas Supreme Court. There was worldwide interest in the case, and for a short time the murder of Sir Harry Oakes took precedence over war news.

Freddie did not get the solicitor of his choice. Shortly after his arrest, he asked the police to contact his lawyer, Sir Alfred Adderley. He was a distinguished barrister with an impressive record of success in the courtroom. Later, Sir Alfred said that he would certainly have taken the case for the defence but the police had never contacted him, which looks like another attempt by the police to ensure de Marigny's conviction. De Marigny's second choice for a defence lawyer was Godfrey Higgs. Instead, the prosecution enlisted the services of Sir Alfred, which must have disconcerted Freddie, as was probably intended.

Early in the trial, Harold Christie described how he had found the body. He said he was a close friend of Oakes and often spent time at his estate. If he was there late in the evening, he often slept over in the bedroom next to Sir Harry's. On the evening before the murder, Oakes had entertained several guests: Christie, Christie's niece and her friend, and two other acquaintances of Sir Harry's who had been guests on earlier occasions, Charles Hubbard and

Mrs Dulcibelle. Christie's niece and her friend left at about seven o'clock, while the rest stayed for dinner. After dinner they played checkers. Hubbard and Dulcibelle left at eleven that evening. Soon after all the guests had gone, Oakes retired to his bedroom to read his newspaper. Christie had gone with him and they had chatted until half past eleven. Then Christie had gone to the guest bedroom to read before going to sleep. Christie said he had woken twice in the night, once to fend off mosquitoes, once by the storm. In each instance, he was only awake for a few minutes before falling asleep.

When he woke in the morning he had breakfast. Seeing no sign of Oakes, he went to his room. Going in rather tentatively, he greeted Oakes, got no reply, then noticed that the mosquito net and a part of the bed were blackened and burnt. Then he rushed over to the bed, and saw Oakes lying aslant on it, half burnt and his head bloodied. Christie did not realize Oakes was dead, and tried to lift his head to give him water. He also tried to wipe Oakes's face clean with a bathroom towel. After that he ran to the bedroom doorway to shout for help, not knowing that the servants were off that day, before going downstairs to telephone. Christie claimed to have seen burn marks on the stairs and saw a little smoke coming from Sir Harry's bedroom.

Christie was cross-questioned by Sir Godfrey Higgs, acting for Freddie, and he asked why Christie had gone out of his way to park his car out of sight of the house when he normally parked it clearly in view. Higgs was implying that Christie had gone to the Oakes house late at night, in secret, did not want Oakes to know he was there and murdered him. Christie said he was trying to save petrol and it seemed a natural thing to do. Then Higgs revealed that Christie had been seen as a passenger in a station wagon arriving from the area of the harbour in Nassau at midnight. In fact a strange boat has been sighted in the harbour on the night of the murder. A night watchman saw two strange men getting off the boat and getting into a car. It is thought that Higgs himself may have been one of the two men. By chance, perhaps, the night watchman was unable to give his testimony at the trial because he was drowned shortly after Freddie's arrest.

Dr Hugh Quackenbush gave evidence for the defence. He noticed blisters at various points round Sir Harry's body. He thought they had been created before death and therefore were unconnected with the fire; they were due to some other, completely unknown, trauma. He put the time of death at between two and five o'clock in the morning on 8 July 1943. Dr Laurence Fitzmaurice, who carried out the post mortem, said that Sir Harry's skull had been cracked by a heavy blunt object. He also found triangular wounds a few inches across on and round the left ear lobe, showing that the blunt instrument had a well-defined edge.

Thomas Lavelle testified that he had overheard part of a conversation between Oakes and de Marigny. Oakes was upset with Freddie, telling him not to write letters to his wife; he also called Freddie a sex maniac.

Barker and Melchen, the American detectives, gave evidence that showed their incompetence, which was so extreme that people wondered if they were deliberately concealing or destroying evidence. They even contradicted one another. Barker claimed he discovered Freddie's fingerprint on the screen on 9 July, and it was that discovery that led directly to Freddie's arrest. Now Melchen revealed that Barker did not mention to him that the fingerprint was identifiable as Freddie's until 15 July. Even more bizarre, this contradicted his own earlier statement that he had been unaware of the identification until 19 or 20 July. There were also inconsistencies regarding the time of their interview with Freddie.

Higgs poured scorn over the method Barker had used for lifting the fingerprint on the screen. He had used an abnormal method which destroyed the print. Higgs accused Barker of lying. What Barker had really done was to lift Freddie's print, not from the screen beside Sir Harry's bed, but from a glass Freddie was drinking from during the interview. Barker insisted that he had taken the print from the screen. Then, when Higgs confronted Barker with the screen in the court room, he asked Barker to show him where exactly he had taken the print. Incredibly, Barker was unable to remember where this crucial piece of evidence had been found. Significantly, Barker was the only person to claim to have seen the fingerprint on the screen.

It was now emerging that the evidence was very likely rigged in order to frame Freddie. Further incompetence was exposed when Barker admitted that he had not dusted for fingerprints on the bed's footboard. He had also missed out several other areas in the room where prints might have been found. He failed to fingerprint all the visitors to the crime scene for elimination purposes. Worse still, he had lied about doing so, first saying that he had and later admitting that he had not. Barker was also asked why he had failed to tell his colleague Melchen about the discovery of the crucial fingerprint for such a long time. Barker was unable to answer.

Overall, Barker did a great deal of damage to his own professional reputation as well as to the case for the prosecution.

Freddie took the stand and gave frank testimony to the strained relationship with his father- and mother-in-law. He said Oakes was often angry with him, apparently for being married to his daughter. He also seemed to have an alibi for the time of the murder. He had entertained several people at his house that evening. Most had gone home at midnight, and he had driven one guest home at one o'clock, returning home at half past one in the morning. His friend Georges was in the house in another room with his girlfriend. Freddie went to bed at about two o'clock. He was woken by the cat (which belonged to Georges) at three o'clock, at which time he heard Georges leaving in his car to take the girlfriend home. Georges returned at a quarter past three and Freddie called him to collect his cat. Then Freddie slept until he was woken up at half past six. It was, in fact, only a partial alibi; there were gaps during which Freddie could have gone to the Oakes house and killed Sir Harry.

He admitted that Melchen and Barker found singed hairs on his hands and beard. He explained that the singeing happened when he lit cigars and when he cooked on the gas cooker. They had asked to see the shirt he had been wearing on the evening of the murder. He could not remember which one, but showed them all his laundry; there was nothing there to incriminate him.

When Georges testified his evidence tallied with Freddie's. But then counsel for the prosecution read from the statement Georges had made to the police; in that he made clear that he did not see Freddie between eleven o'clock in the evening and ten o'clock the next morning. The night appeared to have been enlivened with encounters in order to supply Freddie with an alibi. Then Ernest Callender for the defence read Georges' statement out word for word. Georges said that at half past one he had a conversation with Freddie through the bedroom door; he had not actually seen him, but nevertheless they had words. That meant that Freddie was at his own house at half past one.

Nancy gave evidence of her parents' hostility towards her husband. She added that she had been approached by Barker and Melchen after her father's funeral. They claimed that the prints had been positively identified as Freddie's. They were claiming there was more than one print. This too cast doubt on the truthfulness of Barker and Melchen.

The jury came to the majority verdict (nine out of twelve jurors) of not guilty. The opinion of the islanders had been swayed by the trial and its exposures. Now, instead of being reviled, Freddie de Marigny was exonerated. He had not killed Sir Harry Oakes. But if Freddie had not killed him, who had?

Many theories have been put forward over the years, many of them implicating one or more of Nassau's leading citizens of the time, including Axel Wenner-Gren, Sir Harold Christie and (inevitably) the Duke of Windsor. The Mafia has also been blamed. So far none of the theories has been proved. Sir Harry Oakes was a tough, uncompromising man and it is likely that he made some enemies over the years. Perhaps someone from his chequered past turned up on Nassau to exact revenge. Oakes wielded considerable power on Nassau, and perhaps he seriously disadvantaged someone on the island as a result of his recent decisions and strategies. It is also worth remembering that Nassau had a high crime rate, and that maybe Oakes was just a victim of a casual break-in, that it was no more significant than an aggravated robbery.

Christie may have seen the possibility of making an enormous amount of money from casinos, and become angry at being blocked by Oakes. Christie could have murdered Oakes himself or hired someone else to do; he was certainly rich enough to hire a killer. Alternatively, Frank Marshall may have seen Oakes as the major obstacle in the way of the casino plan. Marshall, it is alleged, had connections with Lucky Luciano and his associate Meyer Lansky. It is thought that Luciano and Lansky were the masterminds behind the plan to develop casinos in the islands, and that Marshal was their go-between. It may have been extreme pressure from Luciano and Lansky that drove Marshall to kill Oakes in order to facilitate the casino deal, or Luciano and Lansky may have sent in a hit man behind Marshall's back: hence the mysterious unidentified boat. Wenner-Gren may have murdered Oakes because Oakes had found out too much about Wenner-Gren's spying activities. Possibly the Duke of Windsor murdered Oakes for a similar reason. It is thought that Oakes knew about the Duke's links (through Wenner-Gren) with the Nazis.

The possibilities lie in these areas, but the truth of what happened remains curiously elusive. Nothing of any significance, except the Duke's dealings with the Nazis, ever really emerged after the 1940s to shed any light on the murder of Sir Harry Oakes. That in itself implies that somebody very powerful, somebody with a big name to protect, was behind the killing. One question that has never been satisfactorily answered is the key question about Barker and Melchen. Why did the Duke of Windsor send away to Miami for two completely incompetent detectives? Was it a further example of the Duke's legendary bad judgement? Or was the bungled investigation a carefully orchestrated pantomime that would distract people from what had really happened – and incidentally destroy all the forensic evidence along the way? On the face of it, the Duke snubbed his own Bahamian law enforcers in order to bring in Laurel and Hardy to solve the crime, but one suspects there was more to it than that.

PART FIVE

UNSOLVED CRIMES OF THE LATE TWENTIETH CENTURY

(1951–2000)

Death at the Roadside: Sir Jack Drummond

On 4 August 1952, an English family on a camping holiday in the south of France pulled into a layby on the N96 near the village of Lurs, seventy-five miles from Aix. The Drummond family consisted of the scientist Sir Jack Drummond, his wife Ann and their ten-year-old daughter. It was a hot afternoon, and they had decided to camp for the night beside the River Durance. Not long after that, all three of them were violently murdered.

It was a puzzling crime. Sir Jack was a very different character from Sir Harry Oakes. He was sixty-one and a former professor of biochemistry at London University. It seemed very unlikely that a former co-worker would have tracked him down in order to exact revenge. Drummond had been rather more than an ordinary academic, though. During the Second World War he had done some major work on nutrition, which had earned him a knighthood; he had also been a senior researcher at the Boots pharmaceutical laboratory in Nottingham.

On the face of it, the triple murder looked like a casual, opportunist act of violence with robbery as its probably motive. The French police apprehended the peasant farmer whose smallholding was the nearest property to the scene of the crime, and charged him with the murders. He was Gaston Dominici, a man of seventy-five.

First on the scene after the murder was Gaston's son, Gustave Dominici. He initially told the police he had heard shots at one o'clock in the morning on 5 August, and thought there were poachers about. He found the body of the daughter, Elizabeth, at half past five. She was lying near the river, battered to death with a rifle butt. Gustave Dominici had waved down a passing cyclist at six o'clock to tell him to fetch the police. Lady Drummond's body was found close to a Hillman car and Sir Jack's body lay just across the road. Both of them had been shot from behind, as if they had been attempting to run away from their killer. The stock of the gun was found floating in the River Durance; the barrel was later found on the river bed.

But Gustave Dominici changed his story, which aroused serious suspicion. One of his neighbours, Paul Maillet, reported that Gustave Dominici had told that when he found Elizabeth she was still alive. One of Dominici's relatives reported that he had seen Lady Drummond and Elizabeth calling at the Dominici farm with a bucket, to ask for water, when Gustave Dominici, his brother Clovis and their father, Gaston, insisted they had had no contact with the Drummonds. The police were confronted with a wall of silence and deception. Some witnesses were reluctant to say anything. Others made contradictory statements. The police tried to set one family member off against another, which caused even more confusion. The police went on pressing the Dominicis for the truth. Eventually Gustave and Clovis told the police what they wanted to hear, that their father had admitted that he had 'killed the English', and on 13 November 1953, the seventy-five-year-old Gaston confessed to the murders.

But this was a classic case of a confession given after a protracted period of determined police interrogation. If the police go on questioning for long enough, interrogation subjects will confess to anything – just to bring the interrogation to an end. This is what seems to have happened in l'affaire Dominici. Needless to say, confessions squeezed out of people under these conditions are meaningless. Shortly after confessing, Gaston Dominici changed his story again, saying he had not committed the murders and had confessed to them only to protect his family. Gustave withdrew his earlier statement too.

The various different versions of what had happened drew strong suspicion on the Dominici family, and the police went on questioning them for fifteen months, certain that the Dominicis were behind the murders. The French legal system went through the whole process of putting the old man, Gaston Dominici, on trial, but it was hard to see what his motive might have been. He was a pillar of the local community. There were other questions, too. Men were seen in the area at the time of the murder, men who were never identified. The murders were committed with a battered old American Rock-Ola carbine; where had it come from? One promising line of investigation in recent years has been the probability that Drummond was a spy, caught up in the Cold War.

Nevertheless, Gaston Dominici was brought to trial in Digne a year later. In November 1954 he was found guilty of the three murders without any extenuating circumstances and sentenced to death. He faced the guillotine. But there were so many loose ends in the investigation, the total lack of motive being a major worry, and there were several moves from the central government in Paris to overturn the verdict. One such move came from a young minister, François Mitterand, but initially these had no effect. Then, in 1957, the French President René Coty commuted Dominici's sentence to one of life imprisonment. Three years later, Coty's successor Charles de Gaulle set him free. In 1960, de Gaulle watched a television programme about the case. It showed the pathetic eighty-four-year-old man locked up in the prison of Les Baumettes in Marseilles. He affirmed his innocence. It was evident that he was unhappy to be so far away from his farm, and to be separated from his dog. The programme was profoundly influential. As a viewer, de Gaulle was moved by the old man's predicament and granted him a pardon on 13 July 1960.

One reason for believing that Gaston Dominici was innocent is that in his forced 'confession' the reason he gave for killing the whole family was that Sir Jack had caught him offering to have sex with an undressed Lady Drummond, which was completely absurd. Presumably Gaston thought that up, forgetting that he was seventy-five and distinctly past his best, as press photographs of the time clearly show. A second reason is that the US army rifle did not belong to him and he had no idea how to use it.

Some time after the murders, a man called William Bartkowski was arrested in Germany in connection with another crime. He unaccountably and spontaneously admitted to being one of four contract hit men who had been hired to kill Drummond. This confession has never been satisfactorily explained. Bartkowski's scenario involving four hit men would tie in with the sighting by at least four local passers-by of some unidentified men (not Sir Jack and not the Dominicis) on the road near the crime scene. Post mortems on Sir Jack and Lady Drummond revealed that the bullet entry wounds were of different sizes, so two guns were used; by implication, there were at least two killers.

A closer scrutiny of Sir Jack Drummond's past life revealed what may have been a highly significant pattern of activity. The camping holiday had not taken Drummond to Lurs entirely by chance. He had been there at least three times before, in 1947, 1948 and 1951, so he had visited the place four times in five years. Close to the village, about six miles away, was a chemical factory that had started manufacturing advanced insecticides for crops.

410

During the Cold War, insecticides were widely believed to have the potential to be used as a chemical weapon. One possibility is that Drummond was acting as a kind of industrial spy, with a view to reporting back to the authorities in Britain on the chemical production activities at Lurs. The camping holiday was therefore a cover for this espionage. In support of this hypothesis is the fact that Drummond's camera was never found; by implication it was taken by the hit men in order to conceal the nature of Drummond's recent activity.

Sir Jack had a long discussion in Lurs, just two days before he died, with a man called Father Lorenzi. Father Lorenzi was a priest who was known to have been a prominent figure in the French resistance during the Second World War. We can only speculate about the nature of Drummond's conversation with Lorenzi, but it is significant that Paul Maillet was another French resistance fighter and a friend of Gustave Dominici. Maillet is believed to have been the true owner of the US army rifle.

The Dominici family evidently knew things about the murders, or the run-up to the murders, which they were unable to reveal – even though it meant that old Gaston might be guillotined as a result. It may be that their web of friendships in the area gave them some knowledge not only of the French resistance during the war, but also knowledge of what secret activities of resistance fighters were continuing in the Cold War, too. The Dominicis may have been persuaded to help some scheme, perhaps to outwit or block Drummond's espionage work, not knowing that the outcome would be the murder of the whole family. That would certainly be consistent with their confused state of mind in the weeks following the murders.

Gaston Dominici is now long dead, but his family is still fighting to clear his name. William Bartkowski may have been one the four hit men, though there is no corroboration for his confession; the identity of the other three, if indeed there were three more, has never been discovered.

THE A6 MURDER: WAS HANRATTY GUILTY?

One August evening in 1961, a married man called Michael Gregsten drove his girlfriend Valerie Storie out into the country for sex. They worked together at the Road Research Laboratory near Slough in the south of England. Gregsten's wife knew about the affair. Gregsten drove his Morris Minor, as he had driven many times before, to the chosen spot and parked on the roadside next to Taplow Meadow, just outside Maidenhead. As they embraced and kissed in the front of the car, there was a sharp tap at the window behind Valerie. Michael could see the man, but Valerie couldn't. The man threatened Michael with a gun, said, 'I am a desperate man', and climbed into the back seat of the car. Then he ordered Gregsten to drive off, insisting that they keep looking ahead; they were not to turn round and look at him. They set off through the outskirts of Slough, then onto the open road. After a tense two-hour drive, the stranger ordered Michael to stop in a lay-by on the A6. It was fairly sheltered, surrounded by bushes and known as Deadman's Hill. It was a favourite spot for courting couples.

The menacing stranger asked Michael Gregsten to hand him a duffel bag, and either Gregsten saw this as an opportunity to take a look at him or tackle him and disarm him, or the stranger interpreted his movement as a threat. Maybe the gunman had realized that Gregsten had already taken a good look at his face through the passenger window and would be able to identify him; he had had time during the drive to decide that Gregsten could not be trusted to leave the scene alive. Whatever the reason, as Michael Gregsten passed the bag, the stranger fired twice and Gregsten was killed outright instantly.

By now it was dark, and the terrified Valerie found herself alone with a homicidal maniac. The stranger savagely raped her, shot her in the back several times at close range and left her for dead in the lay-by. She in fact survived, but remained disabled for the rest of her life. In spite of spending as much as six hours at close quarters with the gunman, Valerie only really saw his face clearly once, for a few seconds, as it was lit up by the headlights of a passing car. She was able to supply police with a description, but it remains uncertain whether that description is at all reliable. By the time she caught the single glimpse of the gunman's face, she had already been traumatized by the shooting of her lover and terror at her own impending death. The police circulated a picture of the wanted man, based on her description.

Recognition by voice played a key part in the prosecution case at the trial. Just before the man raped her, he said, 'Shut up, will you? I'm thinking'. He spoke with an accent that was very distinct but Valerie could not identify it geographically. It wasn't London. It wasn't Glasgow. But a distinct way of speaking just the same. He pronounced the word 'thinking' as 'finking'.

As soon as Michael's body and the scarcely living Valerie were found in the A6 lay-by, a massive murder hunt was launched. It was a very peculiar case. The man had appeared from nowhere, disappeared into nowhere, seemed to have no connection with Michael or Valerie, and seemed to have no motive whatever. There was really nothing at all to go on, except the knowledge that there was a violent madman on the loose, a man who said 'finking'.

The police had a suspect, a man called Peter Louis Alphon. His face fitted the identikit picture, and he could not give any account of his movements on the night of the murder. The police even got as far as arresting him, and they were probably right.

At this point, bizarre things began to happen in the development of the case. Michael Gregsten's widow happened to be in Blackpool on holiday, after the murder of her husband, when she spotted a man, a total stranger, about whom she had an intuition. She got in touch with the police. The man was James Hanratty. It says something about the strange and desperate mindset of the police involved in this case that they acted on this absurd contact. Mrs Gregsten had not been at the scene of the murder, had no reason to think she had ever seen the murderer, and so could not have expected to recognize him. She only had the identikit picture. The police picked Hanratty up and questioned him. Initially he could not account for his whereabouts on that fateful evening – but how many of us could do that? – and they started investigating his recent movements.

The police discovered two .38 cartridge cases from bullets fired from the murder weapon in the Vienna Hotel; one of the rooms had been occupied by a Mr James Ryan, which was an alias used by James Hanrattty. The police decided they need look no further. There was nevertheless no forensic evidence from the car to connect Hanratty to the murder.

Hanratty was lined up in an identification parade. Valerie was unable to pick anyone out that she recognized. 'I'm sorry. I only saw him for a few seconds. It's very difficult.' She knew and freely admitted that she had been badly traumatized during and after her ordeal and that this had blocked and distorted her memory. The police ran a second identification parade. This time the police asked the men to repeat the line, 'Be quiet will you? I'm thinking'. Valerie felt sure Hanratty was saying 'finking'. The police thought they had got their man.

Hanratty made himself doubly vulnerable at this point by producing an alibi. He had not mentioned Rhyl before, but now he claimed that on the night in question he had been in Rhyl, 250 miles from the murder scene. It looked like an improvised smoke screen, and the police saw no reason to make no more than a cursory check on his alibi.

James Hanratty was arrested in Blackpool on 9 October in 1961, identified by Valerie at an identity parade, and sent for trial at Bedford Assizes. Much of the trial proceedings turned on Hanratty's alibi, that he had been at Rhyl in north Wales on the day in question.

The jury took a long time – nearly ten hours – to come to the decision that Hanratty was guilty. The use of a gun in the murder was crucial. As the law stood at that time, if Hanratty had strangled or poisoned Michael Gregsten he would have been sentenced to life imprisonment; using a gun meant death. He was sentenced to death and, in spite of a petition for clemency bearing 28,000 signatures, he was hanged in Bedford Prison on 4 April 1962.

The conviction and execution of James Hanratty were extremely controversial. Britain was phasing out capital punishment at the time, and Hanratty's was one of only three executions that took place between 1961 and 1965, at which time hanging ceased altogether. Had the suspect been correctly identified? Had enough enquiries been made into the validity of Hanratty's alibi? Had any motive been established for the murder? Had sufficient evidence altogether be gathered to justify a conviction, let alone an execution? Had alternative suspects like Alphon really been investigated properly? Hanratty himself stoutly denied that he was involved in any way with the murder, and went to the gallows protesting his innocence and pleading with his family to clear his name. Many people have campaigned to have the case reopened and get some of these questions answered.

By the time the police check got round to checking Hanratty's alibi they had already decided that he was the killer. They ran only a cursory check which confirmed that they were right. But shortly after the hanging, no fewer than fourteen people came forward to say that they had seen or spoken to Hanratty in Rhyl, and that the police had interviewed none of them. The police enquiries had led them to the Vienna Hotel, where Hanratty had certainly stayed. In the Vienna Hotel, the police found cartridge cases that connected the place to the murder scene. But Hanratty was not the only person who had stayed at the Vienna Hotel. As it turned out, it was for him an unlucky choice. It was a very unlucky coincidence that he chose to stay at the same hotel as the murderer. Also staying at the Vienna Hotel was Peter Louis Alphon, who up to that moment had been the police's main suspect. Alphon was not identified by Valerie at an identification parade, but then neither really was Hanratty. But once the police had decided that Hanratty was the killer, further enquiries into Alphon were dropped.

Unlike Hanratty, Alphon had no alibi at all for the night of the murder. He was a friend of Michael Gregsten's wife and therefore had a previous connection with Michael and Valerie that Hanratty did not. Alphon later claimed that Mrs Gregsten had paid him £5000 to frighten the lovers into separating so that she could get her husband back.

Here – at last – was a possible motive. Alphon pronounced the word 'thinking' as 'finking'. He looked remarkably like the identikit picture.

There was also the manner in which the Morris Minor was being driven as the murderer left the murder scene. Many witnesses saw the car as it drove away from the scene; they noticed it because it drew their attention. It was being driven very erratically. This is very peculiar if the murderer was Hanratty, because Hanratty was an experienced driver. Alphon, on the other hand, had not even passed his driving test, and is therefore far more likely to have been the driver that night.

In a similar way, the personality of Alphon fits the events of the night better. Hanratty was a city character, sociable and well liked by the people he worked with; he had never shown any sign of psychological hang-ups. He does not seem very likely to have behaved in the neurotic and irrational way that the A6 killer behaved that night. Alphon on the other hand was neurotic, psychologically fragile, a petty criminal, a loner, roaming about with no proper job. Even the most rudimentary psychological profiling would have identified Alphon as far likelier to have committed the A6 murder than Hanratty. He also had an odd, distinctive way of speaking. His voice was recorded by investigators years later as he spoke about the A6 shootings – I have heard the tape – and the neurotic peculiarity of his speech fits Valerie's observations.

All this could have been established by the police in

1961. All this could have been presented in court to ensure that the right man went to the gallows. What was not available at the time was Alphon's confession. It was not until many years later, when the events of that summer had preyed on his mind to such an extent that he wanted other people to know what had happened. He claimed in his confession that he was paid a large sum to 'damage' Valerie and Michael. What appears to have happened is that family friends seeking to help Mrs Gregsten by ending Michael's affair with Valerie hired Alphon to surprise and frighten the lovers at Taplow Meadow, where there were known to meet. Maybe Alphon took the gun as a prop, to wave at Gregsten, knowing that it would thoroughly frighten him. Alphon's fundamental instability as a person meant that he got carried away with his gangster role and the situation ran away with him. Maybe he didn't know how to bring the frightening episode to a satisfactory close and panicked. The apparent lack of purpose to the attack is certainly consistent with this scenario. The story is unfortunately muddied by Alphon's retraction later on. By the time Paul Foot interviewed him for his book Who killed Hanratty? He had thought better of his confession, perhaps fearing he would be put on trial.

Whether there would have been a watertight case against Alphon is impossible to tell now, since the forensic trail has gone cold, but if all these facts had been made known to the jury at Hanratty's trial it would have been clear that there was more than 'reasonable doubt' about

Hanratty's guilt. It was not a safe conviction.

Immediately after the execution, many began to wonder whether justice really had been done. Even Mrs Gregsten, who had pointed the finger at Hanratty in the first place, began to have doubts. The gathering uncertainty led the British government further towards the abolition of hanging. At least if a man is given a life sentence for murder there remains the possibility of release and restitution; the mistake can be put right. There is no possibility of putting right a hanging.

Over the years since the murder, Hanratty has increasingly looked like the wrong suspect, Alphon the right suspect. But very recently the situation has become startlingly more complicated with the emergence of some DNA evidence. In 1999, the Hanratty family, which has remained steadfastly convinced of Hanratty's innocence throughout, won their fight to have his case reviewed.

Thirty-seven years after Hanratty was hanged, it emerged that vital evidence that could have saved him from the gallows was deliberately suppressed by senior police officers at the time of his trial, presumably in order to secure a conviction. Hanratty's brother Michael and his sister-in-law Maureen were shocked at the misconduct of the authorities. Because of this and the flaws in the identification process, the case was referred back to the Court of Appeal. Geoffrey Bindman, the Hanratty family's solicitor at the time, commented that the amount of information not disclosed at the trial was substantial, enough to have saved Hanratty from conviction. The identification procedure was seriously flawed, because there was heavy dependence on voice identification and Hanratty was the only person with a London accent asked to speak in front of Valerie Storey. The Rhyl alibi was swept aside by the police, when there were fourteen people who had seen Hanratty or spoken to him in Rhyl at the time of the murder – fourteen potential witnesses for the defence who were studiously ignored by the police.

Several books have been written about the A6 murder, starting with *Who Killed Hanratty?* by Paul Foot in 1971; the most recent exploration of the case is Bob Woffinden's 1997 book *Hanratty: the Final Verdict.* The general view is that there was such intense revulsion at the crime that the authorities felt pushed to get a conviction at any price. When Roy Jenkins was Home Secretary in 1974, he thought there was sufficient justification to review the case and asked the lawyer Lewis Hawser to look into it. Hawser's 1975 report said that there had been access to all the relevant evidence and that therefore the conviction had been safe. In other words, regardless of whether Hanratty was guilty or not, there had been no procedural errors in arriving at the verdict.

Campaigners working for Hanratty's exoneration made new representations to the British Home Office in the 1990s. The case against Hanratty rested partly on the fact that he had been identified on the morning after the murder in the supposedly stolen Morris Minor by two men in Redbridge in East London. But what now emerged was that the stolen car had been spotted a very long way away, in Derbyshire, by as many as eleven people at the same time. The presence of the stolen Morris Minor in Derbyshire had even been formally reported to the police. The police elected not to pass this key information to the defence; it might, after all, have helped to get Hanratty off. This was part of the newly emerging suppressed evidence. Geoffrey Bindman, Paul Foot and Bob Woffinden were astonished to find that a significant amount of material had existed all along which could have helped Hanratty's defence significantly but which had been deliberately with-held from his defence lawyers. Some of it was not shown to the prosecution team either, presumably for fear that the defence might gain access to it.

The former Assistant Chief Constable of the Metro-politan Police, Baden Skitt, led the enquiry and he too was shocked at the suppression of evidence. The Hanratty family were outraged. They now knew that key evidence had been deliberately concealed. Michael Hanratty said, 'All this evidence has been locked away in Scotland Yard. They told us to come back for it in a hundred years. It is a disgrace. We're worse than South Africa.'

In 1991, the Bedfordshire Police allowed Bob Woffinden to see previously undisclosed files on the A6 murder. Baden Skitt's report in addition revealed a significant fact about the Morris Minor. The recorded mileage shown on the clock was too low for Skillett's sighting in Brentwood and Trower's sighting in Redbridge Lane to have been sightings of the Morris Minor in which Gregsten died. There is no evidence that Skillet and Trower even saw the same Morris Minor as each other. The evidence against Hanratty had, in short, been 'cooked'.

The re-emerging evidence was the basis for a formal hearing in the Court of Appeal. A handkerchief Hanratty used to wrap up the gun was subjected to DNA testing. The DNA profile was compared with DNA samples from the Hanratty family. The apparent fit between the handkerchief and Hanratty seriously dented the claim that Hanratty was innocent, but the Hannratty family's solicitor pointed out that the exhibits from the case had not been stored properly. At the time of the trial there had been no question of DNA testing – the technique had yet to be invented – and the exhibits had been stored together, unsealed. Clearly, there was a distinct possibility that Hanratty DNA from other exhibits had been transferred to the handkerchief. Over a period of thirty-nine years, the items had been handled over and over again. The evidence was, once again, but in a very different way, contaminated.

The match between the handkerchief and Hanratty was in any case possible, not definite. As a result, it was decided that an exhumation of Hanratty's body was necessary to resolve the question. If Hanratty's guilt or innocence could be established by modern forensic means, then it should be.

In March 2001, James Hanratty's body was exhumed from Carpenter's Park Cemetery near Bushey in Hertfordshire. DNA from his teeth was found to match two samples found at the scene of the crime (trial exhibits 26 and 35); one was on Valerie Storie's underwear and the other was the handkerchief wrapped round the murder weapon, a .38 revolver. As a result of the DNA matching, the Court of Criminal Appeal ruled that Hanratty's conviction was safe and that there were no grounds for a posthumous pardon. In other words, even though serious errors may have been made in the process of bringing Hanratty to justice, he was nevertheless the man who committed the crime, so justice was done.

The Hanratty family remain unconvinced, though, for the same reasons as before. At the appeal hearing, the barrister acting for the Hanratty family, Michael Mansfield, argued that the exhibits were from the beginning never handled in a forensically sterile environment, and could easily have become cross-contaminated. During the trial at Bedford Assizes, the exhibits were regularly taken to and from court in the same boxes; the samples repeatedly came in contact with one another, including the samples of Valerie Storie's and James Hanratty's clothing. In that context, it would not be at all surprising if some of Hanratty's DNA found its way onto the other trial exhibits, especially in the minute quantities that were actually present. Officers and witnesses took the exhibits and handled them freely; people were not to know at that time about the possibility of damaging the evidence, simply because no one knew about DNA. Michael Mansfield claimed that the exhibits had been handled in a lax way that frustrated modern scientific analysis. The contamination of the exhibits could be accounted for by the broken vial found among the exhibits.

The forensic scientists who carried out the tests counterargue that if Hanratty was not the killer, the killer's DNA is unaccountably missing from the exhibits; no other man's DNA was found. The Appeal judge, Lord Woolf, took the view of the forensic scientists: 'In our judgement . . . the DNA evidence establishes beyond doubt that James Hanratty was the murderer.'

But, if Hanratty did it, why on earth did he do it? And how did Mrs Gregsten identify him in a crowd at Blackpool? The A6 murder remains one of the greatest murder mysteries of modern times. The DNA breakthrough has opened a new phase in the controversy. Maybe further new techniques, not yet invented, will solve the mystery in the future. Let us hope so, for the sake of justice. Even if Hanratty was guilty of the crime, his trial was not a fair one. Significant evidence that he was in Rhyl at the time was deliberately suppressed by the police, and on that basis alone his trial must be regarded as a mistrial. Even if guilty, James Hanratty did not get justice. If innocent, he was the victim of a gross miscarriage of justice.

THE MURDERED SUSSEX SCHOOLBOY: KEITH LYON

The still-unsolved murder of a Sussex schoolboy in 1967 is a classic cold case. After a few years, the trail evaporates and even the most conscientious detectives sense that the file has to be closed. The murder of Keith Lyon was one of those cases.

Keith Lyon, who was twelve years old, was walking along a bridle way up Happy Valley, a small area of downland between Ovingdean and Woodingdean near Brighton in Sussex, to buy a geometry set for his home-work when he was set upon by some youths and killed. His body was found on 6 May 1967 on the bridle path. He had been stabbed eleven times. The murder weapon, a kitchen knife, was found some days later a mile away in the grounds of a school. The knife was forensically tested at the time and it was found to carry traces of blood of Keith's blood group and also traces of another blood group as well. It was not known who the second blood sample came from.

The police questioned a number of people, and they had their suspects, but there was no evidence. The case petered out and then the material was boxed up and put into store.

Recently some workmen were modernizing a sprinkler system in Brighton Police Station when, quite by chance, they uncovered the evidence from the Keith Lyon case locked in a basement. What they stumbled on was several boxes of items relating to the case. The collection had been lost for thirty-five years. When the evidence was re-examined, detectives realized that forensic tests devised since 1967 might reveal rather more than could have been hoped at the time. Among the finds in the boxes was the murder weapon, still stained with both Keith's blood and the blood of another, unknown, person.

With the advent of DNA profiling, it may at last be possible to tie the second blood sample to a particular individual, and the police believe that that person was the murderer.

As Detective Inspector Bill Warner of Brighton and Hove City CID has commented, the murder happened so long ago that it is possible the murderer may be dead by now, but it may still be the case that his profile is on the National DNA Database. The door has opened on the possibility, even after all this time, that the killer of Keith Lyon may yet be brought to justice. It is a distinct possibility that the youth who so casually and brutally stabbed Keith to death went on to commit other crimes, which raises the chances of finding his DNA profile on the UK database. If, on the other hand, the youth was so shaken and appalled by what he did that he never committed another offence, then his DNA will not appear in the records.

Detective Inspector Warner said, 'The most disturbing fact was we mislaid the exhibits. The case was reviewed several years after the initial inquiry and again in the mid-1970s. It was always thought that the knife had been mislaid somewhere. The significance of the find is that we have got the evidence now and we have got the chance of forensic retrieval to identify the offender.'

Sussex detectives are now re-examining the list of original suspects in the case, to see if they can find a DNA match. They already know that one of the suspects has died. But, as DI Warner said, 'provided we have his DNA, we can find out who did it.' DNA has opened the door on clearing up this and tens of thousands of other cold cases – murders and other serious crimes that the police had previously lost hope of solving.

TEN YEARS IN SAN FRANCISCO: THE ZODIAC KILLINGS

Sometimes journalists think up sensational nicknames for serial killers. The practice gives the unidentified killer an identity of sorts, or at least a persona – and it helps to animate the sequence of news stories. It was the press who invented the name 'The Night Stalker' for a Californian serial killer. It was the press who gave Peter Sutcliffe the name 'The Yorkshire Ripper'. The killer who struck again and again in the San Francisco area for a decade beginning in 1968 thought up his own name. He was 'Zodiac'. In the same way, Jack the Ripper invented his own persona. Zodiac had other points in common with Jack the Ripper, too. He sent the police clues and information in polite letters; he taunted them. He also went undetected, unidentified, uncaught, unconvicted, unpunished.

For more than ten years Zodiac stalked the San Francisco area. The reign of terror started at Christmas in 1968. A couple of teenagers had drawn their car up in an open space next to a pump house in the Vallejo Hills above San

Francisco. It was a favourite spot for lovers. David Faraday and Bettilou Jensen hardly noticed the cold on that chilly, cloudless and moonlit night. They were so involved in each other that they scarcely noticed another car pulling up ten feet away. Suddenly a bullet smashed through their rear window, showering them with broken glass, and then a second slammed into the bodywork. Bettilou instinctively jumped out of the car and started to run away. David put his hand on the door handle, preparing to follow her, when the gunman reached in through the open door window and shot him in the head. Then the gunman ran after Bettilou. She had only run about forty feet when he fired five shots at her. She fell, dead, and the gunman got back into his car and drove away.

Perhaps a minute later a third car came along. The woman who was driving it saw Bettilou's body lying on the ground and, instead of stopping, she resourcefully stepped on her accelerator to get help quickly from the next town. She met a police patrol car coming the other way and flashed her headlights to make it stop; she told the patrolman about the body and together they went back to the pump-house. They found Bettilou dead, and David still alive but unconscious. They got him to hospital, but he died shortly after arrival.

There was very little for the police to go on. David had not been robbed. Bettilou had not been sexually assaulted or raped. The police looked at the possibility that the murderer was the jilted lover of either Bettilou or David, someone determined on revenge. But investigation failed to yield any suspects. The two teenagers had been ordinary students leading straightforward lives that concealed no secrets, no past. It was to be an unsolved double murder.

Six months later the killer struck again at another spot favoured by lovers, this time at Blue Rock Park, just two miles from the place where David and Bettilou were murdered. Michael Mageau was sitting in his car with his girlfriend, a twenty-two-year-old waitress called Darlene Ferrin. They were not alone at Blue Rock Park, as there were other courting couples who had driven there for the same reason. They did not notice when a white car pulled up beside them for a few minutes. It drove off, then came back and stopped on the far side of the road. A spotlight was suddenly shone onto them and Mike saw a figure approaching. He assumed it was a policeman and reached for his driving licence, which the policeman would ask to see. Instead the approaching figure opened fire on them, shooting Darlene first, then Mike. The gunman walked back to his car, fired some more shots at them from there, then drove off at speed.

A few minutes later the killer phoned the Vallejo County police station to report a murder on Columbus Parkway. He said, 'You will find the kids in a brown car. They are shot with a 9mm Luger. I also killed those kids last year. Goodbye.' When the police arrived, Darlene was dead. Mike was still alive, but the bullet had damaged his tongue and he could not speak.

There was one more possible lead, though. Four months before the murder, Darlene's babysitter had been aware of a white car parked outside Darlene's apartment, and she had felt uncomfortable about it. She mentioned it to Darlene, who said, 'He's checking up on me again. He doesn't want anyone to know what I saw him do. I saw him murder someone.' The babysitter had seen the driver of the white car and could describe him. She told the police – too late to save Darlene's life – that he was a middle-aged man with brown wavy hair and a round face. As Mike recovered, he regained the use of his voice and was able to confirm that the gunman had brown hair and a round face. The stalker watching outside Darlene's apartment had been the man who killed her four months later.

About two months after the shooting that left Darlene dead and Mike seriously injured, handwritten messages arrived at the offices of three local newspapers. They were written in capital letters. For some reason mad people often write in capital letters – perhaps the written equivalent of shouting. Either the writer of these notes was mad or he was trying to disguise his handwriting and prevent the police from identifying him.

The three notes all opened in the same polite way: 'DEAR EDITOR, THIS IS THE MURDERER OF THE TWO TEENAGERS LAST CHRISTMAS AT LAKE HERMAN AND THE GIRL ON THE 4TH OF JULY.' He went on to give exact details of the gun and the ammunition he had used, to make it clear to the police that he really was the murderer.

He also sent an extra sheet of paper covered in a strange code, together with the demand that the editors publish it on their front pages. If they did not, he threatened to go on killing people in the night. The letters were signed with the killer's logo, a cross inside a circle: it was a gunsight.

The three newspapers went along with the mad gunman's request; from a purely journalistic point of view it was a good story. Cryptographers worked to decode the secret message, and eventually a teacher called Dale Harden cracked it. He looked for a group of symbols that could stand for the word 'kill'; in the circumstances it was the word most likely to be used. He found it and after many hours of work he deciphered the whole message: 'I like killing people because it is so much more fun than killing wild game in the forest because man is the most dangerous of all to kill.' He boasted that he had killed five people in the San Francisco area; when he was reborn in paradise, he believed, his victims would be his slaves.

When the killer's strange message was published, it produced a massive public response. Newspaper readers volunteered all kinds of information, none of which led anywhere. Then the killer himself volunteered a clue of a kind, a nickname for himself that he must have known would ensure headlines; 'DEAR EDITOR, THIS IS ZODIAC SPEAKING.' The police were being fed clues, but no positive leads. Meanwhile the killings continued.

On 28 September 1969, another young couple were having a picnic on the shore of Lake Berryessa, about fifteen miles north of Vallejo. They were twenty-year-old Bryan Hartnell and his twenty-two-year-old girlfriend Cecelia Shepard. It was half past four in the afternoon and they had finished eating. They were lying on a rug, kissing, when they saw a stocky man with brown hair walking towards them across the clearing. He disappeared for a moment into a wood, then reappeared wearing a mask and carrying a gun. As this alarming figure approached, Bryan saw that the mask had painted on it a circle with a cross inside it.

The gunman had a soft voice and his manner was not particularly threatening. But it was all deception, and the encounter quickly turned into an horrific nightmare. He allayed the couple's worst fears by pretending that he had a simple robbery in mind. He said, 'I want your money and your car keys.' Bryan explained that he only had less than a dollar, but that the gunman was welcome to that. The gunman started to chat, explaining that he was an escaped convict and that he would have to tie them up. After tying them up, the awful truth of what he was dawned. He said, 'I am going to have to stab you people.' Bryan asked him to stab him first, because he couldn't bear to watch his girlfriend being stabbed. The gunman agreed, knelt calmly down beside Bryan and stabbed him several times in the back with a hunting knife. Bryan felt dizzy and sick, but was still conscious when the madman turned to Cecelia. After the first stab, he went berserk, stabbing again and again while she frantically thrashed about to try to avoid the blows.

Finally the girl lay still. Zodiac regained his composure, walked over to their car, pulled a felt pen from his pocket, drew something on the car door. A fisherman heard their screams and ran over to find that Bryan and Cecelia were still alive. The police arrived almost immediately, having had an anonymous tip-off; 'I want to report a double murder.' The caller had given them the exact location. When the police arrived, Cecelia was unconscious. She died two days later in hospital, without regaining consciousness. Bryan made a full recovery and was able to describe the killer. The symbol the maniac had drawn on the car door was a gunsight, so it was obviously Zodiac again. The police identified the telephone where the tip-off call had been made, and were able to lift three high-quality fingerprints from it. Unfortunately the owner of these prints did not have a criminal record. Still the police were unable to identify this dangerous killer.

Two weeks later, on 11 October 1969, a fourteen-year-old girl was looking out of the window at her home in San Francisco. She saw a stocky man sitting in the passenger seat of a parked taxi, going through the pockets of the driver, who appeared to be dead. She called her brothers to come and watch. Together, they watched the man get out of the taxi, leaving the driver slumped across the seat, wiping the door handle with a piece of cloth before walking off.

They called the police but the details were not taken down correctly, possibly because the children were over-excited, and the police understood – mistakenly – that they were looking for an NMA, a negro male adult. The killer was actually white. A police patrolman stopped a stocky white man near the scene of the crime to ask him if he had seen anything unusual; he had not, he said, so the policeman let him go. There was a kind of irony in this exchange. What to most of us would be extremely unusual and grotesque would register as normal in the mind of a psychopath like Zodiac. He wasn't lying to the police; he had seen nothing unusual; the grisly murder he had just committed was an integral part of his way of life. The patrolman thought nothing of the encounter, because the man did not answer the description of the suspect. The taxi driver was found to be dead from a gunshot wound in the head. He was Paul Stine, and he was only twenty-eight.

Then Zodiac wrote a letter to one of the San Francisco newspapers. 'THIS IS THE ZODIAC SPEAKING. I AM THE MURDERER OF THE TAXI DRIVER OVER BY WASHING-TON ST AND MALE ST LAST NIGHT, TO PROVE IT HERE IS A BLOOD STAINED PIECE OF HIS SHIRT.' The piece of cloth did indeed match the shirt of the taxi driver. The bullet was a .22 fired from the same gun that had killed Bettilou Jensen and David Faraday. Just like Jack the Ripper, he had started sending the police souvenirs of his crimes, little bits of forensic evidence that he was the murderer.

Just like Jack the Ripper, he taunted the police with their incompetence. 'THE S. F. POLICE COULD HAVE CAUGHT ME LAST NIGHT. SCHOOL CHILDREN MAKE NICE

TARGETS. I THINK I SHALL WIPE OUT A SCHOOL BUS SOME MORNING. JUST SHOOT OUT THE TIRES AND THEN PICK OFF ALL THE KIDDIES AS THEY COME BOUNDING OUT.' The letter was signed with the now-familiar gunsight symbol. The state of mind he was parading was remarkable. It was the exact opposite of what any normal human being thinks and feels. The normal human response to children is to want to nurture them and protect them, to love them. He wanted to kill them. What Zodiac saw was easy prey. His way of talking about children was very far from 'nice'. Whether he actually thought this, or was being deliberately provocative for the sake of publicity is hard to tell. His flamboyant outreach to the media suggests that he wanted cheap notoriety more than anything else; he wanted to be seen as Jack the Ripper, or the Phantom of the Opera, or Spring Heeled Jack. The more outrageous the better.

The descriptions from the children who had seen the murder of the taxi driver and the descriptions from the earlier victims all matched. A composite image of Zodiac could now be drawn up and issued to the public. The killer was a white male between thirty-five and forty-five years old, with short brown hair, possibly with a red tint. He was five feet eight inches tall, heavily built, wearing glasses.

Someone claiming to be Zodiac called the police in the middle of the night on 21–22 October 1969. The caller wanted the police to fix up an 'appearance' for him on a talk show. He wanted to talk, on air, to F. Lee Bailey or

Mel Belli, the leading criminal lawyers in the United States at the time. Mel Belli agreed to appear on Jim Dunbar's early morning talk show. At twenty past seven in the morning the man phoned in, saying that he was Zodiac, though he preferred to be called Sam. Then he blurted out, 'I'm sick. I have headaches.' The call was traced back to Napa State Hospital. The caller was a psychiatric patient, and so probably not the real Zodiac.

Two months later, at Christmas, Mel Belli received a card from Zodiac. 'DEAR MELVIN, THIS IS THE ZODIAC SPEAKING. I WISH YOU A HAPPY CHRISTMAS, THE ONE THING I ASK OF YOU IS THIS, PLEASE HELP ME. I AM AFRAID I WILL LOSE CONTROL AND TAKE MY NINTH AND POSSIBLY TENTH VICTIM.'

It was very much a call for help. The killer knew that ahead must lie capture and trial, and that he would be needing help from a first rate criminal lawyer. But he was also admitting that he was running out of control and needed to be stopped. It was classic psychopathic serial killer territory. He had reached a point where he wanted to be stopped, wanted to be caught. In fact, the whole business of writing letters and giving the police clues was to do, at some level, with wanting or needing to be caught. A handwriting expert looked at the card and said that Zodiac's mental state was deteriorating.

On 17 March 1970, Kathleen Johns was driving through the Vallejo area, with her baby in the back of the car, when a white Chevrolet drew up beside her. The driver indicated that she had something wrong with her rear wheel, and she pulled over to see what it was. Kathleen said afterwards that he was a neatly dressed, clean-shaven man. He said her wheel was wobbling and offered to tighten the wheel nuts for her. She agreed to let him do this, but when she drove off the wheel came off altogether; she realized he must have loosened them rather than tightened them. Then the neat man offered to give her a lift to a service station, but when they reached it he drove straight past.

'You know I am going to kill you,' he said. When he slowed down on a bend, Kathleen had the courage and presence of mind to open the door and jump out, with her baby in her arms. She landed safely and ran and hid in an irrigation ditch. Zodiac stopped his Chevrolet and started searching for her with a torch. He was approaching the ditch where she was crouching when, luckily for her, a lorry came along and caught him in its headlights. This distracted him and he gave up looking for her. He got back in his car and drove off. Kathleen made her way to a police station to report the incident and while she was in the police station she saw the Zodiac 'wanted' poster on the wall; she identified the man on the poster as the man who had just abducted and threatened her. The police drove her back to her car and found that Zodiac had been back to it and, in frustration and revenge, set it on fire.

In spite of the long series of incidents, the police were still a long way from identifying Zodiac. Detective Sergeant Lundblatt had an idea that he was Andy Walker, who had known Darlene Ferrin. Darlene's sister had also identified him as the man who had waited outside Darlene's apartment in the white car. Andy Walker also bore a strong resemblance to the man who stabbed Cecelia Shepard to death. Walker was known to suffer from bad headaches and said to get on badly with female colleagues. He had also been in the army where he had studied codes.

This seemed promising, but there was a problem. Not everything matched. Andy Walker's fingerprints did not match the one left in Paul Stine's taxi. His handwriting did not match the writing in Zodiac's notes. The police then discovered that Andy Walker was ambidextrous, and his handwriting varied according to which hand he used. It was also possible, the police believed, that the murder of Paul Stine had been planned so that Zodiac used the severed finger of an unknown victim to plant 'fake' fingerprints in the taxi in order to fool the police. It was a desperate line of thought.

The police decided they needed to match Walker's palm print with the one they found on the telephone after the Paul Stine murder. They decided to try to get a sample of Walker's palm prints without arousing his suspicion. An under cover policeman managed to get Andy Walker to carry a goldfish bowl for him, but the palm prints he left on the bowl were not clear enough to be of any use. Naturally, Andy Walker realized he was being targeted by the police, and very properly got a court order to stop the police pestering him any more.

More Zodiac letters arrived, again containing all sorts of clues, though none of them were crucial. It seemed he was a Gilbert and Sullivan fan, as he was taunting the police with a parody of a G & S song, listing those he wanted to kill with the chorus, 'Titwillo, titwillo, titwillo.' There were no killings during the entire run of The Mikado at the Presentation Theatre in San Francisco. He also seemed to be preoccupied with water and flooding, leading the police to believe that he might live in a low-lying area.

The mad serial killer's demands became more absurd with time. He was obviously a fantasist and a megalomaniac. He demanded that everyone in San Francisco must wear lapel badges carrying his symbol. They didn't, of course, and when he realized it was not going to happen he arbitrarily threatened to kill Paul Avery, the crime writer on the San Francisco Chronicle. Journalists started semi-facetiously wearing, not the required gunsight badges, but badges bearing the slogan 'I am not Paul Avery'. Avery unsportingly wore one too and took to carrying a gun.

There were few new leads, though one correspondent suggested that Zodiac was responsible for an earlier murder, the killing of Cheri Jo Bates in November 1966. That murder, just like the later ones, had been followed up with crank letters.

On 7 April 1972, a law secretary called Isobel Watson was getting off a bus when a white Chevrolet swerved across the road and nearly hit her. The car stopped, the driver apologized and offered to give her a lift. She wisely declined. Then he jumped out and stabbed her in the back. She screamed and her neighbours ran out to help. The Chevrolet driver drove off. Isobel was able to describe her attacker. He was five feet nine inches tall, white, in his early forties and wearing black-rimmed glasses. He was almost certainly the Zodiac Killer.

Time passed and the case was no nearer resolution. The inquiry was wound down. Eventually there was only Inspector David Toschi left on the case. Zodiac's correspondence ceased for almost four years. It was possible he had committed suicide, which is what sometimes happens with psychopaths who recognize that they are beyond control and, at some level, want to be stopped. But Toschi believed that Zodiac got his kicks from the publicity rather than from the killings themselves. If he had killed himself, it was likely that he would have drawn attention to the fact by leaving a note or writing a letter to the press. On 25 April 1978, Toschi got confirmation that he was right; Zodiac was indeed still alive. Zodiac sent a letter to the *San Francisco Chronicle*. There were references in the letters to films, so it seemed likely that the killer was a film enthusiast. One of the local cinemas had the constellations painted on the ceiling, and that was probably the origin of Zodiac's name for himself. It was hard to see any other origin. It was also possible that the gunsight logo was not intended to be a gunsight at all, but the symbol that appears on a cinema screen as a projectionist's guide. A love of film would also match up with the killer's evident love of display and mass communication. Perhaps he even saw his serial crimes in cinematic terms; the story of his career as a killer was in itself a kind of screenplay.

The police hoped to use the killer's obvious love of publicity to trap him. A film was made about the Zodiac killings, and when it was shown in San Francisco a suggestion box was set up in the foyer, where people could leave any information or ideas they had about the identity of the killer. It was a big box, big enough to have a detective hidden inside it. The detective read each letter with the aid of a torch as it was dropped in and the idea was that he would raise the alarm if there was anything that looked as if it might have come from Zodiac himself.

The Oakland police thought they had the killer at one point. The suspect had seen the film three times and had been observed acting strangely during the showings. But it turned out he was a Vietnam War veteran who was sexually excited by the scenes of violence – and his handwriting did not match.

Police in San Francisco came to think that Zodiac was either dead or in prison for a crime in another state. But one criminologist at least thought the killing had continued – in a new location. There were several murders of young women, often students or hitch-hikers, in the Santa Barbara area in the early 1970s. Like Zodiac's victims, none of them had been sexually molested.

One possible suspect was a former boyfriend of Darlene Ferrin, who lived at Riverside at the time when Cheri Jo

Bates was murdered. The suspect lived with his mother, whom he hated, and cut up small mammals as a hobby. During the period of three years when the Zodiac Killer was completely inactive, 1975–1978, the suspect had been in a psychiatric hospital after being charged with child molesting. In spite of these promising-sounding leads, it has proved impossible to identify the Zodiac Killer with any certainty.

Over the years, many people were investigated as suspects. The lead suspect was Arthur Leigh Allen (1933–1992). In 1971, a friend of Allen's reported to the police his suspicion that Allen was the killer. It seemed to the police that there was a good deal of circumstantial incriminating evidence that agreed with this. Arthur Allen was a convicted criminal and there were components of weapons in his home. When asked if he had read a short story called The Most Dangerous Game, he said he had and that it had impressed him. The police thought this significant, as the cipher code Zodiac used appears to refer to this story. The police kept returning to Allen as their prime suspect, searching his home three times, in 1972, 1991 and again in 1992, just two days after his death. Arthur Allen always denied any connection with the crimes, and the police were unable to find any physical evidence of his involvement. It was one of those cases where the police were convinced they had the right man, but could not prove it. It is worrying that policemen can see reading books – and being impressed by them – as indicating or reinforcing criminal tendencies. One of my own books was recently found in the home of a murderer, and the local sheriff observed that it was 'not normal reading matter'. I suppose much depends upon your point of view.

The Vallejo County Police Department wisely decided not to proceed with charges against Arthur Allen. Allen's handwriting did not match Zodiac's; his DNA did not match the DNA on Zodiac's letters either. In this remarkable case, in which there seem to be no shortage of witness reports, descriptions and physical evidence, even the prime suspect evaporated into thin air.

THE VANISHING EARL: LORD LUCAN AND THE MURDER OF SANDRA RIVETT

London. 1974. It was the middle of the evening of Thursday 7 November, and Lady Lucan began to wonder what had happened to her nanny. Five minutes before nine o'clock, the twenty-nine-year-old nanny, Sandra Rivett, had gone downstairs to the basement kitchen of 46 Lower Belgrave Street to make some tea for Lady Lucan. A quarter of an hour had passed, and Veronica, wife of the seventh Earl of Lucan, was concerned that Sandra had not returned. She left her three children upstairs and went down to the ground floor to find her.

The house was a typical upmarket London town house, with its rooms spread across six floors, including a basement where the kitchen and breakfast room were situated. The ground floor, where Lady Lucan now was, accommodated the dining room, living room and a cloakroom. The upper floors were mostly bedrooms. Lady Lucan noticed that the basement light was off. When she tried the switch, it did not work. Lady Lucan called Sandra's name, but there was no answer. She could hear faint noises, which she thought might be coming from the cloakroom, and wondered if that was where Sandra was.

Suddenly she was attacked, bludgeoned repeatedly over the head. She screamed and was told forcefully to shut up. She was a small, slight woman only five foot two inches tall, and she found herself struggling with a large and threatening figure, which stuck three gloved fingers down her throat. He tried to strangle her. He tried to gouge out her eyes. She found herself fighting for her life. She grabbed and squeezed her attacker's testicles, which made him back away momentarily and she was able to get away.

Lady Lucan managed eventually to get out into the street and stagger to the nearest pub. The Plumbers' Arms was just thirty yards along the street, and she knew there would be people there who could help her; it was a place of safety. She burst in, gasping, 'Murder, murder! I think my neck has been broken! He's tried to kill me. I've just escaped being murdered. He's in the house. He's murdered the nanny.' She managed to explain that her children were still in the house, but no-one went to save them. Instead, the police were called, while Lady Lucan slumped to the floor in a faint and was taken to hospital.

The police forced open the door and noticed a lot of blood on the stairwell. Then they went upstairs to check that the children were unharmed. The seven-year-old boy and the four-year-old girl were asleep in their bedrooms.

The ten-year-old Frances was quietly watching television in a bedroom on the second floor. They were far enough up the building not to have been disturbed by the violent incident in the basement.

The police noticed that the basement door was open. Close to it they found a twisted length of lead pipe, about nine inches long and wrapped in tape. In the breakfast room there was more blood, with pieces of smashed china. On one of the basement chairs, there was an unscrewed light bulb; the police suspected that the intruder removed the bulb so that the victim would be unable to see him. In the basement there was a canvas mailbag resting in a large pool of blood. Inside they discovered the battered body of Sandra Rivett. She had died of blows to the back of her head.

At midnight, the police went to find Lord Lucan. They thought this would be a simple matter of going to his apartment in Elizabeth Street, where he had lived since separating from his wife over a year before. He was not there.

The following evening, the police visited Lady Lucan in hospital. She was in a poor state, suffering from the effects of seven head wounds, loss of blood and shock. Her injuries had been examined. There was a suspicion, never really followed up, that the injuries inside her mouth had been self-inflicted; it is extremely unusual for an attacker to put his fingers inside his victim's mouth. Perhaps there was a clue here to what really happened, but for the moment the police were ready to accept Lady Lucan's version of events. She was able to tell them that she had put the two youngest children to bed and then watched television with Frances. Sandra had knocked and come in shortly before nine to ask if they would like some tea. Then she described going downstairs to meet her attacker, who she was certain was her husband.

She said that after the struggle they had both fallen to the floor exhausted and her husband had admitted accidentally killing the nanny. Sandra normally took Thursday evening off, and Lucan was expecting to find his wife, alone, in the basement. Typically, it was Lady Lucan herself who made the tea in the evening, as her husband would have known, and her husband had intended to kill her. Because of the change of routine he had killed Sandra by mistake.

The Lucans got up off the floor and went upstairs to the bedroom where Frances was still watching television. Frances told the police she noticed her mother had blood on her face when her parents came into the room; then Frances was sent to her own room. After that, according to Lady Lucan, the Lucans went into the bathroom, where 'Lucky' Lucan inspected her injuries before laying a towel on the bed for her to rest on. When he went to the bathroom for more towels to clean her up, and she was on her own for a moment, she took her chance and ran out of the house.

A difficulty with all of this is that there is only one available version of what passed between Lady Lucan and her attacker. We have only Lady Lucan's word that her attacker was Lord Lucan, and there were no witnesses to the conversation. One possibility is that Lady Lucan tried to calm her husband down by pretending to collude with him. She persuaded him that Sandra would not be missed. They could hide the body and she could tell the police that a burglar had broken in. She was terrified that he was going to kill her too and was ready to agree to anything. Lucan suggested that she should take some sleeping pills. She agreed, but only if she could lie down for a while upstairs on her bed.

Lord Lucan, Richard John Bingham, was born in 1934, the son of George Bingham, the sixth Earl of Lucan. He was the second of four children, with a younger brother and two older sisters. During the Second World War, the children were evacuated to the United States, where they lived in luxury in mansions in Florida and New York. After the war, Lucan went to Eton, developing into an imposing figure six foot four inches tall. He did his National Service in the Coldstream Guards before joining a merchant bank. He spent most of his free time gambling at the casino tables at the Claremont Club in Berkeley Square. After winning £26,000 in two days, Lucan decided to devote himself full-time to gambling. He left the bank.

Lucan met his wife, Veronica Duncan, in 1963. By chance, Veronica's sister married Bill Shand Kydd, who was a wealthy friend of Lucan's. Just two months after they married, Lucan's father died and he inherited the title and a large amount of money. The seventh Earl of Lucan was not the first to acquire a spectacularly bad reputation. His great-great-grandfather, the third Earl, was responsible ordering the catastrophic Charge of the Light Brigade at the Battle of Balaclava.

After the birth of their children, Veronica developed severe post-natal depression, which was unfortunately incorrectly diagnosed and inadequately treated. As a result, her mental condition gradually deteriorated, though she was still able to run the household and care for the children. Lord Lucan was supportive and keen to help her out of the depression. He researched the subject and tried to persuade her to seek professional help. In 1967, he urged her go into a psychiatric hospital, but she refused treatment. It seems he tried again in 1971 to have her admitted to hospital after she experienced hallucinations. He got her as far as the front door of the hospital before she ran off in a fright.

The pressure on their marriage brought it to breaking point in 1972. Lucan became increasingly impatient with Veronica's illness and her refusal to do anything constructive about it. He spent more and more time with his friends at the gambling tables. There he lost a great deal of the money he had inherited.

According to one of the nannies they employed, Stefania Sawicka, Lord Lucan beat his wife, pushed her down the stairs and tried to strangle her. Lady Lucan was frightened and told Sawicka, 'Don't be surprised if he kills me one day.' She acknowledged that her husband had a violent streak and that sometimes he would beat her with a stick wrapped in tape.

It was in 1973 that Lord Lucan moved out, taking up residence in a basement flat in Elizabeth Street. He confided in his friends that he was worried about the well-being of the children. Veronica was in such a poor state mentally that she was incapable of looking after them properly. He decided that the children would be safer living with him, and launched a formal battle for custody. The custody hearing was to take place in May 1973. In March that year he decided he would not wait. He followed the nanny when she took the children into a park and persuaded them to go back with him to Elizabeth Street – to stay. For several weeks the children lived with their father while he waited for the custody hearing. He hired a private detective to follow his wife, with the idea of collecting information about her that would help him to secure permanent custody. He also taped his wife's emotional outbursts so that he could demonstrate her instability.

When the custody hearing came to an end in June 1973, Lucan lost. The judge described his behaviour as lawless and decided that Lady Lucan should have custody of the children. Lucan's luck seemed to be running out. He had been spending fast on the maintenance of his family and two homes, detectives, medics and lawyers; he now had debts amounting to over £40,000. He too began to have psychological problems. He could not sleep, and he started drinking heavily. He also blamed his wife for his predicament, sometimes openly expressing hatred for her.

It is alleged that in October 1974, Lucan confided to his close friend John Aspinall that he wanted to kill her. A few weeks before the murder of Sandra Rivett, he told another friend that he would like to kill his wife and drop her body into the Solent. People said overheated things like this when they were drunk, and nobody took them very seriously, at least until the awful events of 7 November.

After Sandra Rivett's murder, the police combed Lucan's apartment for clues. They found that his car keys, driving licence, wallet, address books and passport were all still there. The address books were a starting point, and the police started ringing his friends. One of the people they made contact with in this way was Susan Maxwell-Scott. She gave an account of the events of 7 November that differed from Lady Lucan's, and this is where the case becomes a maze of speculation. Up to this point we really have only Lady Lucan's version of what happened in her house that evening, backed up at one point by the evidence of her ten-year-old daughter. Lady Lucan's version of events may have been completely accurate, or it may have been a complete travesty of what really happened. Now that Susan Maxwell-Scott gave different version of some key facts, doubts began to arise in many people's minds about the reliability of Lady Lucan's version.

According to Susan Maxwell-Scott, Lord Lucan knocked on her door at 11.30 p.m. He was dishevelled and had evidently recently washed his trousers: they were still wet.

She naturally offered him a drink and asked what was wrong. He said he had been walking past the house where his wife lived on his way to his own apartment, where he intended to change for dinner. He said he peered into the basement window and saw his wife locked in a struggle with a man. He let himself into the house with his key and went down to the basement. He slipped and fell into a pool of blood as he approached the man wrestling with his wife. The man ran off when he saw Lucan. His wife became hysterical and blamed him for hiring a hit man to kill her. He had helped his wife to clean herself up, but while he was fetching more towels she ran out of the house. He was afraid she would tell the police that he, Lucan, was responsible for injuring her and that he had decided to lie low. Susan Maxwell-Scott said Lucan told her he had made three phone calls, one to his friend Madeleine Floorman, one to his mother, one to Bill Shand Kydd.

Possibly Lucan had visited Madeleine Floorman's place before going to Susan Maxwell-Scott's. She had been woken up by someone knocking hard at her door at ten o'clock in the evening, and she had decided not to answer. A little later she had a phone call from someone she believed to be Lord Lucan. He sounded distressed and incoherent and she eventually hung up and went back to sleep.

Some time between ten o'clock and half past ten, Lucan phoned his mother to tell her there had been a catastrophe at Belgrave Street. He wanted his mother to collect the children and take them to her own house for safety. He told her that his wife and Sandra had been injured. It was of interest to the police that the story he told his mother exactly matched the story he told Susan Maxwell-Scott, which added to its credibility. Before going to see Susan Maxwell-Scott, Lucan tried to phone Bill Shand Kydd but could not speak to him.

He wrote two letters to Shand Kydd. The first was a brief description of the evening's events and the second dealt with financial matters. The letters, in their blood-stained envelopes, were posted on 8 November. The first letter ran as follows:

Dear Bill,

The most ghastly circumstances arose tonight, which I briefly described to my mother, when I interrupted the fight at Lower Belgrave St and the man left.

V. accused me of having hired him. I took her upstairs and sent Frances up to bed and tried to clean her up. She lay doggo for a bit. I went into the bathroom then left the house.

The circumstantial evidence against me is strong in that V. will say it was all my doing and I will lie doggo for a while, but I am only concerned about the children. If you can manage it I want them to live with you – Coutts St Martins Lane will handle school fees.

V. has demonstrated her hatred of me in the past and would do anything to see me accused.

For George & Frances to go through life knowing their father had stood in the dock for attempted murder would be too much. When they are old enough to understand, explain to them the dream of paranoia and look after them.

Yours ever,
Lucky.

Lord Lucan left Susan Maxwell-Scott at quarter past one in the morning, driving off in a Ford Corsair after saying that he had to 'get back'. On Sunday 10 November, Newhaven police found the Ford Corsair parked in a residential street, Norman Road, a short walk from Newhaven Marina. There were lots of bloodstains in the car. The Ford belonged to his friend Michael Stoop, and Lucan had borrowed it because the battery in his own car was faulty. When they opened the car's boot the police found a length of lead piping similar to the one found at the scene of the crime. Inside the car was a notepad from which a page had been torn. The missing page was delivered by post to Michael Stoop; it bore a note from Lord Lucan.

My dear Michael,
I have had a traumatic night of unbelievable coincidences. However I won't bore you with anything or involve you except to say that when you come across my children, which I hope you will, please tell them that you knew me and that all I cared about was them.
The fact that a crooked solicitor and a rotten psychiatrist

destroyed me between them will be of no importance to the children.

I gave Bill Shand Kydd an account of what actually happened but judging by my last effort in court no one, let alone a sixty-seven-year-old judge, would believe – and I no longer care, except that my children should be protected.
Yours ever,
John

After the discovery of the car in Newhaven, the police combed the area between it and the sea, including the docks, the marina and the ruined nineteenth-century fort. Fishermen on the quay thought they saw someone near the marina in the early hours of the morning on 8 November. Lord Lucan was nowhere to be found. Possibly he had boarded a cross-Channel ferry. Possibly he had taken a boat from the marina. Possibly he had gone up into the fort and committed suicide in the maze of unexplored underground passages there.

Because there was an expectation that Lucan would at some point reappear and resolve some of the questions about the death of Sandra Rivett, the inquest was delayed. After seven months, it began to look as though Lord Lucan had made a determined effort to disappear. Sandra Rivett's inquest was opened on 5 June 1975 at Westminster Coroner's Court.

The major available source of evidence was Lady Lucan, but she made it clear in her statements to the police that she intended to incriminate her husband. At that time, English law prevented wives from testifying against their husbands unless they were charged with assault. Lucan had not been charged, since he was not available to be charged, so it looked as if, strictly keeping to the law, Lady Lucan would be unable to give evidence. Given the peculiar circumstances, the coroner made an exception. Lady Lucan gave her account of what happened. Then a statement by the daughter, Frances, was read out.

Frances had heard her mother scream from what sounded a long way away. Frances was unafraid: she assumed the cat had scratched her mother. Later, her parents walked in together. Her mother's face was bloody and her father was wearing an overcoat. Frances was sent to bed, then she heard her father calling her mother; she saw her father looking for her mother before he went downstairs.

The pathologist Keith Simpson said that Sandra Rivett had suffocated by choking on her own blood, dying within minutes of the attack. This was quicker than the police surgeon's version of events; Dr Smith, the police surgeon, thought Sandra was alive until shortly before she was discovered. Lord Lucan's mother said her son had called her twice during the evening, but that he was incoherent. He had talked of blood and mess, but gave no detail. She said her son had asked her to pick up the children, which she did at a quarter to eleven. When he called a second time, he asked about the children, but his mother would say little because she had police in the house. The inquest also heard evidence from Susan Maxwell-Scott, Bill Shand Kydd and Michael Stoop.

The police forensic experts reported on their blood analyses. Sandra Rivett's blood (type B) and Lady Lucan's blood (type A) were found in two main areas of the house. Sandra's blood was found mainly in the basement. Lady Lucan's was concentrated mainly in the ground floor hallway at the top of the stairs down to the basement. There were also hairs in that blood which matched Lady Lucan's, supporting the idea that she had been attacked at the top of the stairs. But there was also blood of Lady Lucan's type on the mailbag containing Sandra's body. Possibly the attacker had the same blood type as Lady Lucan. Both Lady Lucan's blood type and Sandra Rivett's blood type were found on the lead pipe and also in the Ford Corsair. The piece of bent pipe wrapped in tape that was assumed to be the murder weapon, used in fact to batter both women over the head, contained no hairs belonging to either of the women. This was very strange, and suggested that the lead piping was not the murder weapon at all.

The envelopes sent to Bill Shand Kydd carried blood-stains of type AB, though this could have been a mixture of two separate blood samples, in other words the blood of Sandra and Veronica mixed. Further bloodstains of Sandra Rivett's blood type were found in the back garden. A bloodstained footprint was found in the basement, leading towards the garden. It had been made by a man's shoe, and it gives some corroboration for Lord Lucan's story that he disturbed an unidentified intruder.

Some fibres found in the house and in the Ford Corsair were a focus of interest at the inquest. Some blue-grey wool was found in the car, in the basement, on a blood-stained towel and on the lead pipe allegedly used to bludgeon Sandra and Veronica. These blue-grey wool fibres were believed to come from the attacker's clothing and the forensic evidence was made to imply that whoever attacked the women had also been in the Ford Corsair. Similarly, the rather crude (pre-DNA) analysis of the blood samples seemed to prove that Lord Lucan's story about his intervention in the basement in a struggle between his wife and her attacker was untrue; 'her' blood samples were found on the floor above the basement, which was where she said she had been attacked.

The investigators explored Lord Lucan's claim that he had seen the attack on his wife from outside. They tried to re-enact what he described and found that it was difficult to see anything at all from a standing position outside the basement window. Lucan would have had to stoop down to see in and even then he could only have seen the bottom four steps of the staircase into the basement. Given that the incident happened in the middle of a November evening and the light bulb had been removed, the basement would have been plunged in darkness anyway. Things looked very black indeed for Lord Lucan's version of what happened.

The timing of the events, on the other hand, favoured Lord Lucan. He had made reservations for four at his club for half past eight that evening. The club doorman said Lucan had arrived in his Mercedes at a quarter to nine, asking if his friends had arrived. Lucan was dressed casually, as if for golf and seemed untroubled. The doorman had the impression that Lord Lucan was on his way to his apartment to change for dinner. These timings made it virtually impossible for Lucan to reach the basement, take out the light bulb, wait for his wife to come down and commit the murder at nine o'clock. He would have had a bare ten minutes to drive two miles through city traffic to his apartment, park his Mercedes and walk (or run) back to 46 Lower Belgrave Street, which was half a mile away from his apartment. In fact the only way Lord Lucan could have been guilty of the murder is for the doorman's timings to have been wrong. But they would have had to be wrong by fifteen minutes or more, and it is difficult to see how Mr Edgson, the doorman, could have carried out his duties at all if he was as clueless about time as that.

The inquest on Sandra Rivett was a remarkable event in its own right. An inquest is held solely to decide the cause of death. Yet this inquest heard a lot of evidence that went well beyond that. There was widespread interest in the murder and people wanted to know whether Lord Lucan really was the murderer, but the inquest was not the proper place to determine that. There was, in effect, a large-scale impropriety in turning the inquest into a trial for murder, and the person put on trial was not even present to defend himself. The evidence presented was heavily slanted against Lord Lucan, because, characteristically, the police decided prematurely who was to blame and slanted the evidence accordingly.

The inquest lasted four days. The coroner decided that the jury had heard enough and it took them thirty-one minutes to return a sensational verdict. The verdict was that Sandra Rivett had been murdered by Lord Lucan. The general and widespread reaction to this was that the inquest had gone a step further than was appropriate – or just. As a direct result of this, a month later a bill was passed to prevent coroner's courts from naming murderers. It pre-empted the result of a trial; if Lucan had then been found, he would have been condemned in his absence, without having had the opportunity to defend himself, or appoint lawyers to present his case.

But the most sensational and remarkable aspect of the whole case is that Lord Lucan was never found. To this day, what happened to him after he left the car in Norman Road in Newhaven and walked down towards the marina is a complete mystery. Lord Lucan was able to disappear so efficiently because, for some reason, a warrant for his arrest was not issued immediately. This is odd, because the police seem to have had little doubt from the beginning that he was Sandra Rivett's murderer. They waited a week before issuing the warrant, and by then he had escaped, many think, abroad. If the warrant had been issued at once, the houses of his friends might have been searched.

Some think Lucan boarded a ferry and slipped over the side, drowning himself in the Channel. Others think he waded into the sea or jumped off the long harbour breakwater at Newhaven. But no body was washed ashore and police divers explored the waters of the harbour in vain. Others thought he might have gone up into the fort at Newhaven or onto the open shrubland beside it to commit suicide, but sniffer dogs failed to pick up Lord Lucan's scent there; heat detection devices found nothing either. Detectives went to France to interview immigration and security staff, but there had been no sightings of him getting off the ferry there.

There were nevertheless reported sightings from various places abroad. Interpol picked up a report that a hotel owner in Cherbourg recognized a frequent guest at the hotel as Lord Lucan. When members of the hotel staff were shown photos of Lucan, they confirmed that this was so. The mystery guest spoke fluent French. It is known that Lucan made a point of improving his French, taking French coaching several times a week. From then on, reports of sightings came from almost every country in the world. The British police were actively interested in tracing Lucan, but they never succeeded in tracking him down.

He had relatives in Zimbabwe, whom he visited before his disappearance. It may be that when he needed to disappear, he chose southern Africa. There are several persuasive stories of sightings there. The police became interested in these when they discovered that Lord Lucan's children were spending significant amounts of time there when they entered adulthood, and therefore became free to travel. In 1995, there were press reports that Scotland Yard detectives were convinced that Lucan was alive and living in Johannesburg. There was still no confirmation of this. Lucan was never apprehended, never brought back.

One former Scotland Yard detective, Duncan MacLaughlin, thought he had traced Lucan to the sub-continent of India. Lucan had lived in Goa under the name Barry Halpin until he died in 1996. But Barry Halpin turned out to be Barry Halpin, a Merseyside folk musician who had taken the hippy trail to India in the 1970s. It was another false scent.

By October 1999, the High Court decided that the seventh Earl of Lucan was, for all legal purposes, officially dead. His estate, amounting to less than £15,000, was scarcely worth inheriting. Lady Lucan commented that she hoped that would be an end to it. She believes that her husband is dead, referring to herself as 'the dowager countess'. Lucan's son, George Bingham, also believes his father is dead. He declared his intention of becoming the eighth Earl but, because the Lord Chancellor ruled that there was still no definitive proof that his father was dead, he was unable to take his seat in the House of Lords.

The ultimate question of Lord Lucan's guilt remains unanswered. Perhaps some of his friends, who saw him after the murder, know the answer. But they have said nothing. The inquest verdict is plainly unsatisfactory, because the inquest developed into a trial in the absence of the accused, and because no one was there to present Lord Lucan's case for him. By disappearing, Lord Lucan created an almost unprecedented legal and ethical situation, where the verdict has to be suspended – apparently for ever.

DEATH IN JEDDAH: HELEN SMITH

Helen Smith was born in Britain in 1956. She was working as a nurse in Jeddah in Saudi Arabia when she met her death at the age of twenty-three in 1979. She had been working in Saudi Arabia for only four months. The circumstances of her death are still unclear, though it is known that she died violently.

On the evening of 19 May 1979, she went to a party at the house of Dr Richard Arnot and his wife Penny. In the morning, after the party, her body was found in the street seventy feet below the balcony of the Arnots' third floor apartment. Beside her, impaled on the spiked railings that surrounded the apartment block, was the body of Johannes Otten, a thirty-five year old Dutch tugboat captain. They had clearly died in the same catastrophic accident or act of violence.

There were some clues as to what might have preceded Helen's death. Although she was fully clothed, the trousers and underpants of Johannes Otten were round his ankles, implying that some sort of sexual activity or attempted sexual activity took place immediately before their deaths.

There was an official Saudi investigation into the incident. Its conclusion was that the couple had accidentally fallen from the balcony while they were drunk, perhaps during a sexual encounter on the balcony. At the time, this finding was endorsed by the British Foreign Office.

Helen's father, a retired policeman called Ron Smith, was unable to accept the official version of events, which he saw as a cover-up for murder. He believed that the cover-up came from a high level in the British establishment. He spent twenty-five years trying to uncover what really happened that night in Jeddah, and get justice for those who, he believes, killed his daughter. While he pursued this quest, Ron Smith refused to allow his daughter's body to be buried. Instead it was preserved at Leeds General Infirmary so that it was available for forensic tests. During the long years following Helen's death, her body was investigated in no less than six post mortem examinations, which did not all arrive at the same conclusions.

Ron Smith attempted to have an inquest into his daughter's death in Britain. The autopsy report he ordered after inspecting her body in Jeddah was kept by the British Foreign Office, and he was refused a copy in spite of requesting one. When it was finally released, one vital page was missing; eventually that too was passed to Mr Smith. He tried to have an inquest opened in West Yorkshire, but coroner Philip Gill refused to hold an inquest on the grounds that the death occurred outside his jurisdiction. A Home Office pathologist examined Helen Smith's body and found evidence that she had injuries that were not consistent with a fall from the balcony. She had received a series of blows to her head and face. Two other pathologists, one of the British, the other Danish, carried out their own post mortems and they too concluded that the injuries were not consistent with a fall. There was an implication that the two victims had been murdered and then thrown from the balcony to make the double murder look like an accident.

In March 1982, there was a High Court hearing to decide whether the West Yorkshire coroner was right, and it neither upheld the coroner's decision nor overruled it, which was frustrating for Mr Smith. The High Court judges, Lord Justice Ormrod and Mr Justice Forbes, reserved judgment because of the complexities of the case. The eventual inquest returned an open verdict.

In July 2002, Ian Lucas MP asked a question in the House of Commons about the case. He asked the Secretary of State for the Home Department if he would order a new inquiry into the death of Helen Smith. Hilary Benn MP, answering, said, 'An inquest was held into Helen Smith's death in 1982. Inquest proceedings can be reviewed by the courts and we are not aware of any grounds for the government to take further action.'

Ron Smith still refuses to have his daughter buried until her killers are brought to justice. He remains convinced that she was murdered and that the murder was made to look like an accident. 'People say it is a mystery, but there is no mystery. She was murdered and I know who murdered her. I will just keep up the fight. What else can I do?'

At the root of the problem in Jeddah is the clash between the lifestyles of Western migrant workers, like the doctors and nurses at the expatriate party, and the official, Islamic code of conducted expected by the Saudi authorities. When individuals are caught out, for example consuming alcohol, their Western embassies often fail to support them strenuously. It is possible that something of this kind happened regarding Helen Smith. However she actually died, the Saudi version of events clearly indicated that as far as the Saudi authorities were concerned she was behaving badly, by drinking and engaging in casual extra-marital sex. She was in the wrong. What Ron Smith found when he went to Jeddah is that both Saudi and British authorities were uncommunicative. The Embassy's subdued response implied that Helen should not have been at the party in the first place. That naturally made Ron Smith suspicious. But was he right to assume foul play?

His hypothesis, that Helen was raped and then murdered, was openly supported by many of the people she worked with at the Baksh Hospital. Naturally, the other guests at the party did not wish to incriminate themselves or their friends and they all insisted that Helen's death was an accident. Some of the people at the party were in fact surprisingly frank. One woman admitted that she did not know what was happening to Helen because she (the non-witness) was in another room having sex with a man who was not her husband. It was an extraordinary admission to make, in a country where the punishment for adultery is death by stoning. Given the drinking at the party and the other violations of Saudi law, the expatriates at the party were given, by Saudi standards, light sentences. The host was sentenced to a year's imprisonment; the others were sentenced to public flogging.

The testimonies of the guests at the party give cause for suspicion in that they contradict one another in many important details. Something was being concealed. Could it have been the presence there of a Saudi? Ron Smith had great difficulties in finding out anything at all. The press helped, sniffing the scent of a good story, and dug out one or two more crumbs of information. One significant fact was that Johannes Otten's clothing and belongings had been tampered with to cover up the fact that he had been murdered. Another was the arrival of a mysterious Saudi at the crime scene shortly after it was discovered.

We may never know what happened to Helen Smith – unless one of the guests at the party one day decides to tell the whole truth about that evening in Jeddah.

I THOUGHT I WAS DOING YOU GUYS A FAVOUR: THE GREEN RIVER KILLER

The Green River killer was a serial killer operating in the state of Washington, in the north-west of the United States. He murdered at least forty-two women, and for a long time it looked as if he would never be caught. The public record of the serial killer, the string of perhaps sadistic and brutal killings with all their peculiar circumstances that make up the hallmark of the particular psychopath, is very often widely at variance with his everyday persona. The serial killer is often a quiet, ordinary-looking and ordinary-behaving person holding down an ordinary job. This mismatch is why he often remains unidentifiable, why he often remains uncaught for a long time.

In July 1982, two boys were cycling beside the Green River close to the Seattle-Tacoma Airport. They were carrying their fishing gear with them and contemplating an afternoon's fishing in the river, when one of them noticed what he thought was a log floating in the shallow water near Peck Bridge. He was curious about it and waded in with the idea of rolling it in to the bank to get a better look. He was shaken when he saw that it was a girl's body. In fact it was the body of a sixteen year old called Wendy Coffield and she was the first victim, as far as was then known, of the Green River Killer.

At first the police treated it as a fairly straightforward sex killing. Police officer Lieutenant Jackson Berd speculated that it was probably the usual case of a man who had had too much to drink, picked up a girl for sex, encountered resistance to his advances and tried to use force; the girl started screaming; the man tried to silence her, instinctively putting his hands to her mouth and throat (the source of the noise); the girl died by suffocation or strangulation and then her body was dumped. It was crime that happened all too often, a nasty crime, but far removed from the cold-blooded serial killing this would turn out to be.

Wendy Coffield was a runaway, a child prostitute who had been missing for three months when her body was found. She fitted Jackson Berd's sex killing pattern. It was thought at the time that Wendy Coffield was the Green River Killer's first victim, but there may have been others earlier. Six months before, the body of Wendy Coffield's friend Leanne Wilcox was found on waste ground several miles from the river. As the investigation progressed and more women fell victim to the killer, it began to look as if the murder of Leanne Wilcox was one of the series.

Five weeks later, the picture in any case changed significantly. In one day, the bodies of three more young women were found at separate locations along the same river. In August, forty-one year old Robert Ainsworth was in his rubber raft drifting down the Green River, south towards the outer edge of Seattle, a trip he had made many times. This time he noticed a balding middle-aged man standing on the river bank and another sitting nearby on a pickup truck. He assumed they were there for the fishing and asked the older man if he had caught anything. The man said he hadn't and asked Ainsworth if he had found anything, which was an odd question. The two men left in the old pickup truck and a few moments later Robert Ainsworth looked down into the water to see the eyes of a young black woman staring back up at him just below the surface of the water.

At first Ainsworth thought it was a mannequin and tried to catch it with a pole. In trying to dislodge it from a rock he overturned his raft and fell into the river. Then he realized that it was a woman's body. Just seconds later, he saw a second corpse floating by, a half-naked black woman. Ainsworth swam to the river bank where the truck had been standing a minute earlier. He sat down, badly shaken and waited for help to arrive. Eventually a man with two children on bicycles came by and he sent them off to get the police. When the police arrived, they sealed off the area and found a third body in the grass no more than thirty feet from where the other two had been floating in the water. This young woman had a pair of blue under-pants knotted round her neck. She had bruises on her arms and legs, showing that there had been a struggle before she was overpowered. She was identified as Opal Mills. She was sixteen. The other two young women were thirty-one-year-old Marcia Chapman and seventeen-year-old Cynthia Hinds. They were both weighted down with rocks and, peculiarly, both had pyramid-shaped stones inserted into their vaginas.

The post mortem examinations showed that although the bodies were all found in the same place at the same time, they had not all died at the same time. Cynthia Hinds had been dead for a few hours only, while Marcia Chapman had been dead for several days. The implication is that the men in the pick-up had killed the three women one by one over a period of time, stored their bodies somewhere else, and then taken them to a quiet spot on the bank of the Green River to dump them – perhaps only minutes before Robert Ainsworth arrived. Yet the bodies in the water had evidently been immersed for quite long time. Just possibly the men in the pickup were nothing to do with the three murders.

A few days before the discovery of the three bodies, a single body was found, strangled and slumped over a log; she was Deborah Bonner. During the years that followed, more bodies appeared, all of women between the ages of fifteen and thirty-six, all across King County, the district crossed by the Green River. Two bodies were found just across the state border, in Oregon.

A huge police investigation costing more than £14 million was set up to identify and capture the Green River

Killer. A Green River Task force was set up, working in shifts round the clock. A major problem faced by the King County police was the attitude of the local people. They were very frightened of being attacked by the serial killer who was on the rampage. But at the same time there was an unhealthy complacency; because many of the victims were prostitutes, and they were the killer's target group, the great moral majority had nothing to worry about. But the Yorkshire Ripper murders were to show how false that kind of thinking can be. You do not have to be a prostitute to fall victim to a committed prostitute-slayer; you only have to be mistaken for a prostitute by someone who, by definition, is not thinking straight. It may be that in the killer's mind a particular hairstyle or location is associated with prostitutes. Then, just by virtue of having long dark hair or walking along a particular street, you become a prostitute in the killer's warped imagination. Complacency can be very dangerous.

Another problem for the investigation was that prostitutes were understandably reluctant to co-operate with the police. The police discovered that many of the murder victims knew one another. It seemed likely that the killer would be found operating in the area frequented by the girls, that he was picking them up in the same relatively small area. Police interviewed many of the prostitutes working central Seattle, to get information on their clients. Not surprisingly, the women were unwilling to share this information.

One prostitute reported a man to the police. He had raped her and talked about the Green River murders; she suspected that he was the murderer. On 20 August 1982, the police announced that they had taken into custody the man she reported. They were unable to find anything that definitely connected him with the murders and had to release him.

Two separate incidents seemed likelier leads. One young prostitute was picked up by a middle-aged man in a blue and white truck. Once she was in the truck, he pointed a gun at her and drove her at speed to a remote spot, where he raped her violently. Afterwards, he was driving her either back or on somewhere else, and she managed to escape when he stopped at a traffic light. She was able to make out part of the registration number as the truck sped off.

A girl of fifteen had a similar experience. A man in a blue and white truck approached her and offered her a lift. Once she was inside, he became aggressive, pulling a gun out and pointing it at her head. He drove her to some woodland, where he forced her to give him oral sex. Then he handcuffed her and released her in the woods. If these young women were victims of the killer, they were lucky to escape with their lives.

Shortly afterwards, a butcher called Charles Clinton Clark was stopped by police in the centre of Seattle. He was driving a blue and white truck. The police did a check on Clark's background and found that he owned two handguns. The investigators thought they had found the

Green River Killer. They showed Clark's driving licence photo to the two young women who had been raped. Both identified him as their attacker. Charles Clark was arrested. His truck and house were searched, and the two handguns were found. After police interrogation, Clark admitted attacking the women.

The two sex crimes were solved, but was Clark the Green River Killer? The fact that Clark allowed his victims to escape made him different from the Green River Killer, so there was some doubt. It also emerged that Clark had strong alibis for the times when many of the murders had taken place. In fact, one of the victims, Mary Meehan, went missing while Clark was in custody being charged with rape.

One of the detectives on the Task Force, Detective Reichert, became suspicious that one of the civilian volunteers working on the case might be the killer. A forty-four-year-old unemployed taxi driver became the prime suspect, because his profile was thought to fit the profile assembled by FBI agent John Douglas. Douglas asserted that the killer was a confident but impulsive middle-aged man who would be likely to frequent the murder scenes in order to re-enact and relive the crimes more vividly in his imagination. The killer would be familiar with the area. He would be interested in police work and might even contact the police under the pretence of assisting the investigation. Unfortunately, this profile was likely to incriminate anyone who came forward to try to help the police. Little wonder, then, that people are increasingly wary of police officers!

Detective Reichert's hunch, based on agent Douglas's profile, led to the close monitoring of the taxi driver's movements though the winter of 1982. During this time, he continuously denied having any connection with the Green River murders, but remained the Task Force's prime suspect. After weeks of scrutiny, it was plain that there was no evidence against him whatsoever, except that he knew five of the victims. The Task Force could not pin the murders on him, so they arrested him for failing to pay parking tickets instead.

The mother of one of the victims made a very interesting observation. She complained that people were missing the point by demanding tougher action against prostitution. 'Our kids are being penalized again. It sounds silly, but how can you be penalized any more after you've been murdered? We admit that our kids had problems but Tracy didn't deserve to die because she wasn't living what was perceived to be a perfect life. The issue was and is this maniac out there, not the lives that some of his victims were leading.'

The Green River Killer was believed to be of the same psychological type as the Zodiac Killer and Jack the Ripper, a psychopathic sex killer who goes on killing until he is stopped. Lieutenant Nolan was second-in-command of the Green River Task Force. He developed a strong feeling about the type of man he was looking for. 'The man we are looking for is a shade of grey. He is very innocuous, fits right into the community. That is what makes him so very dangerous.'

In order to retain the integrity and effectiveness of the investigation, the Task Force revealed as little as possible of what they have learnt about their nameless suspect. They did, even so, release a photofit picture, so that potential victims at least had a chance of avoiding danger. The Task Force released a few details, though. The killer was middle-aged, an outdoor type who knows the mountains, ravines and streams like the back of his hand. He was physically strong: strong enough to be able to carry the body of a full-grown woman for some distance.

There were a few sightings by witnesses. These were moments when people saw the victims in the company of a strange man shortly before they were murdered. From these fragmentary descriptions, the Task Force assembled what they believed were significant details about the killer. The believed the killer drove a pale blue pickup speckled with primer paint to cover spots of rust – a distinctive-looking vehicle.

The forensic evidence from the victims' bodies gave more specific information about him. The Green River Killer was a sexual psychopath. He was a deeply troubled, disturbed and tormented personality, with a sexual personality twisted by some terrible childhood secret that left him simmering with anger against women. The Task Force decided not to reveal any details of the way he killed his victims, though it emerged that strangulation was his favoured method and that it was favoured so that the killer could watch his victims suffer.

The open country within a radius of forty-five miles of Seattle was the killer's dumping ground, though it is not clear from the information released whether the victims were killed where their bodies were found. The bodies were discovered by a wide variety of visitors to the countryside: walkers, joggers, hunters, fishermen, mushroom pickers and boy scouts.

The Task Force was inundated with 10,000 phone calls offering ideas and information. Inevitably there were several false confessions from insane attention-seekers. Lieutenant Nolan was disappointed not to have caught the killer and brought him to justice, but he and his team got used to the disappointment. By the spring of 1983, the investigation was clearly collapsing. There were more and more killings, there was more and more evidence, but none of the sightings or suspects seemed to lead anywhere. By 1985, the Task Force was calling in clinical psychologists to help them deal with their stress and their sense of failure. Typically, Nolan became obsessed with the killer. 'I would love to capture him, to get him to sit down and tell me just why he did this, what drove him. I don't have any idea what this guy's going to tell me, what his secret is.'

Perhaps inevitably, what did develop within the Task Force was a kind of sneaking admiration for the Green River Killer's intelligence. It is recognized that the killer chose his victims very cunningly, leaving the police very little in the way of witnesses, sightings or clues. The killer was good at concealing corpses, which in turn created a range of difficulties for the police. The longer the time that elapses between the murder and the discovery of the body, the harder it is to determine the time of death, and in some cases even the cause of death, as we shall see in the case of Milly Dowler.

The Green River killings ended in the late 1990s. Why did they come to an end then? It is very unlikely, given the psychological profile, that the Green River Killer would simply voluntarily stop killing because he had had enough – still less seen the error of his ways. Someone who has killed that number of people, forty-two at least, is unlikely to find that he has had enough of killing or decide that he really shouldn't be doing it.

By chance, in 1987, the investigators stumbled on a new suspect. He was taken into custody by the police for trying to pick up a policewoman posing as a prostitute. He was released, but the investigators looked at his background and found that he was accused of throttling a prostitute near the airport in 1980; he had pleaded self-defence and was released. In 1987 the police released him after he had passed a lie detector test. One of the investigators, Detective Haney, decided to pursue this suspect and delved further. He found that in 1982 the suspect had been stopped and questioned by police while he was in his truck with a prostitute. The prostitute was Keli McGinness, who was one of the Green River Killer's victims. The police had interviewed the suspect again in 1983 in connection with the kidnapping of another of the murder victims. A witness, the prostitute's boyfriend, had followed the pickup truck to the suspect's house. Detective Haney realized he was on to something when he interviewed the suspect's ex-wife and discovered that the dumping sites for the bodies were all haunts frequented by the suspect.

The clinching evidence was that when the suspect's work record was examined he was absent from work on every occasion when a victim vanished. On 8 April 1987, police searched the suspect's house. There was still insufficient evidence to justify an arrest and the police had to release him from custody. The suspect's name was Gary Ridgway. He was the Green River Killer, but the police had to let him go.

The Green River killings might have stopped, but the remains of victims came to light intermittently, as if to remind the Task Force that it had still not solved the case. The buried skeleton of a woman was discovered by three boys; she was a seventeen-year-old called Cindy Smith and she had been missing for three years. Two more bodies that came to light were those of Debbie Gonzales, aged fourteen, and Debra Estes, aged fifteen. Debra had gone missing six years before her body was found.

Another new suspect appeared in December 1988. A television true crime detection programme was broadcast and in response several viewers phoned in proposing William J. Stevens as a suspect. When the Task Force investigators checked his background, they found that he had already surfaced before as a suspect. But in spite of having a criminal record, there was nothing at all to tie him to the Green River murders and he was cleared of all suspicion.

Meanwhile, more human remains kept coming to light, some of them with a strange story to tell. In February 1990, the skull of Denise Bush was found in woodland in Tukwila, Washington. The rest of her body was found in Oregon five years later. For some reason, perhaps to confuse the investigators, the murderer was moving body parts around. By 1991, the investigative team had all but admitted total defeat.

In April 2001, with more advanced forensic testing including DNA testing available, Detective Reichert, now Sheriff of King County, reopened the investigation. He was still obsessed with solving the case. All the evidence was re-examined and some semen samples found on the bodies of three victims were tested for their DNA profile. The DNA profiles were compared with samples taken from Gary Leon Ridgway in 1987. On 10 September 2001, the spectacular news came through from the lab: the profiles matched. On 30 November, Gary Ridgway was intercepted on his way home from work and arrested on four counts of aggravated murder. It was a start. At last, the man the police had been hunting for twenty years was in custody.

Ridgway, born in Salt Lake City in 1949, was working for a computer firm when he was arrested. At the time when the murders were committed, and for a period of thirty years, Ridgway was employed as a truck painter at the Kentworth truck factory in Renton, Washington.

Ridgway was sexually insatiable, wanting sex several times a day. He also like having sex in public areas or in woods – even in areas where his victims were dumped. Ridgway had fanatical religious beliefs and these, combined with his strong sex drive, generated the tension within him that resulted in serial murder. He had a love-hate relationship with prostitutes. He complained to neighbours about prostitutes working in the area, but was also a frequent client. He functioned in a typically psychopathic way; he did not regard his victims as real people with separate identities, but wrote them off as disposable thrills.

I killed some of them outside. I killed most of them in my house near Military Road. I killed a lot of them in my truck not far from where I picked them up. I picked prostitutes as my victims because I hate most prostitutes and I did not want to pay them for sex. I also picked prostitutes because they were easy to pick up without being noticed. I picked prostitutes because I thought I could kill as many of them as I wanted without getting caught . . . I thought I was doing you guys a favour.

How much of this plea bargain statement represents what Ridgway actually thought is hard to tell; he was picking up quite a lot from his interrogators and giving them back what he thought they wanted to hear, with a view to winning a significant favour.

On 5 November 2003, Gary Ridgway, then fifty-four years old, avoided the death penalty by confessing to the murders of forty-eight women. Most of the murders took place in 1982–84. The deal struck between Ridgway and the authorities was that he would co-operate with them in closing these cases in exchange for forty-eight life sentences without parole. The problem with plea bargaining is that it does not necessarily lead to the truth. There is little doubt now that Gary Ridgway was responsible for some, possibly most of the Green River murders, but was he really responsible, solely responsible, for all forty-eight of them – and only those forty-eight? That was what the authorities wanted to hear, so that was what Ridgway told them. The possibility remains that someone else may have been involved. The plea bargaining has introduced the added complication that it looks as if justice is being bent, negotiated. US citizens are asking who is eligible for the death penalty if Gary Ridgway isn't?

Why did he do it? It was partly the enormous stress generated by the polarization of his fanatical religious beliefs and his powerful sex drive. It was also to an extent an overwhelming sense of disempowerment. The killing was exciting, dangerous and gave his dull life as a truck painter the colour it otherwise lacked. On the other hand, millions of people feel frustrated and disempowered without resorting to serial killing.

But the pattern of the crimes does not quite add up. We are still not seeing the whole picture. We are being asked to believe by the King County officials, who want to see the case closed, that Gary Ridgway went on a frenzied killing spree in 1982–84, and then stopped killing – completely – until he murdered once more in 1990 and on one final occasion in 1998. If that is what really happened, it is unique in the history of serial killing. What usually happens is that there is a killing spree, which involves one or more murders, followed by a cooling-off period, then another killing spree, and so on, rather like cyclical pattern of activity in a volcano. If Ridgway really killed forty-six women in the space of two years, he could not have gone on for twenty years after that nourished by only two more killings. This is a case that appears to be solved, but is not. The solution is probably that Ridgway killed many more women, outside King County. These are murders which he will never own up to because it is only in King County that he has been exempted from the death penalty.

A MISCARRIAGE OF JUSTICE? THE DEATH OF SHEILA BAMBER

Rural Essex. 1985. It was some time after 3 o'clock in the morning on 7 August that Jeremy Bamber was woken up by his phone ringing. He picked up the phone to hear his father, Ralph Bamber, shouting, 'Sheila's got the gun. She's gone crazy. Come over quickly.' Ralph hung up and though Jeremy tried phoning back he was unable to get through. Ralph's phone was off the hook.

June and Ralph Bamber lived at White House Farm in the village of Tolleshunt D'Arcy, nine miles south-west of Colchester and not far from Jeremy's cottage. The Bambers had adopted both Jeremy and Sheila. Sheila Bamber had been married, become Sheila Caffell, and produced twin sons, Nicholas and Daniel. Now Sheila and her six-year-old twins were living with Ralph and June at White House Farm. Sheila had gone crazy before, but there had never been a gun before. Jeremy decided to ring Chelmsford Police Station and ask them to meet him at the farm. After phoning the police, he phoned his girl friend, Julie Mugford, as he was unsure whether he had done the right thing. Then he drove the short distance to White House Farm, to find the police already there. Armed police officers arrived at 5.30.

There was a lengthy discussion about Sheila's state of mind, the weapons in the house, and other aspects of the situation. Then, at 7.30, the police broke the door down to find a terrible scene of carnage inside. They found Ralph Bamber's body first. He was in the kitchen, where the phone was off the hook, and it looked as if Ralph had been attempting to call for help when he was attacked. His wife June was upstairs in the main bedroom. She had been shot once while in bed, then several more times as she tried to get out of the room. The twins had been shot several times in the head as they lay in bed. Sheila was lying dead beside her parents' bed in the main bedroom. She had died of a single gunshot wound to the throat. She was holding a .22 semi-automatic rifle.

When the police told Jeremy what had happened, he went into shock and vomited.

Sheila Caffell's marriage had broken down. She became depressed and slid further into paranoid schizophrenia, having to enter hospital twice for treatment. She had in fact only been discharged from hospital days before the shootings. Psychiatric reports recorded that her mental illness was centred on the twins, and even more disturbingly that she referred to them as 'the Devil's children'. The psychiatrist noted that she had suicidal tendencies. Before the shootings she had stopped taking the medication prescribed to control her dangerous state of mind.

Jeremy Bamber said that there had been a discussion the day before the shootings, during which it had been proposed that the twins should be fostered, possibly on a part-time basis, or that they needed some other care arrangements. It is quite possible that this could have triggered a schizophrenic episode; Sheila could have decided that killing the children and her parents, and then killing herself, would solve the problem. The police concluded that Sheila Caffell had murdered her sons and her parents and then committed suicide.

It was then that something extraordinary happened, something which took the murder case into a new dimension altogether and ensured its place in the annals of criminal history. During the next few weeks the police came to a different conclusion. They decided that Sheila Caffell had not committed suicide, but that Jeremy Bamber had killed her as well as killing all the other members of the household, finally putting the murder weapon into Sheila's hands. It was a very strange decision to make. Normal, rational people use the reasoning procedure known as Occam's razor; this is the principle that an explanation should entail as few assumptions as possible or, put more colloquially, always go for the simplest explanation. In this case, the profoundly disturbed Sheila Bamber was by far the likeliest suspect for this appalling crime. On this occasion, the police decided not to apply Occam's razor.

Bamber was arrested, questioned and released. Then on 29 September he was re-arrested and charged with the murders.

The police had decided that Bamber had a strong motive for murder. He stood to inherit over £400,000 as well as the Bamber estate, consisting of five farms, a farming co-operative and packaging factory in which Ralph had a twenty percent share, and a caravan park with an annual turnover of about a million pounds. The lure of this considerable wealth was enough to give Jeremy Bamber a motive.

Why did the police change their minds? They interviewed a number of friends, relations, business contacts, some of whom had a vested interest in seeing Jeremy Bamber convicted of the murders so that he could not inherit. The police seem not to have considered that possibility that the statements they were getting might contain bias. There were also problems with Jeremy Bamber's girlfriend's account of his actions. Bamber had broken their relationship off after the murders and it is very hard to know how much credence can be put in her version of events. Had Jeremy Bamber really referred disparagingly referred to his 'old' father, 'mad' mother and a sister with 'nothing to live for'? In the circumstances they were damaging remarks, but we cannot be sure that he even made them. Many people in any case refer to people of their parents' generation as old or mad without meaning them any harm, and usually without intending any disparagement. Had he really made a phone call saying, 'Tonight's the night'? If so, what had had he meant by it? There are obviously serious reasons to doubt hearsay evidence against Jeremy that might have been motivated by cash, revenge, or immunity from prosecution.

The main evidence brought forward by the prosecution was the blood found in the gun's silencer. The victims were shot at close range, so the victims' blood splashed back into the silencer. A test on the blood in the silencer showed that it was of the same group as Sheila's. If that was the case, Sheila could not have committed suicide. With the silencer attached to the rifle, it became too long for anyone to shoot themselves. Obviously Sheila did not shoot herself with the silencer, then detach the silencer and put it in the cupboard downstairs before returning to the bedroom to die. The presence of Sheila's blood in the silencer seemed to prove that someone else - Jeremy - had shot her.

But there was another possibility, that the blood was a mixture of Ralph's blood and June's blood. The forensic evidence did not conclusively prove that Sheila had not killed herself. More recent tests using DNA profiling have produced an interesting result. There is no sign of Sheila's DNA in the blood in the silencer, but there is a trace of June's DNA and that of an unidentified male. This more advanced test proves that Sheila could have carried out the shootings herself, using the silencer, then removed the silencer, knowing that she needed to shorten the rifle in order to kill herself with it.

A piece of evidence that could - and should - have saved Jeremy Bamber from conviction was the sighting of a mysterious figure at the window of the main bedroom at White House Farm. Both Jeremy and the police saw the figure in the bedroom when they first arrived at the house. If the figure had been either June or Ralph, surely he or she would have opened the window to make contact with the police. The figure was too tall to have been either of the twins. It could only have been Sheila, possibly wandering about in the grip of who knows what mental torment as she prepared to kill herself. If it was indeed Sheila, and it is difficult to see who else it could have been, the police who saw her knew perfectly well that Jeremy was with them, outside the house. Given that he was there, with them, he could not possibly have been responsible for Sheila's death, and therefore not for the deaths of the others either. When the police and Jeremy saw the figure in the bedroom, they retreated behind a hedge and moved off about two hundred years along the lane. The .22 rifle does not make a loud noise, so Sheila may very well have shot herself at that moment without the police hearing anything at all.

It was said by some witnesses that Sheila knew nothing about guns, but that was not true. She had been on a shooting holiday in Scotland and taught how to shoot. She had also seen Ralph and Jeremy load that particular gun. She had also lived on a farm most of her life, and would have known perfectly well how to load and fire guns.

Two witnesses claimed that the bathroom window was open, implying that an intruder, Bamber, had broken in, but the police investigators found all the doors and windows secure. On 7 November 1985, Detective Superintendent Ainley wrote in his report,

There was no apparent entry to or exit from the house, Detective Chief Inspector Jones did in fact examine the inside of all the ground floor windows and noted that they were all shut and secure on their latches. . . It seems, however, that after the inspection by DCI Jones some person partially opened the transom window in the kitchen and also opened the catch on the ground floor bathroom window. I have been unable to discover the person responsible.

This is of course a very revealing comment. Someone – after the murders had taken place – was making it their business to make it look as if there had been an intruder. That person is very unlikely to have been Jeremy Bamber, as he was the prime suspect if the killings had been carried out by an intruder.

At Jeremy Bamber's trial, the prosecution alleged that he planned to buy an expensive new Porsche. This, they argued, showed that Bamber knew that he was coming into a lot of money shortly. But what Bamber planned to buy was not a Porsche, which would indeed have required a massive windfall, but a replica Porsche kit car; this would have cost him about £2500, a sum he could have afforded without murdering his parents. Indeed, if he had been planning to kill them for their money, he would have aspired to something more ambitious than a kit car.

Another 'telling detail' the prosecution utilized in the trial was the evidence of a struggle in the kitchen. Ralph Bamber was six feet two inches tall, far too big a man for Sheila to have fought with. The evidence of the struggle clearly showed that Ralph was grappling with a male assailant moments before he was shot. But the signs of disorder that were interpreted as evidence of a fight were explained at the police enquiry in 1991. Walter Cook said then, 'I am aware that [the photographs] might suggest such a struggle, but at the time it did not appear that way to me. I could only see two things broken, one was a lampshade and the other was a plate. There was also brown sugar on the floor, but it was confined to one small area. I later learnt that the chairs and the brown sugar had been knocked over by the firearms squad when they rushed about the house looking for Sheila.' So there was no struggle. Sheila could after all have shot her father, just by taking him completely by surprise.

It has become clear over the twenty years that have passed since the appalling events of August 1985 that the jury at Jeremy Bamber's trial did not hear all the evidence. Nor did the jury hear the evidence straight. The evidence was carefully adapted and selected in order to produce a conviction. It was not only a miscarriage of justice; there were clear signs that attempts were being made, for more than one reason, to frame Jeremy Bamber and get him convicted.

On 29 October 1986, Jeremy Bamber was convicted at Chelmsford Crown Court for the murder of five members of his adoptive family. The judge, passing sentence on him, described him as 'evil almost beyond belief' and recommended that he serve no less than twenty-five years. In 1994 the Home Secretary, Michael Howard, wrote him a letter telling him he would never be released. Jeremy Bamber became one of a small, élite group of convicted murderers whose crimes are deemed so appalling that they can never be released. Bamber has consistently protested his innocence and has tried to have his case reviewed. Two appeals have been rejected, one in 1989, one in 2002.

Did Jeremy Bamber cycle over to his parents' house that August morning, climb in through the bathroom window, shoot his entire family, cycle home, phone the police and then return to White House Farm in his car? Or did Sheila, known to be mentally ill and on the verge of losing her two sons, finally lose control of herself and shoot the family before committing suicide? The open, bloodstained bible beside Sheila's body is consistent with a deranged and suicidal state of mind. But it is not a clear-cut case, and it needs re-hearing. Jeremy Bamber himself has said, 'Let no-one doubt that, in years to come, justice will be achieved and my conviction quashed.'

If he is telling the truth, and he is innocent, then Jeremy Bamber has been the victim of a very serious miscarriage of justice, and the sooner it is put right the better.

THE MISSING ESTATE AGENT: SUZY LAMPLUGH

The body of Suzy Lamplugh has never been found. Her killer has never been identified. There seems, even so, little doubt that she was murdered shortly after she vanished in July 1986. It is rather surprising that after more than twenty years, we still don't know what happened to her.

Suzy Lamplugh was a twenty-five-year-old estate agent. It was her job to show strangers round properties that were often unoccupied. On one of these routine assignments she disappeared. On a normal working day, she left her office in Fulham, west London, to meet a man calling himself Mr Kipper and show him round a house. It was a Victorian property valued at £130,000. When she did not return to the office, and did not return home either, the police launched a large scale search to find her.

At first it seemed likely that she would be found relatively quickly. She had been seen by witnesses getting into a black car driven by the man, Mr Kipper, whom she had met at the house. The neighbours who saw her go were able to give enough information about the driver for a photofit picture of him to be constructed.

But the trail quickly went cold. As the months passed and Suzy still did not reappear it became increasingly likely that she had been abducted and murdered. It became a question of waiting until someone discovered her body. In December 1986, Suzy's mother Diana Lamplugh set up the Suzy Lamplugh Trust, with the aim of promoting personal safety at work and generally creating a safer society. In particular, Diana Lamplugh wanted to make employers more aware of the dangers their staff were exposed to in the course of doing their jobs.

By October 1987, when Suzy's body had still not been found and no suspect had been identified, the police scaled down their inquiry, which had reached a dead end early on. They had no leads at all.

The possibility remained that Suzy's abductor and killer would offend again and that he would then become visible. A candidate emerged in the shape of John Cannan, a convicted murderer who was forty-two at the time of Suzy's disappearance, and who was sent to prison for life in 1989 after raping and murdering Shirley Banks, a twenty-nine-year-old sales manager from Bristol. He had been in prison before and had in fact only been released from prison three days before Suzy vanished. There was speculation that Cannan might be Suzy's killer. In October 1987, just at the time when the first investigation into Suzy Lamplugh's murder was grinding to a halt, and presumably her murderer felt safe, Cannan tried to kidnap a woman at gunpoint in a car park in Bristol. She managed to escape. The very next day, Cannan abducted Shirley Banks, a sales manager in Bristol. Her body was found, naked and badly decomposed, six months later in the Quantock Hills. He skull had been beaten so relentlessly with a brick or a rock that it had smashed like an eggshell.

In 1994, when Suzy had been missing for eight years, she was officially declared dead. In 1998, detectives from Scotland Yard investigated a new lead in the case, after hearing from a woman who said that she knew a man who knew about Suzy. The detectives commented that they would not be organizing any fresh searches for the body after the tip-off. In May the following year, the officer in charge of the Suzy Lamplugh inquiry, Detective Superintendent Brian Edwards, was put in charge of another very high-profile and difficult case, the murder of Jill Dando.

In November 1999, Diana Lamplugh and her husband heard from a secret informer that Suzy was buried at the former Norton army base in Worcestershire. This location matched claims made by John Cannan's girlfriend Gilly Paige in 1989 that Cannan had confessed to murdering Suzy Lamplugh and burying her body there. Gilly Paige later withdrew her statement.

The following month Detective Superintendent Sean Sawyer took over the leadership of the inquiry. In May 2000, the police announced that they had reopened the case. They had a new witness and some new leads. They had found the car that they thought had been used in Suzy's abduction and subjected it to forensic examination.

The car was traced by detectives to a North London dealership, where it had been parked for several years. The police were optimistic that microscopic traces of its occupants might confirm that the car was indeed used to abduct Suzy Lamplugh, and also help in the identification of her killer.

Suzy's mother tried 'not to get too excited about it' but it did seem that she was getting closer to knowing what had happened to her daughter. She was by now convinced that John Cannan was the murderer, and so were the police. They had investigated half a dozen suspects and eliminated all of them. Only one suspect remained, and that was John Cannan. When the murder of Shirley Banks was investigated, three significant links across to the Lamplugh case emerged. Mr Cannan was known to his fellow prisoners as 'Kipper', the very unusual and distinctive alias chosen by Suzy's killer when he made the appointment with her; this in itself is too strong a link to be coincidental. After serving a six-year sentence for rape, Cannan was released from prison three days before Suzy Lamplugh disappeared. John Cannan also bore a strong resemblance to the photofit suspect. But Mr Cannan denied any involvement and has consistently maintained (through several bouts of questioning by the police) that he was not responsible for the abduction of Suzy Lamplugh.

In June 2002, the Metropolitan Police investigators sent a file relating to the case to the Crown Prosecution Service, asking it to consider whether a charge could be brought for the murder of Suzy Lamplugh. The CPS had to assess whether there was enough evidence to justify bringing charges. Often in such cases it is not just a question of whether the right suspect has been targeted, but whether there is enough evidence in the file to stand a good chance of achieving a conviction; if not, it is simply a waste of the courts' time. The CPS saw the presentation of the file as 'a significant step' in the enquiry, but on close examination it became clear that there was not enough evidence to proceed. It decided that there could be no charges.

In 2006, John Cannan appealed for early release from prison. It was now twenty years since Suzy Lamplugh disappeared and was probably murdered. Still no one had been brought trial. But instead of release, Cannan risked facing a second charge of murder. The police conducting the Lamplugh inquiry were extremely anxious at the prospect of a serial violent sex offender and killer being released, possibly to commit further similar crimes; officers like Jim Dickie were very worried at this prospect. If John Cannan killed Suzy Lamplugh, he did so only three days after release from prison; the possibility that that this might happen again was extremely alarming. Dickie was convinced that Cannan stalked Suzy Lamplugh before arranging to meet her. But if that is true, how did he organize that in the three short days after he left prison? There is something not quite right about this hypothesis.

In July 2006, John Cannan was due to have his tariff (the length of time he has to spend in prison) reviewed by an independent judge. It was understood that Cannan, then fifty-three years old, had appealed over his tariff. The police were so alarmed at this prospect that Scotland Yard took the unusual step of announcing publicly that he must never be freed. Officers took the view that attractive, blonde, female twenty-something professionals were at particular risk from him and that even when he is sixty he will still be a grave danger to them.

Clearly there are human rights issues involved in this case. John Cannan can argue that he is being kept in prison for an offence of which he has not been found guilty – and for which he has not even stood trial. He has certainly not confessed to it. The police argument is that the circumstantial evidence is great enough for the interests of public safety to be set above John Cannan's claims.

The Scotland Yard detectives began a new review of the case, with fresh forensic testing, with a view to presenting the CPS with a more convincing case. This is very praiseworthy in terms of its dedicated quest for the truth and justice, but it could, again, from John Cannan's point of view, be seen as a determination to convict – a kind of victimization. On the other hand, this is how police forces operate, utilizing often huge resources in order to secure the conviction of an individual. This time the police are collaborating with the CPS, and now both CPS and police think they are close to uncovering the final pieces of the jigsaw.

It is, even so, very unlikely now that John Cannan will ever brought to trial for the abduction and murder of Suzy

Lamplugh. He and his legal representatives will be able to argue that given the massive amount of publicity that has surrounded the case it would be impossible to find an unprejudiced jury. He would be able to claim, and with some justice, that he would not get a fair trial because the media have already found him guilty. Here we confront the ultimate conundrum of justice in western society – its determination to respect the rights of individual citizens, while ensuring the safety of the rest.

DEATH ON WIMBLEDON COMMON: RACHEL NICKELL

A twenty-three-year-old part-time model, Rachel Nickell, was out on Wimbledon Common on the morning of 15 July 1992, walking her dog. She was attacked, sexually assaulted and stabbed to death; she was stabbed forty-nine times. She had her two-year-old son Alex with her at the time. He was thrown aside into the undergrowth by the attacker. The police were foxed for some days by a piece of paper stuck to Rachel's forehead after the murder. They wondered if this was intended as a symbolic signature by the killer, who was clearly mentally unhinged. Then they realized that the little boy had made his way back to his mother, found her terribly injured and stuck a piece of paper on her because it was the nearest thing he could find to a sticking plaster – to make his mummy better. One of the most horrific aspects of the crime was that it was committed so callously in front of the little boy.

This kind of senseless, out-of-the-blue attack is what we all secretly dread, because we cannot really prepare ourselves for it or protect ourselves from it. We are all vulnerable to random acts of violence from the criminally insane. There was, naturally, a great deal of media coverage. Alongside this, the police felt themselves to be under the spotlight, and under pressure to catch the killer quickly. And this led to serious mistakes.

The police turned to a forensic psychologist called Paul Britton, who was an expert in offender profiling. What he could do was to use the details of the crime to piece together the sort of person the criminal must be. Britton had had some conspicuous earlier successes. He had helped the police to identify the killers of Jamie Bulger in Liverpool. The police had meanwhile come up with someone who looked like a suspect. He was Colin Stagg, who lived in an apartment near Wimbledon Common. The police became interested in him because he appeared to be on the edge of society, a loner with strange interests that included paganism. They became even more interested when they heard from a woman who had made contact with Stagg through a lonely hearts column in a local paper. She showed the police some sexually explicit letters he had written her. Paul Britton analyzed the sexual nature of the Rachel Nickell murder, and also looked at the available evidence about Colin Stagg's psyche. He came to the conclusion that whoever killed Rachel Nickell and Colin Stagg had exactly the same 'sexually deviant based personality disturbance'. He also came to the breathtakingly unjustifiable conclusion that this so-called personality disturbance was so rare that Colin Stagg had to be the killer. This arbitrary decision has in effect ruined Colin Stagg's life.

The police were being told by a highly reputable expert that Colin Stagg was the murderer. All they lacked was evidence. Some evidence had to be found to connect Stagg to the murder. The only witness evidence they had was a single sighting of Stagg on Wimbledon Common later that day, which was of course of no value at all. To make matters worse, two other witnesses were sure they had seen Stagg at two other locations at the same time, so the witness evidence cancelled itself out.

Under Paul Britton's guidance, and with the approval of the Crown Prosecution Service, the police set up a trap for Stagg. Entrapment is always ethically questionable. This particular entrapment amounted to a breach of Stagg's basic human rights. In simple terms, no one should be treated the way Stagg was treated. The trap was dignified with a code name, Operation Edzell. A policewoman, who would be known as Lizzie James, was to contact and befriend Stagg, win his confidence and try to worm a confession out of him. Lizzie James claimed to have spent her teens in a satanic cult, in which she had taken part in the ritual killing of a mother and baby. She could only form a sexually satisfying relationship with someone who had also taken part in such a killing.

Of course, a great many men will agree to anything, anything at all, if it means a woman will agree to have sex with them. It was a honey trap. In effect, Lizzie James was telling Stagg that he could have sex with her if he said he had killed Rachel. It was a disgraceful plan, one the police officers concerned should never have contemplated, and one the Prosecution Service should not have condoned. Colin Stagg fell into the trap. He was so keen to please Lizzie James that he admitted to killing a woman in the New Forest in order to win favour. He made it up. James reported the confession back to her colleagues, who checked it out and found that there had been no such murder. She went back to Stagg and told him she didn't believe his New Forest story, adding, 'If only you had done the Wimbledon Common murder. If only you had killed her it would be all right.' Stagg answered, 'I'm terribly sorry, but I haven't.'

Rumours that Colin Stagg had become the prime suspect in the police investigation filtered out to the press. A tabloid journalist interviewed him and in the interview Stagg emphatically denied having anything at all to do with the Wimbledon Common murder. The police became concerned that the press activity might endanger their Operation Edzell and called it off after several months. They reviewed the evidence they had so far and, almost incredibly, in view of the lack of evidence and the total and utter failure to elicit a confession by way of seduction via Lizzie James, decided to go ahead and arrest Colin Stagg. In August 1993, he was arrested and charged with Rachel's murder.

The unfortunate Colin Stagg spent thirteen months in prison on remand before his case came before Mr Harry Ognall at the Old Bailey on 14 September 1994. It turned out to be a surprisingly short trial. In the pre-trial submissions, Mr Justice Ognall was asked to consider whether the evidence gathered during Operation Edzell was admissible in Stagg's trial. Justice Ognall considered, and then had some very harsh words to say about the police and their 'puppet master' Paul Britton. He denounced them all for setting up what amounted to a conspiracy to incriminate Colin Stagg. It was 'a skilful and sustained enterprise to manipulate the accused, sometimes subtly, sometimes blatantly.' The plan overall was a 'wholly reprehensible' attempt to incriminate Stagg using 'deceptive conduct of the grossest kind'. The judge ruled that the evidence gathered in this way was inadmissible under the Police and Criminal Evidence Act 1984.

The so-called evidence acquired by Lizzie James was of course all the evidence the police had; none of it could be used in court, so the prosecution case collapsed instantly. Colin Stagg was acquitted and set free.

Because of the publicity, Stagg acquired a profile he had not had before and, ironically, acquired a girlfriend too. A woman called Diane started writing to him while he was in prison and later visited him. After he was acquitted, they were married. It was not to be a long-lasting marriage. Stagg commented that Diane 'wasn't all there' and she deserted him after a few months. She then turned out to be a major danger to his security. In 1998, Mrs Stagg gave an interview to the *Mail on Sunday* in which she claimed that there was a 'terrifying anger' inside Colin Stagg, and – most damaging of all – that he had twice told her he was responsible for Rachel's death.

Fortunately for Colin Stagg, the age-old principle of autrefois acquit (already acquitted), sometimes called double jeopardy, meant that he could not be put on trial for the murder a second time. But it would in any case be understandable for Colin Stagg to feel a towering anger at the way he had been treated in the wake of Rachel's murder.

Life after Operation Edzell proved to be difficult for the policewoman who had played the role of Lizzie James. She had a nervous breakdown which was brought on by post-traumatic stress. She was given £125,000 in compensation by her employers, in addition to a pension. No compensation or help of any kind were offered to Colin Stagg.

Life after Edzell was also bumpy for the police officer in charge of the Stagg case, Keith Pedder. He retired from the Metropolitan Police in 1995, but was not in the clear. In March 1998, he was arrested and charged with inciting a police officer (aka Lizzie James) to commit a corrupt act. The charges were later dismissed when the court concluded that he, in his turn, had ironically been the victim of an entrapment operation by the Criminal Investigation Bureau.

Keith Pedder wrote a book about the Rachel Nickell case, which revealed that Operation Edzell had had approval from the highest levels in the Metropolitan Police and the Crown Prosecution Service. It seemed that the functionaries at those senior levels had been unaware of the Police and Criminal Evidence Act 1984; if they had been aware, they must knowingly have conspired to illegal entrapment. Pedder also revealed that the Deputy Assistant Commissioner who was in charge of the investigation into the conduct of the inquiry into the handling of the Nickell case in the wake of the Stagg trial – Ian Johnson – was the very man who had authorized the undercover plan in the first place.

Inevitably, Paul Britton became the subject of a formal allegation of misconduct. This was launched by Colin Stagg's original solicitor. By 2002, when the British Psychological Society eventually got round to considering the question of Britton's alleged misconduct, it decided to waive the complaint because too long a time had elapsed. During the hearing, Stagg and Britton came face to face and Stagg let Britton know what he thought of him. Britton unwisely considered making a formal complaint that Stagg had called him a pervert, but it was not clear who Britton imagined was going to preside or arbitrate, still less how he might emerge unscathed from such a procedure.

As is usual in such cases, the police refused to back down and admit that they were wrong. They injudiciously and unethically (given the court's decision to acquit) made it very clear that they still considered Colin Stagg to be guilty. Sir Paul Condon, the Chief Commissioner of the

Metropolitan Police, publicly announced, 'We are not looking for anyone else.' This was a straightforward contradiction of the acquittal. It also showed a determination to stick with their prime suspect, even though no genuine evidence against him had ever emerged – even during Edzell. They wanted to create the impression that they had got it right; they had identified the killer; that through some tiresome technicality of the British legal system the killer had got off. The press (notably the *Daily Mail* and the *Mail on Sunday*) went along with this, partly because of some off-the-record briefings by the police. Rachel Nickell's parents and her boyfriend were also persuaded that Stagg was guilty in spite of the acquittal.

During the years that followed, more of the 'evidence' gathered during Operation Edzell emerged. The picture of Colin Stagg that came out tended to reinforce the idea that he was innocent, not that he was guilty. He came out as a rather timid, lonely and sensitive person who was keen to have the companionship of a woman. It was clear that he struggled to understand the (completely fake) persona adopted by the policewoman. He begged her, 'If I have disappointed you, please don't dump me. Nothing like this has happened to me before. Please, please tell me what you want in every detail.' Colin Stagg was a bewildered, lonely man who wanted above all to please this woman. Operation Edzell really showed that Colin Stagg was a very long way from having the personality of a killer; there was nothing aggressive about him at all. It really then looked more remarkable than ever that on the strength of Operation Edzell the police decided they had enough evidence to arrest him. More and more people considered the possibility that someone else must have murdered Rachel.

Operation Enigma was an imaginative project that explored 200 unsolved murders to see whether there were serial killers at work. April 1998 brought the news that Operation Enigma had identified a cluster of four murders that were committed by one person: the Wimbledon Common murder was one of them. Subsequently, there were more murders that looked as if they might be the work of the same killer. The murder of Margaret Muller at Victoria Park in Hackney in February 2003 was one; the sexual assault and stabbing of Sally Bowman at Blenheim Crescent in Croydon in September 2005 was another.

But there was one murder in particular that looked very similar indeed to the attack on Rachel and her son. That was the murder of Samantha Bissett and her four year old daughter Jazmine in November 1993. This double murder happened at Samantha's home near Winn's Common at Plumstead. Samantha Bissett was sexually assaulted and then stabbed to death; her body was then mutilated by her killer. The little girl was also sexually abused, then suffocated to death. The mutilation inflicted after death was so grisly that the police photographer, who must have seen some very gruesome sights, was off work for months afterwards.

A mentally ill man was arrested and charged with the

Bissett double murder in May 1994. He was Robert Napper, and he was (eventually) identified on the evidence of fingerprints found at the crime scene. By a strange coincidence, Napper's fingerprints were almost identical to those of his victim, so they were very hard to distinguish from one another. There are in fact renewed doubts about the reliability of fingerprint evidence in general after tests have shown that different fingerprint experts reach different conclusions on the same evidence, and can also be influenced by police expectations. Even so, Napper's and Bissett's fingerprints were almost identical. By another extraordinary coincidence, Napper and Samantha Bissett had the same birthday.

Once in custody, Napper was identified as the perpetrator of a whole string of violent sex crimes against women. The police identified him as the Green Chain rapist, who over an eight-year period had carried out perhaps forty rapes and other sex attacks on a Thamesside path called the Green Chain Walk. Napper went on trial, and was described by the judge as 'highly dangerous'; he was too dangerous to be on the loose and was sentenced to an indefinite sentence in Broadmoor.

There were certainly enough similarities between the murders of Rachel Nickell and Samantha Bissett for the police to conclude that Robert Napper was responsible for killing Rachel. But at the time when Napper was arrested, they had contrived to get Colin Stagg imprisoned on remand. They had someone for the Wimbledon Common murder and did not need the complication of admitting they had the wrong man. While Napper could have killed both Samantha and Rachel, Stagg could not have killed Samantha because he was in prison at the time – the very best of alibis. Napper had no alibi for the time when the Nickell murder took place. Keith Pedder, who was in charge of the Nickell case, later admitted that he and his team had thought of Napper as a possible suspect but 'there was nothing to tie him to the Rachel Nickell murder'. This was an extraordinary comment to make. There had been nothing to tie Colin Stagg to the Nickell murder either, yet the police were ready enough to pin the Nickell murder on him.

At Scotland Yard, there is a Murder Review Group, an elite squad that has the task of investigating cold case murders, murders that have remained unsolved for a long time. It has been known since 2002 that the Murder Review Group considered Robert Napper as a suspect for the Wimbledon Common murder. In 2003 the Group announced they had made a breakthrough in the Nickell case. Using a new DNA technique (DNA Low Copy Number) on Rachel Nickell's clothing taken from the scene of the murder, fragmentary human DNA had been recovered that could belong to the killer. Colin Stagg offered to give a DNA sample, knowing that it would prove his innocence, but his offer was significantly declined, which implied that the investigators were no longer trying to pin the murder on him. A year later it was announced that the analysis had yielded DNA details suggesting a match with Robert Napper. Unfortunately the match was not sufficiently well-defined to amount to proof; it was not going to stand up in a courtroom. Robert Napper could not have been convicted on this DNA evidence. After the Operation Edzell fiasco, the Murder Review Group were treading very cautiously.

The Murder Review Group were keen to interview Napper about the Nickell murder, but they were barred by the Broadmoor psychiatrists. Eventually the psychiatrists relented. In June 2006, detectives from the Murder Review Group questioned 'a forty year old man' at Broadmoor regarding the Nickell murder. It began to look then as if Napper might be charged and tried for the Nickell murder.

For Colin Stagg, this was of paramount importance. If someone else was convicted of Rachel's murder the cloud of suspicion and gossip that still hung over him would disperse. There might even be compensation. Stagg is aware that he has never been able to shake off his association with the Wimbledon Common murder. 'You will always have people who will always believe I had something to do with it in some way. They'll just think there's no smoke without fire, and the police had every reason to arrest me.'

The fragmentary DNA evidence points towards Robert Napper as the murderer, a serial offender now imprisoned in Broadmoor for two other murders. Colin Stagg's situation has changed, and it looks as if he is in line for a large sum in compensation for, among other things, wrongful imprisonment. Stagg's life was irretrievably damaged by his arrest and imprisonment, and by the press campaign against him. The *Daily Mail* described him as 'the violent oddball with a taste for kinky sex and knives.' He was clearly the victim of prejudice. He was a loner with an interest in wicca; he had a picture of the Cerne Giant in his home. These, the police considered, were more than adequate reasons for treating him as a suspect. Then, when they were unable to find any other suspect, he became the prime suspect. But for the probity of Mr Justice Ognall, police and press prejudice would have sent Stagg back to prison – by the law of the lynch mob.

Stagg was unable to get a job for twelve years, unable to go out without fear of abuse and threats, and was virtually a prisoner in his own apartment. And Colin Stagg is not the only victim of the police's determination to pin the Wimbledon Common murder on him. If they had not had a fixation about Colin Stagg, the police might have connected the murder with Robert Napper, and taken Napper into custody before he had the opportunity to kill Samantha Bissett and her daughter.

I'M A CELEBRITY: O. J. SIMPSON

The O. J. Simpson murder case is one of the most highly publicized crime cases of the last few decades. The reason is that the man charged with double murder was a high-profile American football star. He had retired from football in 1979, long before the murders, and since then had pursued a modest career as a sports commentator and a minor film actor. It is one of those unusual cases where the chief suspect is a celebrity, and this ensures saturation coverage by the media.

At the end of a long trial, Simpson was acquitted. The verdict was blurred when afterwards, in a civil court hearing, Simpson was found liable for the wrongful killing of Ronald Goldman. There were therefore two conflicting verdicts on the case, one saying that he didn't do it and one saying that he did.

Just before midnight on 12 June 1994, one of O. J. Simpson's former wives, Nicole Brown Simpson, was found dead outside her home in the Brentwood area of Los Angeles. Beside her body was a second body, that of her boyfriend, Ronald Goldman. Nicole Brown's children was asleep in an upstairs bedroom. The evidence found at the scene by police investigators led the police to think that O. J. Simpson, who had divorced Nicole Brown two years earlier, might have been the murderer.

Simpson's lawyers persuaded the Los Angeles Police Department to let him turn himself in to the police at eleven o'clock in the morning on 17 June. The charge of double murder meant that he would get no bail and, if convicted, the death sentence. In California, double homicide is a capital offence. As events turned out, the prosecution decided to seek a life sentence, not the death penalty.

The case was very large in scale, because of Simpson's celebrity status. He had eleven lawyers working on his defence; another twenty-five lawyers worked for the prosecution. One hundred and fifty witnesses were called. The nine-month trial became the longest running trial in California's history, accumulating costs of more than $20 million. The presiding judge felt sorry for the marathon hearing to which the jurors were subjected, and laid on some diversions for them, including a theatre trip, a sightseeing trip in an airship and a boat trip to Catalania Island. The murder trial attracted more media coverage that any previous criminal trial since the Lindbergh kidnapping case way back in the 1930s.

One major problem in the case was that Orenthal James Simpson was black. There was a presumption within the black community that he would not receive justice, simply because of his colour. There was also a presumption among whites that he would not be found guilty by a jury composed mostly of representatives of minority groups; they would be unlikely to convict a black celebrity, regardless of the weight of evidence against him. It was an insoluble problem. The lost lives of Nicole Brown and Ronald Goodman seemed to dwindle into insignificance as O. J. Simpson took the centre of the stage; his right to justice and his right to be free of bigotry seemed to override the need for justice for the victims.

On 17 June 1994, a thousand journalists waited to see Simpson give himself up to the police and give a media statement. But he failed to appear. At two o'clock the police began to search for him as Robert Kardashian, one of Simpson's lawyers, read out a rambling letter from him that sounded like a suicide note. 'First everyone understand I had nothing to do with Nicole's murder . . . Don't feel sorry for me. I've had a great life.' The journalists joined in the hunt for Simpson.

In the early evening, at a quarter to seven, a police patrol car spotted a white Ford Bronco travelling north on Interstate 405. The car belonged to one of Simpson's friends, Al Cowlings. The officer approached Cowlings, who was driving, and Cowlings shouted that Simpson was naked inside the car and holding a gun to his head. The office backed away and a low-speed chase began. The chase was filmed from helicopters and it was reported live on the media. Many people watched from bridges crossing the highway. Eventually Cowlings drove Simpson back to his home, 360 North Rockingham Avenue, Brentwood.

Simpson did not emerge from the vehicle for another forty-five minutes. When he did, police took from him $8,000 in cash, a passport, a false moustache and beard, and a loaded gun (a Smith and Wesson .357). In spite of the numerous infringements of the law involved in this escapade, Simpson was never charged for any of them.

When Simpson first appeared in court on 20 June he pleaded not guilty to the two murders. Two days later the grand jury was dismissed because of the excessive media coverage, which could have affected the jury's objectivity and so produced a false verdict. At a second court appearance, a month later, Simpson claimed confidently that he was 'one hundred per cent not guilty'.

The trial began on 24 January 1995. The prosecution case, led by Marcia Clark, opened with the assertion that Simpson killed his ex-wife in a jealous rage. Evidence was produced in the form of an emergency phone call made by Nicole Brown Simpson in 1989; she said she was frightened that Simpson would do her physical harm. There were also expert witnesses who gave evidence from fingerprints, shoe prints and DNA that placed Simpson at the crime scene. They also presented a picture of the relationship that gave him a motive for murder.

Allan Park, a limousine driver, said he was unable to contact anyone at Simpson's gate at a quarter to eleven on 12 June, when he was due to pick Simpson up. At ten to eleven he saw a large figure go into the house, some lights were switched on and then Simpson answered Park on the intercom. The two men loaded baggage into the car and left for the airport at a quarter past eleven.

Simpson's expensive defence lawyers argued that Simpson was the victim of police fraud and sloppy handling of evidence which had led to DNA contamination. His lawyers went so far as to accuse LAPD detective Mark Fuhrman of planting evidence at the crime scene. Fuhrman found himself on the stand, having to defence himself against charges of racist language. He denied he had used the word 'nigger' to describe black people during the ten years beforehand, but the defence team had found nine-year-old audio tapes on which he could be heard using the word repeatedly. The tape had been made by a screenwriter gathering background material for a story she was writing on policewomen. The notorious Fuhrman tapes became a cornerstone of the defence case. They showed that some of the testimony at least was biased, and helped Simpson towards acquittal. As a result of his testimony, Fuhrman was later tried for perjury; he did not contest the charge.

A leather glove was found at the crime scene. It was alleged to belong to Simpson. The prosecution team decided not to ask Simpson to try on the glove in the courtroom, to show that it fitted, because they suspected that soaking in blood, alteration by forensic testing and freezing several times would have shrunk it. But the assistant prosecutor, Darden, was goaded by Cochran into asking Simpson to try it on. The glove was now too tight for Simpson to pull on over his latex-gloved hand. The moment was a gift to the defence. Cochran quipped to the jury, as he had several times earlier in the trial relating to evidence in general, 'If it doesn't fit, you must acquit.' The assistant prosecutor, Christopher Darden, told the judge in desperation that Simpson had arthritis and his failure to take anti-inflammatory drugs that day had caused his hand to swell. The prosecution team also knew that the glove had probably shrunk significantly since the crimes were committed.

The prosecution maintained that drops of Simpson's blood found at the crime scene had resulted from cuts on the middle finger of Simpson's left hand, which he (allegedly) sustained in the struggle with Ronald Goldman. The problem with this is that none of Simpson's gloves had any cuts. There was blood on the glove found at the crime scene, but none on the glove found back at Simpson's house. This suggested that someone had fixed the evidence.

In spite of the several major gaffes in their case, the prosecution team was confident of a conviction. In the United States generally, the case was seen in broad socio-political terms. Many black Americans were convinced that Simpson was innocent and that he should be acquitted; a conviction would encourage further police misconduct. Many white Americans believed Simpson was guilty. As a result, racial tensions intensified. Many in authority feared that a guilty verdict might incite a repeat of the 1992 riots in Los Angeles.

The jury considered its verdict for three hours before deciding the Simpson was not guilty. The verdict was announced at ten in the morning on 3 October 1995. But was Simpson really not guilty? There was in fact quite a lot of evidence that incriminated him:

1. Traces of blood belonging to Nicole and Ronald as well as Simpson himself in and on Simpson's car (DNA analysis).
2. The bloodstained socks found in Simpson's bedroom were soaked in Nicole's blood (DNA analysis).
3. Hairs on Ronald's shirt belonged to Simpson, though Simpson claimed never to have met Ronald.
4. Blood on Simpson's gloves belonged to Nicole, Ronald and Simpson.
5. The gloves carried fibres from Ronald's hair and the carpet in Simpson's car.
6. There were documents showing that Simpson had earlier been arrested for beating Nicole. The documents included photos showing her battered face. Simpson was sentenced to three years' community service for this earlier violence.
7. Nicole had lost a set of house keys. She had told family members she was afraid Simpson had taken them in order to get into her house. The keys were found at Simpson's house.
8. Nicole had finally broken with Simpson on the day of the murders; he seemed very disturbed by this.

9. The left hand glove found at Nicole's house matched the right hand glove found at Simpson's house.

10. Under oath, Simpson claimed he did not own any Aris Isotoner gloves, but media photographs show him wearing some.

11. The bloody footprints at the crime scene were made by Bruno Magli shoes. These are expensive and rare. The size twelve prints matched Simpson's shoe size.

12. Under oath, Simpson claimed he did not own any Bruno Magli shoes, but a photo taken at a football game shows him wearing them. Simpson claimed that the photo had been doctored, but another photo emerged also showing him wearing the shoes.

13. Nicole's friends and family were well aware that Simpson was stalking her. Nicole said that Simpson had told her he would kill her if her ever found her with another man.

14. A store receipt showed that Simpson had purchased a twelve-inch knife six weeks before the murders. The type of knife purchased exactly matched the wounds on Ronald and Nicole.

Whether O. J. Simpson was actually guilty of the double murder or not is still not known, but this is an impressive list of evidence for the prosecution. If the accused had been less well-known, if he had been unable to pay for expensive defence lawyers, there can be little doubt that in a routine court hearing he would have been found guilty on this evidence. The team for the prosecution was in fact profoundly shocked at the not guilty verdict, which it had genuinely not expected. Some observers who did not approve of the verdict blamed it on bias or ignorance on the part of the jurors. Apparently only two of the jurors had received a college education, which was cited as an indication of their intelligence (which of course it is not). On the other hand, their lack of education may account for the jurors' lack of awareness of the significance of the DNA evidence. Some of them evidently thought they were being given old-fashioned blood-group information and had no idea of the uniqueness of a DNA profile. Prosecutors heard more than one juror making comments such as, 'Well, lots of people have the same blood type.'

Some jurors were prepared to be interviewed; some said they thought Simpson had probably committed the murders, but the prosecution had bungled the case. In this criticism, they were very much closer to the mark. The high-profile prosecutor Vincent Bugliosi, who numbered the famous Manson trial among his cases, took the same view. He wrote a book with the unequivocal title *Outrage: The Five Reasons O. J. Simpson Got Away With Murder.* In it he roundly criticized the leading members of the prosecution teams, listing their mistakes. He drew attention to the prosecution's mistake in not introducing the note Simpson wrote before trying to escape, pointing out that it 'reeked of guilt'. The prosecution should have shown it to the jury. He also argued that a bigger case should have been made out of Simpson's significant history of physical abuse of Nicole.

O. J. Simpson's skin colour was nothing whatever to do with his guilt or innocence. Bugliosi argued that the defence lawyers had opened a door for the prosecution once they painted a (false) picture of Simpson as a leader in the black community. The defence's remark was clearly designed to elicit sympathy and support from the jury, but the prosecution could have countered that Simpson had had little impact in the black community and had done nothing to help black people less fortunate than himself. Bugliosi argued that the prosecution needed to do this in order to prevent the jury from allowing Simpson's colour to bias their verdict, which it may have done.

This tilting of the jury may have been a major deciding factor, and it has been suggested that if the trial had been held in mainly white Santa Monica, rather than 'minority-rich' Los Angeles, its outcome might have been different.

Since the case, O. J. Simpson has tried to persuade the world of his innocence. He has said that he would look for the real murderer of Nicole. On the other hand, there is little evidence that he has gone to any trouble to track this hit man down. Conspiracy theorists have it that there has been a string of murders of friends of Ronald, Nicole and O. J. A friend of Simpson's, Casimir Sucharski, was murdered shortly after Nicole. But if the double murder was part of a sequence, O. J. himself would have a vested interest in hunting down the killer, which he does not appear to be attempting. A more promising line of enquiry might be the Mafia or drugs. Nicole was apparently planning to open a restaurant with Ronald Goldman and, allegedly, finance it with cocaine profits; rumour had it that the pair of them were well out of their depth in a deal with drug dealers. This is no more than hearsay and speculation, but there were always possibilities other than O. J. Simpson.

William Dear has suggested that O. J's. son Jason might have been the murderer and that all O. J. was guilty of was covering up for him. The hypothesis is that Jason had a crush on Nicole, was jealous of her relationship with Ronald and had no alibi on the night of the murder. It is ingenious but ultimately unconvincing.

In November 2006, Regan Books announced that they were about to publish a book by Simpson entitled *If I Did It*. The idea was that Simpson would explain exactly how he would have committed the murders – if he had committed them. This was seen by some as a back-door route to a confession. But later that month, after a barrage of hostile public reaction, the parent company of Regan Books cancelled Simpson's book.

The case is unique. It may be that O. J. Simpson was guilty; it may even be that many of the people who were involved in engineering his acquittal thought that he was guilty, too. There were, even so, many reasons for deciding to find him innocent.

DEATH OF A PAGEANT QUEEN: JONBENET RAMSEY

There is nothing so upsetting as the murder of a child, and nothing so alarming as a child murder that goes unsolved; the idea of a child killer on the loose, unpunished and free to kill again is not just a personal nightmare but society's worst nightmare. This is an horrific case of the cruel and cold-blooded murder of a six-year old girl. The case was so horrific that it distorted the judgement of the police and led to suspicion falling on the wrong people. The murder eventually went unsolved.

On Christmas night in 1996, a couple in Boulder City, Colorado, found that their daughter was missing from her bedroom. John and Patsy Ramsey were alarmed, then terrified when they found a hand-written ransom note left for them to read on the stairs by their daughter's kidnapper. It began, 'Mr Ramsey, Listen carefully! We are a group of individuals that represent a small foreign faction. We do respect your business but not the country that it serves. At this time we have your daughter in our possession ... You will draw $118,000 from your account ...'

Apart from bearing all the hallmarks of the criminally insane, the amount demanded was an odd figure. Why $118,000 and not $100,000 or $150,000? The eccentricities of the note alone must have made John Ramsey realize he was dealing with a madman, which was frightening in itself, and his little girl was in the clutches of that madman. Moments later Patsy Ramsey called the police, who arrived within minutes. The police carried out a brief search of the main rooms in the house, did not find the girl and did not find any sign of a forced entry. The tone of the ransom note implied that the collection of the ransom would be monitored and that the girl would be returned once the money had been paid. John Ramsey made arrangements to pay the ransom and a friend of his, John Fernie, picked up the ransom from the bank during the morning.

That afternoon, Linda Arndt, one of the Boulder Police detectives, asked Fleet White, who was a friend of the Ramseys, to search the entire house with John Ramsey for 'anything unusual'. This was an odd request in that police detectives should have undertaken the search. Ramsey and Fleet decided to begin their search in the basement. First they searched the bathroom and 'train room'. Then they went into the room they called the wine cellar although the Ramsey's did not use it for that purpose. It was there that John Ramsey discovered his daughter's body under a white blanket.

The post mortem showed that JonBenet had died as a result of strangulation and skull fracture. She had been garrotted with a length of nylon cord and the handle of a paintbrush. She had also been sexually assaulted, though not raped. It was noted that the method of garrotting required a special knowledge of knots. A peculiarity of the post mortem was the revelation that JonBenet had eaten pineapple a few hours before the murder, yet her mother was unaware of this; it is difficult to understand how a six-year-old child could have consumed anything without her parents knowing. Photos taken of the Ramseys' home the day JonBenet's body was found show a bowl of pineapple on the kitchen table with a spoon in it. Neither Patsy nor John could remember putting the bowl on the table – or feeding it to JonBenet. Was this something the murderer did?

The police interpreted everything as indicating that the Ramseys were guilty. The odd sum of $118,000 showed up on his home computer as his annual bonus. His financial liabilities came to exactly $1,118,000. It looked to the police as if the figure of $118,000 might have stuck in John Ramsey's mind; it looked as if he had drafted the ransom note. The police also thought the ransom figure was pitched too low in relation the Ramsey's income and capital. The household's net worth, also visible on the Ramsey computer screen, was over $6 million. The handwriting on the ransom note did not really match that of any family member, though it bore some resemblance to Patsy's.

From the very beginning the police suspected that John and Patsy were responsible for their daughter's disappearance. By the time the little girl's body had been removed from the house a few hours later the Boulder Police had made up their minds. The Ramseys were guilty of killing their daughter.

To compound this injustice, the police leaked to the local media a few key facts about the case. One fact was that there was no evidence of a break-in. Another was that there was no possibility of anyone from outside the house getting in. This disinformation was intended to signal clearly to the people of Boulder that the Ramseys must be guilty. It ensured that they could not have a fair trial. It also ensured that their lives in Boulder would be unendurable from that moment on.

Further leaks to the press revealed the discovery of child pornography and evidence of child sex abuse at the Ramsey house. This misinformation was based on the completely unfounded hypothesis that John Ramsey had been abusing his daughter and murdered her to escape detection. Another leak included the idea that Patsy had accidentally killed her daughter in a fit of temper over JonBenet's bedwetting and made up the kidnap story to avoid detection. When police are investigating a serious crime they need to have working hypotheses about what happened. But leaking these speculations to the press is very destructive, as it turns speculation into pseudo-fact. Leaking the working hypothesis about the death of JonBenet seriously damaged the Ramsey's future lives and the truth, which may have lain somewhere else altogether.

The conviction that the Ramseys had killed their

daughter blinded the police to the implications of some of the evidence. Photographs of the child's body show the distinctive paired burn marks left by a stun gun. The very fact that JonBenet was cold-bloodedly stunned before she was killed is far more in keeping with a planned abduction than with murder or accidental killing by the parents. This was forensic evidence that did not fit the police scenario, so it was ignored.

A videotape of the police interrogation shows a police officer outlining the police hypothesis to a bewildered and angry Patsy Ramsey. Patsy listens, shaking her head in anger, frustration and disbelief, saying very emphatically, 'You're on the wrong path, buddy.' The police officer tries bluff, telling her there is 'trace evidence, scientific evidence' that proves Patsy's connection to the murder. This infuriates Patsy, who knows perfectly well that this cannot possibly be true, because she knows she didn't commit the murder. She tells the officer that her daughter was the most precious thing she had and that her life has been hell ever since she died. She erupts: 'Quit screwing around asking me questions and find the person who did this!' The tape is a moving document, a compelling piece of evidence in itself that Patsy Ramsey was innocent.

But the police would not budge from their scenario. As in so many other cases, they had decided what had happened, and it was just a question of wearing down the suspects until they went along with it. A move was made to indict the Ramseys, but the indictment was dropped because it was seen that the case would not hold up in court. A great deal of the alleged evidence was spurious and untrue. There was, for example, no evidence whatever of child pornography or child abuse at the Ramseys' house; that was pure invention. Police photos taken on the day of the crime show clear evidence of a break-in at the cellar window. The post mortem evidence showed that JonBenet was not killed by a single blow to the back of the head, which was necessary to fit the police hypothesis, but had died a more complicated and tortured death. The little girl had been immobilized with a stun gun, sexually assaulted, strangled and finally hit over the head. That (real) scenario did not fit the case the police had been struggling to build against the Ramseys. The indictment had to be dropped 'for lack of evidence'.

The actions of the police up to this point meant that, as far as the community was concerned, the Ramseys were not only guilty but had been in effect condemned and convicted by the law. It was trial by mischief-making rumour. The calculated leaks and the consequent media frenzy meant that the lives of the unfortunate couple and their eleven-year-old son had been wrecked. Not only had they lost JonBenet, a delightful little girl who had won beauty contests: they now stood to lose everything else, too.

A few people went on having faith in the Ramseys. A television documentary drew attention to the solid evidence from the crime scene, which pointed clearly and unequivocally to a break-in. It went on to suggest that the abductors may have intended to take the child out through the window where they broke in, but for some reason decided not to abduct her but to kill her there in the cellar. The ransom note implies a change of mind, as it proposes a finely judged figure for the ransom. Or it may have been that more than one person was involved in the attack and the two (or more) men had different motives. Perhaps while one man, economically motivated, was writing the ransom note another, sexually motivated, was assaulting and strangling the child. The documentary led to a new investigation co-ordinated through the District Attorney's office, though on limited funds.

The new investigators were concerned that there were several other suspects who had not been pursued by the police in 1996, simply because they had decided the Ramseys were guilty. No routine house-to-house search of the neighbourhood had been carried out, for the same reason. There had been two men living close by, both with criminal records, who moved away straight after the murder. There were also two paedophiles in the area who were not checked out. The police had prematurely decided on Patsy and John Ramsey as their prime suspect – their only suspects – when there was plenty of evidence pointing elsewhere.

There were two small spots of blood on JonBenet's clothing. One of the bloodspots contained her DNA, but also traces of some DNA belonging to someone else. There was similar 'alien' DNA under one of her fingernails.

The 'alien' DNA belonged to neither John nor Patsy Ramsey, but to someone else. The DNA from the second blood spot was from the same stranger, a white male, who should have been the police's main suspect. These blood samples were available in 1996 but the implications were not followed through. The investigators tried unsuccessfully to match the stranger's DNA through the US national DNA database. It looks as if the killer was a first offender, or just an offender who had never been caught. He still hasn't been caught.

The investigators found a dozen new suspects, and one of those became the prime suspect. Thirty-eight registered sex offenders were living within a two-mile radius of the Ramseys' home, an area that encompasses half the population of the city of Boulder; the statistic was in itself alarming. The investigators called a press conference at which they gave the impression that they now knew who they were looking for and that the net was closing in on him. They hoped that this pressure might push the suspect into coming out into the open. It had an immediate and melodramatic effect that they could not have foreseen.

A mechanic called John Kennedy lived in Boulder. He went to the police to say that he thought he knew who the killer was – a man called Michael Helgos, who had committed suicide the day after the press conference at which the investigators hinted heavily that they knew their man and would soon have him behind bars. Kennedy thought the timing of the suicide was significant. He also knew that Helgos was a bizarre, deranged, violent man who took pleasure from shooting cats and speculated what it would be like to crack a human skull. Helgos had also said in the period just before the murder that he was going to make a lot of money, which could have been a reference to the ransom he hoped to get.

In fact, the police had been informed about Helgos shortly before the murder. Home videos were found showing him playing with a very young girl. A neighbour had returned home to find him naked with her daughter. He had a video collection containing some very violent scenes, but it also included a Disney film in which a very young girl was shown being woken up by Santa Claus; was this a scenario Helgos wanted to re-enact, and the mainspring of the decision to wake JonBenet up on Christmas night?

Michael Helgos owned several stun guns, one of which was of the same type as was used on JonBenet. Two footprints were found in the Ramsey house. One was a print of a HITEC trainer; Helgos owned a matching pair.

There were peculiar circumstances surrounding the death of Michael Helgos. The fatal shot was fired through a pillow. Why would Helgos have wanted to muffle the shot? It would not have mattered to him, when dead, whether anyone heard the shot. But perhaps Helgos's death was not suicide at all. Perhaps someone else shot him. The bullet passed right through his chest from left to right, an odd wound for a right-handed man to inflict on himself, especially given that most people killing themselves with a gun shoot themselves in the head.

Given that the ransom note uses the word 'we' and there were two different footprints in the house, it looks as if two people were involved in the murder. Michael Helgos was one. Who the other was remains a mystery. Was Helgos sufficiently unnerved after the press conference for his associate to fear that he would give them both away and could not afford to let him live? The associate's name is known to the case investigators (though not to me) and they even know where he lives. Inevitably there has been endless speculation and accusation over the years, some of it leading to litigation.

As Patsy Ramsey feared, the man or men who attacked her daughter went on to attack again. In an affluent part of Boulder, nine months after the Ramsey murder, a girl of about the same age as JonBenet and who even went to the same dance studio as JonBenet was attacked in her own home. Her parents found an intruder in the house who presumably got in while they were out. The parents went to bed, and then some time later the intruder went into the little girl's room, put his hand over her mouth, called her by her name and sexually assaulted her. Luckily the mother was a light sleeper and woke up, sensing something was wrong. She went into her daughter's room and saw the intruder, who ran past her and jumped out of the window and off the roof to get away. He was dressed completely in black. Michael Helgos is known to have liked dressing completely in black and stalking people at night. This attack is very likely indeed to be linked to the Ramsey case, though the Boulder police denied any connection. The later investigators discovered that although the second attack was known in full detail to the police, they had taken no action on it; in view of the seriousness of the offence, this is in itself very strange.

There was an unexpected new development in August 2006. A forty-one-year-old schoolteacher called John Mark Karr was arrested in Bangkok on child pornography charges. Apparently the US authorities traced him by using the Internet after he sent e-mails about the Ramsey case to a professor of journalism. When he was arrested, he confessed to being with JonBenet when she died. He said her death had been an accident. Asked if he was innocent, he said, 'No.'

But only twelve days after Karr's arrest it was announced that his DNA did not match that of the 'stranger' at the crime scene and the authorities decided that no charges would be brought against Karr for the child's murder. Even so, four months later it was revealed that federal investigators were still looking into the possibility that Karr was an accomplice.

The case appears to be tantalizingly close to being solved. One of the major suspects, Michael Helgos, is dead, probably killed by his even more dangerous associate. David Williams, one of the detectives involved in the case, says the killer could be taken into custody. They have his

DNA. 'It's a travesty that it isn't happening.' It would take six detectives six months to solve the crime. But the District Attorney's office does not have unlimited funds and the case may have to be closed before the final solution is reached.

Meanwhile the Ramsey family has had to endure the horrible bereavement inflicted on them by total strangers, the loss of JonBenet. They have also had to endure a painful hostile interrogation by the authorities. They have been vilified in the press. They have been assumed to be guilty by their neighbours. They were forced to move away and try to make a new home for themselves in Atlanta, where they lived in reduced circumstances. Their lives have been destroyed.

Patsy Ramsey died of ovarian cancer in June 2006, at the age of forty-nine. She was aware at the time of her death that the Boulder County District Attorney was investigating a suspect in Bangkok, and this gave her the satisfaction of believing that her daughter's killer had finally been traced and would be brought to justice. For her, it was a resolution of a kind.

DEATH ON THE PATIO: THE MURDER OF BILLIE-JO JENKINS

On 15 February 1997, a thirteen-year-old English girl was brutally bludgeoned to death as she painted the French windows opening onto her own back garden in Lower Park Road, Hastings. Her name was Billie-Jo Jenkins, and from shortly after the discovery of her body was reported by her forty-year-old foster-father, Sion Jenkins, he was the prime suspect. Was it another case of the police jumping to too hasty a conclusion, deciding too quickly who the murderer was, and gathering only evidence that would gain his conviction? Or was Sion Jenkins really guilty as charged? As we shall see, the police did briefly consider another possibility, but dismissed it at a fairly early stage.

Billie-Jo was born in March 1984 and initially brought up by her natural family in east London. She was then, from the age of nine, fostered by Sion and Lois Jenkins, who lived in Hastings. At the time of her death she was attending Helenswood School in Hastings. Sion Jenkins was Deputy Head at another Hastings school, the William Parker School, a comprehensive school for boys. Jenkins

540

was a devout Baptist, had stood for the local council and was generally regarded as a pillar of the community, and therefore certainly not an obvious murder suspect.

Sion Jenkins gave his initial statement to Sergeant Steve Hutt, who took notes as Jenkins recalled what had happened. On the day of the murder, Billie-Jo had arranged to meet a friend at four o'clock. The family had lunch together and after that Sion's wife Lois had taken their two youngest children to a seafront playground. Jenkins took his ten-year-old daughter Lottie to a clarinet lesson and returned home at quarter past two to give Billie-Jo and his twelve-year-old daughter some domestic chores. Jenkins told Billie-Jo to paint the French windows opening onto the patio at the back of the house, and Annie was given the job of washing the car at the front. Jenkins noticed that Billie-Jo was painting the inside of the French windows and told her he wanted the outside painted (as well or instead). Billie-Jo was getting paint on the floor, and Jenkins had no white spirit to remove it. He told Billie-Jo to be careful, presumably meaning he did not want her to get any more paint on the floor.

At about three o'clock, according to Sergeant Hutt's notes, Sion Jenkins left Billie-Jo alone in the back garden of the family home, painting the French windows and listening to Oasis, while he took Annie with him to collect Lottie from her clarinet lesson. He shouted 'Bye' to Billie-Jo and told her he would be gone about fifteen minutes. He returned at twenty-five minutes past three and then decided to go and buy some white spirit. He set off in the car with Lottie and Annie but realised after they had set off that he had no cash. He returned home after this abortive trip between three thirty-nine and a quarter to four. They went in through the front door, Lottie first, then Annie, then Jenkins himself. They went into the dining room. Lottie screamed when she saw Billie-Jo's leg. Jenkins went to see what had happened and found Billie-Jo laying face down with blood on her head. He held her and tried in vain to revive her. While he had been out of the house for no more than ten minutes she had been hit over the head at least ten times with a metal tent peg.

Sion Jenkins and his wife Lois were encouraged to appear on television to appeal to the public for witnesses to come forward. This is a common police practice in the wake of a murder. One motive is to create an appearance of purposeful activity for the benefit of the general public: to make it appear that the police are 'doing something'. Another is to subject close relatives who are suspects to the pressure of appearing in public; it is an extension of the police interrogation technique. Close examination of the suspects' body language and tone of voice on the videotape suggest to the police investigators whether suspects are being truthful or not. It is to a great extent a test of suspects' acting skills and as such it is a very questionable practice.

Initially, the police thought the murder looked like the work of an intruder but, after questioning Jenkins, they believed there were inconsistencies and implausibilities in what he said. They began to suspect that he was the murderer. The house was set back from the road by a flight of steps. Because it was semi-detached, with houses at the back, the only entry and exit point for an intruder would have been up the front steps and round the side of the house. Jenkins was not out of the house for very long, and in that short time it would scarcely have been possible for an intruder to approach the house from the front, mount the steps, go round the side of the house, climb over the side gate, get round the back of the house to the patio, kill Billie-Jo and then leave by the same route. There was also the question of the murder weapon. An attacker could not have known that a metal tent peg would be lying there.

The intruder scenario no longer seemed a reasonable option, and that left Sion Jenkins as the prime suspect. Nine days after the murder, Jenkins was arrested and released on bail. On 14 March he was formally charged with Billie-Jo's murder.

The police were dissatisfied with the account Jenkins gave of the shopping trip, which seemed designed to get him conveniently away from the crime scene for the ten minutes when the crime was committed. He claimed he had driven off with the intention of buying white spirit, when there was already enough white spirit in the house. He in any case returned home empty-handed as (he said) he had forgotten to take any money with him. This may not be as suspicious as it seems, as his wife commented that he had done the same thing earlier that day. It may be best explained as a simple piece of low-level domestic disorganization, the sort of off-duty incompetence that makes us (most of us) sometimes absent-mindedly lock ourselves out of our own houses; or remember while swimming that we have forgotten to take a towel; or indeed, as I have done several times, buy a bottle of white spirit when there is already a bottle in the house. The fact that a murder was being committed has inflated the significance of Sion Jenkins's wasted trip out of proportion. We all waste trips.

The police were also concerned at Jenkins's behaviour after finding Billie-Jo's body. He did not dial 999 straight away. Instead he phoned a neighbour. When the neighbour arrived, she naturally insisted that he dial 999, which he did. It seems he also opened the door to a colleague after finding Billie-Jo, but did not mention what had happened. He also, very strangely, went out to his car, a convertible, to put the roof up. It was odd behaviour, the police thought, but in fact easily explicable in terms of displacement activity while in shock. Jenkins commented that while he was putting the roof up he wondered, 'What the bloody hell am I doing here?' When he phoned the emergency services, he was advised to put Billie-Jo into the recovery position. He did not follow this advice. He afterwards explained this by saying that he knew she was dead; the recorded 999 phone call shows that he did not know whether she was breathing or not, so he could not have known whether she was dead or not. On the other hand, he may have thought Billie-Jo was dead, but not wanted the emergency services to think so. At an unconscious level he may have sensed that the emergency services would react more quickly if they thought her life could still be saved. Or maybe he just felt vulnerable and helpless and wanted to pass on to the emergency services the awful responsibility of saying that his daughter was dead.

Jenkins's two daughters apparently gave versions of events that were different enough from each other to be considered unusable at the trial. It would be interesting to know why they contradicted one another.

Overall, there were enough peculiarities about Sion Jenkins's behaviour to arouse suspicion. Then, when the police routinely explored Jenkins's professional life, they uncovered a certain amount of dishonesty. He had lied about his qualifications – most of them, in fact - in order to get his job as a Deputy Head, and he was currently repeating those lies in the process of applying for a headship. The court rightly ruled that this evidence could not be used to prove that he was a murderer and did not bear on the case in any way. But the revelation did cast doubt on Sion Jenkins's honesty and probity. It also has to be borne in mind that a false claim to professional qualifications amounts to serious misconduct. In the teaching profession it is a dismissable offence. There may well be former colleagues of Sion Jenkins who now believe that he got his promotion to Deputy Head ahead of other candidates under false pretences. It is no small matter. In spite of the evidence offered that he was a pillar of the community, a devout Baptist and so on, he was prepared to tell lies in order to advance his position, and that must reflect on the reliability of his testimony.

This accumulation of suspicion and doubt led to Sion Jenkins's being accused of murdering Billie-Jo by hitting her repeatedly over the head with an eighteen-inch long metal tent spike. At Lewes Crown Court on 2 July, he was found guilty by a jury of four women and eight men and sentenced to life imprisonment. The jury's unanimous verdict drew shouts of approval from the packed public gallery, where Bille-Jo's natural parents were sitting. A problem was that Sion Jenkins was a man of good reputation, a man with no previous convictions, a man with no formal record of violence – and he had no known motive for such an angry, vicious attack. If he did kill Billie-Jo, the motive was known only to Jenkins; the courts never revealed one.

In spite of this, the judge said at the conclusion of his case, 'Sion Jenkins, the jury have convicted you of murder on what in my judgement was compelling evidence. On the 15th February last year you battered your foster daughter with an iron bar. It was a furious assault, the motive for which only you now know. The fact that you committed this crime, the circumstances in which it was committed and the way in which it was committed lead me to conclude that you are a very considerable danger to the community.'

Jenkins decided at once to appeal against the verdict; he had steadfastly maintained his innocence. On 30 November 1999, he made his first appeal, challenging the prosecution's forensic evidence, or rather their interpretation of that evidence. This appeal failed.

He claimed that he discovered Billie-Jo's body by chance when returning from a shopping trip with two of his children. The prosecution claimed that the abortive shopping trip was a thinly disguised alibi to make it appear that he was out of the house (and with witnesses to prove it) at the time of the murder.

The most damning evidence against Jenkins was a spray of tiny blood droplets on his clothing. The prosecution claimed that the 158 blood droplets landed on him when he hit Billie-Jo with the tent peg. The defence claimed that while Jenkins was, in his shocked and bewildered state, trying to nurse and revive Billie-Jo, a bubble of air in her blood-filled nose burst, sending out a fine spray of droplets. At the trial much depended on the experts called to give evidence about the blood. One expert witness called by the prosecution said it was impossible for the blood to have been sprayed by exhalation. Another, also called for the prosecution, said the pattern of blood on Jenkins's clothes was consistent with Jenkins delivering several blows over Billie-Jo's head. But there was an alternative way that the blood could have been transferred, and it was to form the basis of a retrial.

In 2003, Jenkins won the right to mount a second appeal. His lawyer at the time, Clare Montgomery, said that Jenkins had spent six years in prison 'in appalling conditions as a child killer'. She was referring to the fact that people convicted of crimes against children are routinely subjected to hostile treatment by fellow-prisoners. She also drew attention to the fact that his arrest had led directly to separation and divorce proceedings initiated by his wife, Lois, and estrangement from his daughters. His life had been ruined by a wrongful accusation and a wrongful conviction.

The appeal led by Clare Montgomery, the lawyer acting for Sion Jenkins, hinged on a challenge to the evidence given by Home Office pathologist Dr Ian Hill, who had carried out the post mortem on Billie-Jo. She described Dr Hill's evidence as incomplete and incorrect. Dr Hill, she claimed, had not carried out a microscopic examination of Billie-Jo's lungs. At the trial, Dr Hill had refused to countenance the defence's claim that the blood specks on Jenkins's clothing might have an innocent explanation, that they did not prove that Jenkins was guilty. The defence hypothesis was that at the time of death Billie-Jo's airways had become temporarily blocked and that when Jenkins had raised Billie-Jo up in an attempt to revive her they had been freed; the sudden release of trapped air through her nose had sprayed an aerosol of blood onto his clothing. Dr Hill had wrongly ruled this out as a possibility. The effect of Dr Hill's presentation of the evidence had been that the jury concluded that Jenkins could have acquired the blood stains only by killing Billie-Jo.

The second appeal hearing was told that if a

microscopic examination of the tissue round the lungs had been carried out it would have revealed that Billie-Jo was suffering from interstitial emphysema. Her lungs would have been full of air. Professor David Dennison, a lung specialist, carried out a new test which showed that in this condition Billie-Jo would have been able to release an aerosol-type spray of blood if her body was moved. And Sion Jenkins said that he had indeed moved her in his futile attempt to save her life. The new evidence of Professor Dennison was reviewed and supported by Professor Robert Schroter of Imperial College, London. He concluded that the fine spray of blood could have been expelled from Billie-Jo's dead body, just by leaning on it or turning it, as Jenkins testified that he did. It was also possible that the fine spray could have been carried in any direction by minor local air currents on the patio. Dr Hill was confronted with the new evidence and agreed with it.

The result of the appeal in 2004 was the ordering of a retrial. The jury in the retrial, which was held in 2005 and lasted three months, could not reach a verdict. A second retrial was held, and this too ended with the jury unable to reach a verdict, after thirty-nine hours of deliberation, in February 2006. As a result, Sion Jenkins was formally acquitted. He will not be put on trial again.

Billie-Jo's natural family were furious at Jenkins's acquittal. One woman shouted, apparently at his second wife, Christina, 'It's not over yet, you slag.' As Sion Jenkins sat outside Court Seven at the Old Bailey, two of Billie-

Jo's aunts ran up and started hitting him, leaving him with blood on his chin. The aunts were led away chanting, 'Justice for Billie-Jo!' The family's anger arose partly from the fact that some evidence that was potentially very damaging to Sion Jenkins was not heard in court. There were Lois's claims that he had been violent towards her and the children. There was a statement from his daughter Annie that in a fit of rage he had punched her in the stomach. There was an allegation that in the weeks before the murder he had had an affair with a seventeen-year-old girl bearing more than a passing resemblance to Billie-Jo. These claims, which may or may not have been true, might have shown Sion Jenkins in a rather different light. There was a hint, buried within them, that Sion Jenkins was in a stressed state and may have reacted to Billie-Jo's carelessness in getting paint on the floor with more than normal irritation, a hint that he may have snapped and, in a fit of uncontrolled rage, beaten her with the tent-peg.

In fact, one of Billie-Jo's friends and contemporaries, Holly Prior, told the jury at the retrial that Billie-Jo had confided in her that her foster father had hit her. Billie-Jo had asked Holly not to tell anyone. Holly noticed that she had scratches on her neck and bruises on her face. When Holly asked how she had got them she said Mr Jenkins had been hitting her dog, Buster; when she remonstrated with him 'he pinned against the wall and scratched her face.' Sion Jenkins denied this but agreed that on one occasion he slapped Billie-Jo round the face. Jenkins came to believe that it was reports like this – coming from his wife – that led to his arrest.

But the neat explanation that Sion Jenkins was given to fits of violent rage and simply killed Billie-Jo when she annoyed him scarcely fits the timings. Jenkins and his two natural daughters left the house to get into the car to go shopping. He returned to the house to tell Billie-Jo they would be back in a quarter of an hour. He was gone for three minutes. Those who believe Jenkins carried out the murder have to believe that he went through the house, immediately and without provocation started raining blows on Billie-Jo's head, went upstairs to change into clean but identical clothes and returned to the children waiting in the car – all in those three minutes. It is not credible.

This is a rare and remarkable case of a person charged with murder in effect being put on trial three times for the same crime (at a total estimated cost of £10 million), at the end of which there was still no verdict. The British legal system, elaborate and expensive though it is, has been unable to determine whether Sion Jenkins is guilty or innocent of murdering Billie-Jo.

Is there an alternative suspect? There was always the possibility, never discounted, that an untraced prowler got into the back garden and killed Billie-Jo. The police discounted this as they regarded the only access to the back garden as being from the front and round the side of the house. Any prowler approaching from the front and leaving again by the same route would have risked being seen. It would have been almost impossible for a prowler to have done that, and committed a violent murder, all within the space of, at most, the ten minutes allowed by Jenkins's alibi. It would also have been impossible for a prowler approaching from the front to have known that there was a young girl, a potential victim, in the back garden at the time.

The police were sceptical about the prowler but, when he was first questioned by the police after the murder, Sion Jenkins told them he had had a confrontation with a prowler. He had spotted the intruder in the bushes in the back garden one night just a few weeks before the murder; he had chased the man off and then took the dog out to look for him in the local park. A mysterious footprint was found in the back garden. The police examined it and found that it did not match any members of the Jenkins household; it was a stranger's.

A close family friend, Peter Gaimster, gave evidence at the trial that supported the prowler scenario. He described how at a dinner party just days before Billie-Jo died, Sion and Lois Jenkins had spoken about a prowler who was causing them some anxiety. 'At one point, Sion took me outside and we discussed at length how the prowler could have got round the back of the house. Sion and Lois were very concerned about this, but had not reported the matter to the police.' It was to Mr Gaimster's house that the Jenkins family went immediately after the murder. He described 'scenes of chaos' as the Jenkins family tried to cope with the situation.

The only plausible scenario is that the hypothetical prowler did not approach from the front, but climbed into the back garden from the rear, from a neighbouring back garden, and left the same way. It is also possible that Billie-Jo had been stalked. It is not at all uncommon for paedophiles to watch their prey and learn their characteristic routines, establish where they are likely to be at certain times. So it may not have been a coincidence at all that Billie-Jo was alone in the back garden when the attacker struck. He may have been watching and waiting, perhaps behind the bushes in the garden, until he heard Jenkins shout something like, 'Bye, Billie. Back in fifteen minutes,' and knew she was alone.

Jenkins claimed that he and his wife had become anxious about prowlers and break-ins in the area, that it made him have security lights and window locks fitted. On the other hand, this was contradicted by other residents who said there was very little crime in the area other than vandalism to cars.

The person who committed the murder did so in an insane frenzy. There is one forensic detail, one piece of solid evidence, that lends support to the idea of a mentally unbalanced intruder. Two pieces of bin liner were found inserted into Billie-Jo's nostrils. They were not mentioned until near the end of the trial and they were given very little attention, but they do imply an attack by a madman. There were claims that a man escaped from a mental hospital on the day of the murder, and that he was seen in

553

the area. The police responded to this by saying that he had an alibi. They said that he had no traces of Billie-Jo's blood on his clothing and was not involved in the murder, but this may be a case of the police having, by this stage, decided who the murderer was and not wanting any further suspects.

It is nevertheless the case that a middle-aged man referred to only as 'Mr B' was seen near the house, and a wild-looking man was seen running through the park away from the direction of the property at about the time of the murder. Mr B was said to be mentally ill, with an obsession with stuffing plastic bags into his nose and mouth. In spite of the police dismissal of this line of enquiry, it seems that Mr B did not have a watertight alibi at the time of the murder. An e-fit picture of a man acting suspiciously in the area was circulated by the police, but no-one was ever identified from it.

The pieces of plastic bin liner turn out to be crucially significant pieces of evidence. Overall, the frenzied nature of the crime is more consistent with a maniacal attack by an obsessive and deranged stalker. If that is what happened, there must be people in Hastings who either know, or have strong suspicions.

After he was arrested, Sion Jenkins remarried and moved to Hampshire. His former wife, Lois, and their four natural daughters emigrated to Tasmania. Lois Jenkins claimed that her ex-husband was violent towards her and their daughters. It is not known how much truth there was in these allegations, but the judge ruled them inadmissible because in his view they had no direct bearing on the Billie-Jo case.

The Sussex police have vowed never to close the Billie-Jo case. There is still, in spite of everything that has happened, a strong police commitment to bring to justice the killer of Billie-Jo, 'a bright, lively thirteen-year-old girl with everything to live for who was brutally murdered on the patio of her foster parents' home, a place where she ought to have been safe.'

PART SIX

RECENT UNSOLVED CRIMES
(2001–PRESENT)

WALKING HOME FROM SCHOOL: MILLY DOWLER

Milly Dowler was a thirteen-year-old English schoolgirl who was on her way home from school in Walton-on-Thames on 21 March 2002 when she disappeared without trace. Her family and friends had no idea what had happened to her. A large-scale search was launched, and teams of police officers combed the roads, streams and rivers round Hersham, where she lived. Detectives who had been involved in the earlier abduction of Sarah Payne in Sussex were brought in to assist. There were several appeals to the public for information, including a reconstruction on the television programme Crimewatch of Milly's interrupted journey home. The singer Will Young made an appeal on the ITN news programme. Milly was a fan of Will Young's and had been to a concert of his just the day before she disappeared. There was a possibility that she had run away from home and the appeals on the media were made partly in the hope that Milly would see them and return home.

Milly's family had no idea what had happened. Her father expressed the fear that she had been abducted. Her mother nursed the hope that Milly had run away, though she could think of no reason why she would want to do that. When, one week after her disappearance she had still not reappeared, the police speculated that she had been abducted, though probably not taken by force. She would probably not have gone off with a total stranger, so there was an implication that she had been abducted by someone she knew. There were several sightings of Milly just before she vanished, but none of the witnesses saw or heard any kind of struggle; it looked as if she had just stepped into someone's car without anyone else noticing what was happening.

On 23 April 2002, a month after Milly disappeared, a body was found in the Thames, only two miles from the place where Milly disappeared. There was naturally widespread speculation that this must be Milly Dowler's body, but the next day it was identified as that of a seventy-three year old woman called Maisie Thomas, who had been missing for a whole year. By June, Milly had still not turned up, alive or dead, in spite of a £100,000 reward offered by The Sun newspaper. Milly's parents went on sending her texts in the hope that she was alive and would phone them on her mobile, but the police sensed that the girl was dead and warned the Dowlers that they should prepare themselves for that eventuality.

It was not until six months later that her remains were discovered; then it became apparent that she had been abducted and murdered. On 18 September, Milly's skeleton was found in Yateley Heath Forest not far from Fleet; pathologists confirmed two days later from dental records that the remains really were Milly's. There were no traces of any of her clothing or belongings with the skeletal remains. Presumably her killer had stripped the body of anything that might help to identify her. Her purse, rucksack and mobile phone had gone. They are still missing.

Milly suddenly became the focus of a major media campaign as well as a major police operation, Operation Ruby, to find her killer. The police investigation involved more than 100 officers, who conducted 120 searches and interviewed more than 2,800 people. In spite of this intensity of effort, no one has been charged with the murder.

Milly Dowler attended Heathside School. On what was to be her last day there, she left at three o'clock and boarded a train to take her home. Usually, she got off the train at her home stop, Hersham, but on 21 March she got off one stop early at the Ashley Park station, Walton-on-Thames, to visit a cafe with her friends. She conscientiously phoned her father at three forty-seven to let him know where she was (about one mile from home) and that she would be home in half an hour. She set off for home on foot along Station Avenue, the road leading north-east from the station. She was last seen about fifteen minutes later, still walking north-eastwards, close to the junction with the A244 and less than a quarter of the way home. The police believe Milly was picked up, killed and buried shortly after this final sighting at around four o'clock.

There have been several arrests in relation to Milly Dowler's murder, but no charge has been brought. A twenty-year old woman from Tewkesbury, made repeated phone calls to the police, Milly's school and Milly's parents (Sally and Robert Dowler), pretending to be Milly. She was imprisoned for five months for making phone calls to cause annoyance, inconvenience or needless anxiety. In a similar way, a forty-nine-year-old man sent repeated e-mails from Nottinghamshire claiming that Milly had been smuggled out of Britain to work as a prostitute in Polish nightclubs. He had a history of paranoid schizophrenia and was sectioned under the Mental Health Act for being a danger to the public.

On 6 May, police searched woodland near Milly's home, but found nothing. On 16 May, a thirty-six-year-old man was arrested in Chertsey and questioned but later released without being charged. On 13 June another man, this time from Ashford, was questioned by police but also released without charge. At about this time, police discussed the case with other officers investigating the disappearance of two women in West London; possibly the abduction (and murder?) of Milly was not an isolated crime but one in a series. On 29 July 2002, a third man was questioned; this time the man was arrested and released on police bail. On 8 July 2005, yet another man was questioned. He was thirty-six, from West Drayton in Middlesex, and he too was released after questioning by the police.

On 12 September, it seemed as if a breakthrough had

been made. Closed-circuit television footage taken in the street at the time of Milly's disappearance was analyzed by the FBI. Although the image was very poor the FBI experts believe the figure standing near a dark saloon car might be Milly. The police asked the driver of the car to come forward.

In October, after Milly's remains were discovered in Hampshire, police appealed for witnesses who saw two men with a schoolgirl in a field near the spot where Milly's body was found. This significant sighting was made about half an hour after she went missing twenty miles away in Walton-on-Thames, and about 300 yards north of the place where she was found.

In January, a strange new lead emerged. A DNA match was found between a sample taken from a coffee cup found after a 2002 break-in at a church at Ryhope in Sunderland and a stain on a bodice found in Milly's bedroom. Officers travelled to Ryhope and took DNA samples from fifty-five men connected with Ryhope church: none matched the coffee cup sample. The Surrey Police came to the conclusion that the apparent match was just a coincidence and discontinued that line of enquiry. It would have been very odd indeed for Milly to have had any intimate contact with a Sunderland burglar; it is a cautionary tale about the value of DNA samples for identification purposes. Those who want to preserve the integrity of DNA testing argue that the top, which Milly bought at the New Look store in Kingston, Surrey, was never worn by her and that it was originally sold in Sunderland, returned to the shop and then redistributed for sale in the south. Maybe.

The CCTV footage from various business premises in the street leading from the station was closely examined by police investigators as it showed what was happening there around the time of Milly's disappearance. Most of the people and vehicles visible on the footage were eliminated from the enquiry. A few were of interest and the police wanted to interview the people concerned, believing that they may have seen Milly at the moment when she accepted a lift. One image, timed at six minutes past four in the afternoon, which is just about when Milly disappeared, showed a man in a white or pale blue shirt, walking along the road away from the station carrying a guitar in a black case. He was crossing the junction with Copenhagen Way. Another, timed at eight minutes past four, showed a woman or girl with long blonde hair and wearing dark trousers and top walking in the same direction. At eleven minutes past four a group of four people walked in the opposite direction, towards the station and carrying assorted bags and cases. Another CCTV image showed a red N registration Daewoo Nexia turning into the road Milly was walking along. The police were keen to identify its owner.

After failing to identify even a possible suspect, the Surrey Police cast a wider net. It was possible that the murder of Milly Dowler was not an isolated, one-off killing but the work of a serial killer. The team of detectives made contact with the team investigating the murder of the French student Amelie Delagrange. They looked for possible links, but found nothing definite.

Amelie Delagrange, who was twenty-two, was found battered to death at Twickenham Green in south-west London. It seems that she may have been murdered by the same man who committed five other attacks in that part of London, including the murder of Marsha McDonnell in Hampton. Marsha was only nineteen. The team investigating Milly Dowler's murder have had to keep and open mind, as there is no proof either way. On the other hand, someone who makes one random attack on a stranger is very likely to commit another. A possible link between the two murders is that a few days after her murder some of Marsha's possessions were found, dumped in the River Thames at Walton-on-Thames, in other words close to where Milly lived.

The red Daewoo is regarded by the police as a very significant element in the disappearance. It was caught on CCTV a few yards from where Milly was last seen and at the right time, but it was never traced.

In July 2005, the Surrey Police started to look at David Atkinson as a possible suspect for the murder of Milly Dowler, as well as the murder of Sally Geeson. David Atkinson was a thirty-one-year-old Scottish soldier serving with an engineer regiment at the Waterbeach base near Cambridge. He dropped some friends off at the Fountain

Bar in Cambridge on New Year's Eve, 2004. Atkinson's friends described him as 'spaced' that night. He was grasping the Range Rover steering wheel and staring at the girls in their New Year party clothes. Atkinson was a dangerous sexual predator, and the muscle-building steroids he was taking made him doubly dangerous. As is so often the case, he did not arouse the suspicions of those around him; instead of being closely watched, for everyone's sake, he was left on his own. Atkinson seized Sally Geeson, a twenty-two year old student, and raped her a few minutes into the New Year (2005); then he strangled her.

David Atkinson lived on for only a few more days, committing suicide in a hotel in Glasgow. He left a note saying that he had killed a woman with his bare hands. That murder case at least was solved, but Atkinson's suicide left a great many questions. The armed forces, today as always, shelter significant numbers of misfits and fugitives. The newspaper Scotland on Sunday disclosed that the armed forces employ at least eleven convicted sex offenders. An implication is that a significant number of potential rapists and sex killers are being given a safe haven. There is the distinct possibility, given the violence of the Geeson murder, that Atkinson might have killed before. Was the army protecting him?

The police speculated that Atkinson might have been responsible for murdering Milly Dowler. He had been stationed with the Royal Engineers at Minley in Surrey for ten months, very close to the spot where Milly disappeared. The Ministry of Defence cannot account for his whereabouts at the time of Milly's disappearance; he had just finished a training course at Chatham in Kent and had yet to embark on another course, so he was probably on leave – and free to kill.

Another telling fact is that Milly Dowler's body was found on a track beside Ministry of Defence land. It was only a hundred yards from where the Royal Engineers conducted their training exercises. In other words, Yateley Heath Forest was not a place that was right off the map as far as David Atkinson was concerned; it was an area he would have known well.

The Surrey Police said that Atkinson was 'of interest' as a potential suspect. His history meant that he was someone who might have committed the crime. The time and the location fitted too. In fact, at the time when the body was discovered, the police noted the fact that there was MoD land adjacent and speculated that the killer could have connections with the military. David Atkinson fitted into that hypothesis perfectly. Records of military personnel were explored at the time, but Atkinson was not spotted.

However strong the suspicion might be that David Atkinson was Milly's killer, there remains the fundamental problem – lack of proof. Because of the skeletal state of Milly's remains after six months, it was not possible to ascertain exactly how she died. Nor was it possible to find out whether she had been sexually assaulted. No traces of the killer's DNA remained; and Atkinson's DNA was not on the data base for correlation anyway, so it is hard to see how the police could have picked Atkinson out as even a potential suspect until after his suicide and confession.

Other violent sex offenders present themselves as potential suspects, too. The Soham killer, Ian Huntley, who killed the two young girls Holly Wells and Jessica Chapman, was investigated as a possibility. The M25 rapist, Antoni Imiela, was also investigated.

The Milly Dowler murder remains unsolved. The 'best-fit' hypothesis is that David Atkinson was the murderer. He had a history of violence, which first emerged on a tour of duty in Germany. He married a German woman, Liane Haake, and she actually reported him to the military police for his assaults on her. She said that he raped her and threatened her with an axe. The charges were later withdrawn. In 1997, Atkinson carried out a violent attack on an eighteen-year old Polish woman called Katrin Schyroki. He was court martialled for this, but Katrin condemned the hearing as 'a whitewash'. Like Sally Geeson, Katrin Schyroki was attacked in a car. In each of these attacks, Atkinson managed to trap the young woman in the car. Katrin thinks her life was saved when some bystanders saw what was happening and rushed to her rescue. The initial charges included indecent assault and kidnapping, but they were dropped and Atkinson was found guilty on a lesser charge of false imprisonment. He was fined and allowed to carry on with his military career. The leniency with which he was treated may have exposed Milly Dowler and other girls and young women to extreme danger. It is possible that the outcome was unintentional, that the army authorities had not intended to be lenient, but that the result was produced by the way the local German authorities gathered evidence on behalf of the victim. Even so, given the seriousness of the false imprisonment conviction, the British military police in Germany were entitled to pass Atkinson's DNA on the British Home Office's burgeoning DNA database. Atkinson was a violent criminal who clearly needed watching and storing his DNA profile would have been a wise precaution. The reasons why that did not happen are being explored by the MoD.

As it is, the police forces in three towns in Germany are keen to check Atkinson's DNA against forensic evidence they have collected from a string of unsolved sex crimes, including at least one murder. The main focus of their inquiry is the 1998 murder in Krefeld of a thirty-five-year-old prostitute called Jacqueline. She was found strangled in her flat in the town centre. Not only was Atkinson on his tour of duty in Germany at the time, he was living in Krefeld.

Whether Atkinson's DNA had been on the British national DNA database or not has made no difference as far as solving the Milly Dowler case is concerned, as there is no scene of crime sample with which to compare it. The strong suspicion nevertheless remains that David Atkinson is the nearest thing we currently have to a suspect for Milly's murder, though proof that he did it is still lacking.

The nagging question that still remains at the back of my mind relates to the second man. There was, as mentioned earlier, a significant sighting close to the place where Milly's body was later found, a sighting of two men with a schoolgirl. Does this mean that David Atkinson had an accomplice when he murdered Milly? And does this perhaps explain why Milly felt it was safe to get into the car? She may, like all well-trained youngsters, have hesitated to get into a car with a stranger, but getting into a car with two young soldiers offering her a lift may have seemed to her to be somehow safer.

KILLING THE CRICKET COACH: BOB WOOLMER

On Saturday 17 March 2007, the Pakistan cricket team was knocked out of the World Cup when it was defeated by the Ireland team. The defeat was all the more mortifying for Pakistan because the Ireland team was made up of part-time players. At a quarter to eleven the following morning, Sunday 18 March, a chambermaid at the Pegasus Hotel in Kingston, Jamaica, found the Pakistan cricket team's fifty-eight year old coach, Bob Woolmer, naked on the floor in his bathroom. He was taken to hospital but shortly afterwards pronounced dead.

It was four days later that the Jamaican police announced that Woolmer had not died of natural causes as at first thought: he had been murdered. He had been strangled with enough force to break a bone in his neck and splatter the walls with vomit. There was no sign of a forced entry into the hotel room, implying that Woolmer had known his murderer and let him in. The police had to wait some weeks before the results of toxicology tests came through. These might establish whether Woolmer was to some extent disabled with poison before being strangled.

British experts wondered whether their Jamaican counterparts had too quickly jumped to the conclusion that Woolmer died by manual strangulation. A British pathologist spoke contemptuously of the standards of Jamaican pathologists. If Woolmer had indeed died by manual strangulation, it was very odd that there were no bruises or scratches on his neck. His last meal had been lasagne, which was delivered to his room by room service. The Jamaican police had not ruled out the possibility that death was due to aconite poisoning, which can cause asphyxia.

The Interpol forensic expert, Susan Hitchin, took the view that the post mortem examination was bungled. She believed that the evidence pointed towards Woolmer dying from natural causes. He was a diabetic, and his blood testing kit was found on the floor near the body, which was leaning against the door. This had made it difficult for the chambermaid to push the door open. The fact that Woolmer's body was propped up against the door raises the question of how a killer could have escaped. He would have needed to push the body out of the way to get out, but how would he then have got the body back up against the door? The location of the body alone suggests that no killer entered the bathroom. Woolmer could therefore not have been strangled – though he could have been poisoned.

Police investigators travelled to Pakistan to clear up discrepancies between the statements given by officials and team members. The scale of the investigation expanded when a team of detectives from Scotland Yard arrived, and an Interpol forensic expert. The British police carefully searched the twelfth floor hotel room, looked through the witness statements, and scrutinized the closed-circuit television footage showing the corridor outside Woolmer's room.

The police had no particular suspect in the frame, but it was not hard to guess that Bob Woolmer's death was closely connected to the humiliating defeat of his team the previous day. The performance of Pakistan's cricket team was closely followed, with an almost hysterical zeal, by its millions of supporters. Any one of them could have felt sufficiently let down to want to wreak revenge on a scapegoat – and who better than the coach who trained the team? Pakistan's defeat by Ireland was the most humiliating in the team's history. It was greeted in Pakistan by the ritual burning of effigies of Bob Woolmer, and chants of 'Death to Woolmer'. With feelings among the team's fans running this high, it is a distinct possibility that an over-zealous fan could have taken the chanting literally.

The Kingston police began looking for three Pakistani fans in particular: the three who checked out of the Pegasus Hotel immediately after the murder. It would have been quite in character for Woolmer to have opened his door to chat to a fan, or even a trio of fans. He was friendly, approachable, good-natured and freely mixed with fans. He would have thought nothing of opening the door, wearing only a towel after his morning shower, to oblige an autograph hunter.

But there are other possibilities. Woolmer was white, not a Muslim, and something of an outsider as far as the Pakistan team were concerned. Allegations of match-fixing had circled round the sport for many years. The match with Ireland was regarded in cricketing circles as a very strange game. Pakistan's opening match against the West Indies was similar. Bob Woolmer may have had his suspicions that team members had accepted bribes to throw these games. Given his strength of character, he would have confronted his players with these suspicions.

Gambling on the outcome of cricket matches and even on individual batsmen's scores is a major activity in the subcontinent of India. It is estimated that as much as £20 billion a year is gambled on cricket matches in India alone. Such large sums are staked that there is an enormous temptation to fix matches. For significant bribes, players may produce the desired outcome. Both the Pakistan and the South Africa teams have been involved in match-fixing in the past. Bob Woolmer had acted as manager to both teams and he knew all about match-fixing. He had also written about the sport, and it was rumoured that he was about to write a book that would reveal the extent of the match-fixing. If that rumour was believed, it is possible that one of the illegal betting syndicates hired a professional killer to silence Woolmer before he got round to publishing. On the other hand, the book Woolmer was writing is said to have contained no such material. Following his death, his co-writer said that match-fixing would be included.

Match-fixing is a possibility, but at the same time the Pakistan players had their reputation as players to consider, and it seems unlikely that they would have exposed themselves to humiliation and ridicule for the sake of bribes. It would be a very short-term gain. Tim Noakes, Woolmer's co-author, does not believe that Woolmer was murdered because of the match-fixing. In his view it is match-fixers and not coaches who are killed by other match-fixers.

The book Bob Woolmer was working on when he was murdered will have a section on match-fixing added to it prior to publication, its co-author has revealed. At the time of his death, Woolmer was working on a book with Tim Noakes, who was at one time doctor to the South African team and a sports science professor at Cape Town University. Woolmer was editing the original 600 pages, of which he wrote over three-quarters in the week before he died. The page proofs arrived at the Pegasus Hotel the day after he died. These were clearly not the manuscripts that were said to have been stolen from his room. Noakes decided to let it be known that there would be a chapter on match-fixing in their jointly-written book. He also made it known that the print-run would be increased from 5,000 to 100,000 copies, anticipating a huge surge of interest in what Woolmer might have to say about the sport. The rumour that Woolmer might have been murdered because he was about to blow the whistle on match-fixing led to the decision to examine the match-fixing phenomenon statistically. Thomas C. Gilfillan was recruited by Noakes to analyze all the data relating to South Africa's one-day matches in the 1990s. For much of that time the team was coached by Woolmer. Gilfillan worked on the assumption that if you know the form of both of the teams playing, it is possible to predict the outcome of seventy per cent of matches. Noakes commented that the results would shed light on the character of the team captain.

A third possibility is that Bob Woolmer was an incidental victim of Kingston's high crime rate. Murder is not an uncommon crime there and this might have been a random killing completely unconnected with cricket or Pakistan. Meanwhile, the Pakistan cricket coach's body remains at four degrees Celsius in a zipped-up black bag in a cold room in the basement of a Kingston funeral parlour. The body, like the case itself, is going nowhere. It stays in Jamaica until the coroner decides to release it to the family in South Africa. Nothing of any substance has so far emerged to resolve the mystery. Woolmer's final e-mail messages give no hint of concern about match-fixing. There is no hint of any fear, either.